'This is a timely study of the regulation of public order before and after the development of human rights legislation, showing the influence of both official and especially secret forms of policing on the control of public space. The longer perspective of two hundred years punctuated by incidents and "moments" in history creates a critical interdisciplinary chronology of public order legislation which will inform students and academics working in the history of law, criminology, and social history.'

Barry Godfrey, Professor of Social Justice,
Liverpool University, UK

'A thought-provoking and impressively detailed survey of the often strained relationship between the law, policing, and public order in Britain over the last two centuries. Dr Channing is to be congratulated on his carefully researched and apposite interdisciplinary study. This book deserves to be required reading for those interested in the historical and legal balance between freedom of expression and public safety.'

David J. Cox, Fellow of the Royal Historical Society
and Reader in Criminal Justice History,
University of Wolverhampton, UK

'This is a very welcome study of the policing of public order in Britain. The book charts the relationship between the historical development of legislation, dealing with public order offences, and the practice and application of that law on the ground. By taking a long view (from the passage of the Metropolitan Police Act 1829 to the present) this study offers an original and exciting analysis of the policing of public protest and political activism.'

Dr Heather Shore, Reader in History,
Leeds Beckett University, UK

The Police and the Expansion of Public Order Law in Britain, 1829–2014

Incidences of public disorder, and the manner in which they have been suppressed, have repeatedly ignited debate on the role of policing, the effectiveness of current legislation and the implications for human rights and civil liberties. These same issues have reverberated throughout British history, and have frequently resulted in the enactment of new legislation that reactively aimed to counter the specific concern of that era. This book offers a detailed analysis on the expansion of public order law in the context of the historical and political developments in British society.

The correlation of key historical events and the enactment of consequent legislation is a key theme that resonates throughout the book and demonstrates the expanding influence of the law on public assemblies and protest, which has continued to criminalise and prohibit certain social behaviours. Crucial movements in Britain's social and political history that have all engaged in, or have provoked, public disorder, are examined in the book. Other incidents of riot and disorder, such as the Featherstone Riot 1893, the Battle of Cable Street 1936, the Urban Riots 1981 and the UK Riots 2011 are also covered.

Positioning legal developments within their historical context demonstrates the ebb and flow between the prominence of the competing demands of the liberties of free expression and assembly on the one hand and the protection of the general public and property on the other. This book is essential reading for academics and students in the fields of criminology, history and law.

Iain Channing is an interdisciplinary researcher at Plymouth University. Dr Channing's research traverses the fields of law, criminology and history and he has presented his research at various conferences around the UK. He is the membership secretary of SOLON and has a particular interest in the history of public order, political extremism and the police.

Routledge SOLON Explorations in Crime and Criminal Justice Histories

Edited by Kim Stevenson, *University of Plymouth*;
Judith Rowbotham, *University of Plymouth*;
David Nash, *Oxford Brookes University* and
David J. Cox, *University of Wolverhampton*

This series is a collaboration between Routledge and the SOLON consortium (promoting studies in law, crime and history), to present cutting edge interdisciplinary research in crime and criminal justice history, through monographs and thematic collected editions which reflect on key issues and dilemmas in criminology and socio-legal studies by locating them within a historical dimension. The emphasis here is on inspiring use of historical and historiographical methodological approaches to the contextualising and understanding of current priorities and problems. This series aims to highlight the best, most innovative interdisciplinary work from both new and established scholars in the field, through focusing on the enduring historical resonances to current core criminological and socio-legal issues.

The Police and the Expansion of Public Order Law in Britain, 1829–2014

Iain Channing

Routledge
Taylor & Francis Group

LONDON AND NEW YORK

First published 2015
by Routledge
2 Park Square, Milton Park, Abingdon, Oxfordshire OX14 4RN

Simultaneously published in the USA and Canada
by Routledge
711 Third Avenue, New York, NY 10017

First issued in paperback 2017

*Routledge is an imprint of the Taylor & Francis Group,
an informa business*

British Library Cataloguing in Publication Data
A catalogue record for this book is available from the British Library

Library of Congress Cataloging-in-Publication Data
A catalog record has been requested for this book

ISBN 13: 978-1-138-06587-1 (pbk)
ISBN 13: 978-0-415-64077-0 (hbk)

Typeset in Times New Roman
by Apex CoVantage, LLC

Contents

Illustrations

Acknowledgements

First, as much of this book has expanded upon my research that was conducted for my doctoral thesis, I would like to thank my supervisors Kim Stevenson, Kevin Jefferys and Daniel Gilling. Their guidance and expertise has been invaluable. Also, I would like to extend this thanks to my examiners Chris Williams and Candida Harris for their much-appreciated input and comments. A special mention is also needed for Kim (again), Judith Rowbotham and David Nash for their guidance as series editors of this innovative collection of research projects under the title Routledge SOLON Explorations in Crime and Criminal Justice Histories, of which I am proud to be part. Others who, at some point or another, have helped me through their advice, discussions and offering a listening ear include Henry Yeomans, Neil Chappell, Sharon Beckett and Oliver Cowan. I would also like to thank Angela Sutton-Vane at the Devon & Cornwall Constabulary's Heritage & Learning Resource, and the archivists and librarians at the Hull History Centre, the National Archives, the Bishopsgate Institute and the History Room at Plymouth Central Library for their assistance and advice. I must also like to thank Nigel Mace, Bob Keys and David Gadien for helping nurture my interest and love of history.

My dearest thanks go to my partner Demelza and my son Shaun, for their love, patience and understanding throughout this process. Their support and inspiration has been invaluable. My parents and parents-in-law have also provided me with unlimited encouragement, love and support. Thank you.

Series editor introduction

The volumes in this series contribute to the unashamedly interdisciplinary exercise in which SOLON has engaged since its inception in 2000: something now enhanced by the collaboration with Routledge to present cutting-edge interdisciplinary research in crime and criminal justice history. The focus is on issues which, while rooted in the past, have also a crucial current resonance and so the volumes reflect on key issues and dilemmas which persist in terms of contemporary priorities.

*****

This is a particularly welcome addition to the series, where one of the early volumes dealt with policing in Northern Ireland, because it returns specifically to a policing focus. One of its strengths is its interdisciplinarity, notably the way in which it brings together perspectives on policing which are valuable to history and law as well as criminology – and with implications for social policy and other disciplines as well. There are key texts on the theme – and the work of the police history team at the Open University has been admirable in creating policing studies as an academic theme for research in its own right. But despite the number of texts produced or inspired by that grouping, which has added the historical dimension to policing studies, too little has been done on the topic in a way which adds the historical perspective to considerations of policing and its challenges when the studies are primarily within the fields of law and criminology. With some honourable exceptions, notably the work by Godfrey, Emsley, Cox and Farrall, criminological and legal texts on policing have still tended to look inwards to the preoccupations of those disciplines, rather than looking out. Where history has been invoked, it has largely been in a chronological rather than in a thematic sense. This volume provides a template for other studies on aspects of policing, past and present – and we look to future texts on themes such as, for example, road traffic management, domestic violence and common assault, to identify three of the most obvious areas which would benefit from similar treatment to that presented here.

This is a wide-ranging book, both in terms of its chronology and its thematic remit – the issue of order and disorder, and how (and why) it has been managed by communities has been and remains a problematic phenomenon. The development of strategies relying on the modern uniformed police as the key agent on the community front line, interacting also with the formal legal process, have never previously been explored in ways that focus on that three-way interaction. Incidents explored within this study have, of course, been covered in previous scholarship – from the Chartists to the EDF, via the Fenians and the Blackshirts. But such a *longue durée* study, identifying commonalities of response and management, has not been undertaken. This volume reveals a surprising level of continuity, rather than discontinuity, in terms of formal responses by the police and the justice system – all framed by the political contingencies of a particular period. Home Secretaries have come and gone – but the issues have largely remained the same and individuals have, in practice – despite rhetoric proclaiming innovation and difference – reacted to disorder and public demands for a restoration of order in very similar ways.

This book reveals also a range of interesting commonalities between types of public disorder – from riots to strikes, via political and trade union protests. Further, one of the legal themes that Channing shows as underpinning official responses to these superficially different challenges to public order has been a sustained reliance on the common law principles surrounding use of the breach of the peace concept. While this has been recognised previously, what this book does is to examine this use in its broader socio-legal setting, revealing the extent to which the management of disorder has consistently been contingent, rather than being inspired by new ideas and policing principles. But it does also reveal the extent to which this management has been centralised since the nineteenth century – through a series of statutory innovations such as policing and public order legislation. As his exploration of *Hansard* and Parliamentary Papers, as well as other official sources underline, central government has been increasingly determined to set the public order agenda, essentially for reasons of political popularity. It is a book that will be of importance to criminologists, lawyers and crime historians – but also to social policy and political studies analysts as well as to socio-cultural historians in general. We are delighted to have it in this series.

Abbreviations

ACPO	Association of Chief Police Officers
BF	Britain First
BUF	British Union of Fascists
CEGB	Central Electricity Generating Board
CPGB	Communist Party of Great Britain
ECHR	European Convention on Human Rights
ECtHR	European Court of Human Rights
EDL	English Defence League
ESIM	Elaborated Social Identity Model
HHC	Hull History Centre
HMIC	Her Majesty's Inspector of Constabulary
HRA	Human Rights Act
IFL	Imperial Fascist League
ILP	Independent Labour Party
JPC	Jewish People's Council
KKK	Ku Klux Klan
LCC	London County Council
LEL	League of Empire Loyalists
MAC	Muslims Against Crusades
NCCL	National Council for Civil Liberties
Netpol	Network for Police Monitoring
NUWM	National Unemployed Workers Movement
PACE	Police and Criminal Evidence Act 1984
PLT	Police Liaison Team
PSU	Police Support Unit
SCP	Social Credit Party
SDF	Social Democratic Federation
TNA	The National Archives
TUC	Trades Union Congress
UAF	Unite Against Fascism
UM	Union Movement

Statutes

Cases

Introduction

In *Keeping the Peace*, David Williams asserted that the law of public order was a compromise which sought to balance the 'competing demands of freedom of speech and assembly on the one hand and the preservation of the Queen's Peace on the other.'[1] Historically, this compromise has repeatedly failed, resulting in a considerable catalogue of public disorder and riot. As 'keepers of the peace', the police and their tactics are intrinsically scrutinised by the media in any event of disorder. At the same time, effective public order policing does not attract the same attention. In this respect, Reicher *et al.* state, 'public order policing is a no-win situation.'[2] The intention of this book is not to serve as a chronological record of events denigrating police tactics, but to provide a critical analysis of the development of public order law and the different approaches that have been utilised by the police from 1829 through 2014. By contextualising this historical development it serves as a stark warning towards future Government policy which aims to regulate public order by restricting fundamental rights and liberties. The relationship between such extensions of public order law and developing police tactics is integral to this investigation.

A historico-legal methodological framework

In recent years, interdisciplinary approaches to academic research have been championed by universities and funding councils, yet it is not certain that such methodologies produce meaningful results.[3] Despite this, individual academic fields still have the capacity to offer knowledge, understanding and specialised insights to 'rival' disciplines whose methodologies would otherwise disregard or mistreat valuable sources or approaches. In her polemic article, 'On

---

1 D. Williams, *Keeping the Peace: The Police and Public Order*, Hutchinson & Co Ltd: London (1967), p. 9.
2 S. Reicher, C. Stott, P. Cronin and O. Adang, (2004), 'An integrated approach to crowd psychology and public order policing', *Policing: An International Journal of Police Strategies & Management* 27, no. 4, p. 559.
3 See P. Bartlett, '"On Historical Contextualisation": A Lawyer Responds', *Crimes and Misdemeanours 1*, no. 2 (2007), p. 104.

Historical Contextualisation', academic lawyer Lorie Charlesworth argues that 'the very process of studying law in action cannot forsake a historical form of analysis.' Indeed, a critical view of the present law of public order and the policing of it is enhanced by the analysis and contextualisation of their development over the past two centuries. Historical contextualisation is needed, argues Charlesworth, 'in order to appreciate the extent to which the guiding ideas, beliefs and values contained within, or otherwise attributed to or associated with, the research topic, have come to be constituted in their present but still developing form.'[4] It is this recognition that the law is continually evolving that renders the analysis of its development particularly imperative. In the realm of public order law this is especially true, as reactive legal remedies have the potential power to restrict or deny rights and liberties that are essential to democratic freedom.

Within the discipline of law, whether black-letter or socio-legal, academic lawyer Peter Bartlett contends that, 'While law is of course about the present, more than any other social science discipline, it cannot escape the past.'[5] The recognition of the importance of legal scholarship within the school of history itself is less decisive, as Bartlett later explains, 'History is itself a contested ground, and that creates difficulties for its integration into socio-legal studies.'[6] Within mainstream historical study, John Tosh argues that legal history 'arouses relatively little interest among historians at present' but highlights that court records are 'probably the single most important source' for the social history of the medieval and early modern periods.[7] This is because a vast majority of the population were illiterate and left no records. However, historians should also not neglect the value of legal history to nineteenth and twentieth century research. This book demonstrates the value of legal sources in gaining a critical understanding of attitudes of the Government, the police and the judiciary towards competing political groups and protest movements, and reveals that assumptions about institutional partiality among these bodies of authority are misplaced. Analysis of Statute and common law will offer an understanding of how the criminal justice system operated throughout this era and how the authorities used these existing powers to deal with issues related to public disorder.

A critical analysis of the development of public order law requires the contextualisation of the past in order to understand the legal systems evolving form, as well as those who amended it, enforced it, and operated within it. The result is a methodology that embraces the disciplines of law, history and criminology. This historico-legal analysis draws on a wealth of primary source material including political publications, memoirs, newspaper reportage, police reports,

---

4 L. Charlesworth, 'On Historical Contextualisation: Some Critical Socio-Legal Reflections', *Crimes and Misdemeanours 1*, no. 1 (2007), p. 8.

5 Bartlett, 'A Lawyer Responds', p. 102.

6 Ibid., pp. 102 and 104.

7 J. Tosh, *The Pursuit of History*, Pearson Education Limited: Harlow (2006) p. 106.

Parliamentary debates, Home Office reports and correspondence, as well as legal sources such as case law, legislation and statutory developments.

This book's primary objective is to provide a narrative that adds value to the disciplines of law, criminology and history. This is achieved by providing a clear historico-legal study of the development of public order law and police tactics utilised to prevent disorder and maintain order. This historical study of public protest and political activism utilises a critical legal lens to analyse the responses of the Government, judiciary and the police. The question arises: with such broad and imprecise powers relating to public order, how could the police fulfil their role consistently, impartially and democratically? The tactics employed by the police and the use of their discretion are examined in order to question the principle of police impartiality. The last 200 years of British history have provided a fertile ground from which to select episodes of disorder for an examination of the development of public order law. This superfluity of potential incidents and sources is largely addressed by the methodology adopted within this book. This book is primarily concerned with the law relating to England and Wales. Although incidents in Scotland and Northern Ireland are referred to, their differences in legal provisions made it unfeasible to direct significant attention to them. For instance, breach of the peace in Scottish Law has its own historical progression, which contrasts with its counterpart in England and Wales.[8] Also, the law in Northern Ireland[9] has its own distinct history since its union with the United Kingdom, which commenced with oppressive laws such as the Suppression of Rebellion Act 1801 and Habeas Corpus Suspension Act 1801.

While the area of public order law itself could include anything from a riot to a person acting drunk and disorderly, this book primarily investigates incidents associated with public protest and/or political activism. Also, the substantive chapters are themed to particular areas of public disorder. Within each of these chapters a chronological analysis deliberates incidents and legal developments significant to that theme. Furthermore, there is a particular focus on the events surrounding the passing of Public Order Act 1936, which was the first Act to specifically incorporate several existing provisions as well as to establish new offences which directly related to forms of public protest and political activism. It also laid the foundations for the Public Order Act 1986 which provides the police with the major statutory powers related to preventing disorder and restoring order today.

Chapter one provides a brief chronological overview of the main legislative and common law developments which have provided police officers of all ranks with the tools to preserve the peace and to restore public order. In chapter two, the role of police officers and their ability to utilise wide discretionary powers

---

8 For significant cases which define breach of the peace in Scotland, see *Deakin v Milne* (1882) 10 R(J) 22; *Raffaelli v Heatly* [1949] ScotHC HCJ1, 1949 SLT 284, and *Smith v Donnelly (Procurator Fiscal, Dumbarton)* [2001] ScotHC 121.

9 As well as the island of Ireland before the establishment of the Irish Republic in 1919.

under the breach of the peace doctrine is examined. This chapter analyses selected incidents of police responses to activists whose methods may have debatably provoked a breach of the peace, but where the lawfulness of their individual actions were ambiguous. Chapter three examines the powers and attitudes of the State and the police towards the crowd in scenes of serious disorder and riot. It assesses instances of the use of the Riot Act 1714 and the common law offence of riotous assembly. An important aspect of this chapter is the development of crowd psychology, which offers vital understandings of how different courses of police action can limit the potential for disorder or either escalate or provoke it. The following five chapters each take a key theme within public order law and chronologically analyse legal developments throughout this period. Chapters four and five both focus on public processions and public assembly. The period covered by chapter four climaxes with the Battle of Cable Street 1936, while chapter five continues from this point with the enactment of the Public Order Act 1936 to the present day. The emphasis in chapters six, seven and eight are on public meetings and freedom of speech, disorder in the private domain and the prohibition of particular styles of dress, respectively. These chapters examine the responses to particular groups and movements such as the Chartists, the suffragettes, the British Union of Fascists (BUF), the Communist Party of Great Britain (CPGB), Union Movement (UM), and the English Defence League (EDL). There is a particular focus in chapters five to eight on how police tactics were utilised and how they adapted to legislative developments such as the Public Order Acts of 1936 and 1986 and the Human Rights Act (HRA), as well as influential precedents laid down by the courts.

Public order law and the historiography of civil disorder

Lawyers, historians and sociologists have all found interest in events of public disorder, rebellion and riot. Guided by the different methodologies of their academic backgrounds, these writers produced literature that is wide and diverse. In contrasting the legal and historical views of the Constitution, constitutional lawyer Albert Dicey declared that historians are concerned with the question of 'origins', while the primary object of lawyers is the study of the law 'as it now stands'.[10] In this review of the leading literature on public order this will be substantiated, yet important developments in interdisciplinary methodologies will also demonstrate the influence of socio-legal scholarship and historical research.

Leading texts on public order law, such as Richard Card's *Public Order Law*,[11] Peter Thornton *et al. The Law of Public Order and Protest*,[12] and John Beggs *et al.*

---

10 A. V. Dicey, *An Introduction to the Study of the Law of the Constitution*, tenth edition, Macmillan Press Ltd: London (1959), p. 15.

11 R. Card, *Public Order Law*, Jordans Ltd: Bristol (2000).

12 HHJ P. Thornton QC, R. Brander, R. Thomas, D. Rhodes, M. Schwarz and E. Rees, *The Law of Public Order and Protest*, Oxford University Press: Oxford (2010).

Public Order: Law and Practice[13] are at the forefront of contributing towards our understanding of the law of public order. They all offer significant detail on explaining the current laws, and analysing how they have been utilised by police and interpreted by judges. Yet the question of how we ended up here, with these sets of laws, is beyond the scope of such legal texts. Some form of historical contextualisation is required to reveal these answers. The most significant texts to delve into the history of public order have been David Williams' *Keeping the Peace*, Charles Townshend's *Making the Peace*[14] and Richard Vogler's *Reading the Riot Act.*[15]

In *Keeping the Peace: The Police and Public Order*, David Williams combined the disciplines of law and history to produce a volume on public order that spans the 1850s to the 1960s. Written in 1967, its contemporary relevance is stimulated by the inclusion of the then-recent disturbances between the Mods and Rockers. Williams approached the issue of public order as the struggle between maintaining freedom of speech and assembly and the preservation of the Queen's Peace. The legal discussion offered adds vital understanding of the law. For example, in discussing the nature of preventive justice he highlighted the vagueness of legislation and the wide discretionary powers exercised by magistrates to bind people over for behavior which is not necessarily criminal in order to exert social control. Yet despite this inconsistency from the courts, Williams concedes that preventive justice 'remains a valuable deterrent in the preservation of the Queen's Peace.'[16]

Charles Townshend's *Making the Peace: Public Order and Public Security in Modern Britain* is a more recent account which principally uses a historical approach to examining disorder, particularly from the legal framework of public order policy and state management in Britain from the mid-nineteenth century to the 1980s. A theme of the book is of the tension that grew between the police and the public in the 1970s and 1980s during violent clashes at protests and industrial disputes, and the growth of police militarism. This escalation in retaliatory violence towards the police is further attributed to the realisation that a 'right' to public meeting did not exist, although it was once believed to have. Townshend claimed that in losing this once-perceived right, the 'right' to order was gained, although no right existed in legislative terms.

Townshend dispels the myths of a 'golden age' in public order, highlighting the flawed perception from the 1990s standpoint that the 50 years between the Public Order Act 1936 and the subsequent Public Order Act 1986 could be split into two unequal parts; the first being a relatively peaceful era before the disorders at

---

13 J. Beggs QC, G. Thomas and S. Rickard, *Public Order: Law and Practice*, Oxford University Press: Oxford (2012).
14 C. Townshend, *Making the Peace: Public Order and Public Security in Modern Britain*, Oxford University Press: Oxford (1993).
15 R. Vogler, *Reading the Riot Act: The Magistracy, the Police and the Army in Civil Disorder*, Open University Press: Milton Keynes (1991).
16 Williams, *Keeping the Peace*, p. 113.

Brixton in 1981. From Brixton onwards Townshend highlighted the disorders at Southall, Toxteth, Handsworth, St Paul's and Tottenham, as well as a continuing decade of football hooliganism, terrorism and strike battles. Townshend argues that public perceptions had frequently created a myth of deterioration in security and a growth in violent crime which celebrates a 'golden age' of order that had existed about 20 years previous. Reminding the reader of the 1974 Red Lion Square disorder and the 1972 miners' strike, Townshend contends that the division is less clear cut and questions whether there may be a 'mismatch between concept and reality'.[17]

In *Reading the Riot Act*, Vogler uses specific examples of disorder which span from the Bristol Riot 1832 to the Urban Riots 1981 to examine the evolving relationship between the magistracy, the police and the army. At different times these separate agencies competed for dominance, yet by the 1981 disorders Vogler asserts that the police had gained supremacy in the control of civil disorder.

In addition to the texts with a particular focus on public disorder are Clive Emsley's influential police histories such as *The English Police* and *The Great British Bobby*.[18] These books offer valuable historical insights into the development of the police throughout this period. They examine important changes within the structure of the police against the backdrop of political and social change, adding valuable insight into our understanding of the development of police organization and culture. Another significant text which considers developments in public order law is *The Struggle for Civil Liberties* by lawyers Keith Ewing and Conner Gearty.[19] They significantly examine the legal responses to political extremism between 1914 and 1945, with an important account on the passing of the Public Order Act 1936. Yet the authors' argument is intermittently hindered by their partiality and their neglect of critical sources. The author's prejudice is highlighted most clearly by historian Richard Thurlow, who accuses Ewing and Gearty of looking favourably upon the parts of the Public Order Act that directly affected the BUF while at the same time criticising the increased powers of the police relating to marches and demonstrations that also hindered the anti-fascists as well as the fascists.[20] Ewing and Gearty contend that the police were pro-fascist and anti-Left in this period, and they selected evidence which supported this claim. However, it is this partiality that potentially led to the neglect of divergent sources and to the nonchalant comparison of policing tactics at fascist and anti-fascist or Left-wing events. By neglecting certain historical perspectives, Ewing and Gearty

17 Townshend, *Making the Peace*, p. 133.
18 C. Emsley, *The English Police: A Political and Social History,* second edition, Pearson Education Limited: Harlow (1996), and C. Emsley, *The Great British Bobby: A History of British Policing from the 18th Century to the Present*, Querus: London (2010).
19 K. D. Ewing and C. A. Gearty, *The Struggle for Civil Liberties: Political Freedom and the Rule of Law in Britain, 1914–1945*, Oxford University Press: Oxford (2004).
20 R. Thurlow, review of *The Struggle for Civil Liberties: Political Freedom and the Rule of Law in Britain, 1914–1945* by K. D. Ewing and C. A. Gearty in *Albion: A Quarterly Journal Concerned with British Studies 33*, no. 2 (Summer 2001) pp. 350–351.

do not differentiate between the extreme political movements' methods and do not evaluate the contemporary popular cultural and social attitudes. Such factors offer important rationales for why the police acted more frequently against the anti-fascists and communists as opposed to the fascists. In addition, the lack of historical scrutiny of highly subjective sources, such as those written by contemporary anti-fascists, emphasises the bias of the authors and their agenda of amplifying the claim of pro-fascist policing.[21]

The analysis of policing tactics in this book attempts to avoid the pitfalls of any such partiality by creating an objective analytical framework which evaluates contemporary social and political attitudes, questions important sources and selects contrasting incidents of police practice which demonstrate a wider understanding of the varied and inconsistent nature of provincial policing through the last two centuries.

---

21 For example, see Ewing and Gearty, *The Struggle*, p. 284, n. 54, where the authors note that for 'a good account' of the Olympia meeting, see I. Montagu, *Blackshirt Brutality. The Story of Olympia* (1934). Montagu was a member of the CPGB, an anti-fascist and a maker of socialist films.

1 The development of public order law

'The police will become the arbiter of the right of people to manifest their views. This represents a serious change in liberty of assembly and police powers.'[1]

Introduction

The introduction of new public order legislation is usually challenged in Parliament on the grounds that it endangers the valued liberties of public assembly and protest. This is demonstrated in the introductory quote by Plaid Cymru MP Dafydd Elis-Thomas, who signalled his warning over clauses 11 and 14 of the Public Order Bill 1986 which provided police with the discretion to apply conditions on assemblies. At the same time, other Members of Parliament have argued in favour of the liberties of others. For instance, in the same debate Conservative MP Nicholas Lyell praised the Bill, arguing 'I believe that it will protect and enhance the liberty of our society as a whole.'[2] New legislation is also usually a response to some failings in public order management or a new perceived threat from radical groups. This chapter first examines the concept of residual freedom and human rights in English law and then provides an overview of the principal Statutes related to public order which are examined in more detail throughout this book.

Residual freedom, civil liberties and human rights

Notions which identify the state's obligation to preserve public order are necessarily associated with the protection or the suppression of civil liberties and human rights. Yet whose liberty should be protected? The concept of liberty in the late eighteenth century was appropriated by both the establishment and the radical alike. E. P. Thompson revealed the popular belief that the Revolutionary settlement of 1688 and the subsequent Constitution of King, Lords and Commons

---

1 *Hansard, HC Deb*, 13 Jan 1986, vol 89 cc792–869 at 844.
2 Ibid., at 853.

guaranteed the liberty of free-born Englishmen. Nevertheless, decisive definitions of liberty itself are obscured by subjective philosophies and values. For instance, in the name of freedom Burke denounced the French Revolution while Paine championed it.[3] Furthermore, Thompson stated, 'Patriotism, nationalism, even bigotry and repression, were all clothed in the rhetoric of liberty.'[4] This inherent ambiguity in notions of late eighteenth century and early nineteenth century liberty was interpreted by Thompson to mean freedom from foreign domination, absolutism and arbitrary searches of one's home and arrest. It also included equality before the law and the limited liberties of thought, speech and conscience.[5]

Within this 'top-down' hierarchy of liberties was a structure which was directed to preserve the power of the state. From this perspective, freedoms such as speech and thought were necessarily limited in order to manage and suppress radical thinkers and militants who threatened the stability of the Constitution. Yet to the political activist or public protester, absolute freedom of speech was fundamental to their philosophy of liberty. Without it there could be no challenge to state autocracy. These diverse perceptions of liberty have been the mainspring between several violent clashes between the state and its subjects. Without the right to vote, the political involvement of the working classes was particularly limited. Yet, as Thompson observed, the people could still 'parade, huzza and jeer on the hustings', and reformers and radical candidates received overwhelming support during election times, while the 'authorities were forced to build barracks and take precautions against the 'revolutionary crowd'.[6]

Before the Human Rights Act 1998 (HRA) and the incorporation of the European Convention on Human Rights (ECHR), there was no legally defined 'right' of public meeting or freedom of speech. Previously, people were at liberty to exercise freedom of speech or assembly, provided that their actions did not contravene any existing law. Since the HRA, Articles 10 and 11 of the ECHR (freedom of expression and freedom of assembly and association respectively) have provided positive legal protection of these rights in UK law. Nevertheless, Article 9 Bill of Rights 1688 provides MPs with freedom of speech in Parliament. Without a written Constitution that guaranteed such 'rights', the notion of residual freedom was prevalent in English law. Since the nineteenth century there have been various legal references to such rights, but as lawyer Davis Mead suggests, there 'is no time at which one can easily plot the entry of a right of assembly and protest into legal and judicial discourse in England.'[7] Mead cites *Bonnard v Perryman*[8]

---

3 See E. Burke, *Reflections on the Revolution in France* (1790), and T. Paine, *Rights of Man*, J. S. Jordan: London (1791).
4 E. P. Thompson, *The Making of the English Working Class*, Penguin Books: London (1991), p. 85.
5 Ibid., p. 86.
6 Ibid., pp. 85–86.
7 D. Mead, *The New Law of Peaceful Protest: Rights and Regulation in the Human Rights Act Era*, Hart Publishing Ltd: Oxford (2010), p. 4.
8 *Bonnard v Perryman* [1891] 2 Ch 269 (CA).

as possibly the earliest mention of a right of free speech.[9] Here Lord Coleridge CJ stated, 'The right of free speech is one which it is for the public interest that individuals should possess, and, indeed, that they should exercise without impediment, so long as no wrongful act is done'.[10]

In *An Introduction to the Study of the Law of the Constitution*, A. V. Dicey offered a contradictory view. Although the first edition of this work fell six years before *Bonnard*, Dicey continued to amend the text until 1908, and his latest version omitted this case. Dicey clearly rejected the notion that any rights to freedom of speech existed in English law.

> The phrases "freedom of discussion" or "liberty of the press" are rarely found in any part of the Statute-book nor among the maxims of the common law . . . At no time has there in England been any proclamation of the right to liberty of thought or to freedom of speech.[11]

Similarly, in respect of the right of public meeting, Dicey also stated that the constitution did not recognise any specific right of public meeting.[12]

In the 1930s, when the issue was directly related to political protest and activism, Lord Hewart CJ emphatically quashed any notion of such rights in *Duncan v Jones*,[13] ruling that 'English Law does not recognise any special right of public meeting for political or other purposes.'[14] This particular case is discussed in more detail in chapter three. However, 40 years later in *Hubbard v Pitt*[15] Lord Denning cited *Bonnard v Perryman* to convey the importance of the right to protest, 'As long as all is done peaceably and in good order, without threats or incitement to violence or obstruction to traffic'.[16] Despite these sporadic and inconsistent references to the rights of free speech and public assembly, the confusion is often caused by the terms *right* and *liberty*. In *Hubbard*, Stamp LJ agreed with Denning and described it as the 'liberty to speak, [and] the liberty to assemble',[17] which is more consistent with the notion of residual freedom than expressly defined and legally protected rights. David Mead emphasises the difference that the HRA had made, by stating that the move from a 'residual, liberty based system to one based on positive rights brings a shift in the burden of proof.'[18] This means that public authorities must now provide an objective basis for any ban or condition that they

---

9 Mead, *The New Law*, p. 4. However, the right to public assembly was also previously discussed in *Ex parte Lewis* (1888) 21 QBD 191 and is discussed in chapter four.
10 *Bonnard v Perryman*, at 284.
11 Dicey, *An Introduction*, pp. 239–240.
12 Ibid., p. 271.
13 *Duncan v Jones* [1936] 1 KB 218.
14 Ibid., at 222.
15 *Hubbard v Pitt* [1976] QB 142.
16 Ibid., at 178.
17 Ibid., at 187.
18 Mead, *The New Law*, p. 204.

impose on public assemblies and all restrictions must be justified in relation to Article 11(2) of the ECHR. Effectively Chief Constables are required to enforce the least restrictive measures open to them in relation to the potential for disorder, when imposing conditions on public assemblies.

The development of public order law

While these contested arguments on the status of civil liberties and human rights evolved during the last 200 years, restrictive public order legislation has had a significant impact on such liberties being enjoyed. These developments were usually a reaction to particular concerns that faced successive governments during this period. This book examines these developments by identifying particular themes which public order legislation has been mandated to regulate.

Under the common law, the breach of the peace doctrine empowers the police to make an arrest without warrant when such a breach is committed in their presence or is reasonably anticipated. This was significantly authorised by Watkins LJ in *R v Howell*,[19] although in his judgment he also acknowledged previous common law authority on the powers of arrest in the anticipation of a breach of the peace such as *R v Light*.[20] It is a significant power which has provided the police with wide discretionary powers due to its ambiguous meaning. The powers of the police relating to the common law offence of breach of the peace are analysed in more detail in the next chapter.

The Riot Act 1714 is the first significant Act of Parliament which traverses a substantial portion of this time period. It was enacted during a period of considerable disorder across England which was highlighted by the Sacheverell Riots 1710 and the Coronation Riots 1714. The Riot Act represented the ultimate power of the State: its reading at a scene of disorder by a magistrate created a felony punishable by death to any person who had not dispersed within an hour. Most significantly, mere presence at the scene was enough to warrant the death penalty and no specific act or intention was necessary to prove guilt. This is analysed in chapter three.

The Riot Act was finally repealed with the passing of the Criminal Law Act 1967. During the Criminal Law Bill's progress through Parliament the opportunity for the Riot Act to be read before its ultimate repeal presented itself in Stockport, as a crowd of 1,000 trade unionists were reported to have caused disorder outside a factory in the Cheshire town. The District Secretary for the Amalgamated Engineering Union argued that the union members only responded with violence because of police provocation which included some 'roughness' and three police charges on the initially peaceful protest. Interestingly, although the authority of reading the Riot Act fell to the 'head officer' of the town or city, the influence of the Chief Constable on whether the Act was read in this case was dominant. The

---

19 *R v Howell* [1982] Q.B. 416.
20 *R v Light* (1857) Dears. & B. 332.

Town Clerk revealed to *The Times* that he discussed the issue with the Chief Constable and ultimately took his advice not to read the Act as reinforcements were expected.[21] In the House of Lords, Labour peer Lord Stonham argued that the Riot Act ceased to be wanted with the establishment of modern police forces and no longer served any useful purpose.[22] Although the Riot Act was still utilised after the creation of the modern police force, this use did diminish and its last recorded use was in 1919 during the police strikes. In the Liverpool area there were a significant number of police officers that supported the strike and widespread looting occurred. The Riot Act was read in Birkenhead where 96 police officers, from the total force strength of 225, were on strike. Despite there being '700 military with machine guns in the town', *The Times* recorded that although the Riot Act was read, 'extreme measures were not resorted to.'[23] With the repeal of the Riot Act, the magistrates also lost their influence in times of serious disorder. Writing in the same year the Criminal Law Act was passed, Williams highlighted how the Chief Constable, rather than the magistrate, was now more likely to cooperate with the military authorities during severe disorder.[24]

Following a period of public discontent and economic instability, there was a series of civil disorders which culminated with the Peterloo massacre. Because of the State's concern over radical political activity, a flurry of legislation was passed to counter the Government's fear of revolutionary movements. Most significant among these Acts were the Unlawful Drilling Act 1819 and the Seditious Meetings Act 1819. While the latter had most of its provisions repealed in 1824, the main provisions of the Unlawful Drilling Act, which proscribed the practicing of military exercise by unauthorised bodies, was not repealed until 2008 with the passing of the Statute Law (Repeals) Act. These Acts represent the Government's fear of insurgency and its responses to it. These were highlighted most urgently by the Earl of Strathmore when discussing the Training Prevention Bill[25] who argued that the laws they were enacting were not strong enough to deal with the disturbances which affected the country. In recognition of the effects these laws had on civil liberties, he stated that 'there was not a man in the House more unwilling than he was to restrict or to suspend the constitutional rights of the people without the necessity.'[26] The urgency declared in this instance was reflected by reports suggesting that there were 100,000 men who had arms which were ready to rise and unite together in the Tyne and the Wear and Carlisle. The 'necessity' to suspend the 'constitutional rights' of the people, as the Earl of Strathmore phrased it, could then arguably have been a measure directed to preserve the political structure rather than wider society from radical activism. These Acts can be seen as largely

---

21 *The Times*, 23 Feb 1967.
22 *Hansard, HL Deb*, 24 Nov 1966, vol 278 cc392–471 at 469.
23 *The Times*, 4 Aug 1919.
24 Williams, *Keeping the Peace*, p. 35.
25 This Bill became more commonly known as the Unlawful Drilling Act 1819.
26 *Hansard, HL Deb*, 3 Dec 1819, vol 41 cc697–698.

preventative, as they aimed to restrict the meetings and training which could have potentially led to a revolutionary threat. Yet at the same time these measures also gave the State power to restrict the liberty of political radicals which may not have threatened disorder or engaged in unlawful activity.

In 1829, the creation of the 'new' police under the Metropolitan Police Act 1829 was a measure primarily mandated to prevent crime. Sir Robert Peel highlighted the rise in crime in London and the inefficiency of the current policing system in Parliament in 1828. This was countered by radical MP Joseph Hume who argued that the cause of rising crime was excessive taxation and the decreased wages paid to labourers. Modelling the Metropolitan Police as civilians in uniform for the purposes of crime prevention was intended to counter the public resistance of a State-controlled police force along the European lines. However, ten years later the Metropolitan Police Act 1839 provided the police with additional powers of search and arrest. By 1842, the first Detective Branch was established as criminal investigation slowly gained more prominence among police duties.[27] While the emphasis on such investigations had traditionally been left to the victim and their community, the active participation of the police had a role in limiting the part of the 'thief takers' who received rewards for helping victims recover stolen items. Yet the increasing prominence of crime detection within the Metropolitan Police led to the diversification and specialisation of investigatory practice. This is highlighted by the establishment of the Special Branch between 1881 and 1883, whose aims were to protect the country from political subversion, terrorism and extremism. With such preventive aims, the Special Branch prominently placed police activity within the political realm as it then used covert methods to gain information on socialists, communists, fascists and other groups considered to have anti-democratic or revolutionary intentions. Nonetheless, it should not be thought that Special Branch heralded a start of political infiltration. As early as 1832, Sergeant Popay of the Metropolitan Police attended meetings of the Political Union in plain clothes, took notes of the speeches, insinuated himself in the private lives of members, altered resolutions to make them more inflammatory, and offered to train members in target practice and sword fighting.[28]

In addition to the creation of the Metropolitan Police, the Municipal Corporations Act 1835 had reformed local governance and placed a statutory duty on newly elected councils to establish watch committees to run their police forces. The County Police Act 1839 provided the Justices of the Peace with the power to establish police forces in their areas. Where authorities had not established their own police forces, it became common practice to utilise the resources of the Metropolitan Police to assist in public order scenarios. In 1839, the gathering of large crowds in Birmingham, which had not established a police force at this time, highlighted the problems associated with dealing with potential public

---

27 P. Stelfox, *Criminal Investigation: an Introduction to Principles and Practice*, Routledge: Cullompton (2009), p. 32.

28 J. Winter, *London's Teeming Streets: 1830–1914*, Routledge: London and New York (1993), p. 51.

disorder without adequate resources. In order to deal with processions of up to 5,000 Chartists, the Birmingham magistrates asked the Home Secretary, Lord John Russell, for permission to swear in a number of Metropolitan Police officers as special constables on 13 July 1839.[29] Although this measure was more favourable than using the military, it demonstrated the depth of anti-police feelings of this time. Historian Malcom Chase describes the use of the Metropolitan Police at Birmingham, who were tasked to arrest any Chartist who addressed the crowd, as 'catastrophic'. The sixty Metropolitan Police officers were 'routed in a pitched battle' by local opposition and the army intervened to restore order.[30] Chase also admits that Birmingham Chartist John Fussell's argument that the magistrates' use of the Metropolitan Police was to provoke an outbreak rather than protect the peace of the town remains 'a plausible view'.[31] An Act of Parliament was passed within a month which ensured that Birmingham had an adequate police force. The Government also took control over the policing arrangements in Manchester and Bolton for a period of two years in response to Chartist activity. The Birmingham Town Council resisted the measure which was introduced by the Home Secretary, warning that upon one pretence or other all the municipal bodies throughout the country will, before long, be stripped of their rightful privileges and authorities and reduced to a state of slavish submission to the Government.[32]

The County and Borough Police Act 1856 made it compulsory for all local authorities at county and borough level to establish a police force. Despite this statutory compulsion, the forces themselves remained under control of the local government. The Act also provided for the creation of three Inspectors of Constabulary who made annual inspections and police forces were only to be awarded with a grant from the Treasury if they were awarded with a certificate of efficiency.[33] Yet historian Chris Williams highlights that the State had wanted to extend its influence over the provincial police forces even further to ensure uniformity, but this was fiercely rejected by local government during the 1850s.[34]

Since the establishment of the modern police service, the police have taken a prominent role in maintaining public order. This book focuses on how they have utilised their legal powers to do this, and how their powers developed to aid them in managing new and developing situations. Under s72 Highway Act 1835, s52 Metropolitan Police Act 1839, and s21 Town Police Clauses Act 1847, the police were provided with powers to regulate the public highways and to prevent obstructions. Although these powers were not specifically tailored to regulate public assemblies, their existence did provide the police with a valuable method

---

29 *Hansard, HC Deb*, 23 Jul 1839, vol 49 cc691–707 at 696.
30 M. Chase, *Chartism: A New History*, Manchester University Press: Manchester (2007), p. 81.
31 Ibid., pp. 81–82.
32 *Birmingham Journal*, 7 Sep 1839.
33 C. Emsley, *The English Police*, p. 54.
34 C. Williams, 'Rotten Boroughs: the Crisis of Urban Policing and the Decline of Municipal Independence 1914–64', in J. Moore and J. Smith (eds), *Corruption in Urban Politics and Society, Britain 1780–1950*, Ashgate: Surrey (2007), pp. 156–157.

of regulating them.[35] Also, there were provisions under s54(13) Metropolitan Police Act 1839, and in certain areas under local bylaws, which provided the police with the power to arrest members of the public who used threatening, abusive or insulting words or behaviour with intent to provoke a breach of the peace, or whereby a breach of the peace may be occasioned. Although this provision was specifically mandated to prevent the fighting and assaults that occurred among the lower classes following such behaviour (see chapter six), it gained prominent use in the prevention of disorder at political meetings.

The activism of the Chartists instigated a response which included the use of old legislation like the Tumultuous Petitioning Act 1661 and the common law offence of high treason as methods to either prevent or punish their activism. A popular response to assist in the management of large crowds in this era was for local authorities to appoint special constables, which had the benefit of being cheaper than establishing a larger force and could also be 'justified on the grounds that an unpaid amateur force was a safeguard of personal liberty'.[36] Later in the century, socialist meetings were broken up by the police and speakers were arrested on the grounds of causing an obstruction. This method of controlling the activism of the far-Left led to complaints that the police were specifically targeting the socialists; other speakers, such as those from the Salvation Army, would hold meetings in the same spots without any police interference.[37] As the law relating to the obstruction of the highways and the use of threatening behaviour or language heavily rely on the discretion of the police, the potential to use these powers impartially to either allow or restrict certain types of political expression has been a prominent feature of public order policing which still exists today.

In the early twentieth century, the suffragettes were frequently targeted by coercive police tactics. While some methods of their activism, such as vandalism and arson, were decisively against the law, they also found themselves on the receiving end of police action when the unlawfulness of their activism was more questionable. For instance, when they heckled political speakers they would be removed from the building by police.[38] Although heckling speakers was part of the contemporary political culture, the response of the Liberal Government was to introduce a hastily passed Statute, the Public Meeting Act 1908. This was a knee-jerk reaction to the suffragettes' heckling and disorderly conduct, yet during this

---

35 See chapter four.
36 R. Swift, 'Policing Chartism, 1839–1848: The Role of the "Specials" Reconsidered' *English Historical Review CXXII*, no. 497 (2007), p. 699.
37 This was raised in Parliament by the Liberal MP Llewellyn Atherley-Jones, *Hansard, HC Deb*, 21 Sep 1886, vol 309 c1103. Evidence suggests that socialists were still targeted twenty years later; see *The South Western Labour Journal*, Special Supplement, 11 Aug 1906, for details of the prosecution of John Tamlyn of the Social Democratic Federation (SDF) for causing an obstruction. This incident is cited in I. Channing, *Poverty and the Poor Law in Plymouth, 1900–1930: Guardians of the Poor or Guardians of the Ratepayers?*, unpublished MRes thesis, Plymouth University, pp. 32–33.
38 See chapter seven.

period disorder and disruption in politics was common, and public opinion largely refused to condemn the practice of breaking up meetings.[39]

Section 54 Metropolitan Police Act 1839 was increasingly used in the interwar period as the rival meetings of the fascists and communists produced disorder on a large scale. It was during this period that the first Act of Parliament which specifically provided the police with a range of powers to manage various public order situations was passed. Although the Public Order Bill was quickly rushed through Parliament in the wake of the Battle of Cable Street 1936, the provisions within it were a combination of responses to both fascist and anti-fascist violence, as well as the disorder and activism associated with the Communist Party of Great Britain (CPGB) and the National Unemployed Workers Movement (NUWM). The resulting Public Order Act 1936 provided the police with the power to prohibit processions in advance; it proscribed the wearing of political uniforms; it banned paramilitary organisations; and it revised and nationalised existing local provisions related to threatening, abusive, and insulting words and behaviour. The measures enacted in this Bill, despite its relatively quick passage through Parliament, generated significant debate about the role of the police and the tension between ensuring the political liberty of the individual and the safety and security of the community. However, given the disorder caused by the competing politically extreme movements, many MPs saw that supporting the Public Order Bill was a regretful necessity. This is demonstrated by Independent Labour Party MP, James Maxton, who summed up during the debate when he said, 'Sometimes in this House when we attempt to evade the evils of dictatorship we are just in danger of imposing upon ourselves all the essential evils of dictatorship.'[40]

In the period after the Second World War, the Home Office continued to remove the police from local control. Chris Williams argues that the Home Office had invoked efficiency, economy and national security in an attempt to achieve these goals since 1919, but it eventually succeeded in 1964 by arguing that provincial policing was hindered by local corruption. The Police Act of that year assimilated the city forces into the counties, removing the more powerful watch committees and enforcing the Home Office's centralist agenda.[41] However, despite this change in governance, the police still had a wide range of ambiguous public order powers to draw upon. In 1980 the *Review of the Public Order Act 1936 and Related Legislation* addressed wide range of public order legislation. The Home Secretary and the Secretary of State for Scotland acknowledged that 'the law needs to balance the freedom to demonstrate with the sometimes conflicting interests of those who

---

39 See A. L. Lowell, *The Government of England* (two vols., New York, 1908), ii. 65, quoted in J. Lawrence, 'Fascist Violence and the Politics of Public Order in Inter-war Britain: the Olympia Debate Revisited, *Historical Research 76*, no. 192 (May 2003), p. 240.

40 *Hansard, HC Deb*, 7 Dec 1936, vol 318 c1764. The debates on specific clauses of the Public Order Bill are discussed in chapters five to eight.

41 See C. Williams, 'Rotten Boroughs', and C. Williams, 'Britain's Police Forces: Forever Removed from Democratic Control?' *History and Policy* (5 Nov 2003), accessed from www.historyandpolicy.org/policy-papers/papers/britains-police-forces-forever-removed-from-democratic-control.

do not wish to do so.'[42] It was highlighted in the *Review* that neither the police nor the Government wanted to abandon the traditional tactic of officers in ordinary uniform passively containing crowds in favour of more aggressive methods such as tear gas and water cannons.[43]

Fifty years later, the Public Order Act 1986 amended much of the 1936 Act. The civil disorder that preceded this Act included the Miners' Strike (1984–1985), disorder involving the National Front and anti-fascists (including Southall 1979), football hooliganism, and the Urban Riots in Bristol, Brixton, Manchester and Liverpool (1980–1981). The diversity of these disorders is reflected in the scope of the new Public Order Act, which provided further powers to the police to regulate public assemblies and processions. The common law offences of riot, rout, unlawful assembly and affray were abolished under s9 and replaced with statutory offences of riot, violent disorder and affray under ss1–3 respectively. The old s5 was also abolished and new offences under s4, s4A and s5 extended the conditions which criminalised words and behaviour which was threatening, abusive and insulting. These are examined in chapter six. The Act also included additional offences relating to racial hatred under Part III.

Since the Human Rights Act 1998 (HRA) has provided positive legal rights with the incorporation of the European Convention of Human Rights (ECHR) into UK law, this has offered some optimism that political activism and public protest will benefit from the now-protected rights of freedom of assembly and freedom of expression under Articles 10 and 11 respectively. Paradoxically, despite the possibility for human rights to now have legal protection, a sequence of counter-terrorism legislation has been enacted which has further damaged civil liberties and individual freedoms. The Terrorism Act 2000 widened the definition of terrorism and made further powers available for the proscription of organisations that were believed to be involved with terrorism. Since the terror attacks on New York and Washington DC on 11 September 2001, the Anti-Terrorism, Crime and Security Act 2001 and the Prevention of Terrorism Act 2005 have made provisions for terror suspects to be submitted to precharge detention and control orders respectively. More legislation followed the terror attacks in London on 7 July 2005, including the Terrorism Act 2006, Identity Cards Act 2006 and the Counter Terrorism Act 2008.

Amongst the implications of these further Act, was the continued assault on freedom of expression which came in s1(3) and s2(4) Terrorism Act 2006. This Act created an offence to glorify the commission or preparation of terrorism under both the encouragement of terrorism and dissemination of terrorist publications. Liberty challenged Clause 2 of the Draft Bill, stating that it criminalised opinions, a measure that should not be tolerated in a democracy as it was both 'repressive and counterproductive'.[44] Ewing criticises the scope of s2 and highlights the concerns

---

42 Cmnd. 7891, *Review of the Public Order Act 1936 and Related Legislation* (1980), p. iii.
43 Ibid., p. 5.
44 G. Crossman, *Draft Terrorism Bill: Liberties Briefing*, Sep 2005, p. 9.

of academics and librarians whose courses may concern terrorism or international relations.[45] Hunt also expressed concern regarding the Act's potentially 'chilling effect' on speech: it could reasonably be expected that broadcasters, Internet Service Providers and other organisations and individuals may consequently practise self-censorship. However, Hunt accurately anticipated that the creation of new terrorism-related offences of publication and dissemination, under s1 and s2 of the 2006 Act would not 'precipitate a rush of criminal prosecutions and/or convictions' due to the uncertainty of outcome faced by prosecutors relating to publications where the nature of the 'encouragement' element is ambiguous.[46]

The Anti-Terrorism, Crime and Security Act 2001 also placed further restrictions on freedom of expression by amendments made to the Crime and Disorder Act 1998. Where the 1998 Act created offences of racially aggravated harassment, the amendments under the 2001 Act added the new offence of religiously aggravated harassment. In 2004, when a committee of nine Law Lords reviewed the Anti-Terrorism, Crime and Security Act 2001, Lord Hoffmann declared that 'the real threat to the life of the nation . . . comes not from terrorism but from laws such as these.'[47] In the following chapters, the growing legislative framework and changing court precedents are analysed against the history of public order policing tactics and responses to particular events.

45 K. D. Ewing, *Bonfire of the Liberties: New Labour, Human Rights, and the Rule of Law*, Oxford University Press: Oxford (2010), p. 219.
46 A. Hunt, 'Criminal prohibitions on direct and indirect encouragement of terrorism' *Criminal Law Review* (Jun 2007), p. 457.
47 *A and others v Secretary of State for the Home Department; X and another v Secretary of State for the Home Department* [2004] UKHL 56, at 96.

2 'I predict a breach of the peace'[1]

Police discretion and the tension
between liberty and order

'I regret very much his biased references to the police. It seems to me to be perfectly futile to take one or two particular instances by one or two individuals and then to stigmatise the whole of the wonderful Metropolitan Police.'[2]

Introduction

At the core of the police officer's duty to keep the peace and maintain public order are the choices they make from the range of powers they have at their disposal. However, enforcing the law on a systematic and impassive basis provides an impossible mandate for law enforcers that will be discussed in this chapter. The police are therefore provided with varying amounts of discretion in order to fulfil their duty. Yet it is the availability of this discretion which can be both a valuable device in the prevention of public disorder or a liability which can bring the actions of the police into disrepute and reveal inconsistencies in police practice which can be criticised on grounds of class, politics, race or gender discrimination. The opening quote from Sir Herbert Holdsworth during a discussion in Parliament on civil and political liberty reveals the dangers: instances of inconsistent policing can bring the whole force into disrepute. In relation to public order law in the United Kingdom, the police have wide powers under the common law to prevent a breach of the peace. The controversial breach of the peace doctrine nullifies any sense of clarity or uniformity in public order law as it provides the police with extensive discretionary powers which limit the understanding of protestors and political activists of how the police will respond to their actions. First, this chapter analyses the definitions of breach of the peace and police discretion. Second, it examines how the police have used their discretion in a number of public order situations.

---

1 Apologies must be made to the Kaiser Chiefs here for parodying their song 'I Predict a Riot' for the purposes of this chapter title.
2 *Hansard, HC Debs*, 15 Dec 1937, vol 330 cc1239–1297 at 1279.

The breach of the peace doctrine

The breach of the peace doctrine empowers the police to make an arrest without warrant when such a breach is committed in their presence, or is reasonably anticipated. However, breach of the peace is not a substantive criminal offence in England and Wales, although it is recognised as a crime in Scotland.[3] Under this ill-defined doctrine, the police have a duty to preserve the peace and are provided with an arrest power which can be used when no substantive criminal offence has taken place. In the use of this power as a preventative measure, the police must demonstrate to the court that their actions were justified by the facts as well as in theory. As the nature of the breach of the peace doctrine is broad, and largely subjective, the discretion of the police officer and the interpretation of the judge do not necessarily harmonise. David Williams scrutinised the basic foundation of the doctrine with these questions" 'what, for instance, is a "breach of the peace", or what is meant by "in their presence", or what grounds are sufficient to justify an arrest in anticipation of a breach?'[4] Since these questions were posed by Williams, the Divisional Court has since provided what has become the standard definition that is referred to today. In *R v Howell*[5] Watkins LJ stated:

> We are emboldened to say that there is a breach of the peace whenever harm is actually done or is likely to be done to a person or in his presence to his property or a person is in fear of being so harmed through an assault, an affray, a riot, unlawful assembly or other disturbance. It is for this breach of the peace when done in his presence or the reasonable apprehension of it taking place that a constable, or anyone else, may arrest an offender without warrant.[6]

In the same year, Lord Denning MR offered a broader definition of breach of the peace in *R v Chief Constable of the Devon and Cornwall Constabulary, ex parte Central Electricity Generating Board*[7] stating, 'There is a breach of the peace whenever a person who is lawfully carrying out his work is unlawfully and physically prevented by another from doing it.'[8] Before these judgments there was a tendency to equate breach of the peace with any sort of disturbance. Criticism on the lack of definition and certainty of breach of the peace has frequently reoccurred in legal scholarship. In 1954, Glanville Williams remarked that there was a 'surprising lack of authoritative definition of what one would suppose to be

---

3 In Scotland, a *breach of the peace* is defined as 'conduct severe enough to cause alarm to ordinary people and threaten serious disturbance to the community'.

4 D. Williams, *Keeping the Peace: the police and public order*, Hutchinson and Co (1967), p. 116.

5 *R v Howell* [1982] QB 416.

6 Ibid. at 427.

7 *R v Chief Constable of the Devon and Cornwall Constabulary, ex parte Central Electricity Generating Board* [1982] QB 458.

8 Ibid. at 471.

a fundamental concept in criminal law'.[9] There was still an element of confusion in Brownlie's *Law of Public Order and National Security* in 1981, which stated, 'the creation of a breach of the peace is probably not a substantive crime.'[10] In 1983, the Law Commissioners' Report, *Offences Relating to Public Order,* recommended that, because of the changeability at common law of what constituted a breach of the peace, the term should not be used in statutory form, such as in s5 Public Order Act 1936.[11]

The modern argument for the abolition of the breach of the peace doctrine has been led by academic lawyers Richard Stone and Helen Fenwick. Stone defines the current position, with regard to police powers, stating '[a] police constable may take any reasonable action to stop a breach of the peace which is occurring, or to prevent one which the constable reasonably anticipates will occur in the near future.'[12] The focus of Stone's argument is centred upon the desirability of certainty within the law, the retaining of proportionality when infringements of individual rights and freedoms are created, and the undesirability of duplicated legal powers. He concludes that the wealth of statutory provisions presently available has made the breach of the peace doctrine an 'anachronism'. He argues that its vagueness was not consistent with the ECHR, which stipulates that certain Convention rights can only be restricted where the constraint is 'prescribed by law'. Fenwick also criticises that, despite the wide use of powers available for policing public protest under the Public Order Act 1986, the police still utilised the 'immensely broad and bewilderingly imprecise powers under the breach of the peace doctrine.'[13]

Police discretion

Without clearly defined legislation, and vague powers available under the breach of the peace doctrine, police officers are afforded wide discretion in fulfilling their duty. But what limitations are there on such discretion? Why does discretion exist, and does it aid or hinder effective policing?

Jeffrey Reiman, American philosopher of the criminal justice system, led an authoritative attack on police discretion in 1996, defining police discretion as:

> the freedom of police officers to decide whether or not to arrest an individual when the conditions that would legally justify that arrest are present

---

9 M. Supperstone, *Brownlie's Law of Public Order and National Security*, second edition, Butterworth and Co: London (1981), p. 2.

10 Ibid., p. 1.

11 Law Com No. 123, *Report on Criminal Law; Offences Relating to Public Order* (1983), para 5.14.

12 R. Stone, 'Breach of the Peace: The Case for Abolition', (2001), 2 *Web JCLI* accessed at http://webjcli.ncl.ac.uk/2001/issue2/stone2.html

13 H. Fenwick, 'Marginalising Human Rights: Breach of the Peace, "Kettling", the Human Rights Act and Public Protest', *Public Law 4* (2009), p. 737.

and when the officer can make the arrest without sacrificing other equally or more pressing legal duties.[14]

There is recognition here that sometimes limited resources effectively mean that a police officer must prioritise where the law is enforced. However, Reiman argued that the legislature should keep the number of laws down, enabling the police opportunity to successfully enforce them. Reiman criticises the existence of discretion, highlighting four key reasons. First, it renders the law vague and uncertain. Second, it amends laws passed by the people's representatives, therefore removing power from the legislative authority. Third, it is used in ways which will discriminate against minorities within society such as the poor, powerless and unpopular. And fourth, it provides police officers with leverage over citizens, such as the power to threaten arrest for information.[15] He later added to these four elements by stating that 'it is incompatible with treating us as citizen-sovereigns of a liberal democratic polity'.[16] These elements combine to provide a precarious basis for the consistent and effective policing of political activism and public protest.

The legal scope of police action

With regard to the policing of political activism or public protest, this book highlights accusations of police discrimination against particular political groups or causes. It is the existence of police discretion, which enables individual officers with legitimate and legal options on how to enforce certain vague laws, that creates an opportunity for the police to discriminate, either consciously or subconsciously, against certain groups or individuals. The scope of the decision making process in relation to police discretion has been most distinctly evaluated by academic lawyer Laurence Lustgarten. He argued that the degree of discretion that existed within the police force was higher at the lower levels of the hierarchy as 'they act within an almost infinite range of lawful possibilities.'[17] The decision making process for a police officer includes many variables of both 'action and inaction'. For instance, when a constable had been summoned to the scene of a minor fight, Lustgarten demonstrated the breadth of police discretion by highlighting the following options available. First, the constable could break it up and issue informal warnings. Second, the constable could break it up and attempt to mediate between them. The third option was to formally caution either or both of them. Fourth, the constable could attempt to inquire into the start of the fight and

---

14 J. Reiman, 'Is Police Discretion Justified in a Free Society?' in J. Kleinig (ed), *Handled with Discretion: Ethical Issues in Police Decision Making*, Rowman & Littlefield Publishers: Maryland, USA (1996), p. 71.
15 Ibid., pp. 78–79.
16 J. Reiman, 'Against Police Discretion: Reply to John Kleinig', *Journal of Social Philosophy 29*, no. 1 (1998), p. 132.
17 L. Lustgarten, *The Governance of Police*, Sweet and Maxwell: London (1986), p. 10.

only arrest the one he or she believed responsible. Finally, the constable could arrest both participants utilising a wide range of charges relating to public order or varying degrees of assault.[18]

Despite their vast variation, Lustgarten expressed that all these options were in the scope of the constable's legal powers. Although both men in the fight may have committed common assault by law in this instance, it is perhaps the availability of the first two options that demonstrate the breadth of this discretion. Lustgarten stated that the police constable has a greater amount of discretion 'when he chooses *not* to invoke the law . . . [as] that will seldom come to his superiors' notice.' In contrast, when a constable wishes to invoke the law, as in the case of Constable Joy of the Kent Constabulary, who arrested an MP for a traffic offence, his superiors were 'able to substitute their discretion for his' overruling Joy's wish to prosecute in favour of a caution.[19]

Police partiality and culture

In consideration of the wide legal powers available and the police officer's own potential prejudice towards particular groups (which could be a result of previous experiences, media representations or their own political ideologies), the idea that the police enforce the law impartially must be questioned. Criminologist Tony Jefferson criticises the conservative notion of police 'impartiality', stating that, 'it is based on very unrealistic sociology . . . [and] constitutes an "impossible mandate".'[20] He states that Chief Constables necessarily make choices and select priorities, which are based on limited knowledge and restricted by time and resources. Similarly, in situations where the law does not supply any clear guidance, police constables on the street must, 'make an inevitably subjective (and hence partial) judgement about the right course of action.'[21] Criminologist Robert Reiner's research on police culture can be utilised to demonstrate how these prejudices may influence their use of discretionary powers. He asserts that police bias and prejudice exist in police work, but argues that it was not necessarily the 'product of peculiarities of the individual personalities of police officers, but a reflection of wider societal prejudice, accentuated by the characteristics of police work'.[22] These influences leave some groups more vulnerable than others, especially in the arena of public protest and political activism.

In public order law, legal powers and regulation are defined by vague terms, such as breach of the peace; threatening, abusive or insulting words or behaviour;

---

18 Ibid.
19 Ibid., p. 12. Despite this, Joy still led a successful private prosecution.
20 T. Jefferson, *The Case Against Paramilitary Policing*, Open University Press: Milton Keynes (1990), p. 47. Citation from P. K. Manning, 'The Police: Mandate, Strategies and Appearances' in J. D. Douglas (ed.), *Crime and Justice in American Society*, Bobbs-Merrill: Indiana, USA (1971).
21 Ibid.
22 R. Reiner, *The Politics of the Police*. second edition, Harvester Wheatsheaf: Hertfordshire (1992), p. 159.

and causing harassment, alarm or distress. Therefore, the police's discretionary powers are so wide that 'virtually any action can, depending on its context, be plausibly branded as criminal so as to justify an arrest.'[23] Lustgarten asserted that common-sense discretion is needed in such situations and underenforcement becomes the norm. However, the danger that arises from underenforcement is that it becomes 'a cloak for conscious or unconscious discrimination on the basis of political opinion, personal appearance, demeanour, social status or race'.[24] Consequently, the resulting selective enforcement has the power to discriminate against those that Reiner highlights as victims of 'societal prejudice'. Commonly known as 'police property', these are the low status, powerless groups that the dominant powers in society leave for the police to deal with and 'turn a blind eye to the manner in which this is done'. These groups include 'vagrants, skid row alcoholics, the unemployed or casually employed residuum, youth adopting a deviant cultural style, ethnic minorities, gays, prostitutes and radical political organisations'.[25] The use of police discretion to underenforce or selectively enforce the law, therefore, means that individuals that fall within the broad category of 'police property' are more at risk from arrest.

The power of the police *not* to make an arrest and to exercise restraint from enforcing the full extent of their legal powers can be a particularly useful tool in the police constable's armoury in defusing a situation or preventing a minor disorder from escalating. As discretion ultimately leads to selective enforcement, however, it can also prove controversial, especially if an individual or group of people feel as though more clemency is afforded to others than themselves. The debate on police discretion demonstrates that not only does partiality exist as part of the inherent nature of police work at all levels, but certain levels of bias and prejudice towards minority groups (such as ethnic minorities or lower-working-class youth) can also be institutionally manufactured. Reiner warns that a vicious circle can develop from such encounters between the police and their 'property', generating hostility and suspicion on both sides, which only exacerbates the situation.[26] This can be witnessed by the often volatile relationship that has existed between the police and the political Left, which is marked by a history of confrontations, violence and distrust. Many incidents involving Chartists, socialist movements, the Communist Party of Great Britain, the suffragettes, Trade Unionists, and anti-fascist activists explored in this book demonstrate these often explosive interactions. In some cases the police's methods of law enforcement can be criticised or perceived as politically motivated, while in others the criminality of the activists justifiably warranted a police response. It is this knowledge or experience that police officers may possess about different groups which, either consciously or subconsciously, determines their discretionary judgments in public order situations. The leaders

23 Lustgarten, *The Governance*, p. 15.
24 Ibid.
25 Reiner, *Politics*, p. 118.
26 Ibid., p. 170.

of far-Right groups, such as Sir Oswald Mosley of the BUF and Kevin Carroll of the EDL, spoke highly of the police and praised them in public, encouraging their supporters to obey the law and police instruction.[27] However, it must be acknowledged that this does not mean that their members obeyed these instructions: it has frequently been seen that members of the BUF and the EDL frequently committed anti-Semitic and anti-Islamic hate crimes, respectively. But contrasted with activists on the Left and their more confrontational attitude towards the police,[28] that confrontational attitude helps demonstrate how the police officers' partiality can be compromised. This has been substantiated by former Devon and Cornwall Chief Constable John Alderson, who stated:

> Though both extremes have similar characteristics . . . they differ in the targets which they aim to attack. Where the Right attacks minorities and non-conformist groups in its assertion of nationalism, the Left attacks the establishment, particularly the police.[29]

Therefore, these different relationships that the far Left and the far Right fashioned with the police, and the manner of their interactions, are significant factors which potentially influenced the use of police discretion, leading to the selective enforcement of the law which is examined further in this book.

Dominique Wisler and Marco Tackenberg propose that the style of public order policing utilised is also influenced by the public sphere. Here the representations of the police and the policed that are produced by the mass media and the political establishment are crucial factors in how the events of a protest or demonstration unfold. In the public sphere, the actions of the police can be seen as 'disproportionate and brutal or, alternatively, as correct and tolerant'.[30] It is these representations that influence future action. To demonstrate this, Wisler and Tackenberg analysed two separate riots in Zurich, Switzerland, to demonstrate the influence of the public sphere. At the Globus Riot 1968, the police used 'tough – even unconstitutional – public-order measures . . . without provoking a public outcry' as these excesses were underplayed by most political parties and journalists. In comparison, the Opera Riot 1980, which did not include the same police excesses, split the attitudes within the public sphere. Consequently, during the public political

27 See BUF leader Sir Oswald Mosley's speech at the Royal Albert Hall 1934 at MEPO 2/3077, Fascist meetings, parade through West End and march past (1934–1935), p. 4, and Kevin Carroll of the EDL at Dewsbury 30 Jun 2012 at www.youtube.com/watch?v=Pa2TO7zYYZQ accessed on 19 Nov 2014.
28 See the Chartists who violently eject the police from their meeting (chapter seven), the Hunger Marchers who heckle and boo the police at Hyde Park in October 1932 (chapter four) and the anti-fascists chant of 'Down with the coppers; smash Mosley's body-guard' in *The Times*, 6 Jul 1937.
29 J. Alderson, *Law and Disorder*, Hamish Hamilton Ltd: London (1984), p. 48.
30 D. Wisler and M. Tackenberg, 'The Role of the Police: Image or Reality?' in R. Bessel and C. Emsley (eds), *Patterns of Provocation: Police and Public Disorder*, Berghahn Books: Oxford and New York (2000), p. 122.

battle that ensued, there were seventy-three demonstrations over the next year. It was not until the leading left wing party. the Social Democrats, and the *Tages-Anzeiger*, an independent but traditionally liberal newspaper, 'turned the spotlight and criticism away from the police, the latter began to flex their repressive muscle on the streets'.[31] The movement then declined, showing that without significant support in the public sphere the police feel legitimised in using more force to restore order. This notion of 'legitimisation' also supports Reiner's idea of police property and thus, for some minority groups the spotlight of the public sphere will offer them little protection from police excesses.

The professional political model of the good police officer

How individual police officers utilise their discretion will also include various other factors. William Ker Muir Jr identified four categories of police officer in a study which identified that the paradoxes of coercive power determine how differently police officers react to the psychological side of their role.[32] These typologies within Muir's professional political model project different explanations behind the inconsistency of police action in public order scenarios. These categories are examined with reference to how they may determine different police responses to public order situations.

The first category is the 'Avoider'. Avoiders evade responsibility either because they have an ethical difficulty arresting or exercising their power, have low self-defence skills and hence low self-confidence, or their ability to avoid conflict is aided by meagre supervision.[33] Muir highlighted that avoiders were likely to resign from the force after a short spell, while others who stayed were often reluctant to enforce the law. Therefore, an Avoider who comes into contact with a provocative speaker addressing a crowd from a street corner may be less prepared to take action against the speaker, whose speech could potentially cause a breach of the peace or who violated statutory law which regulated words and behaviour.[34] Avoidance in these circumstances would not necessarily be influenced by a police officer's politics or prejudice for or against a speaker's beliefs, but for the preference to avoid confrontation and potential conflict. The benefit for an officer who chooses not to enforce the law is that supervisors find it hard to prove that an avoider was not doing their job.[35]

The second category, 'Reciprocators', enforce their authority with negotiated accommodation. Their values include personal skills and building familiar and stable relationships between themselves and the policed that recognise the existence

---

31 Ibid., p. 132.
32 W. K. Muir Jr, *Police: Streetcorner Politicians*, The University of Chicago Press: Chicago and London (1977).
33 Ibid., p. 292.
34 Such as s54(13) Metropolitan Police Act 1839, s5 Public Order Act 1936, or ss4, 4A and 5 Public Order Act 1986.
35 Muir, *Police*, p. 292.

of a balance of power. Reciprocity could mean servicing the community by legal means using their police skills to benefit others, which could be reciprocated in the form of public support. However, reciprocity could also lead to bribes and the entering into illicit bargains between gamblers and prostitutes. However, these represent the extremes and the personal skills utilised in public order situations may not be so acute. For example, Reciprocators may have demonstrated their power by warning speakers when they believe that the speech was becoming potentially unlawful. This form of 'negotiation' was a frequent occurrence at far-Right meetings, which Renton criticises as demonstrating police collusion.[36] In one sense, it could be argued that collusion had taken place. The negotiation between the police and the fascist in this scenario does represent a consensual agreement that allows the speaker to continue as long as they are more cautious in regulating their words. Therefore, the Reciprocator has acted not with any political consideration but with the objective of preserving the meeting and allowing the speaker the liberty to continue as long as the words used do not breach the law. This establishes a good relationship between the police and the speaker, which helps prevent the disorder that may result from the arrest of the speaker or the closing of the meeting.

The third category, 'Enforcers', are those police officers who fight an 'us against them' battle. These officers are more likely to have 'meagre and biased information' and an 'enhanced belief in the efficiency of coercion.'[37] Officers within this category are more likely to act in a politically partisan way. Considering that the far Left regularly pitted themselves against authoritative powers such as the police, while the far Right (especially under Mosley) aligned themselves with law and order, it would be typical for an 'enforcer' to be aligned to the political Right. Additionally, Robert Reiner highlights that police officers are more likely to be aligned to the political Right as a result of the nature of the job, the routine clients from the bottom layer of the social order and the disciplined, hierarchical structure of the force.[38] Considering Muir's notion of the corruptive influence of coercive power, this potentially suggests that police officers that fall within the Enforcer category are more likely to use their power to support the far-Right speaker than the anti-fascist.

The first three categories mentioned are all nonprofessional categories which demonstrate different ways that the existence of coercive power corrupts the role of the police officer. The fourth category, the 'Professional', represents the 'good' police officer, where instead of power corrupting, it ennobles them. Officers in this category tend to have a 'general notion about the dignity and tragedy of human nature and . . . [have the] ability to integrate the use of 'proportionate' force into [their] principles of morality'.[39] Yet even the Professional, who is not

---

36 D. Renton, *Fascism, Anti-Fascism and Britain in the 1940s*, Macmillan Press Ltd: Hampshire and London (2000), p. 111.
37 Muir, *Police*, p. 294.
38 Reiner, *Politics*, pp. 121–124.
39 Muir, *Police*, p. 56.

corrupted by power but exercises it with morality and empathy, may still allow a provocative meeting to continue, despite their own disapproval of the speech, knowing that a successful prosecution would still be unlikely.[40]

Although the category of 'Professional' may represent the model police officer, Professionals are by no means the dominant. In Muir's qualitative research he identified that 36 per cent of subjects could be categorised under this type while the remaining 64 per cent were split between the nonprofessional typologies.[41] The possible responses debated here using Muir's different police categories demonstrate that there are different motivations and characterisations behind individual police officers that may influence their actions. In some circumstances their actions may even be similar despite different the grounds which influenced them. The consideration of these typologies adds an important dimension to the analysis of police action which helps distinguish the more one-dimensional view of the politically motivated police officer who partially enforces the law.

The police officer in action

The previous discussion on police culture and typologies demonstrates some of the motivating factors which may influence the use of police discretion. The use of discretion is now analysed by examining the actions taken by police officers in public order scenarios in order to prevent a breach of the peace and the responses of the courts in determining the legitimacy of them.

Whom should the police take action against?

A recurring dilemma for the police officer on the spot in making a decision to prevent a breach of the peace is who to take action against. This difficulty is made more problematic by a series of seemingly contradictory court judgments. For instance, in *Beatty v Gillbanks*,[42] the police arrested the Salvation Army leaders for proceeding with their public procession despite a public notice being issued which prohibited them. This was the result of the disorder caused when the Salvationists were attacked by the Skeleton Army. Here the police used their preventative breach of the peace powers against the Salvationists rather than their opponents. At the Queen's Bench Division, Field and Cave JJ judged against this police action, stating that the appellants could not be rightly convicted of unlawful assembly as there was no authority for the proposition that, 'a man may be convicted for doing a lawful act if he knows that his doing it may cause another to do an unlawful act.'[43] Yet further case law such as *Wise v Dunning*[44] has

---

40 See 'The police, anti-Semitism and the Public Order Act' in chapter six on the difficulty of securing a conviction against fascist speakers.
41 Muir, *Police*, p. 56.
42 *Beatty v Gillbanks* [1881–1882] LR 9 QBD 308.
43 Ibid. at 314.
44 *Wise v Dunning* [1902] 1 KB 167. See also chapter four.

recognised that 'there must be an act of the defendant, the natural consequence of which, if his act be not unlawful in itself, would be to produce an unlawful act by other persons.'[45] This was a response to the provocative anti–Roman Catholic lectures in Liverpool by the Protestant George Wise. These cases established that there was an invisible line that separated whether provocative conduct could fall within the remit of police action or not. It was therefore within the remit of police discretion to decide whether they thought that the threat of violence from another would be the 'natural consequence' of the provoker or not.

More recently, the preaching of three female Christian fundamentalists at the steps of Wakefield Cathedral in 1997 attracted a hostile crowd of more than 100. The police officer, fearing a breach of the peace, requested that they stopped preaching. When they failed to do so, he arrested Alison Redmond-Bate with obstructing a police officer in the execution of his duty. The discretion shown here to take action against the provocative speaker, rather than a potentially hostile crowd, mirrored the action taken by Inspector Jones on socialist speaker Kathrine Duncan more than sixty years before. In *Duncan v Jones*[46] this action was upheld by the Divisional Court. Yet, in *Redmond-Bate v DPP*[47] this course of police action no longer found validation from the judiciary.[48]

In each of these cases it must be considered where the threat to disorder comes from. Being provocative is not in itself a criminal offence. Therefore, the police officer on the spot has to consider where the threat is coming from and who is to be arrested; whether the conduct interferes with the rights of others; whether any retaliatory violence was the natural consequence of the conduct or not; or whether the retaliatory violence was wholly unreasonable.[49] These considerations are all dependent on the subjective view of the officer, who has limited time and resources to establish the correct course of action. Using police discretion to prevent a breach of the peace does not, therefore, always correlate with the view of the court. This is most notable in *Redmond-Bate*, where the officer took the most effective course of action available to prevent a breach of the peace by arresting the speaker. Although this action was not supported by the courts, the alternative action was to allow the speech to continue and manage a volatile crowd with insufficient resources.

Taking action against nonviolent protest

Another scenario faced by the police is the management of public protest which interferes with the rights of others. In these cases the protestors may use nonviolent methods which complicate the police officer's judgment on whether their action is likely to lead to a breach of the peace. In 1982, John Alderson, the Chief Constable

45 Ibid. at 175–176. *Beatty v Gillbanks* and *Wise v Dunning* are examined in more detail in chapter four.
46 *Duncan v Jones* [1936] 1 KB 220–221.
47 *Redmond-Bate v DPP* [2000] HRLR 249.
48 These cases are discussed in more detail in chapter six.
49 Beggs *et al., Public Order*, p. 64.

of Devon and Cornwall Police refused to remove the peaceful protestors who were preventing the survey by the Central Electricity Governing Board of a farm at Luxulyan, Cornwall which was shortlisted as a possible site for a nuclear power station. Despite the view of the courts in *R v Chief Constable of the Devon and Cornwall Constabulary, ex parte Central Electricity Generating Board*[50] that the protestors had committed a breach of the peace which would have legitimised any assertive police action, the police continued to monitor the protest, demonstrating that their discretionary power, which was exercised by both the Chief Constable as well as the Chief Inspector on site, who reported that in his opinion there was no likelihood of a breach of the peace. This also demonstrates a scenario where police discretion which was used not take assertive action cannot be counteracted by the courts.

In *Brutus v Cozens*[51] and *Nicol and Selvanayagam v DPP*[52] the protests both involved the interruption of sporting events. In 1971, the South African anti-apartheid activist Dennis Brutus walked onto the court during a Wimbledon men's doubles semi-final blowing a whistle and handing out leaflets. Cozens, a uniformed police officer, asked him to leave the court, but Brutus pushed him aside and sat down on the court. The crowd was reportedly hostile to Brutus, shouting at him and shaking their fists. He was arrested for using insulting behaviour that was likely to cause a breach of the peace under s5 Public Order Act 1936. The police officer deemed it his duty to remove the protestor from the court to allow play to continue and appease the angry crowd rather than facilitate Brutus's protest. The decision to utilise s5 to prosecute Brutus demonstrated the ambiguous meaning of the term *insulting* as well as the potential wideness of this interpretation of how a police officer may utilise this provision when anticipating a breach of the peace. The courts also demonstrated the difficulty in interpreting the use of this provision as the House of Lords allowed an appeal by Brutus, after the Divisional Court had found that his behaviour had been 'insulting'. Even when judged retrospectively, these ambiguous preventive powers still appear opaque.

In 1994, a small group of anti-fishing protestors disrupted an angling competition at a lake in a public park in Middleborough in order to raise public awareness towards the cruelty to fish. They threw sticks and stones at the fishing lines, sounded air horns and tried to verbally persuade the anglers to stop fishing. There was no threat of violence from the protestors. When the police arrived, they told the protestors to stop, but Laura Nicol and Diane Selvanayagam continued and they were arrested. The magistrates found that their behavior was likely to lead to a breach of the peace. In *Nicol and Selvanayagam v DPP*, the High Court agreed with the magistrates and it was determined that the 'natural consequence' of their actions was to provoke violence from the anglers. Here it is important to note that a violent response from the anglers would not have been considered 'wholly

---

50 *R v Chief Constable of the Devon and Cornwall Constabulary, ex parte Central Electricity Generating Board* [1982] QB 458.
51 *Brutus v Cozens* [1973] 1 AC 854.
52 *Nicol and Selvanayagam v DPP* (1996) 160 JP 155.

unreasonable' because the protestors were interfering with their lawful activity. It was decisively noted in *Public Order: Law and Practice* by John Beggs QC *et al.* that the protest would have been lawful it they only held banners and chanted anti-angling slogans, rather than directly interfering with the activity.[53]

These examples demonstrate the scope of discretionary powers of the police and the courts. In *Nicol and Selvanayagam* the arrest for a common law breach of the peace offence demonstrates how effective this power can be. The protestors were removed from the scene of the anticipated disorder and detained by the police between 28–30 May before seeing a magistrate who ordered them to be detained for a further twenty-one days following their refusal to be bound over. The decision to use s5 Public Order Act 1936 to prosecute Brutus, rather than seeking a binding-over order for a breach of the peace was hindered by legal definitions and ambiguities in the legislation. Yet the decision to not interfere with the protest, as was taken by the Devon and Cornwall police during the anti-nuclear protest, demonstrates that although a police operation to remove the protestors would have been supported by the courts, the judiciary did not have the power to instruct the police to do this. This is despite the similarities of this case with *Brutus* and *Nicol and Selvanayagam*, as these protests all involved the interfering of people continuing their lawful duties which may have reasonably provoked a violent reaction. Therefore, the decision of the police officer on the spot on what course of action to take, which has wide consequences for those involved, still remains a largely discretionary one which will often vary in different situations.

Conclusion

This chapter has demonstrated the breadth of police discretion in public order scenarios and examined some of the factors which may influence the decisions that police officers make. In some scenarios the courts have laid down general rules regarding the breach of the peace doctrine, but while establishing some common-sense approaches to some scenarios, the law still remains ambiguous in others. For example, when establishing where the threat is coming from the situation may not be so clear during the coming together of a demonstration and counter-demonstration. In addition, when considering whether someone's conduct interferes with the rights of others, it must also be judged whose rights should be upheld. When does a speaker's right to freedom of expression cease to exist and the violent reaction from a provoked crowd be deemed as either a natural consequence or wholly reasonable? These factors must be considered by the police officer on the spot, but as every scenario is individually constructed by distinct elements that create the public order scenario, police discretion is necessarily used to process the situation and the numerous laws at their disposal to either prevent disorder or restore order. The following chapters examine the development of the law relating to different public order themes while analyzing the inconsistencies which have resulted from the use of police discretion.

---

53 Beggs *et al.*, *Public Order*, p. 66.

3 Riot and violent disorder

Controlling spontaneous disorder and excessive police violence

And with a mighty troop around
With their trampling shook the ground,
Waving each a bloody sword,
For the service of their Lord.[1]

Introduction

On the 16 August 1819 at St Peter's Fields in Manchester, 60,000 people attended an annual festival. Crowds arrived in ceremonial processions which included music, banners and rush carts.[2] At the event 'Orator' Henry Hunt used the gathering to hold a meeting demanding Parliamentary reform.[3] The panicked magistrates, fearing potential insurrection, read the Riot Act. Baring in mind that Hunt was able to address only a small number on the fringes of this gathering, the magistrates' reaction must be seen in the context of previous disorder such as those involving the Luddites just a few years before. Percy Shelley's *The Mask of Anarchy*, quoted above, described the bloody scenes of state oppression which unfolded following the reading of the Riot Act by the Manchester magistrates. Seventeen people lost their lives and hundreds more were wounded by the sabres of the amateur yeomanry who were ordered to seize the speakers.[4] Remembered as the Peterloo Massacre, the events of that day have since been used as a warning against the tyrannical suppression of civil liberties. The massacre was even cited in 1976 by Lord Denning in *Hubbard v Pitt*,[5] who stated, 'Our history is full of warnings against suppression of these rights [assembly and expression]. Most notable was the demonstration at St. Peter's Fields, Manchester, in 1819 in support of universal suffrage.'[6]

---

1 P. Shelley, *The Mask of Anarchy* (1819), verse 11.
2 For an analytical discussion on the festivities at Peterloo and the version put forward by the prosecution of Hunt for sedition see R. Poole, 'The March to Peterloo: Politics and Festivity in Late Georgian England', *Past and Present*, no. 192 (Aug 2006) pp. 109–153.
3 M. Bentley, *Politics Without Democracy 1815–1914*, second edition, Blackwell: Oxford, p. 20.
4 R. Poole, 'The March to Peterloo', p. 112.
5 *Hubbard v Pitt* [1976] QB 142.
6 Ibid., at 174.

Yet Peterloo was just one incident among others in the first half of the nineteenth century. Between 1811 and 1820 there was also significant disorder orchestrated by the Luddites and the Blanketeers as well as the Pentrich Revolution and the Cato Street Conspiracy. David Williams and Charles Townshend both highlight the fear of revolutionary activity that followed in the decades after the French Revolution, which had the effect of stimulating the authorities to respond more coercively than the disorder had perhaps required.[7] The brutality utilised in these incidents was accompanied with alarmism in Government, which hastily passed the 'Six Acts'.[8] Following the gradual introduction of the modern police service, the role of keeping order and restoring the peace has largely become the duty of the police.[9]

This chapter examines the role of the police during various incidents of disorder and analyses the provisions used. Central to the policing of public order events is the evolving understanding of the crowd throughout this period. The historical development of crowd theory is examined and its influence on policing evaluated. First, important terms are defined and the differences in the statutory and common law offences of riot are explained.

Definitions

Common law offences

The common law offences of riot, rout, unlawful assembly and affray were abolished under s9(1) Public Order Act 1986, yet they had been part of English law since the Early Modern period. In Lambard's *Eirenarcha* of 1591, 'Riot, Route, or other Unlawfull Assemblie, etc.' are described as breaches of the peace which were punishable as misdemeanours.[10] In 1840, the Criminal Law Commissioners declared that the division of unlawful assembly, rout and riot as separate offences was considered 'unnecessary and inconvenient' as the element of 'unlawful assembly' was prevalent in all three. Therefore, an unlawful assembly was said to consist of:

(1) An assembly of three or more persons;
(2) A common purpose (a) to commit a crime of violence or (b) to achieve some other object, whether lawful or not, in such a way as to cause reasonable men to apprehend a breach of the peace.[11]

---

7 D. Williams, *Keeping the Peace*, pp. 12–13, and C. Townshend, *Making the Peace*, p. 11.
8 These repressive measures mandated to suppress the merest intimation of trouble included the Unlawful Drilling Act 1819, Seditious Meetings Act 1819 and the Criminal Libel Act 1819.
9 For an excellent account of how the police, the army and the magistracy each vigorously contested for primacy of this role see R. Vogler, *Reading the Riot Act*.
10 Supperstone, *Brownlie's Law*, p. 120.
11 J.C. Smith and B. Hogan, *Criminal Law*, third edition, Butterworths: London (1973), p. 609.

An unlawful assembly then became a rout once members of that assembly *started to move towards* the execution of their 'common purpose' or 'joint design'. Members of the assembly are then guilty of riot when the joint design is either *executed or part executed*. The Commissioners continued:

> [I]t seems to be a simpler and more intelligible principle of arrangement to consider the unlawful assembly as the groundwork of the offence and the part execution of the joint design or the motion towards it as aggravations.[12]

Further factors which indicate when an unlawful assembly became a riot was the necessity that the execution or part execution of their common purpose to 'be such as to be calculated to cause *alarm* in the mind of at least one reasonable person'.[13]

The common law offence of affray occurred when there was unlawful fighting (or a display of force without actual violence) between one or more persons in such a manner that reasonable people might be frightened or intimidated. The second element dictates that unless the violence is seen by persons other than the parties concerned, the offence would only constitute assault. This does not necessarily mean that an affray could be committed only in a public place, as assumed in *Sharp*,[14] as the following judgment in *Button v DPP*[15] demonstrated. There was also a large distinction between the punishments attributed to affray and common assault: while the latter was punishable on indictment with one-year imprisonment, affray was punishable with a fine or imprisonment at the court.[16]

The Riot Act 1714

The Riot Act 1714 created a statutory felony of riot and was repealed by s10(2) Criminal Law Act 1967. Under this legislation, if 12 or more persons were 'unlawfully, riotously, and tumultuously assembled together, to the disturbance of the publick peace', the justices were required to read the Riot Act, which ordered all persons to disperse and depart to their habitation or lawful business. It was a felony for any person to remain in the area 1 hour after the reading of the proclamation. Richard Vogler highlights that the statutory offence of riot differed from the common law offence, as it was not necessary to prove a specific act or intention (common purpose) of those assembled, and presence was merely enough to hang the accused.[17] If those assembled had not dispersed within 1 hour, then the justices were empowered to command all citizens 'of age and ability' to assist

---

12 Supperstone, *Brownlie's Law*, p. 121.
13 P. S. James, *Introduction to English Law*, eighth edition, Butterworths: London (1972), p. 155.
14 *Sharp* [1957] I QB 552.
15 *Button v DPP* [1966] AC 591.
16 Smith and Hogan, *Criminal Law*, p. 617.
17 Vogler, *Reading the Riot Act*, p. 1.

them to seize or apprehend 'such persons so unlawfully, riotously and tumultu-ously continuing together after proclamation made'. Furthermore, if any of the rioters were 'killed, maimed or hurt' then the justices, and those assisting them, 'shall be free, discharged and indemnified' of any crime. The Act was last read in 1919 and was repealed in 1967. Vogler notes that its legacy was still considered in 1981 during the Urban Riots, when the Metropolitan Police Commissioner 'argued vigorously for its re-enactment'.[18]

Understanding the crowd

Antiquated explanations of riotous behaviour have focused on the crowd's 'col-lective mind' to explain incidents of disorder in terms of their irrationality, which has been explained by a domineering mob mentality. Nineteenth-century theo-rists, such as Gustave Le Bon and Gabriel Tarde, have propagated the belief that individuals within a crowd have their own rationality and morality supplanted by a collective identity and mentality.[19] Through this process they lose their own values and reasoning, which makes them vulnerable to the destructive emotional influences that prevail and spread amongst the crowd. This process of losing one's ability to think rationally and exercise good judgment therefore explains the perception that crowds are mindless, unpredictable and potentially danger-ous. Individuals become hypnotised by the crowd's emotions and succumb more willingly to the leader's commands. Although these theories were disseminated towards the end of the nineteenth century, preceding examples of regulating large crowds had also evidently characterised the crowd as a single dangerous entity of unpredictable risk. The Riot Act 1714 was testament to the belief that to deal with the potential threat or disorder from a public assembly, all members of the crowd must be indiscriminately ordered to disperse. Furthermore, as witnessed at the Peterloo Massacre, when the yeomanry used force to disperse the crowd after the reading of the Riot Act, they did so indiscriminately: four of the eleven that were killed were women (one of whom was seven months pregnant) and another victim was a 2-year-old boy.[20]

While still widely cited, the classical approach of understanding crowd theory is largely rejected by criminologists, sociologists and psychologists today. David Waddington responded to Christian Borch's attempted resurrection of the clas-sical view, asserting that 'Such crudely provocative theorising will inevitably mislead and misinform, resulting in dangerously repressive and unenlightened techniques of crowd control.'[21] Stephen Reicher *et al.* also emphatically rejected the approach stating, 'the classical approach to crowd psychology is not only

---

18 Ibid., p. 3.
19 G. Le Bon, *The Crowd: A Study of the Popular Mind*, T. Fisher Unwin: London (1895).
20 J. Marlowe, *The Peterloo Massacre*, Rapp & Whiting: London (1969).
21 D. Waddington, 'The Madness of the Mob? Explaining the 'Irrationality' and Destructiveness of Crowd Violence', *Sociology Compass* 2, no. 2 (2008), p. 685.

wrong, but dangerously wrong.'[22] These dangers are clearly demonstrated with examples of how the police's commitment to classical crowd theory can create and aggravate further disorder rather than calming or restoring it.

Reicher *et al.* argues that 'where the police treat all crowd members the same, they are likely to see themselves as all the same' and, furthermore, they are more likely to form an oppositional front to the police should they be treated in that manner by them.[23] The police's utilisation of classical crowd theory therefore has the power to negatively redefine the collective identity of those within a crowd. This was emphasised by Clifford Stott and John Drury, whose study of the 1990 Poll Tax Riot demonstrated how the dynamics of a generally peaceable and well-intentioned crowd changed following indiscriminate and coercive police tactics, which employed cordons, baton charges and mounted officers. The escalation of the disorder which culminated in the involvement of up to 5,000 people was explained by Stott and Drury in terms of shifts in their collective identity rather than the contagious spread of irrational and violent behaviours:

> When the context changed from 'poll tax protest' to 'police attack', so participants' identities changed from non-violent opposition to the former to self-defence against the latter.[24]

Furthermore, because the crowd perceived the police attack to affect them all, and not just the violent minority, it legitimised such use of 'self-defence'. Subsequently, the policing of the crowd must therefore respect the members of it as individuals and recognise that their own tactics have a significant influence on its future behaviour. However, although it has been established that the police's adoption of the classical crowd theory approach can have a negative influence on crowd behaviour, it appears that public order training has yet to fully incorporate more recent and effective models of crowd management.

James Hoggett and Clifford Stott's research in the public order police training of football crowds acknowledged that the classical approach is still dominant in police training.[25] The research acknowledged that although the *Manual of Guidance for Keeping the Peace* produced by the Association of Chief Police Officers (ACPO) was updated in 2003 to include the principles of the Elaborated Social Identity Model (ESIM), the instructors and students engaged in public order training reflected the classical view that the crowd was irrational and influenced by hooligans. Therefore, if the strategy to remove or contain the hooligan element failed,

22 S. Reicher *et al.*, 'An integrated approach', p. 565.

23 Ibid., p. 564.

24 C. Stott and J. Drury, 'Crowds, context and identity: Dynamic categorization processes in the "poll tax riot"', *Human Relations 53*, no. 2 (2000), p. 266.

25 J. Hoggett and C. Stott, 'Crowd psychology, public order police training and the policing of football crowds', *Policing: An International Journal of Police Strategies and Management 33*, no. 2 (2010), pp. 218–235.

the tactics would be adapted to use force against the crowd as a whole.[26] The ESIM approach is a psychological model which proposes that collective behaviour

> is made possible through the shared salience among crowd participants . . . [and] the form and content of a crowd's identity is viewed as context dependent and therefore can change as a function of the inter-group interactions that occur during a crowd event.[27]

In consideration that the behaviour of the different subgroups within a crowd is reliant on their interactions with each other and the police, it is especially important that police tactics are used to positively influence these interactions. A largely successful initiative that has recognised this is an approach termed by Stott and Hugo Gorringe as *liaison based public order policing.*[28] The introduction of the Police Liaison Teams (PLTs) which aim to create communication and trust with crowds has had mixed results. This has been highlighted by Stott, Gorringe and Martin Scothern, who observed the use of PLTs during six protests.[29] For example, during the 'Occupy' protests on 15 May 2012 a PLT was tasked to establish contact with the protestors and liaise with them, highlighting their role as protest facilitator. Stott *et al.* argued that the Bronze Commander's employment of the PLT as the primary tactic rather than deploying the Police Support Units (PSU) he had available demonstrated that this was a visible signal of the police's rejection of the classical crowd control theory and also involved the toleration of some disruption.[30] Unlike previous 'Occupy' protests, the facilitation of the protest by the PLTs, rather than by any other more autocratic means, meant the protest ended without any arrests or containments taking place. Other uses of PLTs have not kindled the same success. In Sussex a 'UKUncut' activist who was visited at home by liaison officers saw this attempt to establish communication as police intimidation. In the subsequent 'street party' demonstration in Brighton on 1 June 2012 the same PLT officer drew his baton, which further eroded the trust between the police and the activists. Stott *et al.* highlight that these negative experiences led to a media response which claimed that 'PLTs are an insidious and illegitimate form of police surveillance designed to criminalise peaceful protest.'[31] However, their research contends that PLTs offer a positive development in public order policing, as the police start with

---

26 Ibid., pp. 226–227.

27 Ibid., p. 219.

28 C. Stott and H. Gorringe, 'From Peel to PLTs: Adapting to Liaison Based Public Order Policing in England and Wales' in J. Brown (ed.), *The Future of Policing: Papers Prepared for the Stevens Independent Commission into the Future of Policing in England and Wales*, Routledge: London (2013).

29 C. Stott, M. Scothern and H. Gorringe, 'Advances in Liaison Based Public Order Policing in England: Human Rights and Negotiating the Management of Protest?', *Policing 72*, no. 2 (2013), pp. 212–226.

30 Ibid., p. 217.

31 Ibid., p. 219. The media response was a video article posted on the *Guardian* online found at www. theguardian.com/uk/video/2012/sep/04/police-liaison-officers-uk-uncut-video.

an initial tactic of negotiated management. Furthermore, whilst acknowledging that police tactics can quickly shift towards the use of escalated force if they perceive the level of threat or potential criminality to warrant it, these shifts were less likely to occur when liaison officers were deployed.[32] These shifts in public order policing strategy have provided some optimism that the rights to public protest and political activism are beginning to be protected, at least in the initial planning of a public order event, and are now having a positive impact in decreasing the threat of disorder and potential riots. However, these changes in practice have largely evolved since the enactment of the Human Rights Act and the incorporation of the ECHR. During the existence of the Riot Act, there was less emphasis on the protection of rights and facilitation of protest, an adherence to classical crowd theory and a commitment to the use of coercive force when disorder occurred or was anticipated. It will now be demonstrated how this mixture of attitudes provoked and escalated the crowds' participation in disorder.

Reading the Riot Act

By virtue of the Riot Act's provisions, which made it an offence to remain in the area an hour after it was read and discharged and indemnified those assisting the magistrates of any crime even if they killed or maimed remaining protesters, it represented the ultimate authority of the state. These extreme measures acted as a warning for those present to disperse or face severe or mortal punishment. The Riot Act was the authorities' last resort in ending a riotous assembly, yet while this power to force compliance and deter further rioting existed, the process was not always successful.

During the national miners' strike in 1893, there was a delay in finding a magistrate to read the Act at Featherstone. West Riding was particularly affected by the strikes, which began in late July, as there were 80,000 miners out of work from the 253 mines in the region.[33] By early September, the disorder had increased as the mine owners still refused to accept the wage demands of the miners (wages had been cut by 25 per cent in response to the fall in the price of coal). With limited police resources, due to the strikes and the Doncaster races,[34] the authorities requested extra support from the military. At 11:45 on the morning of the riot the Chief Constable of West Riding sent a telegram to the barracks at York requesting cavalry and infantry to come by train as soon as possible.[35] The rioters engaged in stone throwing and setting light to buildings in the colliery; by the evening the police and military were both present in numbers. When it appeared that the

---

32 Ibid., p. 225.
33 *Featherstone Inquiry. Minutes of evidence taken before the Committee appointed to inquire into the circumstances connected with the disturbances at Featherstone on 7th September 1893* [C.7234i], p. 3.
34 There was information that the rioters would march to the races and loot the grandstand which increased the police presence at this event. Ibid., p. 5.
35 Ibid., p. 6.

colliery owner, Mr Holiday, was in danger after he addressed the crowd, Sergeant Sparrow told the crowd that he would withdraw the police if they promised to go home. This quietened the crowd and Holiday was removed from danger. Although this initially had a positive effect on the crowd, when someone shouted 'But how about the soldiers?', Inspector Cordon could only reply that he had no power over them. This response reignited the volley of stones thrown at the police.[36] Another incident that garnered a violent reaction from the crowd was the discovery of the military who were stationed in the engine house.[37] The magistrate, Hartley, arrived at 8:00 p.m. As the disorder did not improve on his arrival, he read the Riot Act 40 minutes later. Although there was another lull in the crowd at this point, the troops had also marched up behind Hartley with fixed bayonets. Again the crowd reacted with stone throwing. The troops marched on the crowd, but were again pulled back as they had little effect. Finally, at 9:15 p.m. Hartley ordered the troops to fire blank cartridges. He was informed that the soldiers were not equipped with these and also it was against regulations. Hartley then asked Captain Barker to fire as little as possible. It was reported that as the rifles were being prepared a voice from the crowd encouraged the others to stay, shouting, 'Go on, it's only blank,' and the stone throwing resumed. After the second firing of rounds it was realised that two men had been shot. Some disorder still continued as a railway bridge was set alight and completely destroyed an hour after the last shots were fired.[38]

Despite the Chief Constable's early acknowledgment that there may be serious disorder, the authorities' inadequate response ended with serious damage to property and the death of two men. Richard Vogler highlights that one potential cause of the seriousness of the disorder was that there were no justices with local knowledge present to give orders.[39] Clive Emsley also states that the presence of the soldiers at the colliery also inflamed the situation.[40] In addition, the evidence provided to the Featherstone Inquiry also reveals moments when the crowd reacted differently to the approaches used by the police and the military. For instance, there were lulls when the police initially withdrew and when the Riot Act was first read. However, the crowd responded violently when troops were discovered in the engine room, when they used coercive tactics with their bayonets and when they loaded their rifles.

As the troops had opened fire and killed two men within an hour of the reading of the Riot Act, the legality of their actions was scrutinised by the Inquiry. It had to be established whether the action taken could be justified under the common law. The Inquiry established that

> The riotous crowd at the Ackton Hall Colliery was one whose danger con-
> sisted in its manifest design violently to set fire and do serious damage to

---

36 *Featherstone Inquiry. Report of the Committee appointed to inquire into the circumstances con-nected with the disturbances at Featherstone on 7th September 1893* [C.7234], p. 5.
37 Ibid. One man even attempted to set fire to the engine house to flame the military out.
38 Ibid., pp. 6–7.
39 Vogler, *Reading the Riot Act*, p. 70.
40 Emsley, *The English Police*, p. 116.

the colliery property, and in pursuit of that object to assault those upon the colliery premises . . . and it became the duty of all peaceable subjects to assist in preventing this.[41]

In accordance with this summary, the Inquiry found that

the fact that an hour had not expired since its reading did not incapacitate the troops from acting when outrage had to be prevented. All their common law duty as citizens and soldiers remained in full force . . . we think that, in the events which had happened, Captain Barker and his troops had no alternative left but to fire, and it seems to us that Mr. Hartley was bound to require them to do so.[42]

Despite the shootings occurring before an hour had passed after the reading of the Riot Act, the Inquiry still supported the actions taken by the magistrate and the troops under the elasticity of common law. However, in an attempt to use the common law offence of riotous assembly to limit the provocative activism of the British Union of Fascists in the 1930s, the magistrates did not rule that such flexibility in the law stretched that far.

The common law offence of riotous assembly

Mosley acquitted of riotous disorder at Worthing 1934

The BUF meeting in Worthing on 9 October resulted in Sir Oswald Mosley, William Joyce, Charles Budd and Bernard Mullans being summonsed on the charge of riotous assembly.[43] Mosley and Mullans were also charged with individual cases of assault.

The five necessary elements for the common law offence of riot were summarised by Phillimore J in *Field v Metropolitan Police Receiver*[44] as:

(1) number of persons, three at least;
(2) common purpose;
(3) execution or inception of the common purpose;
(4) an intent to help one another by force if necessary against any person who may oppose them in the execution of their common purpose;
(5) force or violence not merely used in demolishing, but displayed in such a manner as to alarm at least one person of reasonable firmness and courage.[45]

---

41 *Featherstone Inquiry, Report*, p. 10.
42 Ibid., p. 11.
43 William Joyce was national propaganda officer and later gained notoriety as Lord Haw Haw during the Second World War. Charles Budd was a Blackshirt officer for the West Sussex area and Bernard Mullans was described as a member of the Blackshirt movement.
44 *Field v Metropolitan Police Receiver* [1907] 2 KB 853.
45 Ibid., at 860.

Mosley had conducted an indoor meeting at the pavilion on the seafront, a building he described as 'a large tin tabernacle of flimsy construction'.[46] He alleged that the tin sides of the pavilion were struck by sticks and stones during the meeting. According to the prosecution, the crowd which had assembled outside had been orderly and good humoured, and it was the actions of the fascists that had incited disorder. Prosecuting at Worthing Police Court, John Flowers KC alleged that the four defendants, and other members of the fascist movement acting under their encouragement, walked up and down outside the pavilion and assaulted inoffensive and law-abiding citizens. He continued the prosecution's case, stating, 'there was taking place a perfectly disgraceful and intolerable state of things. Violence was being used by the members of the defendant's party against all and sundry.'[47]

The defence responded with the typical BUF stance of being victims of disorder rather than the instigators. Mosley stated, 'If ever a thing has been proved to the hilt before a Court of Law it is this – that they were more sinned against than sinning.' He then appealed to the bench not to 'stretch the law against freedom of speech, the freedom of expression, and against minorities.'[48] The prosecution's argument countered this by stressing the orderly nature of the crowd and considered that the reason that the BUF dress in uniform and travelled to Worthing with bodyguards and ambulance men was to meet violence with violence.[49]

In one instance, Mosley was alleged to have struck a member of the crowd. In addition, a female witness alleged she was hit on the head by a Blackshirt. Police witnesses also highlighted the orderly conduct of the crowd and stressed the unprovoked use of force by the Blackshirts.[50] Much of the disorder was said to have occurred as Blackshirts violently pushed their way through crowds at either a café, where Mosley had supper, or Warwick Street, outside the local BUF headquarters. Mosley had received reports that an angry mob were 'beleaguering' their headquarters, where there were women inside. On arriving there himself, general fighting ensued and some Blackshirts came out of the office to assist them. The prosecution highlighted that the Blackshirts had taken a fighting attitude to the orderly crowd. An example of the unprovoked attacks included the assault of a solicitor's clerk who was passing through Warwick Street after posting a letter and was struck on his head, nose and jaw by Blackshirts, which left him unconscious and covered in blood. Mosley claimed that he stayed on the streets until order was restored because he did not want to endanger the females within the headquarters. In his autobiography, Mosley's recollections of the event glorify the retribution

---

46 O. Mosley, *My Life*, (Friends of Oswald Mosley, 2006) p. 245, downloaded from www.oswaldmosley. com/downloads/My per cent20Life.pdf on 15 April 2010, p. 296. This incident is discussed here as it the action of the Blackshirts in public that was scrutinised in this case, rather than on the private premises of the meeting hall.

47 *Hull Daily Mail*, 8 Nov 1934.

48 *Daily Telegraph*, 10 Nov 1934. Newspaper clipping from MEPO 2/10651, Case of riotous assembly at Worthing, Sussex against Sir Oswald Mosley, William Joyce, Bernard Mullen and Captain Charles Bentinck Budd: Reports, and correspondence.

49 Ibid.

50 Ibid.

of the Blackshirts, recalling that the 'Reds had arrived in coaches from far away, but after protracted debate left in some disorder . . . [and on the disturbance at Warwick Street stated] the Reds were surprised to see us . . . and again they got the worst of it.'[51] The police court proceedings lasted for 5 days before the Bench retired and committed all four defendants for trial at the Lewes Assizes.

Prosecuting, John Flowers KC stated that this was not a political prosecution but one brought by the West Sussex Police to deal with 'a very disgraceful, discreditable and violent state of affairs in the streets of Worthing'.[52] It was also stressed by the prosecution that none of the witnesses that were assaulted had any particular political views and their evidence was supported by 'respectable persons . . . without any political axe to grind'.[53] Mosley had alleged that the prosecution was brought about by the Government of the day, who he claimed controlled the police. It was for this reason he stated that the police evidence was 'contradictory and false'.[54] Under cross-examination, the police tactics to control any anticipated disorder arising from the BUF meeting were exposed. First, the evidence that the crowd was orderly was challenged by the declaration that the crowd threw things, including tomatoes, through the windows of the café, hitting waitresses in the face. Second, the crowd were also alleged to have been booing and shouting at women and chasing them through the streets. None of the police officers called to testify witnessed these scenes. In addition, only four police officers were originally stationed in the vicinity of the BUF meeting, despite notification from Budd that they expected organised disorder from their opponents. It was argued for the defence that the police did 'practically nothing' in preparation for the meeting despite the crowd numbering the same as that of a general election.[55] Branson J rejected the prosecution's argument that the common purpose in this case which constituted riot was the holding of the meeting and parading the streets. He stated,

> It is not suggested here that anything which happened before the events in Warwick Street constitutes a riot. I cannot find any evidence of any common purpose or object with regard to which they can be inferred to have agreed to use violence.[56]

Furthermore, the violence that occurred at Warwick Street broke out in the absence of the four defendants. Branson J instructed the jury to find a verdict of not guilty. The defence applied for costs against the police. However, Branson J responded stating that although he did not think the police gave evidence with the fairness he expected, he did not think that he should make them pay the costs.[57]

---

51 Mosley, *My Life*, p. 296.
52 *Derby Daily Telegraph*, 17 Dec 1934.
53 *News Chronicle*, 9 Nov 1934.
54 *The Star*, 13 Nov 1934. Newspaper clipping from MEPO 2/10651.
55 *Daily Telegraph*, 19 Nov 1934.
56 Ibid.
57 Ibid.

The policing of Mosley's meeting at Worthing demonstrates the wide discretion that the police had when utilising the common law offence of riotous assembly. For instance, the officers on duty did not take any action against those members of the crowd who did cause disorder by throwing objects and using threatening behaviour such as chasing women in an intimidating way. The officers on the ground and their superiors who proceeded with the charge directed their powers against the BUF. Despite evidence suggesting that some members of the crowd used illegal methods to show their contempt of the fascists' meeting, the police used their discretion to overlook some aspects of the crowd's behaviour as they regarded the BUF as the instigators of the disorder. When policing rival political groups, the police's response will undoubtedly be criticised by either one or both of the parties involved. Keeping rival groups apart while attempting to facilitate political activism and public protest while appearing nonpolitical is an ongoing challenge for public order police. When disorder breaks out that includes the destruction of property and acts of vandalism and looting, the police response is critiqued in its adequacy in restoring order and bringing offenders to justice.

Suppressing the riot

The Urban Riots 1981

An outbreak of violence in Bristol in April 1980 heralded the start of several urban riots across England. In April 1981 there was rioting in Brixton, and in July of that year there was rioting in Moss Side, Manchester and Toxteth, Liverpool. The difficulty that the police faced in controlling the spontaneous disorder was evident during these urban riots. This included the waiting time for reinforcements as well as the inadequacy of their equipment. In particular, their helmets provided insufficient protection to the head and their shields and uniforms caught fire when under fire from petrol bombs. The response was for all police officers to be given training in crowd control; improvements to be made to uniforms, helmets, shields and vehicles; and for CS gas and plastic bullets to be made available. Tony Jefferson highlights the significant shift that the changes in public order policing brought in the wake of the Urban Riots. He acknowledges that Robert Mark's philosophy that the art of policing a free society is winning by appearing to lose has been superseded by a new belligerence which was exemplified by Commissioner McNee's sombre warning that 'if you keep off the streets of London and behave yourself, you won't have the SPG [special patrol group] to worry about'.[58]

On 16 July 1981, Home Secretary William Whitelaw addressed the Commons, responding to calls to reintroduce the Riot Act. In his description of the disorders he stated that there were large violent groups who attacked the police, but more often they were scattered groups who engaged in looting and damage to property.

---

58 Jefferson, *The Case*, p. 8. In-quote quotations taken from R. Reiner, *The politics of the police*, Wheatsheaf: London (1985), p. 54 and *Policing London*, no. 8, 1983, p. 10. Sir Robert Mark was Metropolitan Police Commissioner from 1972 to 1977.

He argued that as the Riot Act was primarily mandated to disperse the first group, the reenactment of it was not necessary as there were other provisions available for this area, including the common law offences of riot, rout and unlawful assembly; the arrest powers under the breach of the peace doctrine; s5 Public Order Act 1936; and the offence of obstructing the police in the execution of their duty.[59]

The riots in Moss Side were brought under control in prompt fashion by the Greater Manchester Police. Stretford MP Winston Churchill[60] praised the tactics used by the Chief Constable James Anderton:

> I much applaud their far more aggressive tactics. They went in during the riot with snatch squads to arrest those responsible for the violence. As a result, the violence was brought under control with the minimum number of police casualties. We should all welcome that.[61]

The Urban Riots of the early 1980s helped change the face of modern policing. Jefferson describes this transformation of practice in public order scenarios as 'from "pushing and shoving" to "search and destroy"'. He emphasises this change as being highlighted by the menacing teams of officers who formed 'snatch squads'. He describes their militarised appearance and tactics, which were emphasised by their visored crash helmets, fireproof overalls and the transparent shields that they would bang with their drawn truncheons as they advanced into crowds of fleeing demonstrators in order to make an arrest or to seize a spot of retributive 'destruction'.[62]

This image emphasised the emergent paramilitary image of the police. In response, this argument of paramilitarism has been refuted by P.A.J. Waddington, who contends that as the uniforms and equipment are defensive they should not be considered as provocative.[63] Although this view must be recognised, it is also imperative to note that such uniforms, which are visibly designed for conflict, will appear confrontational to crowd members.

The Public Order Act 1986

In addition to the miner's strikes of 1985, football hooliganism and the political violence involving the National Front and their opponents, the first major piece of public order legislation was enacted in 1986. Part I of the 1986 Act details new offences and the abolition of old Statute and common law offences. S1 Public Order Act 1986 redefined the common law offence of riot, making it the most serious offence of the 1986 Act and punishable by a maximum of ten years

---

59 *Hansard, HC Deb*, 16 Jul 1981, vol 8 cc1397–1503 at 1402.
60 Grandson of the former Prime Minister, Winston Churchill.
61 *Hansard, HC Deb*, 16 Jul 1981, vol. 8 cc1397–503 at 1452.
62 Jefferson, *The Case*, pp. 1–2.
63 P.A.J. Waddington, 'The case against paramilitary policing considered', *British Journal of Criminology 33*, no. 3 (1993), p. 353.

imprisonment. A major amendment in the statutory definition of riot is that it requires 12 or more persons assembled together to be causing unlawful violence for a common purpose. The previous common law offence of riotous assembly required only the presence and participation of at least three or more persons, and the penalty was life imprisonment – although some riots of a serious nature had been prosecuted as high treason, which carried the death penalty. Under the 1986 Act, the crime of riot can be tried only on indictment and requires the consent of the Director of Public Prosecutions. In the event of a riot, the compensation for any damages to property is still provided by the fund of the local police authority in accordance with the Riot (Damages) Act 1886.

The common law offences of rout and unlawful assembly were abolished under s9 and the new offence of violent disorder was created. Rout was considered to be obsolete by the Law Commission's *Report on Criminal Law; Offences relating to Public Order.*[64] Under s2 violent disorder is defined as '3 or more persons who are present together use or threaten unlawful violence'. The offence is distinguished from riot by the number of people present, and it is not necessary for there to be a common purpose. Also, an individual may be guilty of either using or threatening to use violence, meaning members of a group who used threats only could also be tried on indictment together with those who used actual violence, rather than be left to a separate summary trial under the lesser offence in s4 POA 1986.

S3 replaced the common law offence of affray. The main elements which define it are (1) 'A person is guilty of affray if he uses or threatens unlawful violence towards another' and (2) 'Where 2 or more persons use or threaten the unlawful violence, it is the conduct of them taken together that must be considered for the purposes of subsection (1).'

The 2011 riots

Thirty years later, rioting across urban areas of England and the policing of them again came under national scrutiny. Since the 1981 riots the academic consensus has been that the riots had some legitimacy as a form of protest against a variety of social conditions and experiences. These have included the responses to the austerity measures of Margret Thatcher's Conservative government, which included the reduction of public services in poverty-afflicted areas, high unemployment and the police's predominant use of stop and search powers on young black men, commonly referred to as the 'sus' laws.[65] The oppressive and bleak experiences of these neglected communities provided some legitimacy to the disorder as a form of political protest. Indeed, David Waddington questions the notion that such disorder was mindless vandalism by highlighting the view of one French rioter who set fire to a car during the 2005 Paris riots and explained, 'they burn nicely and

64 Law Com No. 123, *Report on Criminal Law; Offences Relating to Public Order* (1983).
65 E. Smith, 'Once as History, Twice as Farce? The Spectre of the Summer of '81 in Discourses on the August 2011 Riots', *Journal for Cultural Research 17*, no. 2 (2013), p. 125.

Figure 3.1 Rioters and police in Croydon, 8 Aug 2011.

Photograph by Raymond Yau. Source: Flickr: Croydon Riots 2011

the cameras like them. How else are we going to get our message to Sarkozy? It is not as if people like us can just turn up at his office.'[66]

The conditions of 1981 evoke similarities with the more recent disorder across England in summer 2011. The similarities and how they have been utilised to fit the political agendas of politicians, journalists, scholars and activists have been critically analysed by historian Evan Smith.[67] Smith warns against the dangers of such comparisons as they threaten to simplify our understanding of the disorders in 1981 by categorising their causes so neatly to fit a particular political agenda today. His historical research highlights the different political understandings of the riots from those who understood them as a response to the socio-economic policies or as a response by the black community to the racism and discrimination they faced. While some comparisons with the 2011 riots are evident, such as the disproportionate use of stop and search powers on black men, spending cuts by a Conservative government (although in the 2011 case this was a Conservative-led coalition Government) and high unemployment, it must be questioned whether the recent disorders have the same legitimacy.[68] Expectedly, David Cameron neatly described the riots as 'criminality', adding

> These riots were not about race: the perpetrators and the victims were white, black and Asian. These riots were not about government cuts: they

66   Waddington, 'The Madness of the Mob', p. 685.
67   Smith, 'Once as history', pp. 124–143.
68   B. Stanko and P. Dawson, 'Reflections on the Offending Histories of those Arrested during the Disorder', *Policing 7*, no. 1, (2012), p. 5.

were directed at High Street stores, not Parliament. And these riots were not about poverty: that insults the millions of people who, whatever the hardship, would never dream of making others suffer like this. No, this was about behaviour . . . people showing indifference to right and wrong . . . people with a twisted moral code . . . people with a complete absence of self-restraint.[69]

The response from the Left critically maintained a 'tough on crime' stance but also demonstrated an understanding that deeper issues were present, as Ed Miliband declared:

> To seek to explain is not to seek to excuse. Of course these are acts of individual criminality. But we have a duty to ask ourselves why there are people who feel they have nothing to lose, and everything to gain, from wanton vandalism and looting.[70]

Reflecting an understanding of crowd theory and the initial flashpoint of the disorder in Tottenham in the wake of the death of Mark Duggan (who was shot by a police marksman) offers some comprehension. Following Duggan's death and the unsatisfactory and conflicting reports about the details of his death, a 100-person march to the Tottenham Police Station was planned by Duggan's family. During the protest a riot officer had allegedly pushed a 16-year-old girl to the ground, where she was hit by batons and dragged away. Although the girl had purportedly thrown a bottle at the police, these actions had dangerously shifted the identity of those in the crowd. The crowd were understandably angry and frustrated with police action due to the emotional and personal nature of the protest. However, regardless of this discontent, there was no reason to expect that such serious disorder would follow. The emotive effect that this incident had on the crowd was to reinforce the crowd's already sceptical view on police legitimacy and trust. With these barriers being completely shattered by such visible acts of police coercion, groups within the crowd were enabled to change their identity from a protest which demanded answers to the death of Mark Duggan to a violent opposition towards the police. This was further exasperated by the use of social media as a video of the girl being struck by police was uploaded to YouTube, causing further anger, resentment and hostility towards the police from the wider community.

Although there were a significant number of rioters who either had gang affiliation or previous criminal history that were arrested during the whole of the disorder, it is still meaningful to consider the motivations of the 29 per cent of London arrestees who were first-time offenders.[71] The London School of Economics and the *Guardian* conducted 270 confidential interviews with those involved in the

---

69 D. Cameron, *PM's speech on the fightback after the riots*, 15 Aug 2011, accessed from www.gov. uk/government/speeches/pms-speech-on-the-fightback-after-the-riots

70 Politics.co.uk, 'Ed Miliband riot statement in full', accessed from www.politics.co.uk/comment-analysis/2011/08/11/ed-miliband-riot-statement-in-full

71 Stanko and Dawson, 'Reflections', p. 6.

riots across England and questioned the participants' motivations for their involvement. Most significantly, 85 per cent of the interviewees cited that treatment by the police was either an 'important' or 'very important' aspect of why the riots happened. Many described their involvement in looting as opportunism, citing that the breakdown of normal rules meant they were able to 'acquire' otherwise unattainable items. Other grievances included tuition fees, the closure of youth services, the scrapping of the education maintenance allowance, perceived social and economic injustices and anger over the police shooting of Mark Duggan.[72]

Rioting continued in Tottenham throughout the evening, with police vehicles, shops and banks being the targets of vandals and looters. Clive Bloom highlighted how the following day, despite police intelligence reporting that gangs were preparing riots in Tottenham, Enfield, Walthamstow and Hackney at 4 p.m., only seven police officers were stationed at Enfield to keep order. Bloom compared these tactics, which were allegedly used to demonstrate poor police resources, with a similar tactic used in the London Student Riots 2010. Bloom highlights a discrepancy in the narrative of a police van that had been apparently attacked by activists, forcing the police officers to flee for their safety. An alternative explanation alleged that the van was left as 'bait' for the students in order that 'an official media narrative' could be created later. He questions,

> Did the abandonment of the vehicle signal a new police tactic which left the streets to rioters who could not be effectively policed with existing resources, thereby leaving the 'policing' until after the event so that punishment might be swifter and harsher?[73]

Furthermore, although this new police strategy could only be speculated, Bloom links the similarities with the policing of the 2011 riots where police initially appeared under-resourced to prevent widespread damage and looting, but then exercised 'swifter and harsher' tactics. Indeed, the media narrative of the riots stimulated public fear and anger as communities descended into lawlessness with no visible police presence and emergency services withheld through fear of attack.[74]

If the 1981 riots heralded the commencement of a move towards paramilitary policing, the legacy of the 2011 riots are potentially even more far-reaching. The tabloid media narratives of the riots helped peddle a culture of fear which propagated an increase of police powers and armoury in order to respond to future disorder. For instance, *The Sun's* YouGov poll revealed 'that 90 per cent of readers favoured the use of water cannons, 78 per cent wanted tear gas, 77 per cent wanted the army on the streets and at least 33 per cent favoured the use of live

---

72 *The Guardian* and the London School of Economics, *Reading the Riots: Investigating England's Summer of Disorder*, London (2011), available at www.theguardian.com/uk/interactive/2011/dec/14/reading-the-riots-investigating-england-s-summer-of-disorder-full-report, pp. 3–5.

73 C. Bloom, *Riot City: Protest and Rebellion in the Capital*, Palgrave Macmillan: London (2012), p. 61.

74 Ibid., p. 81.

ammunition!'[75] On 6 Jan 2014, the Mayor of London, Boris Johnson, wrote to Home Secretary Theresa May stating that he will make funds in order to provide the Metropolitan Police Service with water cannons, citing the 2011 riots and the public approval of this measure as the reason.[76] Following a public meeting which supported this acquisition, the final decision on authorising the use of the water cannon on the UK mainland now rests with the Home Secretary.[77] Theresa May's response highlighted that she was keen that the Metropolitan Police Service have the tools to maintain order but has refused to provide authorisation until further tests are carried out.[78] The public consultation acknowledged significant support for the police use of water cannons. In a poll, 60 per cent believed that a water cannon would be useful for policing London and 52 per cent said they would be more confident in the police's ability to deal with riot or serious disorder if they were able to use water cannons.[79] The consultation also revealed important criticisms: water cannons are indiscriminate and would effectively be used on innocent protesters as well as violent individuals, and may have the effect of deterring participation in peaceful protest; they may escalate violence; they were just a knee-jerk reaction to the riots in 2011.[80]

Conclusion

The images conjured in Shelly's *Mask of Anarchy* still linger over the policing of public order. Although the tactics and tools used by the police do not present an image as graphically oppressive as a 'bloody sword', the number of protesters who have died or received serious injuries as a result of police's use of force or brutality[81] still presents a worrying situation. As the media narratives of disorder and ill-equipped police services help develop public acceptance of more coercive police tactics, such as the expected advent of the water cannon in London, the future policing tactics of disorder is likely to involve the increased use of force.

Much of the disorder described in this chapter has been treated by the authorities as criminality rather than any form of protest. Indeed, the destruction of

---

75 Ibid., p. 84.
76 B. Johnson, *Letter to Theresa May*, 6 Jan 2014, accessed from www.london.gov.uk/priorities/policing-crime/consultations/water-cannon
77 The water cannon has been authorised for use in Northern Ireland.
78 T. May, *Letter to Boris Johnson*, 23 Jan 2014, accessed from www.london.gov.uk/priorities/policing-crime/consultations/water-cannon. See also *Guardian*, 14 Jul 2014.
79 Mayor of London Office for Policing and Crime, *Water Cannon: Responses to Consultation* (2014) p. 2. Available at www.london.gov.uk/sites/default/files/140318%20-%20Water%20Cannon%20-%20Responses%20to%20Consultation%20_0.pdf
80 Ibid., pp. 3–4.
81 Examples: Kevin Gately who died following a blow to the head (possibly from a police truncheon or being trampled on by police horses) at the Red Lion Square protest in 1974; Blair Peach who was killed at an anti-fascist protest at Southall in 1979; Ian Tomlinson at the G20 summit protests in 2009. Student Alfie Meadows required emergency brain surgery after being struck at the tuition fees protest in December 2010. At the same protests, Jody McIntyre, who suffers from cerebral palsy, was pulled from his wheelchair and dragged across the street by police officers.

property and looting are crimes that need to be punished – yet these acts do have deeper meaning. Legitimate protests before the riots of summer 2011, such as the Trades Union Congress (TUC) anti-cuts rally on 26 March 2011 and the student tuition fees protests in late 2010, achieved nothing and the protesters were likely to have felt ignored and further marginalised. Consistent throughout this chapter is the provocative effect that either the police or the troops have had on crowds throughout history. Signs of force from the authorities only serve to demonstrate the battle lines, reinforcing the collective identities of the crowd against an oppressive authority. While there is hope that the PLTs will have a positive impact in preventing disorder and creating better links between the crowd and the police, when disorder does occur there is a worrying trend that the tactics to contain it will again become more forceful and indiscriminate.

4 Freedom of assembly and public processions

Regulation and policing before the Public Order Act 1936

'Does [s52 Metropolitan Police Act 1839] enable the Commissioner to use his own discretion and, for example, to make a distinction as between the obstruction of traffic . . . by a procession of the British Union of Fascists and a procession organised by the workers?'[1]

Introduction

Public processions have formed an essential part of British political and social history as a channel for the public to mobilise and highlight grievances or demands to Parliament or promote propaganda to the general public. They have also had the potential to provoke or instigate violent disorder. This chapter examines how Statute and the common law have been applied to facilitate, restrict or even prohibit public assemblies and processions in the era before the Public Order Act 1936. It illuminates the historical and legal context of the official responses to public processions and evaluates key legal developments and debates from this era. This will include an examination of the responses of the police, judiciary and Parliament when countering public processions which either threatened the peace or resulted in disorder. This will also comprise the processions of the Chartists, the Salvation Army (which led to the influential legal precedent in *Beatty v Gillbanks*[2]) the NUWM and the BUF. The introductory quote by Labour MP Emanuel Shinwell demonstrates how the political partiality of the police was questioned when they used their discretion to regulate public processions. The chapter climaxes with the Battle of Cable Street in 1936, an event that became a catalyst for legislative action in the form of s3 Public Order Act 1936, which is discussed in chapter five.

The analysis of the official responses to public processions since the early nineteenth century to the present day provides a narrative of inconsistent police action which reveals more about the nature of police discretion and the vagueness of the

---

1 *Hansard, HC Deb*, 5 Nov 1936, vol 317 cc253–254.
2 *Beatty v Gillbanks* [1881–1882] LR 9 QBD 308.

breach of the peace doctrine. Furthermore, Government responses demonstrate an ebb and flow of commitment towards civil liberties which was largely dependent on the perceived threat to national security, yet by the post-war period this was eclipsed by a commitment to collective security.

Legal definitions

Public assembly

By its nature a public procession is a form of public assembly. It is therefore subject to the same common law authority under the breach of the peace doctrine which regulates what would deem an assembly to be either lawful or unlawful. In *Beatty v Gillbanks*, Field J quotes Hawkins' Pleas of the Crown, s. 9:

> An unlawful assembly according to the common opinion is a disturbance of the peace by persons barely assembling together with the intention to do a thing which if it were executed would make them rioters, but neither actually executing it nor making a motion toward the execution of it . . . But this seems to be much too narrow a definition. For any meeting whatever of great numbers of people, with such circumstances of terror as cannot but endanger the public peace and raise fears and jealousies among the king's subjects, seems properly to be called an unlawful assembly, as where great numbers, complaining of a common grievance, meet together, armed in a warlike manner, in order to consult together concerning the most proper means for the recovery of their interests; for no man can foresee what may be the event of such an assembly.[3]

Under this definition, the threat of any potential disorder comes from within those assembled, placing an important emphasis on the purpose and conduct of the assembly itself in judging whether it should be considered either lawful or unlawful. Unless the conduct of the members of a public assembly violates any statutory law, then their assembly must be considered lawful. The freedom to assemble in public was not legally enshrined as a right before the Human Rights Act 1998 and the incorporation of the ECHR – but through the concept of residual freedom, people were at liberty to form public assemblies provided the conduct of its members remained lawful. No statutory law to restrict public assemblies existed until the Public Order Act 1986. Under s14 of this Act, the senior police officer can impose certain conditions upon public assemblies provided certain tests are met. However, a procession is more than just an assembly of persons and further legal consideration of what constitutes a procession is necessary.

---

3 Cited by Field J, in *Beatty v Gillbanks*, at 314, Hawkins' Pleas of the Crown (1716–1824).

Public procession

When debating the Party Processions (Ireland) Bill in the House of Commons in 1832, the problem of defining party processions was highlighted by Tory MP Sir Robert Peel, who stated, 'we can tell well enough, in common parlance, what is the meaning of those words, but it would be extremely difficult to point out the meaning in an Act of Parliament.'[4] The Party Processions (Ireland) Act 1832 was designed to eliminate the disorder caused by the escalating culture of parading, which included the numerous Protestant processions of the Orange Order and Catholic processions of the Ribbonmen. These parades became a trigger for sectarian violence, and the 1832 Act carried the repressive measure of banning such processions. Although this Act did not definitively state what a procession was, it defined what type of procession could be prohibited:

> any Body of Persons who shall meet and Parade together, or join in Procession, for the purpose of celebrating or commemorating any Festival, Anniversary or Political Event relating to or connected with and Religious distinction or difference, and who shall bear, wear, or have amongst them any Firearms or other offensive Weapon, or any Banner, Emblem, Flag or Symbol, the display whereof may be calculated or tend to provoke animosity between His Majesty's Subjects of different Religious Persuasions, or who shall be accompanied by any Music of a like nature or tendency, shall be and be deemed an unlawful Assembly.

This elaborate description was drafted in order to permit other innocent processions to proceed unaffected by the Act. When legislation was introduced in England, Wales and Scotland, to counteract the disorder caused by public processions, under the Public Order Act 1936, the definition provided was more general and far-reaching. The definition of 'public procession' in s9 Public Order Act 1936 was unconstructively termed 'a procession in a public place'. The same definition was again offered in s16 Public Order Act 1986. While further interpretation is given to 'public place', no definition of 'procession' exists in Statute. In legal terms, 'procession' can therefore embrace an extensive range of conditions.[5] At common law, there has been further debate on the definition of procession in relation to an appeal by UM member Alfred Flockhart, who was charged with organising a public procession during the duration of a s3(3) ban. This is discussed in chapter five.

With such a wide legal definition that incorporates any manner of people proceeding in orderly succession or moving along a route, processions can take the form of a ceremonial or military style march, a commemorative parade with music and banners, or a mobile demonstration or protest. It incorporates all political and religious organisations and movements as well as social groups and clubs. This wide ranging description has continued to cause controversy as regional bans

4 *Hansard, HC Deb*, 14 Jun 1832, vol 13 c725.
5 Thornton *et al.*, *The Law of Public Order*, p. 101.

on processions have also affected groups and clubs whose processions would not typically pose any threat to public order. This presents the question: Can it be morally justified to ban all processions, rather than those likely to provoke disorder?

The march of the Chartists 1838–1848

The era of the Chartists marks an important period in the development of public order policing. While the Metropolitan Police had been established almost a decade before the rise of Chartism, disorder across the rest of England and Wales was largely managed by a mixture of the police, special constables and the military. Under the Municipal Corporations Act 1835, it was required that watch committees be established in 178 boroughs by their elected councils in order to provide and supervise a body of police. The establishment of these forces differed between the towns, as some looked towards the Metropolitan Police as a model; others just updated their existing system of watchmen and began calling them policemen.[6] Furthermore, the County Police Act 1839 enabled the Justices of the Peace to establish police forces, although this was not mandatory until the County and Borough Police Act 1856. During the early stages of the Chartist disorder, the Government established centralised forces in Birmingham, Bolton and Manchester, with their respective Chief Constables appointed directly from the Home Office.[7] This arrangement continued for three years.

The Chartist movement united large sections of the working class in order to promote political reforms which were highlighted in the Six Points of the People's Charter. These included the extension of the voting franchise to all men over twenty-one years of age who were of sound mind and not undergoing punishment for crime; the ballot to protect voters' anonymity; and the removal of the property qualification for Members of Parliament. The Chartist-related disorder varied considerably in intensity and participation from 1838 to 1858. Yet in relation to social unrest in the decades before it – such as the Gordon Riots 1780, the Luddites' machine breaking from 1811 to 1816 or the Bristol Riot 1831 – Frederick Mather contends that Chartist activism was much less destructive. He qualifies this by adding that the 'English working class was on the whole better housed, better fed, better educated, and far less degraded than in preceding years.'[8] Dorothy Thompson also questioned 'why the British workers responded to hunger by forming a nation-wide movement around a political programme instead of by more traditional means of protest like food rioting, arson, begging, poaching or praying'. In her response, she also noted the literacy and sophistication of this working-class response yet highlighted the Chartists' rejection of centralising government policies and emphasised their 'common language', which was based

6 Emsley, *The English Police*, p. 37.
7 C. Emsley, 'The birth and development of the police' in T. Newburn (ed), *Handbook of Policing*, second edition, Routledge: London (2011), p. 76.
8 F. C. Mather, *Public Order in the Age of the Chartists*, Manchester University Press: Manchester (1959), pp. 12–13.

upon 'an articulate political and social programme'.[9] Yet this is not to suggest that Chartist activism did not include violence, disorder and intimidation; the Chartists utilised various forms of processing in public. The objectives and motivations behind this method of political activism are ambiguous and the responses from the authorities diverse.

The march on Newport 1839

There has been significant debate on the intentions of the Chartist marchers who were defeated by the soldiers of the 45th Regiment and the 500 special constables on 4 November 1839. It is estimated that twenty Chartists were killed in the disorder and many more were injured. While there is considerable consensus among historians that the Chartist leaders had undoubtably attempted to capture Newport in a military coup, which would have marked the beginning of further militant Chartist activism,[10] some historians have offered a more cautious approach contending that the carrying of arms was defensive and the mass march was intended as a show of strength rather than aggression.[11] Following the violence and bloodshed at Newport, the Chartist leaders (including John Frost, Zephaniah Williams, William Jones and nine others) were indicted and tried for high treason. It was charged that all twelve defendants:

> traitorously did levy and make war against our Lady the Queen within the Realm, and being armed did march in a warlike manner through divers towns, and, with 2,000 and more with offensive weapons, beset houses and force persons to march with them, and seize arms further to arm themselves to destroy the soldiers of the Queen and to levy war against the Queen within the Realm, and thereby subvert the government and alter the laws by force, and did march into the town of Newport and make a warlike attack upon a certain dwelling-house, did fire upon the magistrates, soldiers, and constables there assembled, and did attempt and in a warlike manner to subvert and destroy the constitution and government of this Realm as by law established.[12]

These charges conjure the image of an offensive military force which had a predetermined intention of insurrection. The prosecution also claimed that a scout who was sent to the assembly of Chartists, who were half a mile away from Newport, was shot at and returned 'dangerously wounded'. Following this, the mayor requested military backup to reinforce the special constables who had been sworn in and had taken strategic defensive positions within the town's three principal

---

9 M. Taylor, 'Rethinking the Chartists: Searching for Synthesis in the Historiography of Chartism,' *The Historical Journal 39*, no. 2 (1996), p. 283; and D. Thompson (ed.), *The Early Chartists*, Macmillan: New York (1971).

10 D. Jones, *The Last Rising, The Newport Insurrection of 1839*, Clarendon Press: Oxford (1985), p. 1.

11 See D. Williams, *John Frost. A Study in Chartism*, University of Wales Press: Cardiff (1939).

12 *R v Frost and others* [1835–42] All ER Rep 106, at 108–109.

inns. Furthermore, it was claimed that the military of the 45th Regiment did not load their arms until they were fired on, and if the order to fire had not been given then 'there was every reason to believe that the military must all have been killed.'[13] The case for an attempted insurrection certainly seemed strong, yet there were some reasons for doubt. Primarily, the testimony of Matthew Williams, who claimed to be at a Chartist meeting before the march where the intentions of it were forwarded by a man named Reed, was seen as admissible by Tindal CJ. This was despite the defence's claim that as Reed was not a coconspirator in the trial and the witness did not see Frost until the day of the march. The evidence given against him was being used to show his intent by things done in his absence and had happened anterior to him meeting with the group. In addition, although the Chartists marched in procession with arms, this did not necessarily amount to treason. Although this was recognised by the prosecution, it laid more emphasis on them to prove that there was a premeditated plan, which placed greater prominence on the testimony of Reed.

It was argued for the defence that the intent of the demonstration was to liberate certain prisoners who were in custody at the Westgate Inn and to secure better treatment for a prisoner at Monmouth. The show of strength by a large demonstration was, the defence argued, designed to persuade the Newport magistrates to grant pardons for their political prisoners. This was emphasised by the call of the Chartists to 'surrender up your prisoners' when they arrived at the Westgate Inn.[14] Also, if the accusations of insurrection were to be believed, the defence contended that most of the Chartist marchers would not have been unarmed and fled as soon as shots were fired.[15] However, although there was some certainty that the Chartists expected disorder to achieve their demands, the carrying of weapons did not necessarily determine any intended conflict. In subsequent processions in 1848 (described later in this chapter) the Chartists bore arms without any occurrence of disorder. In *R v Frost and others*,[16] the jury found the defendants guilty. Despite the jury's recommendation for mercy, Tindal CJ sentenced Frost, Williams and Jones to death. The punishments for the other Chartists included transportation for life and prison sentences. For the three prominent Chartist leaders, their sentences were changed to transportation, yet David Jones contended that the reason for this alteration 'is still something of a mystery'.[17]

The march on Newport, whether it was an attempted insurrection or a mass demonstration with the purpose of securing the release of prisoners, undoubtedly constituted an unlawful assembly according to Hawkins' Pleas of the Crown. The prosecution for high treason reflected the authorities' own desire to prevent or suppress other possible uprisings of radical causes.

---

13 Ibid., at 116.
14 Ibid., at 117.
15 Jones, *The Last Rising*, pp. 190–193.
16 *R v Frost and others*.
17 Ibid., p. 197. Jones also highlighted that many of the witnesses called by the prosecution were unreliable and the jury were carefully selected to include those who were hostile to the Chartists.

The third National Petition 1848

On 10 April 1848, the Chartists intended to follow their great meeting at Kennington Common with a procession to the Houses of Parliament to submit their third petition. These arrangements caused some controversy and led to a notice being issued by the Metropolitan Police Commissioners, Charles Rowan and Richard Mayne, declaring that as such a procession was 'calculated to excite terror and alarm in the minds of her Majesty's subjects: all persons are hereby cautioned and strictly enjoined not to attend or take part in, or be present at, any such assemblage or procession.'[18] The Home Secretary, Sir George Grey, who identified that the Government were responsible for the issuing of this notice, declared that any meeting which was 'calculated to inspire just terror and alarm into the minds of Her Majesty's loyal and peaceable subjects – would, I apprehend, be against the common law of England.' He continued to state that if the meeting was assembled for the purpose of forming a procession of an excessive number of people to bring the petition to either House of Parliament, then the procession would be contrary to Statute law. The Tumultuous Petitioning Act 1661 provided that

> no person or persons shall repair to His Majesty, or both, or either of the Houses of Parliament, upon pretence of delivering any petition, &c. accompanied with excessive number of people, nor, at any one time, with above the number of ten persons, on pain of incurring a penalty not exceeding £100, and three months' imprisonment.

This Act was cited in *R v Lord George Gordon*[19] by Lord Mansfield CJ, who declared that, despite the contention of the defence, the Act was not repealed by the Bill of Rights 1688 and was still in full force.[20]

There was significant debate in the House of Commons on whether these oppressive actions (such as the Metropolitan Police Commissioners' warning against taking part in the Chartist procession) were justified. Much of the debate was centred on whether the intentions of the Chartists were to cause a disturbance or not. These repressive measures were unsurprisingly condemned by Chartist MP Feargus O'Connor, who recited several processions of large numbers of people who passed close to the House of Commons, adding:

> as the people have never before been prevented from making demonstrations of this kind, I do say that it is now taking them rather by surprise to declare that they must not look to the common custom hitherto as a guarantee of their right to meet and walk in procession as they contemplated.[21]

---

18 *The Leeds Times*, 8 Apr 1848.

19 *R v Lord George Gordon* (1781) 2 Dougl 590.

20 Ibid., at 593. The Tumultuous Petitioning Act 1661 was finally repealed by the Public Order Act 1986 s40(3), Sch 3.

21 *Hansard, HC Deb*, 7 Apr 1848, vol 98 c11.

He continued to state the peaceful intentions of the demonstrators, who did not have 'any view to endanger the peace of the country, or to violate the law of the land'.[22] Other MPs were not so willing to accept this view and supported the warning issued by the Metropolitan Police Commissioners. The Peelite[23] Sir James Graham issued his support stating that, 'Such a procession as that contemplated has been pronounced illegal, and I am glad that it will not be countenanced by the authorities.'[24] Liberal Sir George De Lacy Evans highlighted previous Chartist meetings at Trafalgar Square that were of a 'contemptible character' and had 'occasioned very great alarm and terror', highlighting that his constituents 'suffered materially in their trade' for days before and after those events.[25] Sir Robert Peel defended the precautions taken by the Government by alluding to the ongoing revolutions in Europe, stating that considering the excited state of mind of the public, 'it is impossible to foresee the consequences.'[26]

Despite the proscription of the procession being made in advance of the meeting at Kennington Common, further preventive measures were taken to counter any Chartist attempt to defy it. These precautions included 12,000 police and military being placed on alert. In addition to this, there were an estimated 85,000 special police officers enrolled to help keep order on the day of the demonstration.[27] On the day of the Chartist assembly at Kennington Common, Police Commissioner Mayne informed O'Connor that the meeting could proceed but there would be no procession. Fearful of further suppression if disorder occurred, O'Connor agreed with the Commissioner's reasoning and informed the gathered crowd to give up the planned procession. The petition was taken to Parliament by O'Connor and a few other leaders that had hired cabs to transport it. Importantly, historian Stanley Palmer acknowledges the tactical precautions of the Metropolitan Police, the military and the number of special constables, which demonstrated the power of the state and which was likely to influence O'Connor's capitulation.[28]

Although the third National Petition in 1848 passed off relatively peacefully, Chartist activism continued over the spring and summer months in London, posing further problems for the authorities. With an increase in Irish emigrants escaping the famine, the Chartists received a short-lived boost as the two radical causes of Irish separatism and English Chartism united. The Government responded to this dual threat by passing the Treason Felony Act 1848. This law remedied the gap in punishments for treason which were either death, or for inferior classes of

---

22   Ibid., at cc13.
23   The Peelites were a faction of the Conservative Party who supported Robert Peel's commitment to free trade.
24   *Hansard, HC Deb*, 7 Apr 1848, vol 98 c14.
25   Ibid., at cc17–18.
26   Ibid., at c20.
27   S. Palmer, *Police and Protest in England and Ireland 1780–1850*, Cambridge University Press: Cambridge (1988), p. 488. Palmer records that contemporary newspaper estimates ranged from 120,000 to 250,000 enrolled specials.
28   Ibid.

sedition, a fine or imprisonment. One of the first activists to be charged and convicted under the new Act was the Irishman John Mitchel.

Following Mitchel's sentencing of fourteen years transportation, the various Chartist and Irish groups organised a meeting and procession at Clerkenwell Green, London, on Monday 29 May 1848 to 'demand from the Queen his release'.[29] It was reported that following the meeting, the speakers organised the crowd to march through the streets, encouraging others to join in. Many of the marchers were reported to have been carrying 'bludgeons, pitchforks and other dangerous implements'. The procession was prevented from continuing on route to Buckingham Palace by a 'strong body of police' and the marchers then headed back to Finsbury Square, where the leaders informed the assembly that they would meet again on Wednesday. The following day the Commissioner of Police issued a notice declaring that 'assemblages and processions are illegal, and will not be allowed . . . [declaring that] all necessary measures will be adopted to prevent such processions taking place, and effectually to protect the public peace, and to suppress any attempt at the disturbance thereof.'[30] No statutory authority was cited in the Commissioner's notice and it must therefore be deduced that he was acting under his common law power to prevent a breach of the peace.

Although the Chartists did not mount a legal challenge to the notice, they still defied its authority by meeting at Clerkenwell Green the following day. This time the police did not allow the gathering to form a marching formation. Media reports suggest that there were no known Chartist leaders at the assembly and that the large crowd of about 2,000 people had engaged in stone throwing, running in different directions and shouting.[31] *The Morning Post* reported that by nine o'clock the area was densely crowded and the police started to disperse the crowd. While many in the crowd did disperse quickly, some were influenced by the demands of activists who called on people to stick together so they could manage the police and who further advocated that the military would not hurt them. The partisan newspaper then declared that because of the actions of these 'deluded people' the police were left with no option but to use their truncheons indiscriminately to clear the Green, which was still occupied by a 'few men, women, and children, [who were] removed only by violent measures'.[32] Mather argued that this was a good example of preventive police action as they had chosen the right moment to intervene, which potentially prevented a riot.[33] Furthermore, the police tactics utilised also reveal their own awareness that their presence also constituted a provocation that could potentially cause a breach of the peace. The police were hidden nearby and had plain-clothed observers at the assembly to report on any disorder, which helped the police time their intervention.[34]

---

29 *The Newcastle Guardian*, 3 Jun 1848.
30 *The Morning Post*, 31 May 1848.
31 *The Newcastle Guardian*, 3 Jun 1848.
32 *The Morning Post*, 1 Jun 1848.
33 Mather, *Public Order*, p. 103.
34 Ibid., p. 104.

Following the dispersal of the assembly, the police tactics to prevent any attempted procession continued. Information had been received that Chartists would meet at their several lodges and rush out to form a procession. As these locations were known to the police, a number of plain-clothed officers were placed within their vicinity and were able to call for the reserves of special constables and the City police who were concealed nearby.[35] The meetings of Chartists continued over the next few evenings. While the police managed these meetings and their dispersals, the Honourable Artillery Company had been assembled in case their services were required. There was also an emphasis on the prohibition of processions. On the 2 June 1848, *The Morning Post* declared, 'owing to the admirable arrangements of the police, no processions were allowed to take place.' On the following day, the provisions utilised by the authorities were reiterated as it was reported, 'the instructions given to Superintendents are that no processions are to be allowed, and if any are attempted, they are to be broken up at all hazards.'[36] These instructions potentially demonstrated how the discretionary powers of the Metropolitan Police Commissioners were utilised to direct police practice at ground level. The late involvement of the police in dispersing the crowds also demonstrated that there was at least some commitment to allow the public assemblies. However, it was more likely that this reflected the attitude of the Whig Government towards civil liberties. Mather argued that the Whigs reacted slowly to Chartist disturbances, issuing orders to the police to watch them.[37] The Home Secretary, Sir George Grey, had also claimed responsibility for the instructions issued to the Police Commissioner to prevent meetings which were held in unsociable hours, which demonstrated the control that the Home Office wielded over the Metropolitan police. Despite any commitment to allow the Chartists to assemble within sociable hours, and police intervention to occur only to prevent disorder, the same commitment was not forthcoming to allow public processions. The notice issued by the Commissioner prohibiting them continued unchallenged.

Beatty v Gillbanks: A common law solution to regulating processions?

The Salvation Army was formed in 1865 by the former Methodist preacher William Booth. It is a Protestant movement which was modelled on military lines, with uniformed members receiving rank as either officer or soldier. With a musical band, they marched in formation playing music and singing Christian songs as they fought a moral crusade against alcohol, gambling and vice. In the early 1880s the Salvation Army's activities came to prominence across Britain after many of their marches ended in violence following the organised disruption of a Skeleton Army.

---

35 Ibid.
36 *The Morning Post*, 3 Jun 1848.
37 F. C. Mather, 'The Government and the Chartists' in A. Briggs (ed), *Chartist Studies*, Macmillan: New York (1967), pp. 396–397.

The various Skeleton Armies which formed across the nation were often led in different communities by disgruntled landlords and brothel owners who were hostile towards the Salvation Army's crusade.[38] In *Beatty v Gillbanks*, the Skeleton Army are simply described as, 'another organized band of persons . . . who also parade the streets, and are antagonistic to the Salvation Army and its processions'.[39]

In several regions the Justices of the Peace took the preventative measure of securing public order by prohibiting the processions of the Salvationists. One of the towns that issued a public notice signed by the Justices of the Peace was Weston-super-Mare. Following a succession of violent incidents at Salvation Army processions, the public notice stated that, 'we do therefore hereby require, order, and direct all persons to abstain from assembling to the disturbance of the public peace in the public streets.'[40] Despite the Justices' public notice, William Beatty led a Salvation Army procession through the town's public thoroughfares. After refusing a police sergeant's order to disperse, Beatty was arrested and charged with 'unlawfully and tumultuously assembling with diverse other persons . . . in a public thoroughfare . . . to the disturbance of the public peace, and against the peace of the Queen'.[41] No statutory authority was stated at the Petty Sessions held at the Weston-super-Mare Town Hall, and the case hinged on the authority of the Justices' public notice and the duty of the police to keep the peace. For the defence, Mr Sutherst 'contended that there had been a very gross violation of constitutional rights' and insisted that it was the duty of the police to protect the defendants during their procession. He continued by rejecting the legality of the public notice by stating, 'The proclamation was so much waste paper' and illustrated this by tearing the document into fragments. He continued, 'if the magistrates convicted these men they would act in an exceedingly unconstitutional manner.'[42] Nevertheless, the magistrates considered that the police did not exceed their duty but acted with a great amount of discretion. Beatty and others were 'severally bound in their own recognizances, with two sureties, to keep the peace and be of good behaviour for the term of twelve calendar months, and in default to be imprisoned for three calendar months, or until they should comply with such order'.[43] Following this conviction, Beatty and two other leaders of the Salvation Army were granted an appeal at the Queen's Bench Division.

The serious disturbances at Weston-super-Mare were not isolated. Opposition to the Salvationists' marches from the Skeleton Army and local communities caused disorder across England and formed the basis of questions in the House of Commons to Sir William Harcourt, Liberal Home Secretary and former Solicitor General, on how to manage the increasing disturbances. Harcourt tentatively

---

38 V. Bailey, *Order and Disorder in Modern Britain: Essays on Riot, Crime, Policing and Punishment*, Breviary Stuff Publications: London (2014), pp. 17–18.
39 *Beatty v Gillbanks* at 309.
40 Ibid., at 312.
41 *The Bristol Mercury and Daily Post*, 30 Mar 1882.
42 Ibid.
43 *Beatty v Gillbanks* at 308.

advised local magistrates to preserve the peace as they thought right, but high-lighted that the issuing of proclamations to forbid processions had been successful in Exeter, Stamford and Salisbury. However, he also ambiguously added:

> I may say that those people cannot be too strongly condemned who attack persons who are only meeting for a lawful and, I may say, laudable object; but, on the other hand, I cannot but condemn the imprudence of those who encourage these processions, which experience has shown must lead to dis-order and violence.[44]

In one instance Harcourt's advice was to prohibit processions if they were likely to cause a breach of the peace. Despite this, he then continued to defend those who met for a lawful and laudable object and condemn those who attack the processions. This indecisiveness prompted a deriding letter to *The Morning Post*, signed by 'One of the Stupid Party'[45] urging Harcourt to clarify the position of the magistrates. The author enquired whether the magistrates should stop the processions or allow them to continue and stop the roughs, questioning whether the Home Secretary only proposed 'to declare the magistrates to be wrong whichever course they pursue'?[46]

It is within this context of ambiguous Home Office advice regarding public pro-cessions that the outcome of *Beatty v Gillbanks* took on such importance. At the Queen's Bench Division, Field and Cave JJ held that the appellants could not be rightly convicted of unlawful assembly as there was no authority for the proposition that, 'a man may be convicted for doing a lawful act if he knows that his doing it may cause another to do an unlawful act.'[47] Although this ruling seemed to have set a new legal precedent which potentially provided legal protection to lawful public assemblies, such as public meetings or processions, the vagueness of the judgment has been criticised by academic lawyers such as Harry Street, who declared that the court did not make it clear whether they were laying down a general rule or whether

> they merely found on the facts of the case that the accused did not cause the disturbance because it was not the natural and probable consequence of their procession that the Skeleton Army should create the commotion.[48]

Neither did this legal victory for the Salvationists guarantee any future protec-tion from their opponents. Victor Bailey highlights that bylaws and Local Acts

---

44 *Hansard, HC Deb*, 16 Mar 1882, vol 267 cc991.

45 This was a sarcastic signature by an anonymous member of the Conservative Party. It refers to the Liberal John Stuart Mill's assertion that the Conservative Party was the stupid party. He famously clarified this statement in a debate in the House of Commons: 'What I stated was, that the Con-servative party was, by the law of its constitution, necessarily the stupidest party. Now, I do not retract this assertion; but I did not mean that Conservatives are generally stupid; I meant, that stupid persons are generally Conservative.' *Hansard, HC Deb*, 31 May 1866, vol 183 c1592.

46 *The Morning Post*, 22 Mar 1882.

47 *Beatty v Gillbanks*.

48 H. Street, *Freedom, The Individual and the Law*, Penguin Books: Middlesex (1963) pp. 53–54.

were used in some areas, which included provisions which were enforced to prevent the Salvation Army processions, such as the prohibition of singing and music. Also, some areas such as Guilford, acknowledging the Salvationists' freedom to form processions, refused to provide police protection if they were attacked by the Skeleton Army. They also warned the Salvationists that if they continued to form processions they did at their own risk.[49]

In practice, subsequent judgments, such as *Wise v Dunning*[50] in 1902, have taken further individual factors into consideration. George Wise was a Protestant lecturer in Liverpool whose speeches regularly caused an obstruction of the highway as well as disorder between his own supporters and his Catholic opponents. It was recognised that he 'used gestures and language which were highly insulting to the religion of the Roman Catholic inhabitants' and on one occasion he told his supporters that the Catholics were going to bring sticks to the next meeting, thereby prompting his own supporters to reciprocate.[51] Lord Alverstone CJ, citing *Beatty v Gillbanks* and *R v Londonderry JJ*,[52] deduced that 'there must be an act of the defendant, the natural consequence of which, if his act be not unlawful in itself, would be to produce an unlawful act by other persons.'[53] The 'natural consequence' element was clarified by Channell J:

> the law does not as a rule regard an illegal act as being the natural consequence of a temptation which may be held out to commit it . . . The proposition is correct and really familiar; but I think the cases with respect to apprehended breaches of the peace shew that the law does regard the infirmity of human temper to the extent of considering that a breach of the peace, although an illegal act, may be the natural consequence of insulting or abusive language or conduct.[54]

Here, the acts of Wise and Beatty can be distinguished. Although the Salvation Army's procession may have ended in violence, the disorder could not be judged to have been a natural consequence of the procession itself. In contrast, any disorder resulting from the insulting and abusive public lectures delivered by Wise and his incitement to violence regarding the use of sticks must be considered as a natural consequence of these actions. This judgment strengthened the breach of the peace doctrine, recognising that public disorder could be the natural consequence of conduct or language that does not necessarily contradict any statutory law.[55] Therefore, a public assembly does not become unlawful

---

49 V. Bailey, *Order and Disorder*, pp. 29–30.
50 *Wise v Dunning* [1902] 1 KB 167. See also chapter six.
51 Ibid.
52 *R v Justices of Londonderry* (1891) 28 LR Ir 440, Ir QBDC.
53 *Wise v Dunning* at 175–176.
54 Ibid., at 179–180.
55 Threatening, abusive and insulting words or behaviour with intent to provoke a breach of the peace, or whereby a breach of the peace is likely to be occasioned was made an offence under s5 Public Order Act 1936. Similar regional offences existed under local acts and in the Metropolitan district under s54(13) Metropolitan Police Act 1839. See chapter six.

simply because some other body threatens to disturb it – but if it is considered that the natural consequence of an assembly is for it to incite disorder, then its prohibition would be supported by the judiciary. Assessing whether disorder is the natural consequence of someone's conduct is highly discretional, which ultimately means that such judgments will often be inconsistent.

Constitutional theorist A. V. Dicey defended the liberty of a group of people to assemble and process together in the public streets in his *Introduction to the Study of the Law of the Constitution*, which was last amended by the author in 1908. He stated:

> if the right of *A* to walk down the High Street is not effected by the threats of *X*, the right of *A*, *B*, and *C* to march down the High Street together is not diminished by the proclamation of X, Y, and Z that they will not suffer *A*, *B*, and *C* to take their walk.[56]

Dicey advocated two limitations towards the freedom of A, B, and C to assemble in public. First, he stated that if the conduct of members assembled was in any way unlawful and provoked a breach of the peace then that would constitute an unlawful assembly; second, he stated that if the conduct of those assembled was lawful, but had provoked a breach of the peace, and the magistrates or constables decided that it was impossible to restore order by any other means, then they have the power to disperse them and any failure of the crowd to disperse would then constitute an unlawful assembly.

The first limitation requires further clarification. For example, what statutory offence may be violated by the members of an assembly to make it unlawful? Although riotous and tumultuous behaviour by members of an assembly would deem it unlawful, the authorities have also frequently utilised Statutes relating to the obstruction of the highways to suppress processions that are otherwise law abiding.

Obstruction of the highway: the use of existing legislation to regulate processions

Since *Beatty v Gillbanks*, the authorities frequently regulated public processions by invoking legislation such as s72 Highway Act 1835 and s28 Town Police Clauses Act 1847. These provisions both deal with the wilful obstruction of the passage of footways or public thoroughfares, yet they were enacted to prevent obstruction caused by livestock, carts or carriages.

The powers relating to processions addressed in s21 Town Police Clauses Act 1847 provide that:

> The commissioners may from time to time make orders . . . for preventing obstruction of the streets within the limits of the special Act in all times of

---

56 A. V. Dicey, *An Introduction*, tenth edition, Macmillan Press Ltd: London (1959), p. 274.

public processions, rejoicings, or illuminations, and in any case when the streets are thronged or liable to be obstructed[.]

A deputation between the Manchester Watch Committee and the Home Office in 1936 revealed that powers relating to the regulation of processions in s213 Manchester Police Act 1844 (a counterpart of the provisions in s21 Town Police Clauses Act 1847 and s52 Metropolitan Police Act 1839) were 'not so valuable as they may on the surface appear to be'. The deputation's resulting memorandum declared that the experience of the police authority was that there was 'often some attempt on the part of the promoters of the procession to disregard the regulations laid down'.[57] It has also been highlighted by Ewing and Gearty that these provisions were more concerned with keeping the thoroughfares clear than with political protest.[58] As these provisions could be utilised against public assemblies, they were equally effective when directed to disperse or prohibit either public processions or public meetings.

The danger of selective law enforcement is highlighted by such legislative measures relating to obstruction of the highway being regularly invoked to disperse socialist meetings. An early example of a prosecution was of W. B. Barker, who appeared at Thames Police Court, London, in 1885. He was charged with 'causing an obstruction by addressing a crowd of persons in a public street', and in reply claimed that, 'it was the right of every Englishman to speak in a public street.'[59] The application of ambiguous or inappropriate statutory powers that infringe the liberty of the subject created the danger that they would be inconsistently applied, which effectively provided opportunities for the police to exercise political partiality and to selectively enforce the law. The magistrates at Thames Police Court even demonstrated such bias as they declared the socialist defendant was 'preaching a very mischievous doctrine' despite the fact that he was not on trial for what he said, but for the obstruction that he caused.

In 1886, Llewellyn Atherley-Jones, a radical Liberal MP and son of the prominent Chartist Ernest Jones, questioned the Home Secretary on the recent prosecutions of socialist lecturers for the alleged obstruction of certain streets in London. The Conservative Home Secretary, Henry Matthews, responded that the Home Office had not given any special instruction to the police regarding meetings in the street and that the 'instructions of the Chief Commissioner seem to me to be quite proper and in accordance with the law.'[60] The police had therefore found a legal, albeit questionable, method of maintaining public order regarding 'lawful' public assemblies. However, as such powers were not specifically directed towards maintaining public order at public assemblies, they were highly discretional and susceptible to selective utilization.

---

57 HO 144/20159, Disturbances: Public Order Bill (1936), 'Memorandum', p. 10.
58 Ewing and Gearty, *The Struggle*, p. 306, n150.
59 *The Huddersfield Daily Chronicle*, 11 Aug 1885, p. 3.
60 *Hansard, HC Deb*, 21 Sep 1886, vol 309 c1103.

The National Unemployed Workers Movement

The Emergency Powers Act 1920

The rise of far-Left activism in the period following the First World War presented a significant challenge to public order and national security. One of the first
peacetime reactions to this threat was the Emergency Powers Act 1920, which
authorises the proclamation of a state of emergency if:

> at any time it appears to His Majesty that any action has been taken or is
> immediately threatened by any persons or body of persons of such a nature
> and on so extensive a scale as to be calculated, by interfering with the supply
> and distribution of food, water, fuel, or light, or with the means of locomo-
> tion, to deprive the community, or any substantial portion of the community,
> of the essentials of life[.]

The proclamation could remain in force for one month and another proclamation would need to be issued to extend the state of emergency. Following the
proclamation being made, s2 provides that 'it shall be lawful for His Majesty in
Council, by Order, to make regulations for securing the essentials of life to the
community.' Richard Thurlow asserts that the use of this state power, which could
'censor news, direct labour, detain or restrict movement of individuals without
due process of law', represented the real 'extremism of the centre'.[61] Among the
regulations that suppressed civil liberties and political freedom was Emergency
Regulation 22, which provided chiefs of police with the power 'to prohibit meetings and marches with the approval of the Home Secretary if they feared disorder
would arise'.[62] This power found favour from Metropolitan Police Commissioner
William Horwood in 1926, after the Emergency Powers had been in force during
the General Strike. In a letter to the Home Secretary, he argued that this power
should be embodied in the general law.[63] This law provided the police with wide
discretion to prohibit political activism on the basis of an anticipated breach of the
peace. These wide powers were naturally opposed by the political Left. Labour
MPs Ernest Thurtle, David Grenfell, James Hudson, John Bromley and Henry
Thomas all advocated for the removal of Regulation 22 in Parliament in May
1926.[64] Thurtle's attack on the Regulation was also accompanied by a condemn-
ing evaluation of the magistrates that challenged their political partiality:

> the magistrates are drawn from political parties hostile to the Labour Party,
> and . . . it is inevitable that their political prejudice or partisanship will come

---

61 R. Thurlow, *The Secret State: British Internal Security in the Twentieth Century*, Blackwell Pub-
    lishers: Oxford (1994), p. 9.
62 J. Morgan, *Conflict and Order: The Police and Labour Disputes in England and Wales, 1900–
    1939*, Clarendon Press: Oxford (1987), p. 254.
63 Ibid., referenced from HO 144/8014, Disturbances: Trade Disputes and Trade Unions Bill, 1927,
    'Commissioner of Metropolitan Police to Home Secretary, 8 Oct 1926.'
64 *Hansard, HC Deb*, 6 May 1926, vol 195 cc453–597, 507–508, 516, 540–541.

into play and they will deliberately make use of the power conferred upon them by this regulation to prevent perfectly legitimate Labour and Socialist meetings and processions.[65]

The motion to delete Regulation 22 from the enforcement of the Emergency Powers Act during the 1926 General Strike was easily defeated, with only 89 votes in favour and 299 against.[66]

In addition to other Left-wing activism, the NUWM organised a series of Hunger Marches around Britain. The NUWM, which was formed in 1921, was not a political organisation but members of the CPGB played a prominent role in its administration. Their first national march was staged in 1922 when the British unemployed from cities as far apart as Glasgow and Plymouth marched to London and requested a deputation with the Conservative Prime Minister Bonar Law. The largely Conservative press had first ignored the marches, but as the processions approached London, NUWM organiser Wal Hannington recalled, 'the whole of the capitalist press became hysterical, and news columns were filled with scare articles about "Secret meetings of the marchers", "Bolshevik gold", "Firebrand leaders", and so on.' He continued to recall an article from the *Pall Mall Gazette* entitled 'The Red Plot' in which, 'The marchers were accused of bearing firearms, and the leaders were made out to be rogues and scoundrels of the worst type, and of course, in the pay of Bolshevik Russia.'[67]

An example of how disorder was sparked occurred during the fourth national Hunger March in October 1932 when 100,000 demonstrators descended on Hyde Park in London. The number of police on duty was 2,600, including 136 mounted police and 750 special constables. The hostile Hunger Marchers at the Marble Arch end of Hyde Park were reported to have been abusive to the special constables stationed by the gates. Accounts state that the special constables became resentful to 'the general attitude of the rabble' and struck out at them with their batons. Unable to then hold their position, the special constables were supported by a mounted baton charge.[68] Two independent observers[69] recorded that the unemployed were booing the police but that there was no sign of disorder or disturbance. They declared that 'People were forced to run for their lives in order to escape being trampled upon by the police horses or beaten by staves.'[70] Seventeen arrests took place and Hannington claimed that there was a general impression within the press

65 Ibid., at c508.

66 Ibid., at c550.

67 W. Hannington, *Unemployed Struggles 1919–1936*, Lawrence and Wishart Ltd: London (1979), p. 84.

68 P. Kingsford, *The Hunger Marches in Britain 1920–1939*, Lawrence and Wishart Ltd: London (1982), p. 154

69 The observers were Reginald Reynolds, general secretary of the No More War Movement, and his friend James Grant, who wanted to witness first-hand 'how much truth there was in the statements that the police treated the unemployed demonstrations as an occasion for beating people up'. Ibid., pp. 154–155.

70 Ibid., p. 155.

that the fighting at Hyde Park and another incident at Trafalgar had been caused by the special constables. Even the *Police Review* stated:

> An excellent fellowship exists [between the constable and the special], but there is a feeling that in this difficult time the appearance of the special is calculated to cause trouble rather than avoid it. At the meetings and hunger marches, the special is an irritant, rather than an antiseptic.

This striking admission regarding the defectiveness of the special constables and a retrospective analysis of the cause of disorder during this incident demonstrates that the Hunger Marchers were not necessarily the instigators of violent clashes between themselves and the police. Historian Jane Morgan argued that the police's statutory powers relating to public processions were weak and their methods may have been found to have had no legal basis if they had been contested in court. She stated that although they could deal with disorder, their preventive powers were inadequate and they could act only when disorder arose. Additionally, when the behaviour of the marchers was not riotous, there was difficulty in proving it to be an unlawful assembly.[71] This led Metropolitan Police Commissioner Lord Trenchard to write to the Home Secretary, declaring:

> I consider that there is a very reasonable case for prohibiting *all* processions (other than ceremonial processions, the Lord Mayor's show etc.) in the central area at any rate on all days but Saturday and Sunday.[72]

This demonstrates that Trenchard believed that the limits of his discretion in dealing with public processions did not extend to the preventive power of proscription and he used his influence to persuade the Home Secretary that new legislation was needed. Furthermore, Morgan's assessment of the uncertain legal capacity to regulate or proscribe public processions in the period before the Public Order Act supports Thurlow's belief that the Home Office were more cautious when managing the activism of the BUF because of Sir Oswald Mosley's ability to mount a legal challenge to oppressive or unlawful police tactics.[73] However, the shortcomings of legislative powers relating to public processions were considered before the era of the BUF and were significantly considered in response to the NUWM.

71 J. Morgan, *Conflict and Order*, p. 254.
72 Ibid., quote referenced from MEPO 2/6269, 'Trenchard to Home Secretary, 27 Oct 1932.'
73 Thurlow, *The Secret State*, p. 198. Here Thurlow states, 'The Home Office was particularly conscious of the fact that Mosley was litigious, stood up for his rights, had never lost a case in court, and was therefore loath to overreach police powers in dealing with him.'

The Processions (Regulations) Bill 1932

The frequent disorder and sporadic fighting that broke out between the Hunger Marchers and the police prompted the drafting of the Processions (Regulations) Bill 1932. The Bill was drafted by the Director of Public Prosecutions, the Metropolitan Police Commissioner, and representatives of the Home Office, the Scottish Office, the Ministry of Health and the Ministry of Labour. These records reveal the Cabinet Committee's debates and several drafts of the proposed Bill.

Clause 1 was directed to suppress the national Hunger Marches of the NUWM. It provided that:

> If the Secretary of State is satisfied that arrangements are about to be made, or are being made, or have been made, for concentrating persons outside the areas in which they ordinarily reside, or for causing persons to go in procession to any place outside the area in which they ordinarily reside, and that the concentration or procession is likely to result – (a) in serious disorder; or (b) in such abnormal demands being made upon poor law authorities as to cause serious derangement in the administration of public assistance, he may by order prohibit the concentration or procession; and, accordingly, any concentration or procession so prohibited shall be unlawful.[74]

The implications of clause 1 were more extensive than just suppressing the Hunger Marches: it potentially provided the authorities with far-reaching powers to prohibit any public assembly in which a breach of the peace could be anticipated or that participants travelled to outside their normal area of residence to take part.

Clause 2 provided local police authorities with the power to temporarily ban either all processions or selected processions, following a successful application to the Secretary of State. The Home Office Memorandum which accompanied the Processions (Regulations) Bill, authored by Permanent Under Secretary of State for the Home Office Sir Russell Scott, recognised that the power to prohibit particular processions could potentially be criticised for unfair discrimination on political grounds. Despite this, Scott declared, 'if no action were possible short of total prohibition of all processions, even the most innocent, the power would be so drastic as to restrict its use within unnecessarily narrow limits, and its usefulness would be seriously impaired.'[75]

The draft Bill demonstrated the dangerous escalation of legal powers that the Home Office were prepared to take in order to prohibit a recurrence of the Hunger Marches. It was also admitted in the Memorandum that there was an opportunity in the drafting of new legislation to not just counter the problem posed by the Hunger Marchers, but also to 'control . . . processions in London itself

---

74 HO 144/18294, 'Police: Powers and duties of the police at meetings, processions and demonstrations'.
75 Ibid., p. 5.

and in other populous areas'.[76] Such provisions as those mentioned in clauses 1 and 2 had the potential to curtail civil liberty, but would also have been open to political abuse, discrimination and selective enforcement. Of those involved in the Bill's drafting, only the representative from the Ministry of Labour voiced concerns whether such legislation would be either practical or effective. The Attorney General declared that the prohibition of processions by the Secretary of State would lead to 'intolerable political difficulty' and suggested that the existing law regarding processions was already adequate. In consideration of the laws regarding the obstruction of the highways, he declared that 'Any new powers to grant or refuse orders for processions should be taken on traffic grounds alone'.[77] In December 1932 the Cabinet decided that 'further legislative measures should not be contemplated until an extended trial had been given to the method of asking courts of summary jurisdiction to bind over the organisers beforehand.'[78]

This tactic was utilised the same month as NUWM organisers Tom Mann and Emrhys Llewellyn were bound over to keep the peace and be of good behaviour in order to prevent an attempted deputation with the Prime Minister. At Bow Street Police Court on 17 December 1932, prosecuting on behalf of the Director of Public Prosecutions, Mr Wallace recited letters sent from Llewellyn to the Prime Minister and several articles from the *Daily Worker* which 'showed clearly that a mass meeting was to take place to enforce the receiving of the deputation mentioned'.[79] The prosecutor cited s23 Seditious Meetings Act 1819, which prohibited meetings of 50 persons or more within a mile of Westminster Hall when Parliament was sitting, demonstrating that the meeting promoted by the NUWM would be illegal. Furthermore, other NUWM activity had also caused concern for the authorities over the legality of their activism.

The month before Mann and Llewellyn were bound over, Sid Elias of the NUWM was sentenced to two years imprisonment for unlawfully soliciting and inciting Llewellyn and Hannington 'to cause discontent, dissatisfaction, and ill-will between different classes of His Majesty's subjects and to create public disturbances against the peace'.[80] The letter, which Elias had sent from Moscow, contained instructions to Llewellyn and Hannington promoting different courses of agitation and activism. Additionally, although the special police were in part culpable of some of the disorder at the NUWM demonstration in Hyde Park on the 28 October, this did not mean that the authorities took the view that the demonstrators were entirely innocent. Many media reports of the disorder mention incidents of stones, mud and coal being thrown from different parts of the crowd, smashing shop windows and striking police vehicles. There were also accounts of several crowd surges from the demonstrators which were reported to have

76 Ibid., Home Office Memorandum 1932, p. 2.
77 Ibid., Attorney-General's Memorandum.
78 Ibid., Duties and Powers of the Commissioner of the Police of the Metropolis, p. 7.
79 *Nottingham Evening Post*, 17 Dec 1932.
80 *The Times*, 5 Nov 1932.

crushed female shoppers.[81] Moreover, reports from Special Branch informants had revealed that the marchers were encouraged to make the march 'as spectacular as possible [with] as many clashes with the police as possible'. The march leaders also advocated that they should create disturbances at Public Assistance Committees, at the Houses of Parliament and at embassies, and to create 'as much trouble as possible for the police'. In addition, it was instructed that 'trade union banners [were] to be used at demonstrations and then used in open conflict with the police.'[82] The evidence here suggests that activists from the NUWM had recently and wilfully engaged in disorder and were encouraged to do so by their leaders. In consideration of this, the authorities' anticipation of further disorder may not have been so questionable.

Despite the recent NUWM disorder, Mann and Llewellyn still wanted to present the petition to Parliament. In anticipating further potential disorder, but this time in the form of an unlawful assembly outside Parliament, the magistrate Sir Chartres Biron 'ordered both defendants to be bound over in their own recognisances in £200, and to find two sureties in £100 each to keep the peace and be of good behaviour for twelve months.' They refused and were each imprisoned for two months.[83] Here, the actions of the Home Office and the magistrates demonstrate the extent of their discretion in preventing an anticipated breach of the peace. Scholars such as Ewing and Gearty keenly identify the injustice to Mann and Llewellyn while dismissing elements of the legal argument used against them in an effort to prove that the National Government's intention was to imprison the four leaders of the NUWM as they were losing patience with the Hunger Marchers.[84]

The Home Secretary defended the action by stating:

> I believe that we were within our rights, that what we did was calculated to cause less disturbance – it was done for that reason and that reason alone – and that these men could have given the undertaking, which was no outrageous undertaking and one which they could have given without any dereliction of their position, without giving away any right of proper free speech or attendance at political meetings. They refused to do it, and they have suffered the consequences.[85]

This defence needs to be questioned on two counts. Were the powers used consistent with other binding-over orders? And was the authorities concern for a potential breach of the peace legitimate?

---

81 *Western Times*, 28 Oct 1932; *Dundee Courier*, 28 Oct 1932.
82 Kingsford, *The Hunger Marchers*, pp. 140–141, citing MEPO 2/3064.
83 Although there is no mention of the instructions for agitation by Elias in the magistrates binding over of Mann and Hannington, Sir Chartres Biron presided over both cases. The letter was also printed in *The Times* on the 5 November 1932.
84 Ewing and Gearty, *The Struggle*, p. 224–227. Elias and Hannington were already imprisoned.
85 *Hansard, HC Deb*, 22 Dec 1932, vol 273 c1300.

The binding over of Mann and Llewellyn was partially consistent with *Wise v Dunning* and *Lansbury v Riley*.[86] In each of these cases, the binding-over order was issued against speakers who had encouraged violence or illegal behaviour. Wise, as discussed earlier, had encouraged his supporters to bring sticks to the next meeting in anticipation that his Roman Catholic opponents would also bring weapons. While campaigning for female suffrage in 1913, George Lansbury, who had resigned his Labour seat in 1912, advocated that the suffragettes continue to use militancy and tactics which involved breaking the law. Where these differed from Mann and Llewellyn's binding over is that it was not proved that Mann and Llewellyn were involved with the previous disorder or of advocating it. Here, it was their association with the NUWM that gave cause for the magistrate to anticipate that their actions would result in a breach of the peace and that sureties would be deemed necessary. While this point seems particularly oppressive, it must be remembered that the 'power to bind over a person before the court to keep the peace or to be of good behaviour does not depend on a conviction'.[87] As a form of preventive justice, it is employed to prevent breaches of the peace rather than to serve as a punishment. However, Harry Street stressed that the requirement to enter into recognizance and find sureties can indeed be a punishment in itself, especially in the case of Lansbury, who was unable to pay the sums fixed by the magistrate, and in default of paying was imprisoned for three months.[88]

Whether Mann and Llewellyn were victimised because of their political allegiances or because of a potentially exaggerated fear of disorder, their martyrdom gave their cause great publicity. Including the other arrests of Hannington and Elias, historian Peter Kingsford reflected that the trials aroused middle-class Labour sympathisers and the conflicts had 'contributed to a three day debate on unemployment and the Government had made a concession with meaning for many unemployed'.[89] It was just fifteen months till the next national Hunger March, but this time the NUWM discarded their former communist slogan of 'Class against Class' and attempted to create a 'People's Front' in opposition to the rise of European fascism. Although the Labour Party and the Trade Unions ignored this call for unity, they successfully harnessed the support of the Independent Labour Party (ILP). The Home Secretary claimed that it was because of the support of four MPs that the 1934 Hunger March differed from the previous one. This is reflected in subsequent policing of the 1934 and 1936 hunger marches as they were stated to have acted with 'more restraint'.[90] Even Lord Trenchard commented in 1936 that 'the meetings were in every case orderly and the conduct of the unemployed marchers beyond reproach'.[91]

---

86   *Lansbury v Riley* [1914] 3 KB 229.
87   M. Supperstone, *Brownlie's Law*, p. 315, n8.
88   Street, *Freedom*, p. 46. Lansbury was required to enter into a personal recognizance of £1,000 and to find two sureties of £500 each.
89   Kingsford, *The Hunger Marchers*, pp. 163–164.
90   N. Branson, *The History of the Communist Party of Great Britain 1927–1941*, Lawrence and Wishart: London (1985), p. 81.
91   Cmd. 5457, *Report of the Commissioner of Police of the Metropolis for the Year 1936*, p. 25.

It was against this backdrop of violent clashes between Hunger Marchers and the police, the selective application of the Highway Act 1835, and the ambiguous interpretations of the common law authority of *Beatty* and *Wise*, that members of the BUF donned their black shirts and began a propaganda campaign, marching in the streets of towns and cities across Britain.

The marching Blackshirts

As a newly formed political movement in 1932, Mosley's BUF aspired to convey the new radical doctrine of fascism to the people of Great Britain via various propaganda techniques. During their public processions, members paraded in tight formation wearing the Blackshirt uniform, which gave the appearance of a military-styled march. The displaying of banners and the inclusion of a musical band were also incorporated in some BUF processions. The importance of effective propaganda methods to the contemporary democratic system was highlighted by jurist Ivor Jennings in 1937. With a newly franchised electorate, Jennings declared that Burke's doctrine of representative government was no longer adequate and that publicity was essential to true democracy. Nonetheless, he continued to state that, as the press and newsreel companies were essentially partial, old forms of political propaganda such as the public street corner meeting, which was instrumental in the rise of socialism, held a cardinal position in democratic government. Moreover, the techniques of publicising such meetings to ensure the largest audience were also imperative.[92] In a practice similar to that of the Salvation Army, the BUF processions were a particularly effective technique of gathering an audience and gaining the movement extensive publicity, yet the military character and appearance of the Blackshirts caused concern over the legality of their processions.

Although the precedent set by *Beatty v Gillbanks* may have reinforced the liberty of the fascists to organise processions in public places, the judgment of *Wise v Dunning* added a further dimension to powers relating to the preservation of the peace. The Blackshirt processions frequently attracted hostile opposition, but it is necessary to question whether or not the resulting disorder was the 'natural consequence' of the BUF's actions. At common law, this consideration would ultimately determine if the judgment of *Beatty* or *Wise* should be adopted and whether the BUF should be permitted the liberty to organise public processions.

As members of the BUF were under strict orders to stay within the law and obey the police, the disorder that resulted from their processions was usually instigated by their political opponents, drawing a similarity with the Salvation Army marches and *Beatty v Gillbanks*. Conversely, when considering the Blackshirts' reputation for violence and brutality, their praise and emulation of European fascist regimes, their aggressive anti-communist policy and the adoption of an openly anti-Semitic policy from late 1934, the level of confrontational opposition

---

92 W. I. Jennings, 'Public Order', *The Political Quarterly in the Thirties 42*, no. 5 (1971), pp. 175–186, pp. 180–182. Originally published as W.I. Jennings, 'Public Order', *The Political Quarterly 8*, no. 1 (1937), pp. 7–20.

to them must be measured in the context of *Wise v Dunning*. Therefore, it must be considered whether the disorder at BUF processions was the natural consequence of the provocation presented by the fascists or not.

The Unlawful Drilling Act 1819

In the House of Commons in May 1933, Labour MP David Grenfell asked the Home Secretary, Sir John Gilmour, if he could share any information on organisations which were drilling adult males on semi-military lines. Gilmour refused to name any organisation, stating that:

> unauthorised meetings of persons for the purpose of being trained or of practising military exercises are prohibited by law and I have no reason to suppose that appropriate action under the provisions of the Unlawful Drilling Act, 1819, will not be taken should occasion arise.[93]

Grenfell's question was a blatant allusion to the BUF's uniformed processions. In response, an article in the *Blackshirt* stated that the BUF were well aware of the 1819 Act and stated that it was:

> frequently impressed on all organisers the necessity of adhering to pure physical training, and of never in any sense stepping outside these limits . . . [adding] Demonstration marching, or practice in such marching, is in no way practising military exercises.[94]

The difficulty of mounting a prosecution under the Act was highlighted by Gilmour, who stated that 'It is difficult to say when physical exercises are really drilling or not. The law is directed against military training.'[95]

In the spring of 1934, the question of the BUF's quasi-military appearance was deliberated by Sir John Gilmour. The necessity to deal with the issue was exposed following violence at a BUF meeting and procession in Bristol in April 1934. Gilmour stated that,

> I think there is no doubt that this disorder was largely due to the adoption of semi-military evolutions by the Fascists, their marching in formation, and their general behaviour, which was regarded by the crowd as provocative.[96]

Following the Home Secretary's comments on the disorder, Sir Oswald Mosley wrote to Gilmour asking him to clarify how the BUF were provocative. He continued to state that the only violence that he was aware of was when 'two negroes attempted

---

93 *Hansard, HC Deb*, 17 May 1933, vol 278 cc356–357.
94 *The Blackshirt*, 16 Jun 1933, p. 2.
95 *Hansard, HC Deb*, 17 May 1933, vol 278 c357.
96 *Hansard, HC Deb*, 9 Apr 1934, vol 288 c15.

to attack me and were knocked down by Fascists. One of these men carried and raised a knife in his hand.' Regarding Gilmour's accusation towards the military character of the BUF, Mosley declared that, 'To march in column of three is not a "semi-military evolution", and the right to march in procession is clearly permissible under the law of this country.'[97] In Gilmour's reply, he stated that such an attack with a knife on Mosley was not witnessed by any police officer but it was reported that one

> half-caste Communist . . . protested to the Fascists, as they marched away from the hall, against the way in which some of his associates had been treated at the meeting, but no assault or threat with a knife by him was observed by the police.[98]

On Mosley's explanation that marching in formation was necessary to protect individual known fascists from attack, Gilmour candidly suggested that 'if members of the British Union of Fascists did not wear a uniform they would not be "well known to be Fascists".'[99]

Processions do offer greater physical protection for political activists as there is safety in numbers and such events usually have a large police presence. Their true value is the publicity and spectacle that they create. A uniformed march is even more effective, psychologically, on both the participant and the spectator. Jennings asserted that uniforms create feelings of security in those that wear them and feelings of insecurity in those who see them, claiming that both ingredients are necessary for the establishment of a dictatorship.[100]

With no effective legal means to prohibit demonstrations, it became the duty of the police to maintain public order by regulating processions to prevent obstruction and preserve the peace. This was achieved by relying principally on s72 Highway Act 1835, s52 Metropolitan Police Act 1839 (or s21 Town Police Clauses Act 1847) and the breach of the peace doctrine. However, when utilizing Breach of the Peace powers, it is required to prove that disorder had been either actual or imminent. Therefore, a large police presence at BUF meetings and processions became a necessary police tactic to preserve order, considering the hostile and organised disruption their activities provoked. A major problem with this police tactic was the appearance that they were protecting the Blackshirts. This was reflected at the highest level by Trenchard who, in a letter to the Home Office, demonstrated his desire for 'doing away with the Fascists':

> The large number of police which it has been found necessary to employ to keep the peace at Fascist demonstrations is creating the impression among anti-Fascists that Sir Oswald Mosley's semi-military organisation is being permitted to develop under police protection.[101]

---

97 *The Times*, 11 Apr 1934.
98 *The Times*, 23 Apr 1934.
99 *The Times*, 23 Apr 1934.
100 Jennings, 'Public Order', p. 177.
101 MEPO 3/2940, Fascist: Disorder at public meetings (1934–1938), Letter from Lord Trenchard to the Under Secretary of State, 28 Sep 1934.

The Public Order Bill 1934

Throughout 1934 there was significant Blackshirt activity and widespread disorder across the country. The increasing rate of fascist-related disorder contributed towards the discussion of new legislation. In July 1934 the Home Secretary debated the existing public order law with the Chief Constables of England and Wales. In his resulting memorandum for the preservation of public order, Gilmour recorded that the Chief Constables were practically unanimous in their desire to see

> that the police should be given the power to prohibit processions which are likely to lead to a breach of the peace or to intimidate other persons, and to regulate the route of processions so as to prevent undue interference with traffic.[102]

Although under the Town Police Clauses Act 1847 this power was available to the magistrates and local authorities, the Chief Constables stressed that for public order to be kept effectively these functions should be held by the police. At this time the Home Office were already becoming aware that the standing joint committees and watch committees in some areas were becoming politically unreliable. Importantly, Chris Williams states that during this period the rising influence of the Labour Party in local government had already 'led to an increase in political battles between police authorities and their chiefs'.[103] The interwar period was a critical time regarding the independence of the local police authorities and the Home Office's battle for centralisation. The period saw a change in definitions used by the Home Office which was highlighted by Permanent Secretary Sir John Anderson, who stated in 1928 that 'the policeman is nobody's servant . . . He executes a public office under the Law.'[104] Therefore, the Chief Constables' request for local autonomy in regards to regulating processions found favour from the Home Office; this was reflected in the drafting of the new Bill.

By October 1934, the Public Order Bill 1934[105] was drafted but, as with the Processions (Regulations) Bill 1932, it did not reach Parliament. The discussion of the committee that drafted the proposed Bill does, however, reveal the steps that they

---

102 HO 45/25386, Disturbances: Wearing of uniform to denote membership of political organisations. Preservation of public order: Disturbances arising out of public meetings and demonstrations, particularly those involving the British Union of Fascists (1933–1936), 'Memorandum by the Home Secretary,' p. 4.

103 C. Williams, 'Rotten boroughs: the crisis of urban policing and the decline of municipal independence 1914–64', in J. Moore and J. Smith (eds), *Corruption in Urban Politics and Society, Britain 1780–1950*, Ashgate (2007) p. 160–161.

104 Ibid.

105 Full title: 'Draft of a Bill to Prohibit the maintenance of certain bodies of persons in connection with political organisations, to restrict and regulate processions, concentrations and public meetings and to facilitate the maintenance to order at meetings'.

were willing to take to maintain public order to the detriment of civil liberty. In addition to this, the Bill neglected the local authorities as the provisions principally provided the Secretary of State and the Chief Constables with wide-reaching powers.

Clause 3 of the draft Bill proposed a wide increase in the powers of the Secretary of State, who would be able to prohibit processions or concentrations of people if he was satisfied that they may either lead to serious disorder or create abnormal demands on the Poor Law authorities. Such a prohibition would make the procession unlawful and those taking part would be guilty of an offence.[106] Interestingly, this clause replicated clause 1 of the failed Processions (Regulations) Bill 1932, and the proposed power lay solely with the Secretary of State and did not require a request from a Chief Constable. This marks a slight departure from the similar power held in Emergency Regulation 22, which placed the onus on chiefs of police to prohibit processions with the approval of the Home Secretary. This departure is likely to reflect that these Bills were primarily mandated to prevent the Hunger Marches which would have traversed through different local authorities and provincial police forces. This would have given the Home Secretary comprehensive control over prohibiting these marches and declaring them as unlawful assemblies without relying on the action of individual local authorities, especially as some had previously shown political support for the Hunger Marchers.

The police were also to have their powers increased by legislation, rather than relying on the questionable use of common law powers or statutory powers relating to traffic obstruction. Clause 4(1) provided that, 'All processions shall follow such route as may be directed by or by authority of the chief officer of police.' This far-reaching power was supplemented by clause 4(2)(3), which provided the further power to impose restrictions on the time and destination of the procession as long as the chief of police is satisfied that such processions may either lead to serious disorder at a public meeting, or interference with the work of a government department or authority.[107]

With a decline in fascist-related public disorder, the urgency to introduce the Bill diminished. In January 1935, the BUF had entered a period of reorganization that concentrated on the recruitment of ideologically committed members and the construction of new electoral machinery.[108] In summarising BUF activity and membership in 1935, historian Stephen Dorril states that the movement had 'degenerated into an organisation increasingly dependent on a localised campaign playing on populist anti-Semitism.' Yet by the end of the year Dorril estimated that paying membership had tripled to around 15,000.[109] By late 1935, organised opposition to the BUF had resurfaced, Blackshirt propaganda now included a provocative anti-Semitic doctrine and in 1936 new legislative public order measures were again discussed by the Home Office.

---

106 MEPO 3/2940, Draft of a Bill . . . clause 3.
107 Ibid., clause 4.
108 D. S. Lewis, *Illusions of Grandeur: Mosley, Fascism and British Society 1931–1981*, Manchester University Press (1987), p. 67.
109 S. Dorril, *Blackshirt: Sir Oswald Mosley and British Fascism*, Viking: London (2006), p. 368.

The Battle of Cable Street 1936

Opposition towards BUF marches became more prominent in 1936.[110] When the political violence resurfaced, the Liberal MP, Sir John Simon, was now Home Secretary; former Air Vice Marshall of the Royal Air Force, Sir Philip Game, was the Metropolitan Police Commissioner.

Mosley's fascist campaign now exploited nationalist ideology with anti-Semitism and had gathered momentum in East London. During October 1936, the resources of the authorities were severely tested regarding three high-profile processions. The first was the BUF's fourth anniversary march in East London, which met large-scale anti-fascist resistance that caused widespread violence and disorder, resulting in the Battle of Cable Street. The second procession was the NUWM's Hunger March, which consisted of unemployed workers from Scotland, Northumberland, Durham, Lancashire, Yorkshire, Nottinghamshire, Derby, Coventry and South Wales. The third march was of 200 unemployed men from Jarrow, which had suffered abnormally high unemployment following the closure of a shipyard the previous year. With the exception of the Jarrow Crusade, which was organised by the Jarrow Council, the marches' relationship to political extremism led to considerable debate by the authorities in how to manage the expected disorder.[111]

The first contingents of the 1936 Hunger March commenced from Scotland on 5 October and were expected to assemble with the other marches in London on 8 November. A memorandum from the Home Secretary to the Cabinet revealed that the march was organised by the Communist Party and the NUWM, who unsuccessfully attempted to procure sponsorship for the march from the Labour Party and the Trades Union Congress but managed to secure support from local trades councils. Simon declared that the organisers were keen to hide the fact that the march was organised by the NUWM and the Communist Party as they did not want a 'communist' label attached to it. The memorandum demonstrated that although there was no legal method of prohibiting the march, every effort was made to hinder and discredit the organisers. Simon reiterated some of the arguments used following the national Hunger Marches of 1932 and 1934. In particular, this included attempting to alienate public sympathy by using the National Publicity Bureau to discredit the march. Simon wanted to demonstrate that the unemployed were being exploited by the communist organisers because the march could not have any constitutional influence on Government policy. Simon stated, 'It is the settled practice that Ministers of the Crown should refuse to receive deputations from such demonstrations.'[112]

In addition to being discredited by Simon, the BUF also faced obstacles in organising their own brand of political activism. Their application for a public procession in Manchester on 19 July 1936 was initially and controversially declined by the

110 MEPO 3/2940.
111 CAB 24/264, March of the unemployed on London: Memorandum by the Home Secretary (1936).
112 Ibid.

Manchester Watch Committee under s213 Manchester Police Act due to the provocative nature of the Blackshirt uniform. The BUF then tested the reason for the prohibition of their procession by responding that they would march without their uniform, an unusual incident which is discussed in more detail in chapter eight. A similar condition was considered by the Hull Chief Constable and Watch Committee when the Blackshirts organised a procession there.[113] These examples demonstrate that different local authorities were prepared to take steps to limit the disorder caused by fascist processions. The uniform ban attempted to remove a proportion of the provocation associated with BUF processions. While some regions attempted to limit such provocation, the Metropolitan Police made little effort to regulate the BUF's fourth anniversary march through prominent Jewish communities.

On 4 October 1936 the BUF planned a large rally in East London. It was scheduled to commence at Royal Mint Street, where the Blackshirts were to assemble and be inspected by Mosley. They then planned to march through East London and divide into four different marching columns, which would each advance to separate open-air meetings located at Shoreditch, Limehouse, Bow and Bethnal Green. Mosley intended to speak at each meeting. The national press highlighted the anxiety and insecurity generated in East London before the Blackshirt rally. The tabloid newspaper the *Daily Mirror* ran headlines such as 'Fascist march plans make Jewish Quarter uneasy'[114] and 'Thousands in terror of great fascist march in East End of London'.[115]

The affected communities took various forms of action regarding the proposed march. The Mayors of Bethnal Green, Hackney, Poplar, Shoreditch and Stepney were received by a Home Office official who referred their request to prohibit the march to the Home Secretary. Mrs Roberts, the Mayor of Stepney, who had previously sent a request to the Home Secretary to ban the march, argued, 'I think the march is extremely provocative.'[116] George Lansbury, Labour MP for Bow and Bromley, wrote the Home Secretary, asking him to divert the march. In a statement to the press, Lansbury stated, 'What I want is to maintain peace and order and I advise those people who are opposed to Fascism to keep away from the demonstration.'[117] The Jewish Peoples Council submitted a petition to the Home Secretary which reportedly contained over 100,000 signatures in an attempt to prohibit the march because of the fear that it would lead to violence. A member of the deputation, headed by the Labour MP James Hall, argued that 'racial incitement and propaganda are likely to cause great disturbance'.[118]

The BUF's anti-Semitic propaganda included a policy for the deportation of Jews who do not put 'Britain first'.[119] When considering the BUF's motives and

113 *Hansard, HC Deb*, 31 Jul 1936, vol 315 cc1856–1857.
114 *The Daily Mirror*, 1 Oct 1936.
115 *The Daily Mirror*, 3 Oct 1936.
116 *The Daily Mirror*, 1 Oct 1936.
117 *The Times*, 1 Oct 1936.
118 *The Daily Mirror*, 3 Oct 1936.
119 O. Mosley, *Fascism: 100 Questions Asked and Answered*, BUF Publications: London (1936).

actions during this period, the legal protection for lawful public assemblies that was attained at common law through *Beatty v Gillbanks* loses its relevance. Taking into account the level of provocation directed by the BUF at the Jewish communities in the East End, the judgment of *Wise v Dunning* must be applied. In that case Lord Alverstone CJ, referred to the 'essential condition . . . that there must be an act of the defendant, the natural consequence of which, if his act be not unlawful in itself, would be to produce an unlawful act by other persons'.[120] Although the Blackshirt march through Jewish communities was not unlawful in itself, a strong argument can be made that the 'natural consequence' of such an act of provocation would result in a breach of the peace. Attention should also be paid to s52 Metropolitan Police Act 1839, which provided the police with the power to regulate the route of processions when occasion required for keeping order and preventing obstruction. Regardless of these legal powers, Simon informed the deputation that he could not intervene.[121] In addition to his uncertainty on the lawful use of such powers, Simon also believed in upholding the tradition of free speech, which he described as 'a grand characteristic of British political life . . . [which] involves a willingness to let others express opinions which we abominate'.[122] Ewing and Gearty dismissed the proposition that any inaction by the Government during the era of the BUF could represent their commitment to political liberty: the Government had also passed the Incitement to Disaffection Act 1934, which created strict limitations on political freedom. However, this Statute related to subversion in the armed forces and addressed a perceived threat to national security which can be greatly contrasted with the public order problems created by the BUF.[123]

Ronald Kidd of the National Council for Civil Liberties (NCCL) rejected Simon's claim that he could not intervene with the Blackshirt procession. He declared that the 1839 Act had been utilised to prohibit a Labour march down Oxford Street in the autumn of that year. In addition, on 22 March the Commissioner regulated an anti-fascist procession by ordering that it would not be allowed within a half-mile radius of the BUF meeting at the Albert Hall. Kidd's deduction was that:

> A word from Sir John Simon to the Commissioner of Police, therefore, would have been sufficient to cause Sir Philip Game to exercise his powers under the Metropolitan Police Act and forbid the Fascist procession to march through the Jewish quarter.[124]

---

120 *Wise v Dunning.*
121 R. Kidd, *British Liberty in Danger*, Lawrence and Wishart Ltd: London (1940), p. 69.
122 J. Simon, *Retrospect: The Memoir of the Rt. Hon. Viscount Simon*, Hutchinson and Co Ltd: London (1952), p. 215.
123 Thurlow highlighted that Major General Sir Vernon Kell of MI5 argued that the measures under the Incitement to Disaffection Act were necessary to promote vigilance as 'discontent in the forces of Hungary, Finland and Russia had played a key role in revolutionary activity in those countries.' See, Thurlow, *The Secret State*, p. 142.
124 Ibid.

The inaction of the authorities was starkly contrasted by the anti-fascist response which mobilised to prevent the Blackshirt march. Communist Phil Piratin recalled the anti-fascist arrangements at the 1991 Witness Seminar on the Battle of Cable Street.[125] As the route of the march was not published, the anti-fascists created contingency plans and used cyclists and motorcyclists to rely information regarding any fascist movement. Additionally, at the sites where Mosley planned to speak, such as Victoria Park Square, two members of the Communist Party occupied the site from five in the morning until the night. Piratin stated that the communists 'kept on speaking and reading books out a bit with two police standing by their side as evidence that they were there all the time.'[126] Therefore, if Mosley's procession had been successful, he would not be able to hold a meeting as the communist meeting would have already been in progress. It is interesting to note that Piratin recalled that two policeman presented evidence that the Communist meeting had occupied the site first. He also spoke favourably of a police inspector who was 'more or less amiable to us at that time' who gave them information on the day regarding Mosley's preferred route.[127]

The events that followed became known as the Battle of Cable Street, as widespread fighting broke out between anti-fascist groups who mobilised to prevent the BUF procession and the police who attempted to disperse them. Contemporary writer and journalist Frederic Mullally reported:

> Never was a more formidable concentration of police seen in London. Six thousand constables, together with the whole of the mounted division, were posted between Tower Hill and Whitechapel, lining the streets or assembled in large groups at strategic points.[128]

Following the erection of barricades along the route by anti-fascists, several baton charges were made by the police to clear the way for the BUF. To prevent further disorder, Sir Philip Game prohibited the Blackshirt march. The fascists were redirected along the Embankment away from the East End and then dispersed. Some Blackshirts regrouped in Trafalgar Square, causing minor disorders. The front page of the *Daily Mirror* recounted the previous day's disorder, highlighting that there were 84 arrests, 268 injured and thousands more involved in riots. One headline announced:

5,000 FASCISTS MASSING TO PARADE HEMMED IN BY A CROWD OF 100,000, INCLUDING THOUSANDS OF ANGRY JEWS AND COMMUNISTS SHOUTING, "THE FASCISTS SHALL NOT PASS."[129]

---

125 Piratin was later to become the last Communist MP and served the Mile End constituency from 1945 to 1950.
126 P. Catterall (ed), 'The Battle of Cable Street: Witness Seminar', *Contemporary Record 8*, no. 1 (Summer 1994), p. 115.
127 Ibid., p. 113.
128 F. Mullally, *Fascism Inside England*, Claud Morris Books Ltd: London (1946), p. 73.
129 *The Daily Mirror*, 5 Oct 1936.

As well as contending that the Metropolitan Police Act 1839 could have been exercised to prevent the BUF procession on the 4 October 1936, Kidd also highlighted the preventative powers that could have been exercised when a breach of the peace was threatened. He questioned why Mosley was not brought before a magistrate 'to show cause why he should not be bound over to be of good behaviour and to keep the peace, when he was in fact threatening so serious a disturbance of the peace'.[130] In comparison, Kidd argued that this was the action taken against Tom Mann, the nominal head of the Hunger March in 1932, despite the situation being less critical than it was regarding the fascist march. Despite not agreeing with the action of preventive justice in principle, he questioned why the authorities did not show as much zeal against Right-wing speakers who deliberately threatened the peace as they did against Left-wing speakers, such as Katherine Duncan,[131] who did not threaten the peace in any way.[132]

Although Kidd's argument was used to demonstrate pro-fascist partiality, this simplistic comparison is not entirely applicable to the situation. The origin of the anticipated breach of the peace at the processions organised by Mann and Mosley reflect this. As described earlier, at NUWM processions it was the conduct of the marchers themselves that caused the authorities concern, while at BUF processions disorder was likely to have been caused by their political opponents. Yet while it must also be acknowledged that the Home Office did actively attempt to reduce support for and participation in NUWM activities, the earlier discussion highlighted that organisers had actively encouraged marchers to engage in disorder with the police and, despite the criticism of the special constables, members of the march had engaged in violent disorder. Additionally, although the incidents were only four years apart, the binding over of NUWM organisers was a particular strategy used at the time which was tested in order to prevent or limit further disorder. As Mann and Llewellyn generated publicity from their imprisonment and became martyrs for their cause, the use of this tactic to control public processions was redundant by 1936.

The legal basis for any prosecution of Mosley ahead of the 4 October demonstration would have been highly contentious. For instance, what law was his proposed action breaking? The potential that his proposed public assembly may be attacked did not in itself make it unlawful. Even if *Wise v Dunning* were to be applied and it was argued that the 'natural consequence' of his actions would be a breach of the peace, there would have been no evidence to suggest that Mosley would have encouraged his supporters to reciprocate as Wise had done. Furthermore, the authorities were more apprehensive about securing convictions along the lines of anti-Semitism, especially after the unsatisfactory outcome against Arnold Leese, head of the IFL.[133]

Perhaps the most significant factor in no action being taken by the authorities to prevent the march was Game's underestimation of how serious the disorder

---

130 Kidd, *Liberty*, p. 70.
131 See *Duncan v Jones* [1936] 1 KB 218, which is discussed in chapter six.
132 Kidd, *Liberty*, p. 70.
133 This is discussed in chapter six.

would be. He advised the Home Office that there would probably be 'the usual few arrests for minor disturbances but I do not anticipate any serious trouble'.[134] Historian Janet Clark suggests that there may have been other motivating factors, as Game had privately welcomed the 'showdown'. Game had written to a friend the day before the proposed fascist march, stating: 'I expect there will be some fun and a few broken heads before the day is out. I shall be glad if it brings things to a head as I hope it might lead to banning processions all over London.'[135] Here the discretion shown by Game to try and facilitate the BUF procession demonstrates the ability of superior police officers to create situations on the ground in order to advocate wider objectives. Game also declared that he was not in favour of binding over leaders of political groups as he did not want them to become martyrs to their cause if they were subsequently sent to prison.[136]

Conclusion

Throughout this analysis of public processions it has been established that gradual shifts in the attitudes and practices of the Government and the police have occurred since the nineteenth century. The brutal suppression of the Newport marchers in 1839 and the proscription of the Chartist processions in 1848 demonstrate that the Government did not tolerate some forms of mobile demonstration which may have been considered to be associated with insurrection, rebellion and revolution. In the case of the proposed 1848 Chartist procession to Parliament, the existence of the Tumultuous Petitioning Act 1661 enabled the Government to direct the Metropolitan Police Commissioner to prohibit the demonstration in advance. At the same time, the freedom to assemble in public was not so severely inhibited. For example, the Chartists were still able to assemble at Kennington Common. In addition, processions held away from Parliament were not subject to such precise legal conditions. Towards the end of the nineteenth century, the ambiguity and uncertainty of the legal powers regarding public processions was highlighted by inconsistent police practice throughout the country. This was highlighted by the confusing and indecisive advice that William Harcourt gave to Chief Constables during the era of disorder associated with the Salvation Army. Yet in that era *Beatty v Gillbanks* offered some optimism that the liberty to hold lawful processions would receive legal protection.

It has also been witnessed that several Metropolitan Police Commissioners – including Horwood, Trenchard and Game – attempted to assert their influence on their respective Home Secretaries for an increase of powers relating to the preservation of order on the occasion of public processions. Furthermore, the experiences

---

134 J. Clark, *Striving to Preserve the Peace: The National Council for Civil Liberties, the Metropolitan Police and the Dynamics of Disorder in Inter-war Britain*, PhD thesis (2008), Open University, p. 196.

135 Ibid., p. 196, which cites A. Moore 'Sir Philip Game's "other life": the making of the 1936 Public Order Act in Britain', *Australian Journal of Politics and History 36*, no. 1 (1990), p. 67.

136 Ibid., p. 197, citing MEPO 3/551, Fascist March and Communist Rally 4 Oct 1936.

of the Hunger Marchers and the BUF demonstrated that they received different levels of police interference across the provinces. This is potentially linked to the political influence of local watch committees and standing joint committees over their police forces. Yet, despite the potential for political partisanship to hinder the activism of radical groups, the differences in police tactics were largely possible only because of the wide discretion available to the police. The Government's reluctance to act in both 1932 and 1934 when bills were drafted to regulate public processions demonstrated a tactful hesitation which saw the concerns over both the Hunger Marches and the Blackshirts fade without introducing oppressive new legislation, albeit only temporarily.

The disorder in East London on 4 October 1936 may have been 'the straw that broke the camel's back',[137] but it was not entirely unexpected, and it became a convenient catalyst in which cross-party support could be drawn upon to pass new legislation. For Game, this had expediently opened the door for his powers to be increased regarding the regulation and prohibition of public processions. While the use of common law powers under the breach of the peace doctrine had been unclear, ambiguous and controversial, the passing of the Public Order Act 1936 was to provide the authorities with more positive powers to prohibit procession in advance.

---

137 R. Thurlow, 'The Straw that Broke the Camel's Back: Public Order, Civil Liberties and the Battle of Cable Street' in T. Kushner and N. Valman (eds.), *Remembering Cable Street: Fascism and Anti-Fascism in British Society*, Vallentine Mitchell: Middlesex (2000), pp. 74–94.

5 Freedom of assembly and public processions

Regulation and policing after the Public Order Act 1936

[I]t is wrong to enact a further series of prohibitions dealing with assemblies without at the same time attempting at long last to enact some positive legislation which gives and defines the right to protest and of peaceful assembly.[1]

Introduction

The passing of the Public Order Act 1936 heralded a new era in public order policing as it significantly provided police with the legal means to apply to the Home Secretary, via their local council, to proscribe public processions in a designated area. This chapter commences with the passing of the Public Order Act 1936 and examines how s3 was utilised up to its repeal under s40(3), Sch 3 Public Order Act 1986. The 1986 Act also extended the police's powers regarding public processions and assemblies under s11–s14. The utilisation of these provisions on the BUF, Union Movement (UM) and the English Defence League (EDL) is included as well as an analysis of *Flockhart v Robinson*[2] and *Kent v Metropolitan Police Commissioner*.[3] The opening quote, from a speech by Liberal MP Alex Carlile during the Public Order Bill 1986 debates, demonstrates that successive legislative measures have inhibited the freedom of assembly rather than sought their protection. Under the New Labour Government, which came to power in 1997, public processions were granted legal protection following the passing of the Human Rights Act (HRA) 1998 and the incorporation of the ECHR in UK law. These constitutional changes will be addressed in relation to the ongoing activism of the EDL and the recent use of cordons under the breach of the peace doctrine, which have been utilised by the police to kettle protesters and which were recently supported by the ECHR in *Austin v UK*.[4]

The Public Order Act 1936

The legacy of the Battle of Cable Street was a hastily passed Statute: the Public Order Act 1936. The Act itself should not be seen solely as a result of fascist

---

1 *Hansard, HC Deb*, 30 Apr 1986, vol 96 cc1020–1027 at 1024.
2 *Flockhart v Robinson* [1950] 2 KB 498.
3 *Kent v Metropolitan Police Commissioner*, unreported, *The Times* 13 May 1981 (Court of Appeal).
4 *Austin v UK* [2012] 55 EHRR 14 (ECHR).

disorder, as it also encompasses suggestions and provisions advocated from Emergency Powers Act 1920 Regulation 22, the Processions (Regulations) Bill 1932 and the Public Order Bill 1934 in response to communist activity and the NUWM. In introducing clause 3, Liberal MP Sir John Simon opposed the general prohibition of processions by stressing their importance as 'an old and well-established method of exhibiting a point of view' although he did concede that they 'may not always be very effective'.[5] Simon clearly explained the necessity for local authorities to be able to regulate the route of processions:

> At present the power is to be found in some rather ancient Statutes. In the case of the Metropolis it is in an Act of 1839; in the Provinces it is in an Act of 1847. The Statutes are in somewhat archaic words. They were passed before the full establishment of modern police forces. They are applied with some little difficulty. It does seem to me that it is much better to put into this Bill a plain provision on the subject.[6]

As enacted, s3(1) provided the chief of police with greater powers to control or regulate public processions. These included the power to prescribe the route of the procession or prohibit it from entering a specified public place. Under s3(2) the chief of police may apply to the council of the borough or district for an order to prohibit all public processions or any class of public procession for a period not exceeding three months; following the consent of the Home Secretary, the order may be made. A similar provision under s3(3) provided the Metropolitan Police Commissioner the power to prohibit public processions with the consent of the Home Secretary, bypassing the need to apply to any local council. The power to prohibit processions could be imposed only if there were reasonable grounds for apprehending that a procession may occasion serious public disorder and the powers under s3(1) were not sufficient in preventing the anticipated disorder.

These powers provided wide discretion for the authorities to restrict political activism and public protest. They echoed Emergency Regulation 22, which also provided chiefs of police with the power to prohibit processions with the consent of the Home Secretary if they anticipated disorder. This power became more extensive as Regulation 22 could be used only when a state of emergency had been declared under the Emergency Powers Act 1920. As mentioned earlier, the general Labour antipathy to the use of this power was demonstrated in 1926 during the General Strike. Yet ten years on the Public Order Bill was supported by the Labour Party, although they would still seek some amendments. This change was in part due to the Labour Party's commitment to opposing fascism. Historian Matthew Worley affirms that Labour had maintained its stance in opposing fascism by advocating reasoned argument and constitutional procedure rather than participate in the anti-fascist activism which was largely organised by the far Left.

5 *Hansard, HC Deb*, 16 Nov 1936, vol 317 c1359.
6 Ibid.

By the 1930s Labour's political arena had been established inside Parliament and City Hall, in contrast to the street politics of the BUF.[7] In part, this contributed to Labour's reluctant support of the Bill in order to control the violence associated with the BUF's street politics. The apprehension was that in doing so the liberty of other groups, including those on the Left, would be restricted in the process.

The statutory powers provided to Chief Constables under s3 were the most controversial of the Act. Even the powers under s3(1) had significantly increased the power of Chief Constables, leading Morgan to reflect that their 'actions in controlling and routeing processions were now, in effect, subject to no extra-judicial control either through local authorities or police authorities or through parliament itself'.[8] The provisions under s3 which gave the authorities the formal power to ban processions in advance remarkably 'survived Parliamentary scrutiny with no substantive modifications'.[9]

Despite this, there were still forceful objections recorded in the House of Commons. Labour MP Mr Buchanan challenged clause 3, stating:

> The Bill was meant to deal with that problem of the Fascist movement and the shocking ill-treatment of the Jews, but this Bill gives the Home Secretary far wider powers, powers to deal with trade disputes and innocent demonstrations and agitations, and I fear that it will put the population of this country in a worse position than they were in before . . . [as the Bill] may well be used, not against the Fascist movement, but against the legitimate aspirations of very poor people.[10]

These concerns on the restrictions of civil liberties were prevalent in the debate. Labour MP for Jarrow, Miss Ellen Wilkinson, made reference to the Chief Constable of York who hindered the Hunger Marchers' procession through the town and prevented them from receiving their provisions. She declared that this clause would 'legalise the present position of these bullying police constables' and criticised the proposed safeguard that the Chief Constable would need his case sanctioned by the local council as inadequate in certain areas: 'the difficulty will arise when there is a Chief Constable and a Council of the same political colour, as happens a very great deal in the Northern districts. In such cases there is [n]o safeguard.'[11] ILP member George Buchanan agreed and stated that Chief Constables should not become involved in making political or religious decisions.

Communist MP William Gallacher made the most outspoken attack, stating, 'this is one of the most dangerous attacks on democracy that has ever been made

7 M. Worley, *Labour Inside the Gate: A History of the British Labour Party between the* Wars, I B Tauris: London (2005), p. 204.

8 Morgan, *Conflict and Order*, pp. 273–274.

9 Ewing and Gearty, *The Struggle*, p. 316.

10 *Hansard, HC Deb*, 26 Nov 1936, vol 318 c602.

11 Ibid., c596.

in this country.'[12] He reminded the House that the Labour Party had developed with the use of demonstrations and processions, and that the Liberals were also responsible for very wild and turbulent demonstrations of their own. He expressed his astonishment that other members could consider 'such an attack on the democratic rights of the people in such an easy manner . . . [we should never] make concessions that mean the sacrifice of democratic rights'.[13] However, not all members from the Left disagreed. Labour MP Herbert Morrison declared that clause 3 was necessary, as clauses 1 and 2 would not prevent the mobilisation of fascist groups entering the East End and causing disruption and provocation or the organisation of another crowd with the purpose of rioting with them.[14]

During a discussion on clause 1, which dealt with the prohibition of uniforms, Captain Ramsey proposed an amendment that would also prohibit the carrying of a 'flag or banner bearing a provocative device or inscription'. Relating this proposal to processions, he described a scenario where Orangemen might march through a Roman Catholic borough, or a Mohammedan procession could march through the Hindu quarter in India, and hoped that some words would be added 'to cover a provocative inscription or device carried in a public procession through the streets'.[15] With reference to the example of Orangemen marching into a purposely provocative area, Labour MP for Liverpool in Scotland,[16] David Logan proposed that there was no need for the amendment. With reference to his own constituency, he stated, 'If people had not the common sense to know that they were hurting the feelings of people in a particular neighbourhood by doing that, they would be taught a lesson and would not go again.' He added to this scenario of self-policing, 'There would be no need for an Act of Parliament to teach them.'[17]

Effectively, the powers under clause 1 offered Chief Constables with wide discretion that could restrict freedom of expression and assembly with very little safeguards. Furthermore, these powers would inevitably entangle the Chief Constables with making decisions which affect political activism. While the political impartiality of the police may be a fine ideal, Jefferson highlights that it is an 'impossible mandate'.[18] In addition, Lustgarten stated that the 1970s and 1980s witnessed the growing politicisation of the police as they became involved in attempting to influence legislation and policy. This constitutional shift changes the role of the police from 'executors of parliamentary command' to the fundamentally politicised role of being significantly responsible for 'the content of the criminal law'.[19] The influence that the Metropolitan Police Commissioners and

---

12 Ibid., c603.
13 Ibid., c606–c607.
14 Ibid., c611.
15 *Hansard, HC Deb*, 23 Nov 1936, vol 318 c66.
16 This was a constituency in the Scotland Road area of Liverpool, England.
17 *Hansard, HC Deb*, 23 Nov 1936, vol 318 c66.
18 Jefferson, *The Case Against Paramilitary Policing*, p. 47.
19 Lustgarten, *Governance*, pp. 168–169.

Chief Constables tried to exert in the 1930s over public order policy established earlier demonstrates that this politicisation was clearly present in the interwar period. The political convictions of Chief Constables together with their police authority, therefore, had the ability to influence their discretion, consciously or unconsciously, and potentially affect the liberty of political activists.

The application of s3 from 1937–1939

In practice the subsequent s3 Public Order Act 1936 obstructed both fascist and communist processions. In 1937 the BUF made an application to hold a procession on 4 July from Limehouse to Trafalgar Square, which would pass through the main Jewish quarter of the East End of London. The new Home Secretary, Sir Samuel Hoare, announced in the House of Commons that under s3(3), a complete prohibition on political processions would be in effect for six weeks in a particular area in the East End of London. This decision was made because the Metropolitan Police Commissioner, Sir Philip Game, was of the opinion that prescribing the route of the procession under s3(1) would not be enough to prevent serious public disorder. The BUF subsequently organised a procession from Kentish Town to Trafalgar Square, which was outside of the prohibited area. Hoare emphasised that the prohibition affected political processions only, irrespective of party, and would not be applied to other organisations such as the Salvation Army or to non-political trade disputes.[20]

The BUF procession on 4 July 1937 passed without any serious disturbances. *The Times* estimated that 6,000 fascists had assembled for the march, but this number was 'dwarfed by the crowd which collected in the locality'.[21] Order was maintained by the 2,383 police officers who were on duty in connection with the fascist demonstrations that day and 19 arrests were made.[22] The majority of those arrests related to s5 Public Order Act offences for insulting words and behaviour. At the Clerkenwell Police Court, the language used by the anti-fascist protestors demonstrated their contempt towards the police and their duty to protect the BUF procession. Among the chants for which protestors were arrested and charged were, 'The police are as bad as Mosley,' and 'Down with the coppers; smash Mosley's body-guard.'[23]

When the ban expired in August 1937, it was renewed for a further six weeks. In September, it was subsequently renewed for three months, the maximum duration under the Act. The three-month ban on political marches in the specified area was continually renewed every three months until the proscription of the BUF in 1940 under Defence Regulation 18B.[24]

---

20 *Hansard, HC Deb*, 21 Jun 1937, vol 325 c847–c848.
21 *The Times*, 5 Jul 1937.
22 *Hansard, HC Deb*, 15 Jul 1937, vol 326 c1455; *The Times*, 5 Jul 1937.
23 *The Times*, 6 Jul 1937.
24 R. Benewick, *Political Violence and Public Order*, Allen Lane The Penguin Press: London (1969), p. 250.

An editorial in the *Times* defended the imposed prohibition of processions in the proscribed area, stating that it 'only puts a restraint on the freedom of demonstration in an area where political licence has threatened to extinguish liberty. It is licence that is restrained in order that larger liberties may be preserved.'[25] Hoare defended the action, stating:

> In those parts there is concentrated a large number of Jews whose memories of racial persecution make them particularly sensitive, and a Fascist procession in centres where these special conditions exist would, in the judgement of the Commissioner and of myself, inevitably have led to serious public disorder.[26]

As the 'special conditions' were not applicable to other parts of London, Hoare was apprehensive to sanction s3(3) elsewhere. On 3 October 1937 the BUF organised their fifth anniversary procession in London. Following the renewal of the ban in East London, the new route was to take the BUF through Bermondsey and South London. A deputation to the Home Secretary (led by Labour MP Ben Smith) to prohibit the procession failed. Hoare stated that the extension of the prohibition to every area that had a 'strong feeling of opposition to a procession demonstrating some unpopular political creed would be contrary to the spirit of the Public Order Act, 1936'.[27]

Hoare's approach to regulating BUF processions under the Public Order Act acknowledged the sensitivities of different communities in reference to fascist provocation. In recognising that 'special circumstances' existed in certain East End districts, Hoare's actions were in line with the *Wise v Dunning* judgment that an unlawful act may be the 'natural consequence' of a legal act in which the language or conduct was insulting or abusive.[28] By sanctioning BUF processions outside of the Jewish communities of the East End, Hoare's decision conceded that prohibiting them would amount to political discrimination. In that case, any attempt to disrupt a BUF procession where the 'special circumstances' did not exist would, therefore, align with *Beatty v Gillbanks*. The distinction between the two judgments is prevalent in Hoare's application of the Public Order Act. A BUF procession can be permitted in one area but proscribed in another because of the different circumstances in which a breach of the peace may be occasioned.

The BUF procession on 3 October 1937 was met with hostile political opposition and created widespread disorder. *The Times* dramatically claimed 'the scenes of disorder yesterday seem to have been quite as bad as those in the East End which induced Parliament to pass the Public Order Act.'[29] When disorder broke, the report stated that the police 'painfully shepherded [the procession] to the place appointed

25 *The Times*, 14 Sep 1937.
26 *The Times*, 29 Jun 1937.
27 *The Times*, 28 Sep 1937.
28 *Wise v Dunning* [1902] 1 KB 167, pp. 179–180.
29 *The Times*, 4 Oct 1937.

for the Fascist meeting amid a continuous series of clashes'.[30] Following the procession, Game capitalised on the disorder by recommending to the Home Secretary that the s3(3) ban should be applied to the whole Metropolitan Police District. He went further, advocating that new legislation should be considered that would make 'processions of all kinds in the streets illegal once and for all'.[31] This pragmatic proposition, which focused on police resources rather than the liberty of the subject, remained in his Annual Report for 1937. He stated that the Public Order Act had a positive effect on the conduct of political meetings and demonstrations but had not reduced their number. He recorded that out of the 11,804 meetings and processions that were policed in 1937, over 7,000 of these were either fascist or anti-fascist. The BUF marches on 4 July and 3 October each required the deployment of 2,500 police officers. Game linked the number of police required to regulate processions with the general increase in crime for the year as an argument to forward the prohibition of all political processions in the Metropolitan Police District.[32]

In September 1938, the BUF application to hold another anniversary procession was not authorised, so they held a public meeting in Lime Grove, Hammersmith, instead.[33] This widened the previous use of the s3(3) ban as the route of the proposed BUF procession did not enter the previously prescribed area. In order to preserve order, the Police Commissioner and the Home Secretary sanctioned the procession ban despite the previous use of s3(3) being justified only in areas where a 'special condition' existed; namely the large Jewish communities situated in the East End. This signalled that, despite Hoare's previous acknowledgement of the 'spirit of the Public Order Act',[34] the potential to widen its application and further restrict the liberty of groups to hold public processions existed. This decision was criticised in the BUF's newspaper *Action*, which in reference to the communist appeals to have the procession prohibited, noted:

> The simple fact is that certain persons having openly threatened to break the law, a democratic chief of police prefers to penalise the law-abiding rather than arrest the known criminals.[35]

Yet the ban seemed to find favour among many of the residents who were regularly affected by the processions. The Conservative Under Secretary of State for the Home Department, Geoffrey Lloyd, stated that he believed that the ban had general approval in East London, adding,

> I would cite only one opinion, that of Dr. Mallon, Warden of Toynbee Hall, who knows the conditions in the area as well as anybody. He says: I do know

30 Ibid.
31 CAB 24/271, 'Prohibition of Political Processions in London: Memorandum by the Home Secretary' (1937).
32 Cmd. 5761, *Report of the Commissioner of Police of the Metropolis for the Year 1937*, pp. 12–13.
33 *The Times*, 24 Sep 1938.
34 *The Times*, 28 Sep 1937.
35 *Action*, No. 137, 1 Oct 1938, p. 2.

the factors here, and I say that the extension of the prohibition is both desirable and necessary.[36]

The new powers available under the Public Order Act had effectively denied the BUF one of their most powerful propaganda tools in the years leading up to the Second World War. Despite this, some success was managed by virtue of their peace campaign, which attracted an audience of over 20,000 at Earl's Court on 16 July 1939.[37] The last national Hunger March was staged in 1936, although it was not the enactment of the Public Order Act that led to its demise. Kingsford argued that other factors drew the far Left away from organising another great march on London. He stated that there were shifts in the patterns of unemployment and a lack of a unifying issue to campaign for. In addition, the energies of many members were focused on the Spanish civil war, and the movement was forced to economise due to its ailing finances.[38] After war was declared on 3 September 1939, public processions and meetings were subject to Regulation 39E under the Defence of the Realm Act 1914. In October 1939 the principle of whether this was necessary was questioned by Dingle Foot. The Liberal MP and barrister Frank Griffith also questioned the necessity of Regulation 39E, following the passing of the Public Order Act. His concern was that the powers of the Secretary of State could be conferred to any mayor, justice of the peace or chief officer of police, in relation to banning processions and public meetings.[39] However, for the BUF the liberty to form a public procession was eclipsed by the interment without trial of many of its leading figures, including Sir Oswald Mosley, in May 1940 under Defence Regulation 18B. Two months later, the BUF was declared a proscribed organisation.

The post-war legacy of s3 Public Order Act 1936

Union Movement and Flockhart v Robinson[40]

In the years following the Second World War, Mosley revived his political ambitions with the Union Movement (UM). Although he never replicated the success of the BUF in terms of membership, the activities of the UM still provoked its share of public disorder. Mosley continued his anti-Semitic politics, which were also now merged with the promotion of a racially white Europe. During the initial stages of Mosley's new movement, the Metropolitan Police utilised different tactics in minimising the disorder. In response to UM's proposed march from Ridley Road to Tottenham, the Commissioner utilised his powers under s3(1) to reroute the march. He deliberately waited until the morning of the procession to

36 *Hansard, HC Deb*, 15 Dec 1937, vol 330 c1284.
37 See chapter seven.
38 Kingsford, *Hunger Marchers*, pp. 223–226.
39 *Hansard, HC Deb*, 31 Oct 1939, vol 352 c1835 and cc1840–1841.
40 *Flockhart v Robinson*.

inform the organisers so the new route could not be advertised. In addition, he also prohibited the use of banners and loud-speaker vans to minimise the provocation. Despite this, there was still considerable disorder: it was reported that 35 arrests were made and 23 people were charged.[41] The Labour Home Secretary, James Chuter Ede, declared that his role comprised of two public duties of equal importance: to maintain order and to preserve traditional liberties. He showed regret that in attempting to balance the two sometimes he had to suspend liberties that had previously been enjoyed.[42] When Chuter Ede was questioned on the provocation caused by the procession, he responded:

> The people who attended at the Home Office did regard the procession as a provocation, but I think that in this country we have to learn both to hear and to see things with which we do not agree, without feeling that we have been unduly provoked.[43]

He also intimated that he was of the opinion that if UM opponents did not turn up and excite interest from passers-by, then the UM would die a natural death as there had not been more that 150 present at any of their demonstrations.[44]

On 11 September 1949, the UM marched through North London and faced anti-fascist opposition at Dalston. There were stones and wood thrown at the procession, and one anti-fascist, James McLeod, broke through the police cordon and attempted to encourage others to do so and fight the members of the UM, shouting: 'Down with Fascism. Let's get at them. We fought six years against this and we must stop it now.' He was charged with using threatening behaviour. The magistrate reminded McLeod that the procession was perfectly legal, declaring: 'This is English law. It is not Jewish law or Communist law or Fascist Law.' Here, the magistrate reinforced the authority of the law, attempting to demonstrate that it does not recognise race or political creeds, but it applies equally to everyone. Despite this, in relation to McLeod's alleged remarks, the magistrate asked him what fighting he did in the war. Following the response of ground crew with the RAF, he stated, 'Do you call that fighting? You will go to prison for six weeks.'[45] However, he later demonstrated his discretion by calling McLeod back and altering his sentence to a £5 fine. Twelve people were charged in connection with the disturbance for offences which included carrying offensive weapons such as a knife and stones, obstruction of a police officer and assault.

Following the continuation of public disorder associated with Mosley's politics, it was not surprising that a month later, on 4 October 1949, the UM's proposed march through the East End of London was proscribed. The date and location, being the anniversary of Cable Street, was provocative in itself. The Metropolitan

41 *Dundee Courier*, 22 Mar 1949.
42 *Hansard, HC Deb*, 21 Mar 1949, vol 463 c42.
43 Ibid.
44 Ibid., at c43.
45 *Evening Telegraph*, 12 Sep 1949.

Police Commissioner, Sir Harold Scott, requested a ban on all political processions for three months under s3(3) as he believed his powers under s3(1) were insufficient to prevent serious disorder. Upon this being granted by the Home Secretary, the UM response echoed BUF propaganda by claiming that the government had 'bowed to mob violence . . . [and deprived] the people of London their traditional rights of public demonstration'.[46]

The use of the s3(3) banning order continued to be an effective weapon against the provocative public processions of the far Right.[47] Yet the definition of a public procession under this provision was still vague. Described by s9 Public Order Act 1936 as 'a procession in a public place', the question still remained on how a procession may be differentiated from a body of people walking to the same destination. On 15 October 1949, UM assistant secretary Alfred Flockhart was charged with organising a public procession while the s3(3) ban was in effect. He had led some members from a newspaper sales drive in Knightsbridge to rendezvous with other officials at Hyde Park Corner. From there, the 150 UM members walked to Piccadilly. It was reported that Flockhart gave signals directing the members following him and as they approached Piccadilly political slogans were shouted. Following a conviction at Bow Street Magistrates Court, Flockhart's appeal at the King's Bench Divisional Court centred on what constituted a procession. In *Flockhart v Robinson*,[48] Lord Goddard CJ placed the emphasis of a procession as being a 'body, of persons moving along a route'. This particularly wide definition was countered by Finnemore J who found that the number of people who proceeded along the same route in loose formation became a public procession only when their ranks closed up due to the traffic at Piccadilly as they then embodied an orderly formation. The magistrate's judgment was held and, as Flockhart had directed the procession, he was judged to have been the organiser. The judgment was held 2:1 with Finnemore J dissenting. He found that the procession had formed spontaneously and Flockhart could not be classed as the organiser because to organise 'meant something in the nature of planning or arranging'.[49]

Kent v Metropolitan Police Commissioner[50]

The position regarding the policing of public processions remained as laid down for half a century. However, before the enactment of the Public Order Act 1986,[51] the s3 power to ban any class of procession was significantly challenged in the Court of Appeal in 1981. Following serious disorder in Brixton, the Home Secretary sanctioned an application from the Metropolitan Police Commissioner to

---

46 *Western Morning News*, 4 Oct 1949.
47 Procession bans had also been implemented in April and May in 1948 to different London boroughs in response to UM activism.
48 *Flockhart v Robinson*.
49 Ibid. at 499 and 505.
50 *Kent v Metropolitan Police Commissioner*.
51 The 1986 Act provided the police with further powers relating to public processions which is beyond the remit of this thesis.

issue a blanket ban on all processions within the Metropolitan Police district, except those traditionally assembled on 1 May to celebrate May Day and those of a religious character customarily held. In *Kent v Metropolitan Police Commissioner*[52] the General Secretary of the Campaign for Nuclear Disarmament (CND), Bruce Kent, a Roman Catholic priest, made an affidavit in support of the application to declare the ban null and void in order to entitle the CND to conduct a procession. Lord Denning MR affirmed the ban, but his judgment demonstrated the scope of such a wide power. The ban covered 786 square miles and prevented community-based processions such as the charity carnival procession through the streets of Fulham, which would have contained 80 floats on a three-mile route. Other processions that fell within the ban included 'a march of students to the House to protest about cuts: and the marches of jobless people who wish to see their Member of Parliament to bring their claims to him'.[53] As the Home Secretary refused to waive the ban to allow the Fulham carnival procession, Lord Denning judged that 'He must have thought that there was a reasonable fear that hooligans and others would attack the police and also perhaps the peaceful people taking part in that charity carnival.' All three judges dismissed the appeal, but Ackner LJ recognised that

> Blanket bans on all marches for however short a time are a serious restriction of a fundamental freedom, and the courts will always be vigilant to see that the power to impose such a ban has not been abused.[54]

Whilst recognising that order had deteriorated in the last five years since the judgment in *Hubbard v Pitt*[55] Ackner acknowledged that to avoid bloodshed and loss of life, it is necessary to restrict some rights and privileges. It would be irresponsible not to exercise that power when serious public disorder is anticipated.[56]

The overwhelming significance of *Kent v Metropolitan Police Commissioner* is that when serious disorder is reasonably anticipated the police and the Home Secretary have the power to impose drastic measures at the cost of fundamental liberties, and this is supported by the courts. Since this judgment, the statutory law relating to public processions has also been largely increased by the Public Order Act 1986.

In addition, Lord Denning emulated Finnemore's definition by referring to the dictionary definition of *procession* as 'proceeding of body of persons . . . in

---

52 *Kent v Metropolitan Police Commissioner.*

53 Ibid.

54 Ibid.

55 *Hubbard v Pitt* [1976] QB 142. In this case Lord Denning promoted the right to demonstrate as long as 'all is done peaceably and in good order, without threats or incitement to violence or obstruction to traffic.' While acknowledging that principle, Ackner LJ is highlighting that the current situation following the Brixton Riot had meant that freedom to demonstrate needed to be curtailed in order to secure the safety of the community.

56 *Kent v Metropolitan Police Commissioner.*

orderly succession'.[57] This wide interpretation indicated that 'any procession was likely to be covered by the definition.' Yet, the phrase 'body of persons' indicates that a procession must be more than one person. Lawyers John Marston and Paul Tain highlight that although an individual may not constitute a procession, that individual may still create disorder if others gather to support or obstruct the person's passage: other provisions to prevent disorder would need to be invoked.[58] By definition it is possible that two people may form a procession.

The current law regarding the regulation of public processions

The Public Order Act 1986

Powers relating to the policing of public processions were significantly expanded by the Public Order Act 1986. In the years preceding the new Act the police and the Home Secretary had utilised the powers of the 1936 Act against various groups. For instance, s3(1) was used to impose conditions on the Hackney Trades Council in December 1979 in order to avoid the National Front's headquarters. The police also re-routed the procession of the British Union for the Abolition of Vivisection to prevent confrontation with the Biorex Laboratories in Islington. In Leicester, the police re-routed National Front (NF) marches away from the parts of the city with a high Asian population.[59] The Home Office's Review of Public Order Law highlighted that the formal imposition of conditions on public processions was rarely used, as police preferred to work together with organisers in an informal capacity to negotiate the route and other matters.[60]

With regard to the power to prohibit public processions in advance, the powers under the 1936 Act were seen as adequate by the Government. This was primarily because the test of whether a ban was necessary or not was the anticipation of serious public disorder. It was advocated that this power to initiate the process should remain with that police and the safeguards of local council and the Home Secretary added the 'necessary elements of local knowledge and political accountability'.[61] In the decade before the new Act there were also significant examples of the use of s3(3) to prohibit processions where it was thought that imposing conditions would not be enough to prevent disorder. Table 5.1 shows the applications received by the Home Office for the prohibition of processions relating to Northern Ireland between 1969 and 1986 under s3(2) Public Order Act 1936.

The table demonstrates that each prohibition has individual circumstances that determine the duration of the order and the geographical coverage. The

57 Ibid.
58 J. Marston and P. Tain, *Public Order: The Criminal Law*, Callow Publishing: London (2001), p. 147.
59 Cmnd. 9510, *Review of Public Order Law* (1985), pp. 26–27
60 Ibid, p. 26.
61 Ibid.

Table 5.1 Table showing the prohibition of processions relating to Northern Ireland between 1969 and 1986. Contains Parliamentary information licensed under the Open Parliament Licence v1.0.[62]

Date order began	Class or classes, of procession banned	Area(s) concerned	Proposed marches or processions known to have been caught by order	Duration of order
20 November 1974	All public processions connected with the death of James McDade	Solihull Birmingham Coventry	Marches associated with funeral of James McDade	one month
26 September 1981	All public processions except those of a religious, education, festive or ceremonial character customarily held	Luton	Marches organised by Irish Republican groups and the British Movement	nine days
30 January 1982	All public processions except those of a religious, educational, festive or ceremonial character customarily held	Coventry	Marches organised by Irish Republican groups and the NF	nine days
27 January 1984	All public processions except those of religious, educational, festive or ceremonial character customarily held	Sheffield North-East Derbyshire Bradford Chesterfield Rotherham	Marches organised by Irish Republican groups and the NF	two days

Government saw its own role in this procedure to 'ensure that orders are as narrowly framed as possible'.[63] The classification of processions that fall under the ban were also seen as an important aspect which had the potential not to deprive some groups of the liberty to form processions while the order was in place.

Despite the general consensus that the 'procedure had stood the test of time' there were still changes made regarding the law of public processions in Part 2 of the 1986 Act. One of the key changes in the law regarding public processions is s11, which provides a national requirement for advance written notice which had only existed before under local Acts of Parliament. Under s12, the conditions which the Chief Constable or Metropolitan Police Commissioner may impose on a procession are also extended. Formerly the senior police officer could impose

---

62 *Hansard, HC Deb*, 27 Jun 1986, vol 100 cc344–5W.
63 Cmnd. 9510, p. 25.

conditions under s3 of the 1936 Act only if they reasonably believed that 'the procession may occasion serious disorder'. S12(1) provides senior police officers with the power to impose conditions if they reasonably believe that:

(a) the procession may result in serious public disorder, serious damage to property or serious disruption to the life of the community, or
(b) the purpose of the persons organising it is the intimidation of others with a view to compelling them not to do an act they have a right to do, or to do an act they have a right not to do.

Similarly to s3(2) and (3) of the 1936 Act, if the senior police officer reasonably believes that the provisions under s12 would not be sufficient in preventing serious public disorder, s13 details the process in which a banning order may be obtained. This could apply to all processions, or class of procession. The 1985 White Paper that preceded the 1986 Act had previously revealed the Government's intention to amend the law to allow for a single procession to be prohibited in order to, 'add to the flexibility of the banning procedure' but this was rejected.[64]

S14 provides a statutory power to impose conditions on public assemblies, such as the stipulation of where the assembly is held, the maximum duration of the assembly, and the maximum number of participants that constitute it. These conditions can be applied by the Chief Officer of Police to prevent disorder, damage, disruption or intimidation if he or she reasonably believes that the assembly may result in serious public disorder, serious damage to property or serious disruption to the life of the community.

The Human Rights Act 1998

While the Public Order Act 1986 effectively placed further restrictions on fundamental personal freedoms, imposing further constraints on public processions, the Human Rights Act 1998, and the incorporation of the ECHR, has provided legal protection for the related rights of freedom of expression under Article 10, and freedom of assembly and association under Article 11. However, these 'rights' are not absolute and are subject to limitations. For example, the right to freedom of assembly is subject to Article 11(2), which states:

> No restrictions shall be placed on the exercise of these rights other than such as are prescribed by law and are necessary in a democratic society in the interests of national security or public safety, for the prevention of disorder or crime, for the protection of health or morals or for the protection of the rights and freedoms of others.

Lawyer David Mead emphasises the impact of the HRA by stating that the move from a 'residual, liberty based system to one based on positive rights brings

64 Ibid., p. 25.

a shift in the burden of proof',[65] This means that public authorities must provide an objective basis for any ban or condition that they impose on public assemblies and all restrictions must be justified in Article 11(2) terms. Effectively, Chief Constables are required to enforce the least restrictive measures open to them in relation to the potential for disorder, when imposing conditions on public assemblies. Lawyer Richard Card highlights that the ECHR acknowledges that there are occasions when a ban can be justified in the interest of public safety. This was witnessed in *Christians against Racism and Fascism v UK*,[66] when it was ruled that disorder could not have been prevented by less stringent measures.[67] However, the police still have a 'positive obligation' to protect peaceful demonstrations from violence. Citing *Plattform 'Ärzte für das Leben' v Austria*,[68] Card argued that the threat of violence alone could not therefore justify the ban of a peaceful demonstration if less stringent methods were available.

The English Defence League

Since their formation in March 2009, the EDL has benefited from the national media attention it has received following their public processions. In a similar manner to the BUF activities that preceded them, the EDL's processions and public meetings have frequently provoked counter-demonstrations by anti-fascist opponents. Unite Against Fascism (UAF) continue to organise counter-protests in an attempt to demonstrate that fascism and racism are not welcome in the community that the EDL selected for a demonstration. These processions and counter-processions demand effective public order policing to keep the opposing factions apart, but despite this they have frequently generated violence and disorder.

The publicity tactic of 'march and grow' is a typical method for far-Right groups to widen their profile. The tactic was also previously utilised by the British National Party (BNP) and the NF. Under the leadership of Nick Griffin, the BNP discontinued exploiting this method as the frequent disorder that occurred was damaging to their electoral campaigns.[69] As a social movement without electoral ambition, the EDL has resurrected the 'march and grow' tactic of the far-Right. Historian Paul Jackson declares that the EDL has rediscovered and updated this strategy by fusing it with the 'new far Right' cause of anti-Muslim sentiment which is 'centralised through internet mobilisation and online networking'.[70] The EDL claim to be a peaceful, non-racist organisation that is opposed to militant

---

65 D. Mead, *The New Law*, p. 204.
66 *Christians against Racism and Fascism v UK* (1980) 21 D&R 138, ECommHR.
67 Ibid.
68 *Plattform 'Ärzte für das Leben' v Austria* (1991) 13 EHRR 204.
69 P. Jackson, M. Pitchford, M. Feldman and T. Preston, *The EDL: Britain's 'New Far Right' Social Movement*, The University of Northampton's Radicalism and New Media Research Group: Northampton (2011), p. 18.
70 Jackson, *The EDL*, p. 19.

Islam only.[71] However, EDL marches and protests have targeted areas with high Muslim populations – such as Luton, Birmingham and Leeds – and members have frequently provoked violence and disorderly confrontations with both the police and anti-fascist groups. Many protests have also involved incidents of racism and Islamophobia.[72]

Table 5.1 demonstrated that the use of powers to proscribe public processions had largely been used to prevent provocative far-Right activism in the years before the legislative changes in the Public Order Act 1986. This was also true in the period immediately after the passing of the 1936 Act, which stifled both the BUF and the UM. Since 2005, proscriptions under s13 Public Order Act 1986 have also been predominantly used to prevent far-Right processions, the only exceptions being the application of s13 in Derby and Sheffield in 2005 to prevent anti-capitalist and anti-globalisation groups. The bans in these cases covered a period of five and three days respectively. The other uses of this provision were used exclusively on far-Right activism. The provision was used three times between 2005 and 2006 to proscribe NF processions and seven times since 2009 in cases involving the EDL.[73] The following analysis examines five demonstrations held by the EDL and contrasts the different approaches by the local authorities in deciding whether to apply for a s13 ban or not.

'The Big One' Bradford, 28 August 2010

In the EDL's first year of activism the 'march and grow' tactic had generated an increasing number of participants at demonstrations with protests at Dudley, Bolton and Newcastle reporting attendances of 2,000 activists. There was also an established track record of violence and disorder which accompanied their protests when the EDL announced their intention to hold a protest in Bradford in August 2010.[74] They billed it as 'The Big One', and the police anticipated that up to 5,000 EDL supporters could potentially protest in the city.[75] This was a highly provocative action as it could have potentially resurrected the fears and insecurities of the communities that experienced the race riots of 2001.[76] Following an application by West Yorkshire Police's Chief Constable, Sir Norman Bettison, to prohibit the EDL procession – which was accompanied by a petition of over 10,000 Bradford residents – the Home Office Minister, James Brokenshire MP,

---

71 See the EDL mission statement at www.englishdefenceleague.org/mission-statement/.
72 *The Guardian*, 23 Sep 2010.
73 Freedom of Information request by the author to the Home Office. Reference: 31049.
74 For information on EDL protests, dates and numbers of arrests see T. Preston, 'Chronology of the English defence League', in Jackson, *The EDL*, pp. 69–73.
75 JUST West Yorkshire, *When Hate Came to Town* (2010), accessed from www.jrf.org.uk/work/work-area/bradford-programme/when-hate-came-to-town.
76 On 7 July 2001, Bradford suffered widespread rioting as growing neo-fascist activism had increased racial tensions within the community. As a result, there were nearly 300 arrests, more than 320 police officers were injured and the riot damages amounted to £7.5m.

on behalf of the Home Secretary, authorised a ban on all marches and processions in Bradford between Saturday 28 and Monday 30 August 2010 under s13 Public Order Act 1986.[77] On 28 August 2010 a static demonstration was still lawfully permitted and only 700 EDL activists took part. Following clashes with the police, fourteen men were detained, two of which were charged with public order violations.

Leicester, 9 October 2010

The Home Secretary, Theresa May, issued a ban on all processions in Leicester to take effect on 9 October 2010 following the EDL's application to demonstrate in the city. This was issued amid fears that the EDL were planning to attack mosques in the area, increasing the likelihood of serious public disorder. This meant that the EDL could demonstrate by way of static protest only, albeit within the protection, or confinement, of heavy police lines. On the same day, a counter-protest by Unite Against Fascism (UAF) was also taking place; the objective of the police was to keep the two groups apart. However, the containment of the EDL within a police cordon to prevent them from causing disorder failed as a large group broke free from the static demonstration, causing damage to property and fighting with the local youth. In its report of the policing of the demonstration, the Network for Police Monitoring (Netpol) emphasised that the EDL had broken through police cordons before and this was anticipated by the local community.[78] The benefit of banning processions was also questioned by Netpol as this led to a shuttle bus service being provided to transport EDL members from their prearranged meeting point to the rally site. Incidentally, the meeting point was an area consisting of three pubs and the provision of alcohol was facilitated for the EDL protestors.[79] Following their transportation to the rally site, there were confrontations with the police 'who deployed riot shields and batons along with dogs and horses'.[80]

The authorisation of a ban on processions, enforcing a static EDL demonstration behind police lines, was not the only preventative tactic that restricted freedom of expression at the Leicester protest. More controversially, the police had blatantly attempted to deter local people from attending the protests. This was done by 'distraction techniques' in which provision was made to local youth clubs and community centres to provide activities that aimed to keep young people away from

---

77 HMIC, 'Policing Public Order: An overview and review of progress against the recommendations of *Adapting to Protest* and *Nurturing the British Model of Policing*' (2011), p. 32.

78 V. Swain, *Report on the Policing of the English Defence League and Counter Protests in Leicester on October 9th 2010*, Network for Police Monitoring (2011), p. 5. Netpol are a network of activists, campaigners, lawyers and researchers who 'aim to effectively challenge policing strategies which are unnecessarily damaging to any sector of our society'. Their report therefore has a critical agenda but still raises important issues regarding the policing of political activism. See http://netpol.org/about/.

79 Swain, *Protests in Leicester*, p. 10; the report also points out that for previous EDL demonstrations licensed premises had been closed.

80 Ibid.

the city centre. Children were also warned that under s46 Children Act 1989 the police would have the power to take any young person into police protection who was at risk of 'significant harm' due to lack of parental care. As this is a provision that aims to keep children safe from exploitation and abuse, Netpol reported that this was the first time they were aware of it being used in the context of political protest.[81] Included in the controversial police tactics aimed at deterring protest was the 'stay at home' message which was largely targeted at the Muslim community.

The prohibition of processions at Bradford and Leicester provided significantly different results. The protest at Bradford was expected to attract the largest assembly of EDL members to date, yet only 700 chose to participate in the static assembly. The police regulated the demonstration and the most significant disorder originated from the EDL protest site as members threw bottles and attacked the police. In Leicester, the prohibition of an EDL procession was questioned as it potentially created further complications. This included the transportation of the EDL from the meeting point to the protest site, and the inadequate facilities to contain the static protest.

'The Homecoming', Luton, 5 February 2011

In contrast to the previous two protests, the EDL rally at Luton on 5 February 2011, which they labelled their 'homecoming', exceeded the size of all previous EDL protests by attracting an estimated 3,000 members.[82] Significantly, a procession ban was not sought and the police facilitated a one-mile march for both the EDL and UAF. Despite no official proscription being applied for, the Home Secretary did receive 'representations from councillors on Luton borough council and members of the public requesting consideration of a ban'.[83] The march hindered local businesses, and shops were boarded up, but the protests caused relatively little violent disorder.[84]

The policing operation in Luton was less autocratic and restrictive than that applied at Leicester and Bradford, and it could be heralded a success due to the fewer incidents of violence. There were only eight arrests and there was significant praise for the police operation that maintained public order. Peter Conniff, Chair of the Bedfordshire Police Authority, declared that

---

81 Swain, *Protests in Leicester*, p. 7.
82 This number is dependent on source used. For example, *The Independent on Sunday* and *Daily Star Sunday*, 6 Feb 2011; *Police Oracle* and *The Guardian*, 7 Feb 2011, declared 3,000 EDL members present; *The News of the World*, 6 Feb 2011, estimated 2,000; while *Luton Today*, 7 Feb 2011, and *Mail on Sunday*, 6 Feb 2011, quoted 1,500 EDL protesters present.
83 House of Commons Written Answers, 24 Jan 2011, col 55W.
84 *The Guardian*, 5 Feb 2011, comments on 'some minor scuffles' and some fireworks and bottles being thrown. *BBC News* accessed from www.bbc.co.uk/news/uk-england-beds-bucks-herts-12372713 at 22 Mar 2011, states that there were seven arrests for weapons offences and assault, while the *Police Oracle* accessed from www.policeoracle.com/news/Police-Prevent-Trouble-At-Luton-EDL-March_30628.html on 22Mar 2011, declared that the demo had 'ended as it began – with no reports of violence'.

Everyone involved in the planning and preparation for this event should be congratulated. It appeared that every eventuality had been taken into account and the day passed off relatively smoothly . . . things were well under control, thanks to the professionalism of the planning team and efficiency of the crowd control.[85]

The decision to facilitate the EDL procession demonstrated a commitment to ensure the rights of the protesters. In a report on the G20 protests[86] in London 2009 by Her Majesty's Inspector of Constabulary (HMIC), it is stated:

We should remember that public protests have been part of British political life for a very long time. Protests are an important safety valve for strongly held views. In addition, the right to protest in public is a synthesis of iconic freedoms: free assembly and free speech.[87]

This notion of an important 'safety valve' can be applied to the facilitation of the EDL's procession in Luton march. Such an unrestrictive approach allowed the demonstrators to consider that their protest had been successfully expressed. Yet the police also have a duty to the wider public summarised by the HMIC report, which stated, 'Presently, the police are required to act as arbiter, balancing the rights of protesters against the rights of the wider public, the business community and local residents.'[88] The duty to maintain public order, when it is anticipated that a protest could lead to a breach of the peace, initiates a large-scale police operation. In Luton, over 1,000 police officers were deployed to maintain order and to keep the opposing protesters apart in an operation that was estimated to have cost £800,000.[89] The size and success of the operation was conveyed by Chief Superintendent Mike Colbourne, who stated:

The policing operation has been in the planning for weeks and the professionalism of the officers was borne out today. We were assisted by 27 forces and it's a great example of how forces can work together in difficult circumstances.[90]

---

85 *Luton on Sunday*, 9 Feb 2011.
86 The G20 protests were focused upon the summit of the Group of Twenty Finance Ministers and Central Bank Governors in London on 2 April 2009, which assembled to discuss the global economy. The protests embraced issues from the War on Terror, economic policy and the banking system. Although many of the protests were peaceful, there was still some disorder (and anticipation of disorder), which led to the use of autocratic police tactics including 'kettling' and the death of newspaper seller Ian Tomlinson after being pushed to the ground by a police officer.
87 Her Majesty's Chief Inspector of Constabulary (HMIC), 'Adapting to Protest' (2009), p. 5.
88 Ibid.
89 *Police Oracle*, 7 Feb 2011. Accessed from www.policeoracle.com/news/Police-Prevent-Trouble-At-Luton-EDL-March_30628.html on 14 Feb 2012.
90 *Luton Today*, 7 Feb 2011.

The large numbers of police employed at EDL and UAF protests is a regular feature of maintaining public order. The EDL procession at Luton was accompanied by a police escort which encircled the protesters. This ensured that the protesters stayed together along the prescribed route as well as protecting them from the potential of an attack by a rival group.

Tower Hamlets, 3 September 2011

In August 2011, the EDL announced its plan to hold a procession on 3 September in Tower Hamlets, East London, which is home to a large Muslim community. In a letter to the press, signed by seventeen MPs, Mayors and Councillors, residents collectively called for a ban on the EDL march solely on the grounds of cost to the Metropolitan Police[91]. This action had no legal basis, as the request to prohibit processions must come from the Commissioner of Police of the Metropolis. However, public petitions reported in the media can highlight particular issues and draw attention to community concerns. On 25 August, the Metropolitan Police Commissioner, Tim Goodwin, announced that he had applied to the Home Secretary to sanction a thirty-day procession ban in the five affected boroughs because of the anticipated violence and disorder.[92] May announced the following day that she had sanctioned the thirty-day ban to protect all groups in the five boroughs. She declared that the decision 'balanced rights to protest against the need to ensure local communities and property are protected'. As s14 Public Order Act only has the power to proscribe processions, a static protest was still lawful. In an astonishingly open statement intended to deter individuals from participating in the protest, Chief Superintendent Julia Pendry stated, 'We have made this decision [to seek the ban] based on specific intelligence and information, and our message is clear: we do not want people coming into the areas to attend these events.'[93]

A significant fear that the thirty-day procession ban was too wide and unnecessarily infringed on the rights to freedom of expression and assembly was raised by philosopher Nina Power in *The Guardian*. She conveyed the fear that other processions that could be affected were the 'East London LGBT [lesbian, gay, bisexual and transgender] Pride, a march against cuts to Homerton Hospital, and, most coincidently, an event to commemorate the 75th anniversary of the battle of Cable Street'.[94] These events and protests were to test the scope and flexibility of the s13 ban. The East London LGBT Pride March was able to proceed despite the ban as it was considered to fall under the exceptions laid out in s11(2) in which processions that were 'commonly or customarily held' were exempt from s11(1), which would require them to give advance notice to the police. The march to

91 *The Guardian*, 23 Aug 2011.
92 *The Guardian*, 25 Aug 2011.
93 *The Guardian*, 26 Aug 2011.
94 *The Guardian*, 30 Aug 2011.

commemorate the battle of Cable Street was also able to proceed, although this was only because it fell on 2 October, the day after the ban ended.

Tower Hamlets, 7 September 2013

The day before the EDL marched in Tower Hamlets in September 2013, the Metropolitan Police Commissioner's decision to impose conditions on the procession was challenged in court by both the EDL and the Mayor of Tower Hamlets. The EDL contested the conditions placed upon them, which included changes to the route, a regulation that the participants could only join or leave the procession at its start and finish point, the location of the assembly point and a time limit of thirty minutes for the assembly. Alternatively, the Mayor's application, in the view of King J, was an attempt to 'obtain a mandatory order from the court, directing the Commissioner to exercise his powers under section 13 to seek the consent of the Home Secretary to ban the march'.[95] These appeals demonstrate the dilemma of public order policing. In this respect Lawyer Neil Parpworth contends that the Metropolitan Police Commissioner is 'between a rock and a hard place'.[96] It is this challenge of satisfying the conflicting rights of activists and the community which is sometimes impossible to achieve when attempting to prevent serious public disorder. As neither the EDL nor the council would have felt happy with the outcome, it could be argued that some balance may have been achieved. Yet the importance for the Police Commissioner was that as King J stated he had 'quite reasonably and rationally and wholly in good faith, [formed the view] that there was a risk of serious public order . . . it is quite impossible in my judgment to say that . . . it was disproportionate [to impose the said conditions]'.[97]

When policing public protests or processions, the appropriate measures available to the police and the authorities to preserve public order are problematic. The police have a duty not to interfere with public assemblies if they do not have justification for doing so under s14(1) Public Order Act 1986. More significantly, they also have a duty to preserve the peace, a duty that may potentially involve protecting a lawful assembly from disruption. The measures taken by the police to ensure the safety of the community whilst also protecting the rights and freedoms of those wishing to protest are frequently in conflict. When the EDL announces the location in which they intend to hold a procession, regional newspapers frequently print letters and articles highlighting the need for a ban.[98] Yet, in accordance with the ECHR, the mere inconvenience, annoyance or offence that a protest or procession may cause is not a sufficient basis for a prohibition of this

95 *R (on the application of Mayor Burgesses of the London Borough of Tower Hamlets) v Commissioner of Police of the Metropolis* [2013] EWHC 3440 (Admin).

96 N. Parpworth, 'Processions or Public Disorder?' *Criminal Law and Justice Weekly 178* (2014), p. 180.

97 *R (on the application of the English Defence League) v Commissioner of Police of the Metropolis* [2013] EWHC 3890 (Admin), at 30.

98 See *Birmingham Evening Mail*, 24 Oct 2011, *Bradford Telegraph and Argus*, 5 Aug 2010, and *Leicester Mercury*, 1 Feb 2012.

Convention right. At the European Court of Human Rights (ECtHR) it was judged in *Plattform 'Ärtze Für das Leben' v Austria*[99] that:

> A demonstration may annoy or give offence to persons opposed to the ideas or claims that it is seeking to promote. The participants must, however, be able to hold the demonstration without having to fear that they will be subjected to physical violence by their opponents; such a fear would be liable to deter associations or other groups supporting common ideas or interests from openly expressing their opinions on highly controversial issues affecting the community. In a democracy the right to counter-demonstrate cannot extend to inhibiting the exercise of the right to demonstrate.[100]

This judgment is resonant of *Beatty v Gillbanks* and places an onus on the authorities to protect a lawful assembly from violent interference, despite any potential offence it may cause.

Applying these conditions to an EDL protest and UAF counter-protest is difficult. Despite the peaceful intentions delivered in the official rhetoric of the EDL and UAF, members of both groups have been responsible for instigating violence on different occasions. At their protests the EDL have caused vandalism, attacked the police, rival protestors and even each other, contradicting their claim to be a peaceful protest movement. But how far does the law extend to protect the Convention rights of free assembly and expression when the group in question frequently engages in public order law violations? Do the criminal actions of some within an EDL protest negate the rights of others who wish to protest peacefully? Is it the responsibility of the protest organisers or the police to ensure that members intent on criminal behaviour are excluded from a public assembly? Who should be held accountable? At an EDL protest at Dewsbury, Lennon's EDL co-leader Kevin Carroll appeared to take some responsibility for the actions of their members by requesting that they behaved themselves and to respect the police and do as they instructed, stating that it was the politicians and the Crown Prosecution Service that were failing them. His praise of the police continued:

> the police officers, they're great fantastic boys and girls, lets respect them, let's do as they say, let's have a big round of applause for the police for fair policing and facilitating us here today, God bless them all.[101]

Despite this rhetoric, the evidence frequently demonstrates that this sentiment is not shared by all EDL members. However, Carroll's public praise of the police also coincided with his own ambitious candidacy for the Bedfordshire Police and Crime Commissioner. Carroll polled fourth with 10.6 per cent of the vote.

---

99 *Plattform 'Ärzte für das Leben' v Austria*.
100 Ibid., at 32.
101 Carroll speech, www.youtube.com/watch?v=Pa2TO7zYYZQ.

The police use of 'strategic incapacitation'

At recent public protests, including the policing of the anti-Capitalist May Day Demonstrations in 2001, the 2009 G20 summit protests and the 2010 student protests in London, the Metropolitan Police Service have controversially utilised police cordons in order to strategically incapacitate crowds. Police cordons are not a new tactic and they have a beneficial and practical function. Richard Glover highlights the routine use of police cordons for the purposes of preserving evidence at a crime scene or separating rival soccer fans has not been questioned and the legality of the practice is assumed. Yet the increasing use of this practice at public protest to contain large crowds for indefinite periods of time has caused controversy.[102] The police are able to utilise such methods of crowd control under the breach of the peace doctrine. The fact that the police consistently use these powers in preference to the provisions available to them under ss12–14A Public Order Act 1986 has been criticised by Helen Fenwick. She contends that 'this is scarcely surprising since its operation on the ground appears to depend largely on police perceptions of the doctrine, informed by unpublished police guidelines.'[103]

At the 2001 demonstrations the police formed a two-kilometre-square cordon which enclosed approximately 3,000 people within it for seven hours. Many of these people were not involved with the protest. One of the protestors, Lois Austin, who continued to lawfully deliver speeches from within the cordon, challenged the legality of this police operation on the grounds of false imprisonment under common law and deprivation of liberty under s8 HRA, contrary to Article 5.[104] Austin lost her claim before all three domestic courts and finally had her case heard at Strasbourg in 2012. Importantly, this case came before the European Court at a time when the 'kettling' tactic had again caused controversy in 2009 and 2010.

Following the tactics of containment used by the Metropolitan Police at the demonstrations against the G20 summit in 2009, protester Joshua Moos challenged the legality of the containment in *R (on the application of Moos and another) v Commissioner of Police of the Metropolis*.[105] At the Queen's Bench Divisional Court, it was accepted that the containment of the Climate Camp protest in Bishopsgate and the police operation to push the protesters back 20–30 meters had been unlawful. Although the judges accepted that there was a risk of disorder when the containment started, they rejected that this was 'imminent'. However, the Metropolitan Police Commissioner's appeal was allowed, and Lord

---

102 R. Glover, 'The Uncertain Blue Line – Police Cordons and the Common Law', *Criminal Law Review* (2012), pp. 245–260.

103 H. Fenwick, 'Marginalising human rights', pp. 737–765.

104 D. Mead, 'Case Comment: Kettling Comes to the Boil before the Strasbourg Court: Is It a Deprivation of Liberty to Contain Protesters En Masse?', *Cambridge Law Journal 71*, no. 3 (2012), pp. 472–475.

105 *R (on the application of Moos and another) v Commissioner of Police of the Metropolis* [2011] EWHC 957.

Neuberger of Abbotsbury MR disagreed with the Divisional Court's assessment that a breach of the peace was not imminent. He stated that 'on the facts as found by the Court, there was no justifiable basis for concluding that Mr Johnson's [Chief Superintendent who was in charge of the operation] apprehension that such a breach was imminent was unreasonable.'[106]

Following Austin's failed appeal at the House of Lords in 2009 and the Metropolitan Police Commissioner's success in the Court of Appeal, *Austin v UK*[107] therefore had the potential to challenge this controversial police power. However, it was held by fourteen votes to three that there was no violation of Article 5 of the Convention. The Court emphasised that it found that there was not a deprivation of liberty owing to the 'specific and exceptional facts of this case'. This highlights that in practice the police do not have a 'free hand' in utilising restrictive cordons, but when they do so it must be proved that it was the least restrictive measure available to them to prevent serious disorder. It was supported in this instance because the court ruled that had 'it not remained necessary for the police to impose and maintain the cordon in order to prevent serious injury or damage, the "type" of the measure would have been different, and its coercive and restrictive nature might have been sufficient to bring it within art 5'.[108]

Hugo Gorringe and Michael Rosie have argued that while the tactic of kettling and other forms of strategic incapacitation such as preventative arrests and surveillance have been deployed on transgressive groups, in Scotland there has been a significant movement towards dialogue policing. This was highlighted by a Smash NATO demonstration and a Stop the War procession in 2009, and a Climate Camp protest in 2010.[109] The organisers of the Smash NATO demonstration had suggested the potential for disorder by putting graphics of a wrench and bolt cutters with the message 'bring what you expect to find' on their website. The police liaised with the protesters, which numbered less than fifty but were treated with suspicion: as one protestor responded to a facilitator, 'We have the right to ineffective protest?' highlighting that such tactics may still be seen as 'control' rather than 'facilitation'.[110] Gorringe and Rosie note that during the Climate Camp protest the liaison policing operation had learned from the previous demonstrations, and effective changes included officers wearing bibs marked 'liaison police' making contact with Climate Camp in advance. They distributed leaflets informing the protestors who they were and also provided contact numbers. Gorringe and Rosie highlight that the value of liaison policing is that it works by building up trust between the police and the protestors, and it de-escalates flashpoints

---

106 *R (on the application of Moos and another) v Commissioner of Police for the Metropolis* [2012] EWCA Civ 12 at para 90.

107 *Austin v UK* [2012] 55 EHRR 14 (ECHR).

108 Ibid., at para 68.

109 H. Gorringe and M. Rosie, '"We *will* facilitate your protest": Experiments with Liaison Policing', *Policing 7*, no. 2 [2013], pp. 204–211.

110 Ibid., p. 207.

rather than preventing them from occurring.[111] Although some disorder must be tolerated in order to ensure the success of the liaison approach, it represents a step forward in democratic policing which aims to facilitate rather than deter participation in public protest.

Conclusion

The enactment of the Public Order Act and the introduction of s3 indicated a significant shift in the Government's attitude regarding the individual liberty of the subject and the collective security of the community. This shift is demonstrated by the subsequent use of s3 to prohibit fascist processions, marking a substantial legal shift from the principle declared in *Beatty v Gillbanks*. Although the BUF's politics attracted and provoked widespread opposition, the BUF were still a lawful political movement. On the occasion of their processions, members of the BUF were typically law abiding and any violent disorder was, by and large, instigated by their opponents. The contrary interpretation to this argument would contend that the prime objective of the BUF was to insult local Jewish communities and incite racial hatred against them. Therefore, the BUF must take responsibility for any violent disorder associated with their political activities, deeming it as the 'natural consequence' of such deliberate provocation and aligning it with *Wise v Dunning*. Yet the provisions introduced in s3 Public Order Act 1936 made any application of previous common law judgments obsolete. The only prerequisite that a Chief Constable needed to impose regulations on public processions, or make an application to prohibit them in a particular area, was that they must have reasonable ground for apprehending that the procession may occasion serious public disorder. This chapter has demonstrated that since the continued disruption of BUF processions in London, which continued in the post-war era of the UM, the power to proscribe them was increasingly utilised. The continual use of the s3 ban, which was initially applied in East London and then across the Metropolitan Police District, demonstrated that far-Right activism was significantly falling from the safeguard of political liberty that they had previously enjoyed. The new legislation provided the authorities with a clearer legal provision which they could utilise against political activism that threatened the security of the community with very little fear of the order being legally challenged. Ewing and Gearty claimed that the Government, by their inaction, tolerated BUF activism and disorder, acting in 1936 only in response to the 'weight of popular opposition to them and the message of Cable Street'.[112] While this may have been a factor that influenced the legislation, it neglects other elements that preceded the statutory response. For instance, successive commissioners and Chief Constables had advocated for an increase in powers relating to public processions in the wake of BUF disorder. Also, the legal astuteness of BUF activism

---

111 Ibid., p. 210.
112 Ewing and Gearty, *The Struggle*, p. 329.

had often impeded the use of preventive measures or restrictive responses, which contrasted with the activism of the far-Left who openly contested police and government authority.

While it was common for local councillors and Mayors to campaign against provocative far-Right activism, it was anti-fascist opposition on the streets which caused concern for the police in maintaining order. This dual anxiety contributed to the acceptance of the wide powers under this Act which also affected other political movements. However, as mentioned in chapter four, many Chief Constables had advocated for more powers to control or prohibit public processions prior to the Public Order Act. Sir Philip Game went even further in his dislike of BUF processions by advocating for the prohibition of all processions. Moreover, when applications for a s3 ban on processions had been submitted to the Home Secretary, they had been consistently sanctioned, and when challenged in the courts, as in *Kent*, they had been supported by the judiciary. This marks a significant shift, not only from the principles of *Beatty v Gillbanks*, but also to Sir Samuel Hoare's description of the 'spirit of the Public Order Act', which acknowledged the existence of special conditions that made proscription of far-Right activism necessary in some areas but not in others.

The legislative developments concerning public processions, both in the Public Order Acts of 1936 and 1986, placed a heavy emphasis on the philosophy of preventative measures. Powers now available to the police to impose conditions or prohibit public processions provide Chief Constables with wide discretionary powers over the liberty of political activists and protestors. It is ultimately their use of available discretion to apply what measure they see as necessary to fulfil their duty to prevent breaches of the peace and protect the public safety. Their discretion can then be applied to either impose conditions or apply to the local council to request a sanction from the Home Secretary to proscribe all processions or any class of processions for a period up to three months. The application of these powers when policing the processions of the EDL demonstrates that there is still some commitment to the right to process in public in accordance with Articles 10 and 11 of the ECHR. While the only banning orders under s13 that have been sought since 2009 have been in relation to the proscription of EDL processions, the numbers of these compared to the locations that have facilitated them are relatively small. Even in the London Borough of Tower Hamlets, where previous prohibitions were sanctioned by the Home Secretary in 2011 and 2012, the Metropolitan Police facilitated an EDL procession there in 2013 but applied conditions in order to prevent disorder.

A further development in the policing of public assemblies, whether mobile or not, has been the use of long containments, or kettling, in order to prevent imminent breaches of the peace. Unlike police powers to ban processions under s13, the use of this tactic is a common law power which has been approved by the courts in cases where it was proved necessary under the individual circumstances. The danger of such coercive tactics being used so frequently is that they indiscriminately contain peaceful, law-abiding protesters and members of the general public for long periods at a time. This not only restricts their liberty but also becomes an influential device which deters people from future participation in public protest. The fundamental freedom to assemble in public and to express one's views, which are affected by the policing of public processions, are also of critical importance to public meetings. Chapter six will analyse the concept of freedom of speech and the legal restrictions placed upon it in relation to public meetings and the preservation of public order.

6 Public meetings and freedom of expression

The criminalisation of words and political censorship

You must recollect that magistrates now have power to punish people who will not keep their tongues within bounds.[1]

Introduction

Public meetings, whether associated with political activism or public protest, have often been a source of disorder throughout Britain. In particular, the words and behaviour of those holding or attending meetings have regularly come to the attention of the police and the magistrates. The introduction of preventative police powers which regulated words and behaviour to prevent a breach of the peace had their origin in the Metropolitan Police Act 1839. The preliminary quote by the Lord Mayor of London, presiding over an early prosecution under s54(13) at Mansion House, highlighted the introduction of this new liberty-constricting law, which was now equipped to criminalise certain words and behaviour which were likely to lead to a breach of the peace.[2] This chapter examines with how these restrictions on freedom of expression developed throughout the period and how the police used their discretion to utilise these ambiguous preventive powers at public meetings.

This chapter begins by evaluating the legal definitions relating to public meetings and freedom of speech. The growth of police powers relating to the restriction of free speech is examined by first analysing the effect of the Metropolitan Police Act 1839. Significant events that motivated legal developments at both Statute and common law level are then examined. This includes the socialist meetings held at Trafalgar Square in the late 1880s and the meetings of the unemployed marchers in 1908. In the interwar period, accusations of partial policing were stimulated as the fascists and communists fought for dominance in the realm of street politics. The provisions under clause 5 of the Public Order Bill 1936, which were drafted to prevent political provocation and disorder, and the Parliamentary

---

1 *London Standard*, 16 Sep 1839.
2 The powers under s54(13) are described later, in the section titled 'S54(13) Metropolitan Police Act 1839'.

debates which accompanied them, are assessed, and subsequent implications to the policing of public meetings are then considered. In the post War period, the reemergence of anti-Semitic far-Right groups brought the use of the power by the police to the forefront. Significant changes in the Public Order Act 1986, as well as subsequent amendments, are then analysed and discussed with reference to the Human Rights Act 1998. Restrictions to these rights are then analysed with reference to extremist groups such as Islam4UK, the BNP and the EDL. Finally, consideration is given to cases such as *Redmond-Bate v DPP*[3] and *R(Laporte) v Chief Constable of Gloucestershire*,[4] which established when the rights to freedom of expression must be permitted.

Legal definitions

Public meetings

Like public processions, public meetings are a form of public assembly and, therefore, subject to the same conditions that would consider such an assembly to be unlawful.[5] This includes statutory and common law offences, such as laws relating to obstruction of the highways,[6] sedition[7] or the use of threatening, abusive or insulting words or behaviour.[8] Other common law offences related to unlawful assembly are riot, rout and affray.[9] The current legal definition for 'public meeting' is found in s9 Public Order Act 1936, which was not repealed by the 1986 Act. First, a meeting is defined as 'a meeting held for the purpose of the discussion of matters of public interest or for the purpose of the expression of views on such matters'. Second, section 9 defines public meeting as 'any meeting in a public place and any meeting which the public or any section thereof are permitted to attend, whether on payment or otherwise'.

---

3 *Redmond-Bate v DPP* [2000] HRLR 249.
4 *R (o/a Laporte) v Chief Constable of Gloucestershire* [2006] UKHL 55.
5 See chapter four for a definition of public assembly.
6 See s72 Highway Act 1835 and s28 Town Police Clauses Act 1847. The offence of wilful obstruction of the highway is now under s137 Highway Act 1980.
7 Smith and Hogan stated, 'There is probably no offence properly described as "sedition" in English law, but the oral or written publication of words with a seditious intention is a common law misdemeanour and an agreement to further a seditious intention by doing any act is a conspiracy.' (Smith, J. C. and Hogan, B., *Criminal Law,* third edition, Butterworths: London [1973], p. 646.) Seditious intention was described in *R v Burns* (1886) 16 Cox CC 355: 'An intention to excite ill-will between different classes of Her Majesty's subjects may be a seditious intention; whether or not it is so in any particular case must be decided upon by the jury after taking into consideration all the circumstances of the case.' See also the Incitement to Disaffection Act 1934 and the Incitement to Mutiny Act 1797.
8 See s54(13) Metropolitan Police Act 1839 and other local bylaws, and s5 Public Order Act 1936, all of which have since been repealed by the Public Order Act 1986 and replaced by ss4, 4A and 5.
9 These are defined in chapter three and, with the exception of rout, are now statutory offences under ss1–3 Public Order Act 1986.

Freedom of expression

Before the HRA, free speech only existed as an absolute 'right' and privilege in Parliament guaranteed by Article 9 of the Bill of Rights 1689, which gave MPs unconditional freedom of expression. Outside of Parliament, freedoms were protected by the common law through the concept of residual freedom, whereby people were free to say what they liked except where the substantive law made it unlawful. As with the claim to free assembly, under the notion of residual freedom, people were free to say what they pleased, but only to the extent that their words or behaviour did not violate any law. This was expressed in 1932 at the Birmingham Quarter Sessions. John Trotter, a labourer who addressed a public meeting, claimed the right to free speech when he was accused of inciting people to steal, assault the police, damage property, engage in unlawful assembly and riotously to assemble together. The Recorder stated in his summing up: 'There is no such thing in a civilised community as the right of free speech . . . You are allowed to express your opinion as far as you keep within the law and no further.'[10]

Police discretion at public meetings

Before the Public Order Act 1986, no provision existed in the substantive criminal law to prohibit the forming of lawful public assemblies.[11] Furthermore, despite the various claims made by public speakers in the nineteenth and twentieth centuries to the Englishman's 'right' to free speech, no legal protection of this notion existed in constitutional terms.[12] The fundamental duty of the police is to preserve the Queen's Peace and uphold the law. In respect of maintaining order at public meetings, the police held wide discretionary powers in order to keep the peace. Therefore, the policing of public meetings was necessarily based on individual factors, such as their existing intelligence on the speakers and the anticipated likelihood of disorder. Once these elements had been analysed, it would be utilised to inform police tactics, such as how many police officers were needed to be on duty and whether note takers were required. When public meetings were in progress the police were also faced with a dilemma: who should action be taken against in the anticipation of disorder, an aggressive or persistent heckler from the crowd, or a provocative speaker who incited discontent and potential violence

10 *Western Daily Press*, 25 Nov 1932.
11 This remained the case until s14 Public Order Act 1986 provided a statutory power to impose conditions on public assemblies which includes the power to stipulate where the assembly is held, the maximum duration of the assembly, and the maximum number of participants that constitute it. These conditions can be applied by the Chief Officer of Police to prevent disorder, damage, disruption or intimidation if they reasonably believe that the assembly may result in serious public disorder, serious damage to property or serious disruption to the life of the community.
12 The right to form a public assembly was not legally protected in constitutional terms until the Human Rights Act 1998. Even following the HRA, and the adoption of the ECHR, the now protected rights to freedom of expression and freedom of assembly under Articles 10 and 11, are not absolute and are subject to the conditions placed in Articles 10(2) and 11(2).

from the audience? The police subsequently had wide discretionary powers under the breach of the peace doctrine at their disposal in order to keep the peace. For criminologist Tony Jefferson, the wide discretion involved in regulating situations such as this necessarily meant that public order policing involved making subjective and therefore partial decisions which ultimately 'exposed a hidden politics of policing'.[13] Yet it is not just the potential of political partiality that needs to be analysed in this context. David Waddington asserts that the very act of invoking legislation could potentially create further problems for the police, requiring the need for police tactics to be measured and the potential consequences of their actions to be calculated.[14] Peter Waddington adds that 'an arrest for a minor offence could spark off a riot in which damage and injury result and an inquiry that threatens careers'.[15] It is in these cases where police officers have to utilise their discretion in deciding when it is appropriate to take assertive action. The resulting history is a continuous narrative of allegations towards the police of partisanship and brutality. With reference to freedom of expression, the first significant provision which provided the police to regulated speech was s54(13) Metropolitan Police Act 1839, which is described in the next section.

The police and the criminalisation of words

Since the introduction of the modern police force, a combination of judicial lawmaking and Acts of Parliament had evolved, informing the provincial police constabularies how to regulate disorder, or the anticipation of disorder, at public meetings. This produced varying results across the country. The introduction of the Metropolitan Police Force was met with fierce resistance in 1829 because of the perceived threat to the individual liberty of 'free-born Englishmen'.[16] However, ten years later the Metropolitan Police Act 1839 provided Metropolitan Police constables with a vast array of statutory powers, which included provisions related to search and arrest, as well as such disparate provisions related to Sunday licencing hours, the destroying of dangerous dogs and 'furious driving', in addition to nuisance behaviors such as knocking on doors and running away, and flying kites in residential streets. The Act also enlarged the Metropolitan Police District as well as absorbing the Thames River Police and the Bow Street Runners into the Metropolitan Police Force. Conservative MP Captain Thomas

13 Jefferson, *Paramilitary Policing*, p. 47.
14 D. Waddington, *Policing Public Order: Theory and Practice*, Willan Publishing: Cullompton (2007), p. 12.
15 P.A.J. Waddington, 'Controlling Protest in Contemporary Historical and Comparative Perspective' in D. della Porta and H. Reiter (eds), *Policing Protest: the Control of Mass Demonstrations in Western Democracies*, University of Minnesota Press: Minneapolis (1998), p. 120.
16 See Thompson, *English Working Class*, chapter four, for a detailed discussion on the free-born Englishman. For a more detailed examination on the resistance to the build up of the Metropolitan Police Act 1829 and the opposition to it, see Emsley, 'Birth and Development of the Police' and C. Emsley, *Policing and Its Context 1750–1870*, Macmillan Press Ltd: London (1983), chapter four.

Wood signalled his opposition to the Bill as it 'tended greatly to increase the powers of the police, and was, in some respects, republican in its tendency'.[17] Before its enactment, the Bill was also criticised in the House of Lords by Lord Ellenborough, who argued that the scope of the Bill was too wide – yet despite his criticism he did not propose any amendments, as it had 'great difficulty' getting through the House of Commons and he did not want to endanger its passing.[18] Newspaper reportage also criticised the measures proposed in the Bill, which provided police constables the power to make arrests without a warrant for sticking post bills on walls; using language which annoyed a passenger; or using threatening, abusive or insulting words or behaviour with intent to provoke a breach of the peace. The *Staffordshire Gazette and County Standard* called the last of these measures the most tyrannical within the Bill, asking 'who is to be the judge?' highlighting the ambiguity and subjectivity of these offences.[19] This provision became law under s54(13).

S54(13) Metropolitan Police Act 1839

Section 54(13) made it an offence to use 'any threatening, abusive or insulting words or behaviour with intent to provoke a breach of the peace, or whereby a breach of the peace may be occasioned'. Outside the Metropolitan Police district, the situation was even more problematic as there were similar bylaws and local Acts in different regions which had inconsistent penalties or procedures. These Acts also required the police to utilise their discretion to decide whether the nature of the words were 'threatening, abusive or insulting', and whether there was the likelihood of a breach of the peace occurring. The Report from the Select Committee on Metropolis Police Offices from 1839 highlights the agenda behind this broad power. James Traill, an acting magistrate at Union Hall who was a witness for the Committee, argued that the magistrates had no power to deal with people who used abusive language or provoking and insulting behaviour. Giving evidence, he estimated that nine-tenths of the assaults brought before the magistrates originated from this behaviour, and he claimed that many people took the law into their own hands because the magistrates could not issue warrants when complaints were made.[20] Traill drafted the clause, using the words 'opprobrious, menacing or insulting words or behaviour', acknowledging that the wording of it was influenced by the Liverpool Street Act 1827.[21]

The preventative nature of this provision is clear. When the Act was passed, the objective was to criminalise the use of words or behaviour which often escalated into violent confrontations or assaults. Furthermore, under the 'reason' for clause

---

17 *Hansard, HC Deb*, 3 Jun 1839, vol 47 cc1291–1292.
18 *Hansard, HL Deb*, 29 Jul 1839, vol 49 cc927–928.
19 *Staffordshire Gazette and County Standard*, 10 Apr 1839.
20 Report from the Select Committee on Metropolis Police Offices; with the minutes of evidence, appendix and index (1837), p. 46.
21 Ibid., p. 79.

8 (as it was when presented to the Committee), it is revealed that it was directed at the 'lower classes'.[22] The clause also featured the power of the Justice of Police to summon the offending person in order to bind him or her to keep the peace towards the aggrieved. The final version of the Act included a power for any Metropolitan Police constable to 'take into custody, without warrant, any person who shall commit any such offence within view of any such constable.' While the intention of introducing this provision was a preventive, to deter violent behavior and assault, its final form would ultimately provide the police with wide discretionary powers of arrest as it criminalised loosely defined words and behavior, which ultimately reduced the residual claim to free speech.

When this provision was amended and became law under s54(13), newspaper research suggests that there was not a flurry of prosecutions, and of the small number reported, the offences principally focused on the threatening aspect of words and behaviour. Offences also arose from small individual disputes. There was no evidence to suggest that the measures were ever considered to maintain order at public meetings. However, this potential was to be realised nearly a century later, during the political battles between the fascists and communists in the interwar period.

The historic claim to the 'right' of public meeting

Public meetings at Trafalgar Square 1886–1888

In the mid-1880s, during a period of severe depression, large groups of unemployed men began to camp in Trafalgar Square. This congregation of disgruntled men without work became a receptive audience for radical political groups such as the Social Democratic Federation (SDF), whose meetings attracted the attention of the authorities. Richard Vogler described this period of suppression of public meetings as being 'the hallmark of careful and strategic planning [by the Home Office and the Metropolitan Police]'.[23] His analysis highlighted the appointment of Sir Charles Warren, who had a military background, as Metropolitan Police Commissioner in 1886, and the Tory Home Secretary, Sir Henry Matthews, as being 'ready to deal with the SDF and the unemployed demonstrators'.[24] Vogler also emphasised the importance of the two magistrates selected to preside over cases brought against any person arrested in connection with the disorder at either Trafalgar Square or Hyde Park. They were 'almost the oldest serving Metropolitan Magistrates . . . and had a record of loyalty to the police'.[25]

On 8 November 1887, Warren issued a public notice that until further intimation, 'no public meetings will be allowed to assemble in Trafalgar Square, nor will

---

22 Ibid., p. 185.
23 Vogler, *Reading the Riot Act*, p. 60.
24 Ibid., p. 61.
25 Ibid., p. 62.

speeches be allowed to be delivered there.'[26] The police subsequently made several arrests of men who attempted to address a crowd. This included one man who was arrested for waving a red handkerchief. The arrest of two journalists, including the well-known war correspondent Bennett Burleigh, who were charged at Bow Street Police Court for being, 'loose, idle, and disorderly persons, disturbing the public peace with intent to commit a felony' and 'obstructing and resisting the police while in the execution of their duty in Trafalgar Square' caused some controversy.[27] Burleigh refused to be bound over to be of good behaviour for six months with sureties of £100, arguing that the presiding magistrate, James Vaughn, did not even listen to the defence. In response, Vaughn replied that he expected the defendant to 'be "pleased" to get off in this way, and remanded him for a week'.[28] Burleigh was granted bail and was discharged a week later. Bodkin Poland, prosecuting, apologised to Burleigh on behalf of the Treasury for his arrest, stating that he had been arrested by mistake.[29] From his analysis, Vogler determined that that the Metropolitan Police were able to exercise independent authority over the magistracy and the military leading up to and including the Trafalgar Square Riot of 13 November 1887, which was in contrast to the experience of the provincial police force during the disorder at Featherstone in 1893. However, the legal and political discussions that arose in this period, as a result of Warren's excessive tactics of suppressing the radical speakers in Trafalgar Square, were critical because they addressed the claim of a 'right' of public meeting.

Following Warren's prohibition, the *Pall Mall Gazette* suggested that:

> [S]omething must be done . . . to defend the legal liberties of the Londoner from the insolent usurpations of Scotland-yard . . . The right of public meeting is one of the most sacred rights which freemen possess. Together with trial by jury, it is the parent of all our liberties.[30]

Many contemporary newspapers referred to the 'right' of public meeting, despite no such legal right being encoded within UK constitutional law. People were at liberty to form a lawful assembly for the purpose of addressing a public meeting because no law had specifically stated that they could not. Despite the liberty to hold public meetings not being a constitutional right, the language utilised by newspapers, politicians and street lecturers demonstrate that there was a traditionally held belief in the 'right' of public meeting. Correspondingly, if the police prohibited a public assembly, their actions must also be legally justified; critics of Warren claim his actions were not. The *Pall Mall Gazette* continued, 'in Central London there is practically but one open space where the poor man can hold a public meeting . . . [But] that one open space is to be now closed against

---

26 *Western Times*, 9 Nov 1887.
27 *Western Times*, 9 Nov 1887.
28 *Aberdeen Journal*, 12 Nov 1887.
29 *Reading Mercury*, 19 Nov 1887.
30 *The Pall Mall Gazette*, 10 Nov 1887.

him – not by law, but the arbitrary edict of a policeman.'[31] Trafalgar Square was a popular place for public meetings in London as speakers could address large crowds without causing significant obstruction of the highway.

Following the Trafalgar Square Riot 1887, Cunninghame Graham, the socialist Liberal MP, and John Burns, who formed the Battersea branch of the SDF, 'were indicted for a riot, an unlawful assembly, and an assault upon William Blunden and John Martell, police-constables, in the execution of their duty'.[32] A crucial part of this case was whether or not Warren's proclamation had any legal authority. If the assembly formed by Graham and Burns was found to be lawful, then the proclamation issued by Warren would be void. In cross-examination by Asquith, who represented Graham, Warren stated that he 'suppose[d]' he issued the proclamation under the common law. Counsel also referred to the Trafalgar Square Act 1844, which 'empowered the Commissioner of Works to make proper regulations for the use of the square' – yet the proclamation was made by the Metropolitan Police Commissioner and not the Commissioner of Works. The Counsel also contended that if Warren used his authority from s52 Metropolitan Police Act, 'that it was ultra vires, as the power given by this section was for making regulations for carriage routes and for the preventing obstruction in the streets . . . The proclamation went far beyond anything of that kind, as it prohibited meetings and speeches'.[33] In advising the jury, Charles J confirmed that although Warren's public notice did not necessarily make a meeting unlawful, his decision was based on the risk to the public peace. The constables therefore fulfilled their duty to disperse those assembled there. He added that if the crowd had gathered for a lawful object, it would not have provided justification for riotous conduct.[34]

Warren's public notice prohibiting public meetings was justified only as a preventive measure to avert a breach of the peace under the common law. However, the defendants had a history of addressing numerous peaceable meetings and there was no imminence of disorder. Regardless of this, the jury found them guilty of unlawful assembly, but not the more serious charges of riot, or for the assault upon the police officers. Charles J concurred with the verdict and sentenced Graham and Burns to six weeks imprisonment without hard labour.[35]

The legal authority of Warren's notice was also subject to the hearing of Mr W Saunders, who was charged at Bow Street Police Court on 17 November 1887 with disorderly conduct for addressing a crowd in Trafalgar Square. Mr Poland, prosecuting on behalf of the Treasury, stated that the Government withdrew the prosecution because there was 'no penalty attached to the disobedience of the proclamation'. The defence pressed for a conviction in order for the case to be

31 Ibid.
32 *Old Bailey Proceedings Online* (www.oldbaileyonline.org, version 7.0, 22 May 2012), Jan 1888, trial of ROBERT GALLINGAD BONTINE CUNNINGHAME GRAHAM JOHN BURNS (t18880109–223).
33 *The Times*, 19 Jan 1888.
34 Ibid.
35 Ibid.

carried into another court. Ingham J discharged the defendant, stating that there was nothing he could do to forward his views.[36]

Edward Lewis, a solicitor who had previously defended many of the accused at Bow Street Police Court, directly attacked the prohibition of meetings held in Trafalgar Square by tendering information in support of his application for summonses against Warren and the Home Secretary, Sir Henry Matthews, 'for having used violence and intimidation with a view to prevent citizens from holding public meetings in Trafalgar Square, for a lawful purpose, without legal authority'. The magistrate, Vaughn, declared that he could not grant the summonses, stating:

> It may be bad law, and if so, you can go to the high court and get the whole of it reviewed and my refusal to grant you summonses considered. If the court says that your judgement is correct, then, of course, I shall be compelled to grant you the summonses.[37]

This led to the hearing *Ex parte Lewis*.[38] Two of Lewis's complaints were that Matthews and Warren had conspired

> by unlawful violence and other unlawful means to prevent divers of Her Majesty's subjects from exercising their constitutional and lawful rights . . . [and to] endanger the public safety and peace, and to injure, annoy, and disturb the public in the enjoyment of their civil rights.[39]

Lewis's claim to establish peaceful public assembly and protest at Trafalgar Square as a constitutional right through the common law failed. However, in his judgment, Wills J stated, 'a great deal was said about the right of public meeting – unnecessarily – inasmuch as it is a right which has long passed out of region of discussion or doubt.'[40] This ambiguous statement has potentially two very different interpretations. It is commonly seen as a judgment which recognises the 'right' to public meetings. In 2010, Peter Thornton QC referenced this quote, arguing that, 'The Law has long recognised the right of public meeting, "a right which has long passed out of the region of discussion or doubt".'[41] Yet, Wills J's summary is not consistent with this interpretation. It is more likely that when he stated that 'it is a right which has long passed out of region of discussion or doubt' he was merely summarising Lewis' argument, which is evidenced by the first clause of his sentence, 'a great deal was said about the right of public meeting'. Therefore, in its full context, Wills J's quote summarises his view that the argument promoting the right of public meeting by Lewis was irrelevant and 'unnecessarily' said.

36 *Reading Mercury*, 19 Nov 1887.
37 *Morning Post*, 16 Feb 1888.
38 *Ex parte Lewis* (1888) 21 QBD 191.
39 Ibid. at 193.
40 Ibid. at 196.
41 Thornton *et al.*, *Law of Public Order*, p. 119.

This interpretation is later reinforced in Wills J's judgment, when he states that there is 'no trace in our law books' of such 'rights'. Referring to Lewis's argument that these rights rested upon 'dedication', Wills J confirmed that:

> The only 'dedication' in the legal sense that we are aware of is that of a public right of passage, of which the legal description is a 'right for all her Majesty's subjects at all seasons of the year freely and at their will to pass and repass without let or hinderence' . . . [and continued to state that a claim to the right of public assembly is] in its nature irreconcilable with the right of free passage, and there is . . . no authority whatever in favour of it.[42]

Furthermore, A. V. Dicey's assessment of the perceived 'right' to public meeting also supports this view. He stated, 'it can hardly be said that our constitution knows of such a thing as any specific right of public meeting.'[43] In ensuing case law this stance is again reiterated.[44]

With regard to meetings at Trafalgar Square, a further point lay in reference to an Act of Parliament which established that 'the Commissioners of Works have a right to say whether or not it shall be so used.'[45] Incidentally, the Works Office later delegated these powers to the Commissioner of Police in 1892.[46] Following the defeat at common law level to establish the right of public meeting, two Bills were later introduced to Parliament in an attempt to guarantee such rights under Statute. The Trafalgar Square (Regulation of Meetings) Bill 1888 was omitted from the Royal Speech in 1889, and an amendment was made to express regret that legislation 'to safeguard the long accustomed right of public meeting in Trafalgar Square' had been discounted.[47]

In July 1888, Cunninghame Graham introduced the Public Meetings in Open Spaces Bill, which was directed to declare and regulate the right of public meeting. Clause 1 stated that where the public had at any time used or enjoyed any open space for the purpose of public meetings in the last twenty years, then the public shall be 'deemed for all purposes to have acquired an absolute and inalienable right to the user thereof for the said purposes.' The penalties stipulated under this Bill demonstrate the intention of its drafters to protect free speech and assembly. Clause 3 stated that the penalty for a breach of the regulations of the Act would be a fine not exceeding £5. Clause 4 provided that, for the unlawful interference, disturbance or molestation of a public meeting, or use of violence or intimidation

---

42 *Ex parte Lewis* (1888) 21 QBD 191, 197.
43 Dicey, *An Introduction*, p. 271. Although Dicey's text was first published in 1885 (three years before *Ex parte Lewis*), it was continuously updated until 1908 and this quote is taken from a 1959 reprint of that text.
44 See *Duncan v Jones* [1936] 1 KB 220–221.
45 *Ex parte Lewis* (1888) 21 QBD 191, 198.
46 L. Keller, *Triumph of Order: Democracy and Public Space in New York and London*, Columbia University Press: New York (2010), p. 139.
47 *Hansard, HC Deb*, 5 Mar 1889, vol 333 cc993–1060.

against a procession, persons or a person proceeding to a meeting, 'shall be guilty of a misdemeanour, and liable on conviction thereof, on indictment, to imprisonment for a term not exceeding *one year*, or to a fine, in the discretion of the Court'. The Bill did not progress past its second reading. Despite the increased debate on public meetings following the Trafalgar Square riots, attempts to secure a constitutional right through both the courts and Parliament failed, leaving the police and local authorities free to utilise the ambiguous and ill-defined powers under the breach of the peace doctrine. The wide discretion this ultimately provided for the police subsequently led to inconsistent practice being applied across the country.

The unemployed Manchester marchers 1908

Before the First World War, the practice of provincial police constabularies relating to public meetings was often inconsistently applied. This is demonstrated by the different receptions received by the unemployed workers of Manchester who marched through the Midlands on route to hand in a petition to Parliament in London in 1908. The contrasting responses of the Birmingham and Coventry police authorities could not be more prominent. When the Manchester men arrived at Birmingham, they were warned by the police that they could not walk in processional order through the streets in the centre of the city or hold an open-air meeting there. The newspaper reportage does not record what legal authority was utilised or question the legality of the police action, but it can be deduced that the police order was a 'loose' interpretation of the common law power to prevent a breach of the peace. Despite the police order, the leaders, Stewart Gray and Jack Williams, declared their 'intention of asserting their rights of free speech'. They wanted to address a crowd at Chamberlain Square. Following the ban Gray was reported to have said to a Police Inspector, 'I tell you frankly that there will be a meeting.'[48] An attempt by Gray to meet with the Mayor to resolve the issue was also reported to have been hindered by the police, who refused him entry to Mansion House. Undeterred, the procession – which consisted of men carrying flags and banners, and a hand cart carrying the petition for local people to sign – proceeded and was met by a 'strong force of police'. After unsuccessful negotiations, the unemployed men began to advance, the police obstructed their progress, and 'a scene of extraordinary violence ensued.'[49] The *Manchester Courier* was in no doubt who to attribute the cause of the violence to, declaring 'A riot, which nearly attained the most serious proportions, occurred . . . owing to the aggressive attitude which was displayed by the body of Manchester unemployed.'[50]

When it became clear that the unemployed men could not break the police cordon, many of them began to march to Coventry. The others attempted to break through the police lines; four men were arrested during the disorder. Two were released on the undertaking that they would leave the city, and the other two men

---

48 *Manchester Courier and Lancashire General Advertiser*, 31 Jan 1908.
49 *Lichfield Mercury*, 31 Jan 1908.
50 *Manchester Courier and Lancashire General Advertiser*, 31 Jan 1908.

were charged with disorderly conduct at the police court. They were subsequently discharged by the magistrates under the assurance that they would leave the city and join the rest of the group. When the unemployed men reached Coventry on Saturday evening they were 'well received by local labour men'. They were provided with sleeping quarters for two nights at the Clarion Club and given three meals on Sunday, including one hot meal. The police were also hospitable: they allowed the unemployed men to hold public meetings and make collections.[51] These contrasting examples illustrate the extent of police discretion available in response to facilitating public meetings in two towns just twenty miles apart.[52]

The previous examples of policing public meetings in 1888 and 1908 demonstrate two key complexities that marked public order policing: First, there was the autocratic police response regarding Trafalgar Square, which heavily relied upon police discretionary powers under the common law to close public meetings and disperse an assembly, or to prohibit public meetings in advance for an undisclosed period of time. The Trafalgar Square incidents also demonstrated the willingness of the courts to approve of such police action. Second, the example from the West Midlands demonstrates how the practice of public order policing varied from one police authority to the next. Both problems can be seen as the result of wide discretionary police powers under the breach of the peace doctrine and demonstrate the susceptibility of these powers to political partiality and discrimination. These considerations must be acknowledged when considering the various police practices utilised in the era of the BUF and their anti-fascist opponents.

The police at BUF meetings

In a manner similar to the examples given from the 1880s and 1908, BUF propaganda also frequently referred to the 'established British right of free speech'.[53] This terminology was used to justify the necessity of using force against political opponents. Sir Oswald Mosley initiated this principle when he formed the New Party in 1931. Arguing that they had experienced organised disruption of their meetings, he declared, 'We are going to defend the right of free speech in this country and will not tamely submit to methods of violence and intimidation.'[54] Referring to his organisation of stewards trained to deal with violent interruption, which the *Western Daily Press* dubbed an 'army', Mosley stated, 'The only methods we shall employ will be English methods. We shall rely on the good old English fist.'[55] When Mosley formed the BUF a year later, these organised stewards became known as the Fascist Defence Force.

---

51 *Lichfield Mercury*, 31 Jan 1908.
52 For other examples on the inconsistent police practice in different regions during this era, see chapter seven and Cd. 4674, 'Report of the Departmental Committee on the Duties of the Police with respect to the Preservation of Order at Public Meetings' (1909).
53 *The Blackshirt*, 15 Jun 1934, issue 60, p. 2.
54 *Western Daily Press*, 16 May 1931.
55 Ibid.

Mosley's concept of 'freedom of speech' was later formulated in an article published in *Action* in 1936. It was a scathing attack on the 'failing' democratic system that, instead of dealing with the assailants of free speech, the Government used the law against the defenders of free speech. Mosley wrote:

> bricks were still whistling freely through the air, and round us, on the ground, were unconscious Blackshirts, savagely mauled by a highly organised Red mob because they had ventured to maintain an "Englishman's right of Free Speech" at their own meeting.[56]

Mosley's reference to free speech as an 'Englishman's right' was an effective propaganda tool, used to justify the use of Blackshirt violence, and to discredit communism as an alien threat to English values. Mosley still referred to free speech as a 'right' in his 1968 autobiography, *My Life*. He mentioned the organised minority who attempted to deny the right of free speech to the people and even claimed of his Blackshirts that, 'These devoted young men saved free speech in Britain.'[57]

Countering Mosley's definition of freedom of speech, the Metropolitan Police Commissioner, Lord Trenchard, stated that free speech did not mean that people could express their views without interruption from political opponents, but that people were free to air their views without *official* interference from the Government, or the police acting on their behalf.[58] However, as free speech was not a legal right, the police did have the common law duty to prevent people from addressing a crowd if it was reasonably anticipated that it would result in a breach of the peace.

In *Justice of the Peace and Local Government Review*, the concept of English 'rights' was addressed in relation to public meetings in public places. It stated that such a right did not exist in legal terms, but it existed as a 'quasi-constitutional right' based on 'practice of very long standing [that was] not lightly to be interfered with'. The right to public meetings in public places was 'only subject to the overriding right of His Majesty's subjects to move freely about the highways . . . and to the duty of the police to prevent breaches of the peace'.[59] This reveals that such freedoms had meaning and importance to the people and the state in principle, but as unwritten rights they had no legal protection.

For Ewing and Gearty, the developments at common law during this period, such as *Thomas v Sawkins* and *Duncan v Jones*, provided the police with the power to select 'apparently on an *ad hoc* and entirely unprincipled basis' which meetings to permit and which to close, with the only requirement being based upon the suspicion of future behaviour.[60] While it cannot be denied that these judgments increased the power of the police in respect of public meetings, it is necessary to examine

---

56 *Action*, 24 Oct 1936, number 36, p. 9.
57 Mosley, *My Life*, p. 245.
58 CAB 24/250, Preservation of Public Order: Memorandum by the Home Secretary and Commissioner of Police of the Metropolis (July 1934), p. 1.
59 'The Right of Public Meeting', *Justice of the Peace and Local Government Review XCIX*, no. 44 (2 Nov 1935), p. 703.
60 Ewing and Gearty, *The Struggle*, p. 328.

wider factors which may have led to the disproportionate arrest of the opponents of fascism rather than the fascists themselves. For instance, in an argument to support the notion of police partisanship, Ewing and Gearty state, 'A protest at an open-air fascist rally in Bristol led to nine arrests, all apparently of demonstrators rather than of fascists.'[61] However, they provide no evidence to suggest that the fascists had engaged in criminal activity, or that the anti-fascist protest was law-abiding and undeserving of such police action. Similarly, an example of disorder at Plymouth highlighted that two anti-fascists had been jailed for assaulting a police officer in the execution of his duty during the officer's attempt to disperse an anti-fascist protest which involved a crowd of 1,000 demonstrators congregating outside the fascist headquarters.[62] Again, Ewing and Gearty do not discuss the behaviour of the crowd. Therefore, these incidents can serve only as evidence of police action against anti-fascist activism, which does not necessarily prove that any partiality was involved. Furthermore, additional examples of the Plymouth Police's action regarding fascist activism at Market Square (in this chapter) and at Plymouth Drill Hall during a meeting addressed by Mosley (in chapter seven) demonstrate that there was no particular partiality towards the fascists on the part of the Plymouth Police.

Assertions by historians Richard Thurlow and Gerald Anderson that the policing of political extremism during the interwar period was hindered by the problems of the interpretation of the law at street level and that the police frequently faced the challenge of keeping the extreme movements apart, provide a more balanced assessment of policing in this era, yet more in-depth historico-legal analysis is required.[63] The analysis presented here will show that not all policing of fascist or anti-fascist activism can be accurately understood as demonstrating political partiality and the use of discretion in selecting when to take assertive action or not has many other pertinent factors.

When the Blackshirts became a recognisable presence on the streets of Britain, the occupation of public space by fascist and communist speakers regularly caused conflict and disorder. BUF meetings frequently attracted opposition from anti-fascist opponents, who responded to their provocative political doctrine by constantly interrupting speakers by cat-calling, singing or throwing missiles. The question of provocation at public meetings raises the same issues discussed in chapter four. The judgments of *Beatty v Gillbanks* and *Wise v Dunning* determine that there is a significant point when the disorder that results from the provocation of an individual or group can be deemed to be a natural consequence or not and it is subsequently possible to identify who was culpable and who the police should direct their action towards. Although anti-Semitism was not part of official BUF policy from the outset, their militaristic appearance, association with the dictatorships of Italy and Germany, disapproval of the political system and

---

61 Ibid., p. 287.
62 Ibid.
63 R. Thurlow, *Fascism in Britain, From Oswald Mosley's Blackshirts to the National Front*, I B Tauris: London (2009), p. 84, and G. D. Anderson, *Fascists, Communists and the National Government: Civil Liberties in Great Britain, 1931–1937*, University of Missouri Press: Colombia and London (1983).

desire to set up the corporate state, outspoken hatred of communism, and fast-growing reputation for political violence generated widespread political opposition. Opposition to BUF activism, whether organised or spontaneous, was a regular feature of their meetings and became a particular feature for the police in devising a strategy that minimised the risk of disorder. This was particularly resonant in the preparations for the policing of a large BUF rally and anti-fascist demonstration at Hyde Park in 1934.

The BUF at Hyde Park 1934

Correspondence between the Home Office and the Metropolitan Police reveals the difficulty in policing large-scale BUF meetings that were advertised in advance. The BUF usually cooperated with the police authorities when planning large-scale meetings and demonstrations. In 1934, the BUF had planned a great rally in London's White City Arena, which had the capacity to hold 80,000–90,000 people. This was later relocated to Hyde Park and rescheduled for 9 September. Martin Pugh attributes this to the deliberate stifling of BUF activity by Hugh Trenchard, stating that 'he intervened to insist that the owners allow police inside.'[64] This was a reaction to the disorder witnessed at the Olympia hall when the police did not enter the hall despite hecklers being evidently assaulted by Blackshirt stewards (this is discussed in chapter seven). BUF propaganda declared that the change in venue was due to the potential damage to the running tracks ahead of the Empire Games staged there the following day.[65] The relocated demonstration, now being in a public place, meant that the Metropolitan Police had more control in maintaining order. Blackshirt stewards had no authority to remove or eject interrupters from a meeting held in a public place. With the anticipation of booing and cat-calling amongst the audience, Frank Newsam, a leading civil servant, declared that it was 'no part of the duty of the Police to preserve quiet at open air meetings, and it is submitted that the Police should not attempt to deal with such conduct, unless disorder arises as a result of it'.[66] Newsam was appointed by the Home Office in 1933 to 'address the problems caused by the disorders resulting from the activities of the British Fascists'.[67]

The Metropolitan Police and the Home Office were attentive to the threat of organised disorder from anti-fascist organisations which had advertised their opposition to the BUF meeting in Hyde Park with pamphlets declaring, 'Answer

64 M. Pugh, '*Hurrah for the Blackshirts! Fascists and Fascism in Britain Between the Wars*', Pimlico: London (2006), p. 170.

65 *The Blackshirt*, no. 64, 13 Jul 1934.

66 HO 45/25383. Disturbances: Anti-fascist activities; anti-fascist demonstrations and activities directed against meeting of the British Union of Fascists in Hyde Park on 9 Sept 1934 (1929–1934).

67 Allen of Abbeydale, 'Newsam, Sir Frank Aubrey (1893–1964)', *Oxford Dictionary of National Biography*, Oxford University Press, 2004; online edition, Jan 2008, www.oxforddnb.com/view/article/35219?docPos=1, accessed 14 February 2015.

the Fascist Challenge in Hyde Park', and that included emotive reminders of the violence utilised by the Blackshirts at Olympia.[68] A major consideration that the authorities contended with in planning the policing of this event was the possibility of large numbers of anti-fascists assembling with the intention of preventing the fascists reaching their platforms. The BUF were already granted permission from the Commissioner of Works to hold a meeting in Hyde Park, with the only stipulation that the police should dictate where their vans, which they used as speaking platforms, should be placed. Newsam had already warned Trenchard and Gilmour that it was likely that the police would be called upon by the fascists to assist them in clearing a path through the crowd to reach their meeting point.[69] He advised that it could be seen as the duty of the police to prevent an obstruction of the thoroughfares and paths of the park only, and not to escort speakers across the grass to their platforms. In this circumstance, it was the fascists' responsibility to get through the crowd without creating disorder. He added that the police should not interfere unless the fascists attempted to launch an attack on the crowd to reach their destination, and that if there was a densely packed crowd around the fascist platform, then the fascists should be informed that the police would not allow them to force their way through. Alternatively, Newsam argued that if Mosley made plans for his supporters to arrive early to keep the path open, then it would be the duty of the police to prevent any hostile elements from jostling them off the ground. This, he stated, could be justified as such action would be likely to lead to a breach of the peace.

Responding to Newsam's memorandum, Trenchard declared that it would be 'ludicrous' if, following the permission granted by the Commissioner of Works and the stipulation given by the police on the location of the platforms, the BUF were prevented from reaching their meeting place by their political opponents. Gilmour also acknowledged this situation and defended the decision that the police would assist the fascists by clearing a path through to the platform, if necessary, giving several reasons. One was that inaction on behalf of the police would only inflame the fascist propaganda that free speech was unattainable in this country. He also compared the situation to May Day demonstrations and insisted that the police would not allow that to be obstructed by Labour supporters. Finally, he added that if the police did not act to prevent the anti-fascists from surrounding the fascist platform, then serious disorder may occur. Regardless of this, Newsam remained opposed to direct police involvement and argued that any view that the police were facilitating the fascists arriving at their platforms may only precipitate disorder.[70]

The debate between the Home Office and Lord Trenchard over how to police the demonstration at Hyde Park demonstrated the scope of discretion available with the competing potential outcomes considered. Despite the view that police facilitation of the BUF meeting would inflame anti-fascist protesters,

---

68 HO 45/25383, 'Remember Olympia' and 'A Woman Tells of Fascist Terror'.
69 HO 45/25383, F. Newsam, Home Office report, 7 Sep 1934.
70 Ibid.

Trenchard's tactic succeeded and the Hyde Park meeting itself passed without serious incident. The problem of anti-fascists crowding the BUF platform was averted by a cordon of police who kept the area clear. The Special Branch report acknowledged that while the opposing meetings were in progress, speakers from each meeting urged their supporters not to go to each other's meeting. It was also reported that all of the anti-fascist speakers, located at four points around Hyde Park, emphasised that 'the counter-demonstration had not been organised as a display of violence, but to show a mass working class opposition to fascism.'[71] The BUF held five separate speaking platforms in Hyde Park until Mosley's address, when the separate audiences congregated together around platform four to hear him speak. It was also recorded that the noise generated by the booing and singing made it impossible for anybody outside of the police cordon to hear the speeches. The majority of the 20,000 audience members were hostile to the BUF. The total number of those who attended Hyde Park was estimated to have been 100,000–150,000.[72] At the close of the proceedings, the police cleared a way through the crowd and escorted the BUF members back to their headquarters, while a crowd of 3,000 followed the procession and booed the Blackshirts. The police then dispersed the crowd and no arrests were made. In Hyde Park, eighteen arrests were made for offences including using insulting words or behaviour, obstructing the police and assault.

Newspaper reportage highlighted the use of new technology utilised by the police. The *Western Morning News* reported that a police autogyro hovered at 1,500 feet for observational purposes and police cars 'fitted with wireless' circled the crowd.[73] There was also significant praise for the police operation. The *Western Daily Press* claimed that the demonstrations passed off peaceably enough, not because of the conduct of the demonstrators, but because of the police, 'who were present in sufficient force to overawe the unruly and quell any incipient attempt to create disorder'.[74]

At the Marlborough Street Police Court the following day, the eighteen charges were heard by the magistrate, Boyd. One significant charge was brought against a fascist who allegedly threw a stone at a police officer which struck him below the eye. The fascist, Hugh Hare, an actor, directed his evidence towards the police officer in question and enquired, 'Did it occur to you that I was giving the fascist salute?' and 'Do I look like the type of person who would wantonly throw a stone?' Following the evidence of Hare and others, Boyd was satisfied that there had been a mistake and Hare was discharged. Another fascist, Thomas Collins, was treated more seriously by Boyd. Following a guilty plea on the charge of using insulting words and behaviour, the magistrate said that to impose a fine would be ridiculous

---

71 HO 45/25383, Disturbances: Anti-fascist activities; anti-fascist demonstrations and activities directed against meeting of the British Union of Fascists in Hyde Park on 9 Sept 1934 (1929–1934).
72 *The Daily Express*, 10 Sep 1934.
73 *Western Morning News*, 10 Sep 1934.
74 *Western Daily Press*, 11 Sep 1934.

and bound him over for twelve months with a surety of £10.[75] The newspaper reports do not declare the political allegiance of Collins, but the Special Branch report claimed him to be the same Thomas Collins who was arrested during the Suffolk Tithe dispute and was convicted with nineteen other members of the BUF for conspiring together to effect an act of public mischief.[76] Interestingly, he was bound over for two years following this charge, but the binding-over order was not mentioned by Boyd following the Hyde Park demonstration.

The Home Office files reveal the tension between Trenchard, Gilmour and Newsam on how to police the fascist event. The tactics utilised by the police to ensure public order were successful and achieved the praise of the press. Newsam's concern that if the police actively aided the fascists it would precipitate disorder did not materialise. Yet the event proved to be a useful propaganda tool for the anti-fascists' claims of pro-fascist police partiality. The communist newspaper, the *Daily Worker*, used the police operation at Hyde Park to demonstrate political bias of the authorities:

> The British Union of Fascists carries on its activities only by gracious permission of Lord Trenchard and His Majesty's Government . . . Mosley was only able to appear in Hyde Park because the entire London police was mobilised in his defence. For every Blackshirt there were three or four policemen.[77]

From the Home Office discussions in preparation of the fascist and anti-fascist rallies at Hyde Park, the conflict in defining appropriate police tactics was a delicate balancing act. The main element of negotiations was to reduce the risk of disorder, although this involved ensuring the fascists were not prevented from holding their meeting. It was also considered vital that the police action did not give fuel to fascist or communist propaganda. Yet in their desire to avoid fascist criticism that free speech was unattainable, it became inevitable that communist propaganda would criticise the police for being pro-fascist. The large-scale events allowed the authorities the time to organise police tactics, liaise with the respective groups and make contingency plans in the event of anticipated disorder. Yet around the country Blackshirts took to the soap boxes on a regular basis to attract the attention of local residents and passers-by. The responses by different police officers on the spot varied between the regions and questions the extent to which free speech was attainable.

Plymouth 1934: 'Go on boys, get stuck into them.'[78]

The typical image of Blackshirt meetings, as portrayed by BUF propaganda, is of fascist speakers lawfully endeavouring to attain a hearing amid the organised

---

75 *Nottingham Evening Post*, 10 Sep 1934.
76 HO 45/25383.
77 *Daily Worker*, 22 Sep 1934.
78 *News Chronicle*, 19 Nov 1934.

disruption of a minority of communists. Although disruption was commonplace at fascist meetings, it was not always organised, and in turn, the behaviour of the fascists was not always lawful. At a meeting in Plymouth Market Square on 11 October 1934, the actions of four Blackshirts resulted in them being charged at the City Police Court. Three of the defendants – William McIntye, George Clarke and Kenneth Davis – were found guilty of committing a breach of the peace and assault. They were sentenced to six weeks hard labour. A fourth defendant, Michael Goulding, who was the speaker at the meeting, had his charge of inciting a breach of the peace dismissed.

It was reported that twenty Blackshirts arrived at the Market Square in a closed van on 11 October when a Trades and Labour Council meeting was already in progress. The crowd was estimated by one witness to have been 7,000–8,000 strong.[79] McIntyre, Clarke and Davis were in plain clothes and walked amongst the audience. Giving evidence, police officer Mitchell stated that Goulding spoke on the roof of the van, surrounded by Blackshirts for ten minutes. The crowd remained noisy. Goulding then instructed McIntyre, Clarke and Davis to attack the crowd by raising his hand and commanding, 'Go on, boys, get stuck into them'.[80] Mitchell then described how the three fascists then struck out and hit anyone within their reach. Other statements describe the particularly brutal nature of the attacks. Chief Constable William Johnson stated that one man, who was struck several times, rushed into the doorway of Woolworths where he was 'further knocked about until he was in a state of collapse'.[81] The three fascists wore insulating tape around their knuckles and all admitted to having reputations as competent boxers. They claimed that they expected disorder and the tape would protect their 'fragile' hands. In the witness box, Police Superintendent Hutchings stated that the tape would 'increase the force of a blow [as the tape would] harden through perspiration'.[82]

It was alleged that Goulding attempted to join in the disorder after giving his instruction but was stopped by the police. For the defence, barrister Fearnley-Whittingstall argued that the disorder started after a brick thrown from the crowd narrowly missed Goulding and a man struck Davis on the back. The provocation towards the fascists was not enough justification for the assaults committed by McIntyre, Clarke and Davis. The presiding magistrate ruled:

> [W]e have no doubt that they came to Plymouth that night with the intention of fighting – at any rate, prepared to do so – on the least provocation. In addition, it has to be remembered that they were all expert boxers . . . Conduct of this sort cannot be tolerated in this city[.][83]

79 *Western Morning News*, 17 Nov 1934.
80 *Western Gazette*, 23 Nov 1934.
81 *Western Morning News*, 13 Oct 1934.
82 *Western Evening Herald*, 16 Oct 1934.
83 *Western Morning News*, 17 Oct 1934.

This incident highlights the trouble that the BUF had in attaining a hearing at public meetings. It also demonstrates the competition for public space. In this case, the Trades Union meeting was already in progress when the Blackshirts arrived. As there was no way of reserving public space, the competing movements could easily hinder each other's meetings. At Plymouth, the police used their discretion to allow the fascists the opportunity to address the public, despite an opposing political meeting already being in progress. Although this action promoted the values of free speech, the jeers, catcalls and singing from the crowd which hindered the Blackshirt meeting also prevented the trade union meeting from continuing. The *Western Independent*, which was critical of fascism, declared that the 'right to freedom of speech was being denied by the holding of these meetings not by their banning'.[84] Yet as soon as disorder occurred, the police responded quickly and the BUF meeting was closed. The Trade Unionists were said to have 'remained quiescent on their rostrum' during the Blackshirt disturbance and 'composedly resumed their speeches' when the fascists had vacated their position.[85] Different public meetings, such as the pre-planned large scale demonstrations at Hyde Park (which was governed by the Home Office and the Metropolitan Police Commissioner) and more spontaneous street-corner meetings (regulated by the police officer on the spot) both present distinct challenges for the maintenance of public order. However, one constant is always present: how do the police prioritise the competing demands of both the speaker and the heckler for the liberty of free speech?

Freedom of speech for the speaker or the heckler?

At public meetings, both the speaker and the heckler claim that they are entitled to share their views. Yet does the claim for free speech refer to the freedom to attain a hearing free from interruption or the freedom to speak unconditionally and without consequence?

While it could be argued that fascist speakers incited disorder or encouraged violence through provocative and anti-Semitic speeches, it appears more common that it was audience members who heckled and showed their contempt for fascism to end up before a magistrate. One incident was reported in *The Times*. At Leytonstone, Greater London, Joseph Bennett, a bookshop manager, shouted 'Go back to Germany and eat German sausage' and 'Fascism means hunger and war' at a BUF meeting.[86] In the opinion of the Metropolitan Police, this was likely to cause a breach of the peace: the heckler was arrested and marched to the police station. At Stratford Police Court, the defendant denied that he intended to break up the meeting but simply wished to express his disapproval of fascist principles, which he declared he was entitled to do. If it was found that his intention was to break up

---

84 T. Gray, *Blackshirts in Devon*, The Mint Press: Exeter (2006), p. 73. Gray's summary from the *Western Independent*, 14 Oct 1934.
85 *Western Independent*, 14 Oct 1934.
86 *The Times*, 22 Oct 1934.

the meeting then he could have been fined a maximum of £5 or up to one month imprisonment under the Public Meetings Act 1908. Bennett was charged with using insulting words contrary to s54 Metropolitan Police Act 1839 and was subsequently fined 40 shillings with an additional £2 and two shillings costs. The use of s54 here demonstrates a departure from the provisions original mandate discussed above.

At an outdoor BUF meeting at the Plymouth Market in February 1934, the *Western Morning News* reported that the BUF area propaganda officer, Arthur Cann, was subject to 'constant interruption, and many unpolite and unprintable remarks', and the 'majority of the three hundred or so who attended the meeting made every possible endeavour to drown Cann's voice with their constant jeers'. The meeting was well attended by the police, and despite the disruption and the local newspaper's claim that the 'hecklers became so persistent that a clash between the Socialist element and the Blackshirt guard which surrounded the lorry seemed imminent' the police did not interfere with the verbal disturbance of the meeting.[87] This is arguably an example of good police practice: although angry words were exchanged, physical hostility did not did materialise and order was kept.

In contrast to the incident at Leytonstone, the exact nature of the heckling at the Plymouth meeting was not reported, and the reader is left to reflect on what the 'unprintable remarks' were. The question that separates these two examples is, at what point should the police act to prevent a breach of the peace? As the actions used by the police in both of these examples were lawful it demonstrates the extent of police discretion in deciding when and when not to act. It also establishes how police practice can vary between provincial forces, which reveals inconsistencies in law enforcement between different regions.

A further option available to the police was to arrest the speaker, yet this happened less frequently at fascist meetings than at the meetings of the far Left. At one meeting in London, known Jew baiter and auctioneer John Penfold was arrested to avert serious disorder after he stated, 'The Jews are taking this country from us by their filthy methods and sweated labour. They are nothing more than usurers and parasites.' He continued to call for the removal of Jews from England.[88] At the Old Street Police Court, Police Constable Gibbs stated that Penfold was addressing 250 people. When the crowd became hostile and started to move towards Penfold, Gibbs stated that he arrested Penfold because he saw that 'a very grave disorder was about to take place.'[89] Penfold claimed that the prosecution was instigated by the Jews. He stated that he was against the magistrate hearing his case and wanted the case to be committed to twelve of 'his countrymen'. The magistrate, Mr F. O. Langley, fined Penfold 40 shillings and ordered him to find a surety of £50 to be of good behaviour for twelve months.

These three responses demonstrate the general range of the police officer's actions at public meetings. Police discretion could be used against the speaker or the heckler, or the officer could decide not to interfere. However, it can be

87 *Western Morning News*, 9 Feb 1934.
88 *Nottingham Evening Post*, 28 Aug 1936.
89 *Western Morning News*, 29 Aug 1936.

questioned whether the arrest of Joseph Bennett for the comments made during the BUF meeting at Leytonstone were appropriate and proportionate. Bennett believed that he was 'entitled' to demonstrate his disapproval of the speaker's principles.[90] Although heckling was usually tolerated at outdoor meetings, police discretion was used to take action when it was anticipated that the words or actions of a heckler were thought to result in a breach of the peace. These discretionary powers were also employed to prevent speakers such as Penfold from addressing a meeting if it was anticipated that it would lead to a breach of the peace. However, the law relating to breaches of the peace was significantly wide to leave police officers on the spot to rely on their discretion in each individual situation. The police tactics of monitoring and surveillance employed at Plymouth ensured that freedom of expression was maintained. Police presence, rather than police action, was enough to ensure that public safety was preserved.

Nevertheless, Ewing and Gearty's claim that BUF speakers were shown a 'remarkable indulgence by the police' must be recognised and the reasons for this considered.[91] It has already been argued that official BUF activism promoted lawful behaviour and the obedience of its members to police instruction. Yet the abhorrent use of anti-Semitism as a political policy presents a more difficult proposition for the frequent use of inaction by the police at fascist meetings. Thurlow has highlighted that there were difficulties in prosecuting anti-Semitic speakers because the 'fascists had developed the technique of criticizing the Jewish people as a whole rather than those present at meetings'.[92] The use of police discretion to act against BUF speakers was therefore impeded by the knowledge that the chance of a successful prosecution was minimal. Indeed, even the 1936 prosecution of the fanatical anti-Semite Arnold Leese of the Imperial Fascist League, who had printed offensive and antagonistic attacks on the Jews, must be seen as a failure as he was acquitted of the most serious charges.[93]

The Director of Public Prosecutions (DPP) needs to consider various factors other than the express enforcing of the law. For example, former BUF member A. K. Chesterton was not prosecuted after he directed threatening comments towards the Jews as the authorities wanted to avoid giving his small far-Right movement, the Nordic League, any publicity.[94] Also, when Leese published another anti-Semitic article, titled *My Irrelevant Defence*, on his release from jail he was not charged because 'a further acquittal might be misunderstood by the public'.[95] The decision making process at all levels of the criminal justice system therefore relies on a variety of factors and is inevitably more complex than

---

90 *The Times*, 22 Oct 1934.
91 Ewing and Gearty, *The Struggle*, p. 329.
92 Thurlow, *The Secret State*, p. 190.
93 See Thurlow, *The Secret State*, pp. 194–195, and I. Channing, *Blackshirts and White Wigs: Reflections on Public Order Law and the Political Activism of the British Union of Fascists*, unpublished PhD thesis, Plymouth University (2014), pp. 174–176.
94 Thurlow, *The Secret State*, p. 195.
95 Ibid.

understanding police action as overtly pro-fascist. Ewing and Gearty criticise the police, stating that there was 'fragrant discrimination against the Left . . . [While the police] were prepared to go to considerable lengths to protect the freedom of the fascists'.[96] Yet this chapter has highlighted the difficulties in achieving a successful prosecution of fascists whose methods of activism are calculatingly conscious of legal boundaries. In contrast, although Ewing and Gearty present a valuable argument for the political discrimination of the Left in this period, the confrontational methods that the Left frequently employed against the police and their frequent promotion of unlawful practices presented extensive reasons for legal action. In addition to the differences in the methods of activism utilised by the far Left and far Right, it must also be remembered that the BUF were not seen as a threat to national security until 1940. In this respect, Thurlow states the BUF were 'an irritant . . . not a serious threat to the establishment'.[97]

Policing communist activism

Communists and seditious publications

In a significant case at the Central Criminal Court in 1933, four communists were charged with conspiring to seduce soldiers from their duty and allegiance to his Majesty. The four Welsh minors had attempted to distribute *The Soldier's Voice*, a newsletter described as the organ of the Communist Soldiers, to servicemen at Newport Barracks. It was argued for the defence that communists had as much right to express their views as anybody else. Although this was not an isolated case regarding communists distributing potentially seditious material,[98] its importance lies in the definition of the limitations of freedom of speech offered by Humphreys J. He stated that people were at liberty to say that the constitution should be changed, that we should have a Republic, or any other kind of Government, as long as

> he does not offend against the law nobody can stop him. What persons cannot do, of course, is in the course of criticisms or suggestions to alter the constitution or the law to advise that they should be done by force or terrorism.[99]

Humphreys dismissed suggestions that the prosecution was based upon the police or the DPP's dislike of the Communist Party as 'ridiculous'. The judgment relied on whether the communists advocated changes by constitutional means, if so then suppression via a criminal prosecution must fail. If they were found guilty of offences against the Incitement to Mutiny Act 1797, their membership of any

---

96 Ewing and Gearty, *The Struggle*, p. 329.
97 Thurlow, *Fascism in Britain*, p. 75.
98 For other examples of communist sedition and the background of the resulting Incitement to Disaffection Act 1934, see Ewing and Gearty, *The Struggle*, chapter five, and C. Andrew, *The Defence of the Realm: The Authorised History of MI5*, Penguin: London (2009), chapter two.
99 *Hull Daily Mail*, 14 Mar 1933.

particular political party was immaterial. All four men were found guilty. Their individual punishments ranged from twelve months hard labour to three years penal servitude.[100]

The activities of extreme communists were treated seriously by the authorities because offences, such as sedition and incitement to violence, were perceived as threats to national security. Communist publications made frequent calls for a class-based civil war. In May 1932, *The Soldiers' Voice* claimed, 'Let us use the knowledge of arms which they give us, when the opportunity presents itself, to overthrow their rule, and, in unity with our fellow-workers, to establish a free Socialist Britain.' In May 1933, the *Red Signal*, the organ for communist sailors, exclaimed, 'If war does come, then it must be turned into a civil war against the capitalist warmongers and their bankrupt system.'[101] These examples were given by the Attorney General during the second reading of the Incitement to Disaffection Bill, and concern was raised that the outcome of recent prosecutions of distributers had the effect of driving the chief offenders underground, which created a 'somewhat sly and almost skulking breed of inciter . . . [that] are too shy or too cowardly to put their names and addresses to the literature which they are in the habit of producing'.[102]

The Trenchard ban and Duncan v Jones[103]

In November 1931, Lord Trenchard issued instructions that forbade public meetings that were held in close proximity to employment exchanges. The Home Secretary defended this action in Parliament, stating: 'recent experience has shown that meetings held in such circumstances are liable to lead to breaches of the peace. There has been in the past, and there still is, ample opportunity for holding meetings elsewhere.'[104] Following these instructions, meetings all over the Metropolitan Police District were broken up by police, some ending in serious disorder.[105] The legal authority that Trenchard used to make this order was vague. Even in the House of Commons, Labour MP and barrister Denis Pritt declared that the ban was

> wrapped in obscurity and secrecy that it is almost as difficult to discover what it is, as it is to discover what are the decrees of the Nazi Government . . . [adding] Lord Trenchard had no more right to do that than I had. He had no right at all, and no sort or kind of justification.[106]

The ban was reminiscent of Warren's prohibition of meetings in Trafalgar Square in the 1880s. A major difference in this scenario, however, was that in

---

100 Ibid.
101 *Hansard, HC Deb*, 16 Apr 1934, vol 288 c742.
102 Ibid. c740.
103 *Duncan v Jones*.
104 *Hansard, HC Deb*, 2 Dec 1931, vol 260 cc1088.
105 *The Times*, 28 Nov 1931.
106 *Hansard HC, Deb* 10 July 1936, vol 314 c1551.

Ex Parte Lewis, it was established that an Act of Parliament had given the power to the Commissioners of Works to declare how the space at Trafalgar Square shall be used. Disregarding this technicality, Wills J had reversed the onus on Lewis to provide that there was a right to public assembly. As Lewis failed to provide this, Wills J concluded that there were no grounds for charging the Metropolitan Police Commissioner or the Home Secretary with a criminal conspiracy or misconduct. Despite criticism of the Trenchard ban from the NCCL, a legal challenge to this authoritarian response to disorder also failed.

Katherine Duncan, a member of the NUWM, attempted to hold a meeting outside a training centre in 1934. Inspector Jones requested that she moved her meeting. On refusing and continuing to speak she was arrested and charged with obstructing the police in the execution of their duty. The NCCL sponsored her failed appeals to the London Quarter Sessions and the Divisional Court. At the Divisional Court, the appellant was represented by Labour MP Denis Pritt KC and Liberal MP Dingle Foot; both were vice-chairmen of the NCCL. They argued that it was not unlawful to hold a public meeting on the highway and that the police officer was not acting 'in the execution of his duty' when he was obstructed by Mrs Duncan.[107] Citing *Beatty v Gillbanks*,[108] he continued to argue that the appellant could not be found guilty of a legal act because of the apprehended illegal actions of others.

Lord Chief Justice Hewart dismissed the appeal and clarified that there was no 'right' to public assembly, and it was 'nothing more than a view taken by the Court of the individual liberty of the subject'.[109] He concluded that the policeman was acting within the execution of his duty and, therefore, the appellant did wilfully obstruct the respondent. He dismissed the appeal. Pritt raised the issue in the Commons, stating that 'it is extremely easy for the police to take repressive measures and find that often they are approved of by the courts.'[110] Thomas Kidd argued that the decision established a precedent:

> [T]he police have power to ban any political meeting in streets or public places at will . . . [and are arbiters] of what political parties and religious sects shall and shall not be accorded the rights of freedom of speech and freedom of assembly – two civil rights which even the judges of earlier times were jealous to protect.[111]

The judicial support for the authoritarian and preventative police tactics highlighted in *Duncan v Jones*[112] and other leading cases of this era such as *Thomas v Sawkins*[113] subsequently strengthened the Breach of the Peace powers utilised by

107 *Duncan v Jones*.
108 *Beatty v Gillbanks* [1881–1882] LR 9 QBD 308.
109 *Duncan v Jones* at 222.
110 *Hansard, HC Deb*, 10 Jul 1936, vol 314 c1561.
111 Kidd, *British Liberty*, p. 24.
112 *Duncan v Jones* [1936] 1 KB 218.
113 *Thomas v Sawkins* [1935] 2 KB 249 (see chapter seven).

the police, widening the parameters of their discretion and providing more opportunity for partial or inconsistent police practice.

The baton charge at Thurloe Square 1936

Thomas Kidd was also at the heart of another incident involving the police treatment of an anti-fascist meeting at Thurloe Square, London. The protest was a response to a BUF meeting held in Albert Hall on 22 March 1936. The anti-fascists assembled half a mile away from Albert Hall, in accordance with an instruction from the Metropolitan Police Commissioner. After the meeting had been in progress for fifty minutes, twenty police officers arrived, some mounted and others on foot. They allegedly proceeded to disperse the crowd without warning, using batons and staves. Following several allegations about police behaviour, Dingle Foot pressed the Government to open an official enquiry. The Home Secretary, Sir John Simon, declared that there was no need for an enquiry and highlighted that the crowd had formed a cordon around the meeting – meaning that the police could not approach the chairman to request that he close the meeting.[114] The NCCL held an unofficial commission of inquiry which they hoped would bring the evidence to the public and induce Simon to order an official inquiry. This approach failed, but the findings recorded that the 'crowd was perfectly peaceable and orderly' and the police would have had no difficulty in approaching the speakers. More significantly, it reported that the crowd offered no resistance to the police:

> [T]here was no necessity whatever for a baton-charge, that the baton-charge was carried out with a totally unnecessary degree of brutality and violence, that serious injuries were caused and that fatal injuries might have been caused.[115]

The responses of the Home Office and the Metropolitan Police to the NCCL's call for an inquiry has been carefully analysed by historian Janet Clark. She noted the contempt that Sir Philip Game had for the organisation. This is illustrated by his opinion of the NCCL as 'a self-constituted body with no authority or statutory powers, whose principal activity is to criticise and attack the police'. He responded to the report of the inquiry by declaring, '[a] more biased judgement I have never read'.[116] Clark highlights that for the Home Office, Sir Arthur Dixon was more sympathetic to the report, and declared that despite its 'one-sidedness . . . the report seems to me to give evidence of careful preparation and to merit careful consideration'.[117] Despite the friction highlighted by Clark between the Home Office and Game, it was agreed that a public inquiry would not be held as the report had 'elicited no new facts of importance'.[118]

114 *Hansard, HC Deb*, 25 Mar 1936, vol 310 cc1361–1378.
115 Kidd, *British Liberty*, p. 130.
116 Clark, *Striving to Preserve the Peace*, p. 185.
117 Ibid., p. 184.
118 Ibid., p. 186.

Although the catalyst for the introduction of the Public Order Bill was the disorder at Cable Street described in chapter four, provisions were also established that were directed towards the conduct and behaviour at public meetings which expanded on the existing provisions to restrain freedom of speech.

Public Order Bill 1936

Several provisions were introduced in the Public Order Bill which created or amended certain offences in relation to public meetings. When Sir John Simon read the Bill a second time on 16 November, he stressed that the object of the Bill was not to legislate against anybody's creed, or to distinguish from one extreme creed or another, but to legislate against the new methods that had recently been adopted by some movements. However, political violence and disturbances were not new to British political meetings. This was recognised by Sir John Simon, who stated that there was 'plenty of noise and roughness in our political methods, but this roughness and this noise have been on the whole tolerant and good humoured'. In the following debate, this view was challenged by those whose experiences of political 'roughness' were neither tolerable nor good humoured.

The most detailed account came from Conservative MP, Commander Bower, who suffered the organised break-up of his meetings by Labour Party supporters in his constituency of Cleveland in North Riding. This included the use of abusive language, the smashing of windows and the breaking of chairs. In addition, female supporters were kicked and clods of earth were thrown at the speakers. He also mentioned that he was physically attacked on stage and his speaker system was damaged.[119] Labour MP for Hackney South, Herbert Morrison recounted his amazement of the 'dangerous vigour' about his public meetings in Cornwall, in which he had to mind his step. He continued to state that he had been shouted down and threatened with violence by Tories, and that the actions of the Communists were notorious.[120] Despite the primary concern of fascist violence, there was a prevailing attitude that the Bill needed to protect the political speakers and prevent all organised public disruption of political meetings. Commander Bower believed the Bill did not successfully tackle this, as he stated, 'This hooliganism has gone on far too long, and I am afraid there is nothing in this Bill which will put an end to it.'[121] In summing up the debate, the Attorney General revisited the question and declared, 'there is no doubt about the feeling which has been voiced on all sides of the House that the organised cold-blooded and persistent interruption of meetings is something to be reprehended.'[122]

William Gallacher made an important distinction between the propaganda of the Left and the significance of the BUF in the East End. Being politically provocative,

---

119 *Hansard, HC Deb*, 16 Nov 1936, vol 317 c1403.
120 Ibid. at c1455.
121 Ibid. at c1404.
122 Ibid. at c1471.

he claimed, was an essential feature of the United Kingdom, but using abusive or insulting language directed at racial or religious sections of the community was entirely different. He stated that the police already had powers to deal with that, but they should be increased if necessary.[123] Thus, it can be determined that the division between these different uses of provocative language was an important factor in framing legislation which would effectively restrict freedom of speech. Yet while the general debate is about how to impose conditions on the British fascists at their meetings, many arguments, including those mentioned earlier, also demonstrate politicians' desire to protect their own political meetings from disruption by political opponents. Political violence, therefore, was not completely marginalised to the radical doctrines of the fascists and the communists – it still played a role in mainstream politics despite the increasing intolerance towards it.

Clause 5 created an offence for any person who in any public place or at any public meeting used threatening, abusive or insulting words or behaviour with intent to provoke a breach of the peace, or whereby a breach of the peace is likely to be occasioned. The only amendment in the wording from s54(13) Metropolitan Police Act 1839 was to change 'in any thoroughfare or public place' to 'any public place or at any public meeting'. This change extended the power of the police to public meetings, which by definition would also include those held on private premises.[124] The 1936 Act introduced the charge of insulting words or behaviour to the whole nation as it had previously existed in London under the 1839 Act only, and in some larger towns and cities under local Acts. Ronald Kidd claimed the Metropolitan Police referred to this power as 'the breathing Act' because to get a conviction under it was 'as easy as breathing'.[125]

The police, anti-Semitism and the Public Order Act

In his report for the year 1937, the Metropolitan Police Commissioner, Sir Philip Game, declared that the Public Order Act 1936 had 'a good effect on the conduct of political meetings . . . but has not reduced their number . . . [asserting] 11,804 meetings and processions have had to be policed, over 7,000 of which were Fascist or anti-Fascist'.[126] However, the Public Order Act did not eliminate anti-Semitic remarks at public meetings, frequent assaults on Jews or the vandalism of their property. Following the London County Council (LCC) elections of March 1937, the secretary of the Jewish People's Council (JPC), J. Pearce, declared in a memorandum sent to the NCCL that the 'Public Order Act as can be seen from the violent anti-Jewish campaign had failed', and had suggested that agitation must now be focused on the demand for a Racial Incitement Bill.[127] The NCCL had recommended an amendment

---

123 *Hansard, HC Deb*, 23 Nov 1936, vol 318 c73.
124 See chapter seven for police powers in relation to public meetings on private premises.
125 Kidd, *British Liberty*, p. 74.
126 Cmd. 5761, *Report of the Commissioner of Police of the Metropolis for the Year 1937*, p. 12.
127 U DCL/75/2, Duplicated circulars issued by NCCL (1937–1938).

to s5 which would have provided that, 'any person who in any public place or at any public meeting uses words calculated to bring any racial or religious community into public hatred or contempt, would be guilty of an offence.'[128]

This agitation was the result of an increasingly violent BUF campaign in East London ahead of the LCC elections. Fascists in East London were reported to have smashed the windows of Jewish-owned shops and chalked anti-Semitic propaganda on walls. The BUF polled 15,278 votes, which amounted to 18% of the poll. The JPC were concerned that their anti-Semitic propaganda could mobilise enough support to return a fascist candidate in the Borough Council elections in November 1937.[129] During BUF public meetings, it was claimed that no attempt was made by the police to stop speakers from Jew baiting, despite this being a clear violation of s5 Public Order Act. A transcript of the BUF's first public meeting following the LCC elections, held at Bethnal Green on 12 March 1937, illustrates the language used by fascist speakers. The first speaker addressed the need to keep on fighting against the Jewish interest, stating, 'We have given the Jews notice to quit and next we'll see the Jews clear out altogether.' BUF candidate Raven Thomson claimed that the number of votes that the BUF received gave them a mandate for their policy based on anti-Semitism. He claimed that Mosley could then claim that he was not a fanatical anti-Semite, and that he was not speaking for himself but a significant section of the population. He continued his attack on the Jews by commenting,

> Here's a British people today, to all intents and purposes lying in a ditch and lousy with Jews. (Police Constable and crowd laughed). The Jew can no more help being a parasite than a louse can be a louse . . . We can't altogether ignore the Jew . . . We will hold him up as a horrible example.[130]

At this time the NCCL was collecting transcripts of fascist speeches and highlighting their perception of a pro-fascist police force which took little or no action against fascist speakers while arresting anti-fascist hecklers or left-wing speakers. An NCCL report from August 1937 entitled 'Disturbances in East London' quoted other fascist speakers as referring to Jews as, 'Hook-nosed, yellow-skinned, dirty Jewish swine' and 'Venereal-ridden vagrants'.[131] Again, no action was taken by the police in relation to these speeches. In a witness statement, collected by the NCCL in relation to police behaviour at a fascist meeting in Stepney Green on 14 July 1937, Alfred Levy described how he was chased by a man in plain clothes who said, 'Get away you Jew bastard', and then he was caught and assaulted by several police officers who threw him into the back of a van. Levy claimed that he was stood at the back of the crowd talking to a friend when the incident took

---

128 Ibid., 'Repressive Tendencies in Recent Legislation in Great Britain', NCCL notes from International Conference held in Paris July 1937, on the curtailment of principles of liberty by recent legislation in certain democratic countries.
129 Ibid.
130 Ibid.
131 Ibid., 'Disturbances in East London'.

place. He stated that he was accused by the police of being a machine gunner.[132] When the police van started to move, he alleged that he heard someone in the van say, 'run these f—— Jews down if they don't get out of the way.' Another statement by local resident Leonard Arundoli remarked that the crowd, measuring many hundreds, were hostile to the fascist speakers and 'indignant that these people should be allowed to come to Stepney Green and preach this racial hatred, protected by the police'.[133] The police later cleared the crowd with a baton charge under the orders of an unnamed inspector, despite many witness statements collected by the NCCL which claimed that the crowd was orderly and that the police took an aggressive stance towards hecklers.[134]

These allegations that the police used anti-Semitic language and laughed at a fascist's Jew baiting at a public meeting raise worrying questions about partiality in the police force. At the higher levels of the police, the successive Metropolitan Police Commissioners, Trenchard and Game, were both outspoken in their desire to suppress the fascist movement. Yet, at street level, disturbing allegations highlight huge inconsistencies in police practice that support the assertion that many members of the police were pro-fascist, anti-Left and even anti-Semitic. However, these accusations must be seen against the wider picture of extreme political activity in Great Britain.

In the Metropolitan Police district alone, there were over 7,000 fascist or antifascist meetings held in 1937.[135] In consideration of the large number of meetings held in the first year of the Public Order Act, events such as this with such strong accusations of police impropriety must be seen as isolated incidents rather than reflecting any normality in their practice. To substantiate this claim, consideration must also be given to how the police were also active in invoking their new legislative powers on BUF speakers in order to limit fascist provocation. Thus, selecting a wider range of sources has the potential to dispel notions of a prevalent police culture of political partiality in favour of the BUF which has been argued by Ewing and Gearty. When considering the nature of police discretion, and the necessarily subjective decisions that police make, other factors in the decision making process are also influential. Therefore, it is not always correct to assume that political partiality is the prime component. While it is important to recognise that some police officers did have fascist or anti-Semitic dispositions, which were reflected in their failure to fulfil their duty impartially, this does not inevitably mean that all police action taken against anti-fascists or communists was politically motivated.

There were arrests of fascist speakers following the Public Order Act which offer some validation that police practice was inconsistent rather than politically motivated. Section 5 was a loosely defined provision which was open to wide discretion. The term 'threatening, abusive or insulting language or behaviour' is

---

132 This was a reference to the Spanish Civil War; Levy did not deny that he had fought in Spain.
133 HHC, U DCL/75/2, 'Police Behaviour in Stepney Green'.
134 Ibid.
135 Cmd. 5761, *Report of the commissioner of police of the metropolis for the year 1937.*

open to interpretation, but it is even more subjective to determine whether language may cause a breach of the peace or was even calculated to cause a breach of the peace.

Inspector James' report from a fascist meeting held on 23 June 1937, again in Bethnal Green, illustrates how the police operation was managed. James was present with one sergeant and ten constables, whom he positioned around the outskirts of the crowd. One constable was stationed near the platform next to a shorthand writer from Special Branch who was taking a transcript of the meeting. The constable could relay information on any provocative language used to James, who roamed the back of the crowd assessing the possibility of a breach of the peace. James' report described the fascist speaker, Earnest Clarke, as 'not a very loud speaker' who usually relied on a loudspeaker van to be heard. On this occasion, the inspector claimed that it was difficult for him to distinctly hear what was said. James' report acknowledged the transcript taken by the shorthand writer, and he declared that he had heard some of what was said but stated that no action was taken against Clarke as the crowd was predominantly fascist sympathisers and were quiet and orderly throughout. He stated that there were no Jews present and no sign of a breach of the peace taking place, adding:

> I am of the opinion that had an arrest been made at this meeting, the crowd would have undoubtedly have become disorderly and the police present would not have been sufficiently strong to have maintained order . . . [He continued to acknowledge a change in tactics since this incident] Since the recent Memorandum on Public Meetings was issued, I have occupied a stationary position alongside the Shorthand Writer, close to the Speakers platform, and all speakers before taking the platform have been cautioned by me against the use of insulting or provocative language.[136]

The Sub-Divisional Inspector added his knowledge of the fascist speaker Clarke, stating that, 'when speaking, [he] closely watches the movements of the Inspector present at his meeting and, in the event of the inspector's attention being distracted from him, seizes the opportunity to attack the Jews.' The Superintendent's report claims that he had attended a large number of Clarke's meetings and 'if a senior officer is present he invariably is informed and moderates his speech accordingly.' The reports demonstrate the difficulty faced when policing fascist meetings. Two days later, Clarke again spoke at Bethnal Green, where he excited the fascist crowd with anti-Semitic remarks, who responded with shouts of 'Jewish scum' and 'Shonks'. Clarke moderated his speech when the inspector began to approach him, but he later made more anti-Semitic references, and was then arrested by an inspector and Sergeant Duncan. The crowd rushed towards the platform and Duncan drew his truncheon, but he did not need to use it. Clarke was taken in the police car and charged under s5. Following Clarke's arrest the

136   MEPO 2/3115, Fascist: provoking a breach of peace with insulting words (1937)

meeting became disorderly and the fascist speaker who followed him could not regain order. The meeting was then closed on the request of the police. It was stated that 150 fascists made their way to the local communist meeting, which created tension. Anticipating a breach of the peace, that meeting was also closed on the request of the police. Another fascist, Henry Burwood, was also arrested for using insulting words and behaviour.

Clarke was later convicted at Old Street Police Court with the evidence of Police Constable Templeman of Special Branch, who took the notes at the meeting on 23 June. In his judgment, the magistrate, Herbert Metcalfe, declared, 'on this occasion you used language of the most gross, insulting, and disgraceful character, language which, from the very word "go", was calculated to insult, not merely the people who were there, but other people.'[137] This conviction was also to have implications for Inspector James, who was present at the meeting on 23 June. In the defence's summing up it was claimed that the meeting 'was so orderly that the uniform police made no attempt to stop the meeting at any time'. The failure of James to take more appropriate action at the meeting was taken seriously by the Deputy Assistant Commissioner. James's report, which mistakenly stated that no inflammatory language was used, was deemed by his superiors to have demonstrated neglect to his duty and he received an official caution. It is likely that James was also on duty at previous fascist meetings, and other speakers may have exploited his 'neglect'. However, James' report, and the tactics he employed at the fascist meeting in question, demonstrates that his priority was in preventing a disturbance that originated from the crowd rather than with what was said on the platform.

Following the passing of the Public Order Act, Mosley suffered several disruptions at public meetings. At Liverpool on 10 October 1937, whilst addressing an estimated crowd of 8,000, Mosley was struck on the head by a large stone and was said to have been unconscious for between five to ten minutes.[138] In an earlier incident at Southampton on 18 July 1937, Mosley attempted to address a crowd of 20,000. Again missiles were thrown at Mosley, and the noise generated by large sections of the crowd also made it impossible for Mosley's speech to be heard.

Two weeks after the Southampton meeting, Mosley sought a deputation with the Home Secretary, Sir Samuel Hoare, regarding public meetings. Following Hoare's refusal, Mosley conducted a series of letters to the Home Office to raise issues regarding the implementation of the Public Order Act by the Metropolitan Police and provincial police forces. Mosley's initial letter began by praising the Metropolitan Police, declaring no one can deny that their arrangements for 'the preservation of order are admirable'.[139] He continued to express his view that fascist speakers were arrested and charged immediately if they said anything provocative while people who attended their meetings and processions were permitted to say anything with the object of provoking a breach of the peace, yet action

137 Ibid., Old Street Police Court, 10 Jul 1937.
138 *Western Daily Press*, 11 Oct 1937.
139 MEPO 2/3116, Disturbances at Fascist meetings: complaint by Sir Oswald Mosley (1937).

was only taken if they were guilty of physical violence. Despite suggesting that the law should be impartially used, Mosley admitted that 'it is only fair to admit that order is now well maintained at outdoor meetings by the London Police.' However, in relation to the provincial police, he claimed that the 'diversity of experience in different areas is extreme and varies on different occasions'.

The Home Office attempted to promote 'even-handedness' in police practice when regulating politically extreme meetings, yet Emsley highlighted that this attempt also meant that left-wing speakers who were little trouble would have action taken against them because 'action had been taken against Blackshirts who were serious trouble.'[140] Furthermore, Emsley states that 'Some senior provincial policemen ignored such directives and, with full support of their local police authority, acted against those whom they considered to be the trouble-makers.'[141] In an example of provincial policing, Mosley recalled the Southampton meeting described earlier, claiming that there were 25,000 members of the audience and only twenty-four police. From the outset, he claimed that 200 men were permitted to stand near the platform and prevent the rest of the crowd hearing the speech by constantly shouting and singing. He also accused the police of not taking action against crowd members who threw missiles, even when one police officer stood beside a stone thrower. He claimed the man was removed only when he drew attention to him and the idle police officer next to him from the platform.

With respect to the policing of their provincial meetings, Mosley wrote to the Home Secretary and declared that, 'it is difficult for the present administration of the law to preserve even a pretence of impartiality.'[142] In response, the reply from the Home Office made it clear that

> So far as the position in the Metropolitan Police District is concerned, the Commissioner of Police has issued definite instructions that the police are to take action in any case in which an offence under Section 5 of the Public Order Act is observed, whether the offender is a speaker at a meeting or a member of the audience.[143]

It was pointed out that there had been twenty-seven arrests in the Metropolitan Police District at BUF meetings between 1 January 1937 and 31 July 1937. Fifteen of these were anti-fascists, while only four were fascist speakers and two were fascists from the crowd; the political persuasion of the other six was unknown. With regard to the provincial Chief Police Officers, A. I. Tudor Esq, on behalf of the Home Secretary, stated that:

> It is not . . . legitimate criticism . . . to suggest that the law is not administered impartially because on occasions, in spite of police arrangements, perfect

---

140 Emsley, *The English Police*, p. 141.
141 Ibid.
142 Ibid.
143 Ibid.

order is not preserved and some stone throwing or assaults take place and some of the offenders escape detection.[144]

The most significant remark in the response to Mosley was the admission that it was 'no part of the duty of the police to secure a hearing for speakers at meetings'. This adds considerable confusion to the provisions under s6 Public Order Act which amended the Public Meeting Act 1908. Under this amendment, the police acquired the power to arrest a person on the direction of the Chairman at a lawful public meeting, whether on private premises or in a public space. This could be implemented if they were acting in a 'disorderly manner for the purpose of preventing the transaction of the business for which the meeting was called together, or incites others so to act' and they failed to give their name and address to a police officer. The discretion available to the police in preserving order, despite its intrinsic faults which lead to inconsistency and alleged partiality, is the ability to adapt to individual situations. Correspondence between the Home Office and the Metropolitan Police in discussing the reply to Mosley highlight that the police could act only if they were instructed by the chairman, and even if names were taken of interrupters, it was 'not necessarily the duty of the police to institute proceedings for a breach of the Act of 1908'.[145]

There was also significant autocratic police action taken against the BUF in Exeter where Prospective Parliamentary Candidate Rafe Temple-Cotton and County Propaganda Officer Captain Hammond were prominent speakers. Chief Inspector Albert Rowsell reported that fascist activity grew during 1937 but it was not till October that year that police observed disorder. His report on 16 October acknowledged that the crowd took a particular dislike to Hammond. Had the police not been there and had 'Hammond continued to address the crowd, injury to person and property would have resulted'.[146] On this occasion the police requested that Hammond close the meeting as they anticipated serious disorder. Hammond obeyed the request and the fascists were shepherded back to their headquarters by the police. Following this, Exeter's Chief Constable, Frederick Tarry, prohibited Hammond from addressing any further meetings except in the open space known as the Triangle. This banning order commenced on 19 October 1937. This very wide interpretation of the police officer's duty to prevent a breach of the peace is highly questionable. In his analysis of this incident, local historian Todd Gray revealed that the Home Office doubted the legality of the police's use of preventative measures:

It certainly seems as though the Chief Constable has overstepped the mark in failing to recognise that, because an individual has used provocative language or conduct on one occasion (apparently not sufficiently serious to warrant a

---

144 Ibid.
145 Ibid.
146 HO 144/21064. Disturbances: British Union of Fascists: Activities.

prosecution under Section 5 of Public Order Act) he is not on that account justified in banning that individual from public speaking.[147]

This incident reveals that while the Home Office recognised that the legality of the preventive powers used by the Chief Constable were highly doubtful, they did not attempt to hold him to account for these actions. Furthermore, the BUF did not legally challenge or disobey this action.

These examples of disorder at public meetings after the Public Order Act reveal several inconsistencies within police practice. First, there was a divide in the policing of fascist activism between some provincial forces and the Metropolitan Police. Second, there was also a notable divide in the actions and attitudes of the senior police officers with their subordinates. For example, Inspector James was cautioned for failing to act when fascist speakers had used insulting words, and some lower level officers had prioritised crowd control over the monitoring of provocative political speeches. Although this may have been influenced by the anti-Semitic attitude of some officers, it must also be considered that in practice it was more difficult to attain a conviction of an anti-Semitic speaker than it was of a protester that caused, or threatened to cause, a disturbance at a meeting. Third, accusations against the police of anti-Semitic and pro-fascist behaviour were also prominent in East London during the BUF's LCC campaign. These instances demonstrate that police officers were not immune from the popular prejudice towards Jews in this period and it also affected how some of them performed their duty.[148] While s5 was a provision that was utilised against both the speaker and the heckler at public meetings, wide discretion was still available in deciding whether the words used were threatening, abusive or insulting and if they were conducive to a breach of the peace. This ambiguity continued in the post war era and the use of police discretion at fascist meetings was again questioned.

Policing public meetings after the Second World War

In the post-War era, fascist activism continued, as did the same debates about police action disproportionately demonstrating pro-fascist partiality at public meetings. Historian David Renton led the most critical condemnation on police action during the 1945–1951 period. Intriguingly, Renton contends that there were three ways the police could have acted in this era: positively, closing down fascist meetings; negatively, intervening with the fascists against the anti-fascists; or neutrally, always upholding the law when choosing between the fascists and anti-fascists, and always upholding the law.[149] His argument contends that the police acted in the second option. This argument suggests that the police are monolithic, and his claim omits any incidents of police action against the fascists.

---

147 HO 144/21064, cited in Gray, *Blackshirts in Devon*, p. 177.
148 Emsley, *The Great British Bobby*, p. 219.
149 Renton, *Fascism*, p. 104.

Furthermore, there is little legal debate on why police action may have more frequently targeted anti-fascists rather than fascists. Yet, more importantly, the third option for police conduct in this period that they acted neutrally is not explored in any great detail because it makes the assumption that the law is absolute. For example, as the earlier discussion on police discretion demonstrated, police officers are provided with wide legal powers to uphold the law and are presented with varying options of action which all may fall within legal boundaries. Therefore, the option to 'always uphold the law' is inherently multifaceted; police officers are inevitably required to use their discretion in order to prioritise what laws to uphold and how to enforce them.

The continuation of fascist anti-Semitism

Despite the defeat of Nazi Germany and the revelations of the Holocaust, anti-Semitic feeling remained high in Great Britain. In August 1947 there was a weekend of anti-Semitic riots in Manchester, Liverpool and Glasgow, and disorder in Bristol, Hull, London and Birkenhead. Throughout the country there was also individual attacks on Jewish property. The resurrection of anti-Semitism just two years after the War was kindled by the *Daily Express* front-page story of the murder of two British soldiers in Mandate Palestine. Although this article may have provided the spark, journalist and analyst of far-Right movements Daniel Trilling has highlights how anti-Semitism festered within British society after the War, even though fascist activism had practically diminished. In addition to the Jewish terrorist violence in Palestine, he highlighted that during the years of austerity, the myth of the Jewish black marketeer and fuel hoarder was kept alive, and soaring unemployment (which reached 1.9 million in 1947) had led to animosity towards Jews and foreigners over claims that they 'were getting jobs'.[150] The far Right quickly capitalised on this wave of denigration towards the Jews and fascist activism was revitalised. Former BUF member Jeffrey Hamm's public meetings for the British League of Ex-Servicemen and Women were given renewed impetus. Also, in November 1947 Mosley held the inaugural UM meeting. Renewed fascist activism also led to the revival of anti-fascism and organisations such as the 43 Group, who emerged to challenge the far Right crusade and physically disrupt their meetings.

A police presence at fascist meetings was a necessity in order to keep the peace. However, an analysis of fascist meetings in this period demonstrates the vagueness of s5 Public Order Act 1936. While the first component stated that it was an offence to use threatening, abusive or insulting words or behaviour, the second part of the section required that it must be proved that the speaker intended to provoke a breach of the peace, or that a breach of the peace was likely to be

---

150 D. Trilling, 'The Lost Weekend', *The New Statesman*, 28 May 2012, p. 33. Trilling interviewed former Jewish refugee and Communist Party councillor Max Levitas, who recalled the general atmosphere of the time.

occasioned. This caveat hindered the prosecution of many fascist speakers. However, there were some successful prosecutions. For instance, Hamm was charged for using insulting words which were likely to cause a breach of the peace for speeches that he delivered on 14 and 21 September 1947 in Dalston, North-East London. The charge relating to the speech on 21 September was dismissed, and the magistrate, Blake Odgers, stated that he 'was perfectly entitled at any political meeting to [verbally] attack any other political meeting . . . [and continued that it] was inoffensive inasmuch as he was not attacking Jews as Jews'. This was in relation to Hamm's criticism of communists and the use of the term 'oriental rabble'. Yet Odgers ruled that Hamm had exceeded the legal boundaries on 14 September when he used the words 'Pale, pink, palpitating pansies' which was phraseology that was likely to cause a breach of the peace.[151] This demonstrates the breath of discretion utilised by magistrates in interpreting which actions were lawful or unlawful under s5. Hamm was bound over in the sum of £25 for twelve months.

Former BUF activist Tommy Moran, mentioned earlier following his arrest in Plymouth in 1934, was also charged with using threatening behaviour at Derby in 1948. Moran, who was addressing a crowd at the Market Place, responded to a shout from the crowd of 'Let's smash the Jews up', by jumping off his platform and running towards a rival meeting. After being charged with threatening behaviour, Moran replied to the police officer, 'I did more than threaten. I hit a Jew. I tried to stop a meeting of the Stern Gang and whatever happens to me I shall always do my best to stop them.'[152] Moran was fined £5. His reference to the Stern Gang directly related to the violence in Palestine. Founded in 1940 by Avraham Stern, the Stern Gang was a Zionist extremist group who were responsible for terrorist attacks on British personnel in Palestine. Although there was relatively little activity in the United Kingdom, the association of Jews with the terrorist group was a valuable propaganda tool for the far Right.[153]

The difficulties in securing a prosecution against an anti-Semitic speaker were not just to prove that the words used were offensive, but were either calculated or likely to provoke a breach of the peace. Even in cases where disorder did occur, the police and the magistrates had the discretion to decide whether it was the direct result of the speech or not. For instance, a political opponent might well attack a fascist meeting despite what was being said, and so the magistrate and the police must use their discretion appropriately to judge if the speaker was responsible for the disorder.

151 *Gloucestershire Echo*, 18 Oct 1947.
152 *Derby Daily Telegraph*, 10 May 1948.
153 Even newspaper reports of the Stern Gang's acts of violence did little to differentiate between Jews and the extremist organisation. For example, on 26 Sep 1947, the *Gloucester Citizen* reported a bank raid by the Stern Gang in Tel Aviv with the headline, 'JEWS KILL FOUR BRITONS' The attack was carried out as British police transferred money from Barclay's Bank to an armoured car. Other contemporary newspaper reports also associate Jews with terrorism. For example, 'JEW TERROR THREATS: BRITAIN'S CLEAR WARNING' *Western Daily Press*, 16 Dec 1946, 'JEWS KILL MORE SOLDIERS', *Aberdeen Journal*, 9 Oct 1946, 'TROOPS READY FOR ANY LONDON JEW TERRORISM', *Hull Daily Mail*, 11 Nov 1946.

The difficulty that faced the authorities in controlling fascist meetings was when a decision was not so clear cut. These less translucent circumstances forced the police to take less affirmative action when faced with anti-Semitic propaganda. Although Renton suggested that a positive use of police power would have been to close fascist meetings, to take such autocratic action in anticipation of anti-fascist retaliation would set a dangerous precedent that would ultimately deny the liberty of free speech to those who had opponents who were prepared to use violence against them. Although the doctrine of the far Right is repugnant and antagonistic, the use of oppositional political violence should not be tolerated because of its potentially commendable ethical status. The violence and disruptive tactics of many of the anti-fascists necessarily warranted police intervention.

Jewish disruption of fascist meetings

On 7 March 1948, a UM meeting at Dalston Road was attacked by several anti-fascists. The police action used here and the proceedings at the Central Criminal Court demonstrate the problems faced by the legal authorities of organised political disruption. The police reports state that while the meeting was in progress thirty to forty Jews arrived in groups of eight to ten and were directed to strategic points by anti-fascist activist Gerald Jacobs.[154] In response to the anticipation of disorder, police reserves were requested – but before they arrived, 'there was a sudden rush forward by the Jews, shouting, "Down with Fascism", "smash them up now". They attacked every person who offered the slightest resistance, surged forward and upset the platform.'[155] Eight arrests were made and the police ordered the fascist speaker, Alexander Raven-Thomson, not to proceed with the meeting after they had re-erected the platform as they anticipated that more disorder would occur. He accepted the order but some UM supporters went to the nearby Commonwealth Party meeting and chanted, 'we want free speech' and 'break up this meeting as well as ours'. Anticipating further disorder, the police also instructed the speaker to close the meeting, which he did reluctantly. A further two arrests were made which included the arrest of Margaret Hutchings of UM for insulting words after she was heard by a police officer shouting, 'Dirty Jew Bastards. They smashed our meeting'. The police believed that the organised attack on the UM meeting was organised by the 43 Group. This is very possible; Renton claimed that in the previous year the 43 Group had disrupted 'hundreds' of fascist

154 Jacobs was known by the police officers of G Division, and it was noted that 'he generally appears to assert some authority. . . [over] the Jewish people who form the opposition'. He was also previously convicted for insulting behaviour at a British League meeting for throwing a tomato at the speaker. He was fined £5. (MEPO 3/3093, Disturbances at Union Movement meetings: result of proceedings against offenders [1948].) The police report's use of the term 'Jew' rather than 'anti-fascist' here is more reflective of the period's deficiency of etiquette regarding political correctness, rather than any stereotyping or discrimination of their subject.

155 MEPO 3/3093, Disturbances at Union Movement meetings: result of proceedings against offenders (1948), Meetings – Resulting in disorder and arrest.

meetings. It was only from the Autumn of 1947 when the attendance at fascist meetings had risen to up to 3,000 that the disruptive tactics of the 100–200 'commandos' of the 43 Group became ineffective. Despite the violence and unlawful tactics of the 43 Group, Renton describes their actions as 'heroic activities' and even ponders why more anti-fascists were arrested in this period than fascists.[156]

Seven of the anti-fascists were indicted for unlawfully assembling for conspiring to commit a breach of the peace. Four also faced additional charges of assaulting a police officer. Two of the defendants were found not guilty by the jury for the charges relating to unlawful assembly, and there was also an acquittal for two of the assault charges. Jacobs' fine of £20 was the largest punishment of the five who were found guilty. The others were given fines which ranged from £3 to £7. Following the sentencing of the defendants, the Recorder of London Sir Gerald Dodson, warned them not to take the law into their own hands and stated,

> You must realise that Police Officers are not your natural foes, they are your friends and provided you behave like reasonable people they will help you . . . [adding] You may not like fascists, whatever they may be, or their meetings, but leave the law to look after them.[157]

Dodson also warned the defendants that although his sentences were light this time, should this should happen again, they would 'undoubtedly' go to prison. The police report also reflected that, although the sentences were considered to be 'comparatively small', the effect of a higher level prosecution at the Central Criminal Court on indictment, rather than the normal practice of being heard by the magistrates had the positive effect. The report, which was written on 14 May, stated that since 7 March there had been no disorder at public meetings in the Ridley Road area, except when Mosley made his first open-air appearance on 1 May, which was regarded as being quite different from the usual meetings held there.[158]

These incidents demonstrate the continuing public order problems faced by the police regarding free speech at far Right meetings. These examples show how the use of police discretion was used to respond to the origin of the disorder. However, other examples are more opaque. Kenneth Younger, the Under Secretary of State for the Home Department, addressed the difficulty of securing a prosecution against fascist speakers using s5:

> I think the House would agree that nothing would do more harm than for the police to bring prosecutions which frequently fail. Indeed they have had some rather unhappy experiences where they have thought a particular sentence or passage in a speech might fall within the mischief of that Section, where they have prosecuted, and where the prosecution has failed, and

---

156 Renton, *Fascism*, pp. 136–137 and Table 4.2 'Arrests, April 1946-December 1947', p. 110.
157 Ibid.
158 Ibid.

where on numerous subsequent occasions the same speaker has used those sentences over and over again, adding that the courts had already said that it was quite all right.[159]

This highlights the difficulty of applying discretion to act against a speaker who uses insulting words. The police officers present would also need to prove that a breach of the peace was either intended or likely. As many of the fascist speeches were directed at the character of the Jews in general, rather than any deliberate direction to the crowd to create disorder, a prosecution on the grounds that the speaker intended to create a breach of the peace was unlikely. Therefore, the offence more likely to secure a prosecution was on the basis that a breach of the peace was likely to be occasioned. This provision relied, somewhat tentatively, on the reaction and behaviour of the crowd. However, even in cases such as the Hamm meeting on 21 September 1947 mentioned earlier – where the police witness declared that 'the crowd were whipped up into a complete frenzy' by the fascist speaker – the magistrate had dismissed the charge.

The challenge of enforcing s5 at public meetings created the detrimental police task of adjudicating what is permitted or prohibited from a political platform. The wide discretion available under s5, as well as the uncertainty of judicial interpretation when deciding whether to initiate a prosecution, led to inconsistent police action. That is not to say that some policing was not politically sympathetic, as some police officers would have undoubtedly identified with the views of far Right speakers, but it would be dangerous to conceive that all policing which seemingly favoured fascist activism was politically motivated.

Academic lawyer Harry Street questioned the extent that proactive police action at fascist meetings would have been desirable. He contended that those who promote unpopular causes which may excite heckling by exaggerating, distorting and vilifying should still receive police protection. Street suggested that any alternative would ultimately see the police as 'the new censors of speech' and the opponents of unpopular causes, such as anti-fascists, would be free to use violence to break up political meetings and subsequently prevent freedom of expression.[160] As an offence under s5 can be committed only if the words or behaviour used were likely to result in a breach of the peace, it must be accepted that anti-Semitic speeches delivered to a completely pro-fascist audience would not lead to disorder. In addition, if an anti-fascist purposely attended and caused disorder at a fascist meeting, the motives of that person must also be questioned in order to determine if a s5 offence had been committed. Did the individual attend the meeting with the intention of causing disorder? Was his or her disruption the result of the speech or of prior dislike of the fascist doctrine? These were important questions which dictated the action of the police and the judiciary. A landmark judgment in 1963 provided new directions at common law on how to treat disruptions at public meetings.

159 *Hansard, HC Deb*, 7 Dec 1949, vol 470 c2050.
160 Street, *Freedom*, p. 51.

The dual existence of s54(13) and s5

Although s5 became the standard provision for police officers to utilise when threatening, abusive or insulting words or behaviour were used at public meetings, the Public Order Act 1936 did not repeal s54(13) and this continued to be used by police officers and prosecutors in other circumstances. The problem was highlighted by Conservative MP Geoffrey Stevens in response to the increasing street disorder involving Teddy Boys in 1958.[161] He stated that there were 4,294 charges brought under s54(13) in 1957, which was nearly a 32 per cent increase in three years. He argued that the maximum fine of 40s was insufficient to deter this 'hooliganism' and stated that the Public Order Act was insufficient to deal with the problem as it was directed to disorder at public meetings, as is stated in the full title of the Act.[162] His Metropolitan Police Act 1839 (Amendment) Bill to increase the penalty under s54 only progressed as far as its second reading. His interpretation of s5 was challenged by Conservative MP and lawyer Major William Whitehead Hicks-Beach, who argued that:

> The heading of the Bill does not lay down the law; that appears in Section 5, which is extremely wide and reads as follows: Any person who in any public place or at any public meeting uses threatening, abusive or insulting words or behaviour with intent to provoke a breach of the peace or whereby a breach of the peace is likely to be occasioned, shall be guilty of an offence. that is to say, an offence under the Act.[163]

National Liberal MP David Renton argued that s5 was not used in such street disorder which involved the Teddy Boys because the Metropolitan Police had been advised by the former Home Secretary, Simon, in a circular:

> to ensure that Section 5 should not be used where the offence could be dealt with adequately under any other enactment . . . [adding] I was asked whether Section 5 had been used otherwise than in the general way intended when the 1936 Act was introduced, and I can tell the House that as far as we know Section 5 has been limited to its original purpose[.][164]

This indicates that although s5 could be utilised as stated by Whitehead Hicks-Beach, the police had adhered to the advice of using other provisions. It was also considered that as the maximum punishment for a s5 offence was three months imprisonment, £50, or both (under s7 Public Order Bill 1936), this was inappropriate for the rising levels of youth delinquency. An example of how s5 was utilised in respect to the intention of the Act was demonstrated four years later, in 1962.

---

161   The Teddy Boys were a youth subculture who wore Edwardian (Teddy) style clothes.
162   *Hansard, HC Deb*, 7 Mar 1958, vol 583 c1579.
163   Ibid., at 1589.
164   Ibid., at 1630.

On 1 July 1962, Colin Jordan of the National Socialist Movement delivered a particularly odious speech to a crowd of 5,000 at Trafalgar Square. In his speech he praised Adolf Hitler and suggested that Great Britain fought the war against the wrong side, submitting that we should have joined Hitler in a war against the Jew. There was a surge towards the platform. Amidst the scenes of disorder, the police closed the meeting and arrested the speaker under s5. The justices convicted the defendant who subsequently appealed to the Quarter Sessions. His appeal was allowed on the grounds that although the words were insulting, they 'were not likely to lead ordinary, reasonable persons, attending the meeting in Trafalgar Square, to commit breaches of the peace by committing assaults'.[165] This indicates the wideness of the provision without any leading common law judgment and the discretion available within the courts in interpreting the meaning of the provision. On appeal at the Queen's Bench Divisional Court, Lord Parker CJ ruled that the speaker must take his or her audience 'as he finds them'. For instance, in referring to Jordan's provocative and insulting remarks to the political Left who were present in the audience, Parker judged that those words 'were intended to be and were deliberately insulting to that body of persons', constituting an offence by itself. On the extent of free speech which is to be allowed, Parker stated:

> A man is entitled to express his own views as strongly as he likes, to criticise his opponents, to say disagreeable things about his opponents and about their policies, and to do anything of that sort. But what he must not do is – and these are the words of the section – he must not threaten, he must not be abusive and he must not insult them, "insult" in the sense of "hit by words".[166]

The importance of this case is that it was explicitly ruled that a speaker who used words which threatened, abused or insulted had to take his audience as he found it. If the words spoken to that audience were likely to provoke a breach of the peace, the speaker was guilty of an offence. Section 54(13) was finally repealed following significant changes to public order law in 1986.

The Public Order Act 1986

Under the Public Order Act 1986, s5 of the old Act was abolished and new offences were created under ss4, 4A and 5. Section 4 replaced the controversial s5 of the 1936 Act. While some of the language remains the same, such as 'threatening, abusive or insulting words or behaviour' the requirement that the words or behavior would or were intended to lead to a breach of the peace was substituted with the prerequisite:

> with intent to cause that person to believe that immediate unlawful violence will be used against him or another by any person, or to provoke the

---

165 *Jordan v Burgoyne* [1963] 2 QB 744 at 746.
166 Ibid., at 749.

immediate use of unlawful violence by that person or another, or whereby that person is likely to believe that such violence will be used or it is likely that such violence will be provoked.

The offence now also included the distribution or writing of any sign which is threatening, abusive or insulting, as well as words or behaviour.

Section 5 Public Order Act 1986 created a lesser offence which provided that:

(1) A person is guilty of an offence if he or she –

   (a) uses threatening [or abusive][167] words or behaviour, or disorderly behaviour, or
   (b) displays any writing, sign or other visible representation which is threatening, abusive or insulting,

   within the hearing or sight of a person likely to be caused harassment, alarm or distress thereby.

The provisions under s5 considerably widened the scope of which words and behaviour could be criminalised. They provide the police with wide powers of arrest in low-level disorder situations. However, s5(3) does provide some guidance for the accused:

It is a defence for the accused to prove – (a) that he had no reason to believe that there was any person within hearing or sight who was likely to be caused harassment, alarm or duress, or (b) that he was inside a dwelling and had no reason to believe that the words or the behaviour used, or the writing, sign or other visible representation displayed, would be heard or seen by a person outside that or any other dwelling, or (c) that his conduct was reasonable.

A Home Office study showed that the police were often the victims that had been caused harassment, alarm or distress in a number of s5 arrests, and it questioned whether the words or behaviour used in many of the cases were deemed sufficient enough to fulfil this requirement. Other concerns included the over-representation of African-Caribbeans in one area of the research, and the doubts whether any real alarm or distress was caused when the victims were members of the public.[168] The overuse of this provision, and in particular the vagueness of the term 'insulting', which dangerously widened the amount of discretion available to the police, was to later be criticised by a campaign to reform this ambiguous power.

167 The original words, 'abusive or insulting' were substituted by Crime and Courts Act 2013 c. 22 Pt 3 s57(2) and came into force on 1 February 2014.
168 D. Brown and T. Ellis, *Policing Low-Level Disorder: Police Use of Section 5 of the Public Order Act 1986*, Home Office Research Study 135 (1994).

Reform Section 5

Peter Thornton argued that s5 is the most controversial of the new statutory offences. Whereas the repealed s5 of the 1936 Act was considered the lowest level public order offence, he stated that the new s5 'extends the criminal law into areas of annoyance, disturbance, and inconvenience.'[169] The most significant change to this provision has been the removal of the word 'insulting'. This follows the prominent campaigning of Reform Section 5, a pressure group with the slogan 'feel free to insult me' who highlighted a number of arrests which attracted national media attention for their trivial nature. This included a 16-year-old protester who held a placard that read, 'Scientology is not a religion, it is a dangerous cult' and a student protester who asked a mounted police officer, 'Excuse me, do you realise your horse is gay?'[170] The reform campaign attracted the support of prominent politicians and MPs such as David Davis, Nigel Farage, Fiona Bruce and Caroline Lucas, civil rights campaigner Peter Tatchell, and comedians Stephen Fry and Rowan Atkinson. Conservative MP for Gainsborough Edward Leigh led the Parliamentary assault for reform by tabling an amendment to remove the word 'insulting' from s5 in May 2011. Although the amendment did not become law, the cross party support shown for this reform forced the Government to hold a consultation on the issue. Since then, under s57 Crime and Courts Act 2013 the term *insulting* has been removed from s5, which came into force on 1 February 2014.

The term *insulting* is largely subjective; Atkinson emphasised this scope when speaking on behalf of Reform Section 5, stating, 'The clear problem of the outlawing of insult is that too many things can be interpreted as such: criticism, ridicule, sarcasm, merely stating an alternative point of view to the orthodoxy.'[171] Yet even after the amendment, the provision still leaves very wide scope for police officers to make arrests. Unlike s4 or 4A, which prohibits behavior which is directed towards a person, or if a person is directly affected by that behavior, s5 does not require that the offending behavior be directed at anyone, but that it is in the hearing or sight of a person likely to be caused harassment, alarm or distress. This still provides the police officer wide discretionary powers to act without any necessary complaint by any member of the public. In other words, it is enough for a criminal offence to be committed if a police officer argues that someone close by may have been caused harassment, alarm or distress, regardless of whether the person close by had been or not.

The removal of the term *insulting* brought the law in England and Wales closer to the recent enactment in Scotland of the Criminal Justice and Licensing (Scotland) Act 2010. The offence under s38 here is limited to 'threatening and abusive' behavior and is also subject to a reasonable person to suffer fear or alarm.

---

169 Thornton *et al., Law of Public Order*, p. 36.
170 See Reform Section 5 website for more examples, http://reformsection5.org.uk/#?sl=3 accessed on 27 June 2014.
171 *The Guardian*, 23 Oct 2012.

Rooney v Brown[172] importantly demonstrates the scope of s38. Iain Rooney appealed a s38 conviction for shouting and threatening police officers when being arrested on the grounds that given the context of his behaviour (being held in custody in a caged van), it was unlikely that a reasonable person would suffer fear or alarm. In addition, it was also argued that only the police officers were present. While acknowledging that context is important in his judgment, Lord Menzies stated that the matter needed to be decided on an objective basis, and the 'court has to consider matters from the standpoint of the reasonable man placed in the shoes of these police officers.' In recognition of the officers' difficulties in arresting and handcuffing the appellant, Menzies stated that because of the continued abusive behaviour and the knowledge that the officers would have to remove him from the van into the police office, the behaviour was likely to 'cause a reasonable person to suffer fear and alarm'.[173] He refused the appeal.

In England and Wales, the question of the extent that a police officer may be caused harassment, alarm or distress was also questioned in *Harvey v DPP*,[174] *Southard v DPP*[175] and *Taylor v DPP*.[176] In *Harvey*, Bean J allowed an appeal after the appellant was convicted of an s5 offence for using swear words to police officers. During a stop and search the appellant had reportedly said, 'Fuck this, man, I ain't been smoking nothing . . . Told you, you won't find fuck all . . . [and] No, I've already fucking told you so.' In judgment, Bean said the police officers were unlikely to feel harassment, alarm or distress because 'they hear such words all too frequently as part of their job.'[177] There is an important distinction between the way the words were used in this case, as opposed to *Southard* and *Taylor*. For example, in *Southard* the appellant used the phrases 'fuck you' and 'fuck off' towards a police officer who was conducting a stop and search on his brother. The court ruled that whether the person addressed in this situation was a police officer or not, the terms used in that context may still be abusive. This differed from *Harvey* as it was considered that the offending words here were likely to cause harassment, although it was acknowledged that 'the facts came near to the borderline as to whether the ingredients of the offence were made . . . [but concluded] that it fell on the side of the line that meant that they had to dismiss the appeal.'[178] In *Taylor*, the appellant had directed the words, 'fucking nigger' and 'fucking coon bitch' towards police officers. As this s5 offence was also racially aggravated it was also contrary to the Crime and Disorder Act 1998 s31(1)(c). In the first instant the appeal was dismissed because 'there must be evidence that there was someone able to hear or see the defendant's conduct, and the prosecution did not have to call evidence that he or she did actually hear the words spoken

---

172 *Rooney v Brown* [2013] SCL 615.
173 Ibid., at 617.
174 *Harvey v DPP* [2011] EWHC 3992 (Admin).
175 *Southard v DPP* [2006] EWHC 3449.
176 *Taylor v DPP* [2006] EWHC 1202 (Admin).
177 *Harvey v DPP* at para 13.
178 *Taylor v DPP* at para 13.

or see the behaviour.' However, it was also added that even if this was not the case, 'it was open to the judge properly to arrive at the conclusion that the officer was a person likely to be caused distress.' Finally, the words used demonstrated hostility towards one member of a racial group and was therefore sufficient to qualify under s28(1)(b) of the 1998 Act as it was judged to have formed part of the motivation for the conduct.[179]

The scope of s5 outlined here demonstrates different circumstances in which the caveat of feeling harassment, alarm and distress may be applied to words or behaviour which are threatening, abusive and (prior to the Crime and Courts Act 2013) insulting. In relation to public protest and political activism, where the words and behaviour of activist gather the attention of large crowds of people, police responses come under further scrutiny and criticism, when the claim to freedom of expression conflicts with Article 17, the abuse of rights.

The Human Rights Act and restrictions on the freedom of expression

Since the HRA, common law judgments have attempted to define the limits of freedom of speech. In 1999, Sedley LJ stated:

> Free speech includes not only the inoffensive but the irritating, the contentious, the eccentric, the heretical, the unwelcome and the provocative provided it does not tend to provoke violence. Freedom only to speak inoffensively is not worth having.[180]

The limit of such provocation was tested by a BNP activist who publicly displayed anti-Islamic propaganda.

Norwood v DPP[181]

Another controversy that challenged the modern right to freedom of expression occurred in Shropshire in 2002. BNP member Mark Norwood was arrested and charged after he visibly displayed a poster in his window bearing the words, 'Islam out of Britain'. In his appeal, Norwood claimed that he was entitled to display the poster and any conviction would infringe Article 10 ECHR. His appeal was dismissed partly due to his unreasonable behaviour in displaying the poster because the High Court took into consideration the proportionality of the conviction. Therefore his freedom of expression was curtailed in order to protect the public interest. *Norwood v DPP* demonstrates the limitations on the right to freedom of speech that have continued irrespective of the Human Rights Act 1998.

---

179 Ibid. at paras 18–20.
180 *Redmond-Bate v DPP* [2000] HRLR 249, 260.
181 *Norwood v DPP* [2003] EWHC 1564.

Norwood appealed on the grounds that his behaviour was 'reasonable' under s5(3) (c). This was rejected by Auld LJ who stated he could not find that 'the appellant's conduct was reasonable so as to enable him to secure an acquittal through the route of section 5(3).'[182] It also reveals the vagueness of the public order legislation that confines it. S5 Public Order Act 1986 provides that,

> (1) a person is guilty of an offence if he (a) uses threatening, abusive or insulting words or behaviour, or disorderly behaviour, or (b) displays any writing, sign or other visible representation which is threatening, abusive or insulting, within the hearing or sight of a person likely to be caused harassment, alarm or distress thereby.

In the case of *Norwood v DPP*, ss28 and 31 Crime and Disorder Act 1998, which adds 'racially or religiously aggravated' motivation to s5 of the 1986 Act, were also applied to reject his appeal. Norwood's appeal claimed that free speech also included, 'the irritating, contentious, eccentric, heretical, unwelcome and provocative, provided that it does not tend to provoke violence'.[183] However, the European Court of Human Rights ruled that the appellant could not enjoy the protection of Article 10 as his action had contradicted Article 17, the abuse of rights, in effect ruling that his application was inadmissible from the beginning. Article 17 is a provision that aims to 'prevent individuals or groups with totalitarian aims from exploiting in their own interests the principles enunciated by the Convention.'[184]

Burning poppies and the Koran

Two very similar incidents involving members of the EDL and Muslims Against Crusades (MAC) have recently resulted in two contrasting punishments. Emdadur Choudhury of MAC, who was convicted for burning replica poppies and chanting slogans such as 'British soldiers burn in hell', during the two-minute silence on Armistice Day in 2010. As Choudhury's protest did not constitute religious or racial harassment, he was charged under the lesser offence of s5 Public Order Act 1986. He denied the charge that his actions were likely to cause harassment, alarm or distress. Judge Riddle acknowledged the ECHR's commitment to freedom of expression but stated that this freedom was not unlimited. Referencing the history of Armistice Day and the symbolic significance of poppies in respect and remembrance of the war dead, he ruled that Choudhury's actions constituted 'behaviour that is bound to be seen as insulting'.[185] Choudhury was fined £50.

Andrew Ryan, an EDL member and a former soldier, was sentenced to seventy days imprisonment for stealing a copy of the Koran from a public library and burning

---

182 Ibid., at 39.
183 *Norwood v UK* (2005) 40 EHRR SE1.
184 Ibid.
185 *Daily Post (Liverpool)*, 8 Mar 2011.

it with a cigarette lighter at Carlisle Town Hall. While burning the Koran, Ryan also shouted derogatory slogans about Islam. District judge Gerald Chalk stated, 'This is a case of theatrical bigotry. It was pre-planned by you as you stole the book deliberately. You went out to cause maximum publicity and to cause distress.'[186] Ryan was convicted of religiously aggravated harassment.[187] Previously, Ryan had an extensive history of public order charges, including racial chanting. Padraig Reidy, writing for *The Guardian*, argued against this conviction, stating that 'harassment' requires targeted action, and as Ryan protested at the town hall, rather than a mosque or Islamic centre, it was 'difficult to see who exactly he was harassing'.[188]

Although the actions of Choudhury and Ryan were very similar, their contexts were hugely different, and that is reflected in the difference in sentences. Newspaper reportage covering these two incidents has not sufficiently acknowledged this difference. The *Daily Mail's* coverage of the Ryan case opened with the statement, 'A man has been jailed for 70 days today after he burnt a copy of the Koran just over a month after a Muslim got away with a paltry £50 fine for a similar offence.'[189] There is no legal argument or attempt to engage in the different charges used in the report. Even the article in the *Guardian* reflected only that, 'judge's decisions are independent' yet, Reidy did however engage in an argument in favour of absolute free speech. He contested that both convictions were wrong, on the grounds that privileging certain types of speech creates grievance and resentment and that the Government and police curbs on free expression do not promote social cohesion.[190]

The actions of Norwood, Choudhury and Ryan can all be regarded as offensive and provocative. They have all been the subject of state interference and invoked legislation which has prohibited or punished their actions. But has the offence and provocation caused warranted such restrictions on freedom of expression? Should communities demonstrate vigilance to ensure the controversial rights of others? Or can preventative measures that prohibit the controversial opinions of others be justified from a human rights perspective as they aim to protect people from discrimination and to maintain public order?

Redmond-Bate v DPP

The extent to which the courts are prepared to permit freedom of expression can be seen in the influential case of *Redmond-Bate v DPP*.[191] The tactics that the police employed in this case placed a strong significance on a preventative strategy. Yet

---

186 *Daily Mail*, 19 Apr 2011.
187 *The Guardian*, 20 Apr 2011. The original article stated that Ryan was convicted of racially aggravated harassment; this has since been amended online at www.guardian.co.uk/commentisfree/belief/2011/apr/20/free-speech-royal-wedding-quran
188 Ibid.
189 *Daily Mail*, 19 Apr 2011.
190 *The Guardian*, 20 Apr 2011.
191 *Redmond-Bate v DPP* [2000] HRLR 249.

since the Human Rights Act 1998, and the adoption of the ECHR, the duty of the police is to enforce the least restrictive measures open to them with regards freedom of expression and the anticipation of disorder. This adds a new dimension to the accountability of the police with reference to their discretional powers such as anticipating a breach of the peace. Indeed, the authority of *Duncan v Jones* has since been mitigated by the ruling of Sedley LJ in *Redmond-Bate*. Like *Duncan*, *Redmond-Bate* also involved an arrest for the wilful obstruction of a police officer in the execution of his duty, as he was acting to preserve the peace. Ms Redmond-Bate was one of three Christian fundamentalists who were preaching on the steps of Wakefield Cathedral, while a crowd of about 100 people gathered, some of whom were hostile to the speakers. The critical question of where the threat to public order came from – being either the speakers or the hostile elements of the crowd – was the decisive issue. It was judged that the police should direct their powers to those responsible for the anticipated or actual breach of the peace, which in this case should have been those in the crowd who were reacting unreasonably to the religious speakers. Despite much of the Human Rights Act 1998 not being in full force at this time, Sedley LJ referred to it in his judgment, stating that in the interregnum, common law and executive action should seek compatibility with the ECHR or risk 'putting the United Kingdom in breach of the Convention and rendering it liable to proceedings before the European Court of Human Rights'.[192] Articles 9 and 10, freedom of thought, conscience and religion and freedom of expression respectively, were mentioned in the judgment in defence of the appellant, which contrasted the inter-war view held by Lord Hewart CJ in *Duncan* that such rights are 'nothing more than a view taken by the court of the individual liberty of the subject'.[193] Sedley also recognised that there was, and had been for a long time, good reason in policing and law to respect the Convention rights, marking a subtle constitutional shift that was cemented by the Human Rights Act 1998.

R (o/a Laporte) v Chief Constable of Gloucestershire

Police powers under the breach of the peace doctrine have been used to significantly corrode the liberty of freedom of expression. However, the scope to challenge these under the HRA has provided some positive results. This is most notably highlighted by *R (o/a Laporte) v Chief Constable of Gloucestershire*[194] where protestors were denied both freedom of expression and freedom of assembly. In 2003, the police stopped and searched three coaches travelling to RAF Fairford to participate in an anti-war demonstration. The Gloucestershire Police used s60 Criminal Justice and Public Order Act 1994 to stop and search those attending. On discovering that eight of the passengers were potentially from a radical group known as the Wombles, they used common law powers of breach of

---

192 Ibid., 255–256.
193 *Duncan v Jones.*
194 *R (o/a Laporte) v Chief Constable of Gloucestershire* [2006] UKHL 55.

the peace to send the coaches back home, denying the passengers to exercise their right to protest. The House of Lords held that the stop and search was legal but that the police had exercised Breach of the Peace powers too early as the threat to public order posed by the passengers was not imminent. The applicant, Jane Laporte, was not one of the Wombles but was also diverted with the other passengers away from the demonstration. In judgment, Lord Bingham stated, 'It was wholly disproportionate to restrict her exercise of her rights under arts 10 and 11 because she was in the company of others, some of whom might, at some time in the future, breach the peace.'[195]

Abdul and others v DPP[196]

In *Laporte* the police acted too soon to prevent a breach of the peace, yet in *Abdul and others v DPP*, the police facilitated a provocative anti-war demonstration in Luton. The decision to prosecute the protestors under s5 came only after the event and consultation with the Complex Trial Unit of the Crown Prosecution Unit.[197] The protestors shouted slogans such as, 'British soldiers go to hell' and 'baby killers'. This case directly questioned the limitations of the right to freedom of expression against the restrictions to words and behaviour under s5. Quoting the district judge, Gross LJ found that the words used were threatening and abusive, and they had 'crossed the threshold of legitimate protest'.[198] This case demonstrates the compatability of the Article 10 right to freedom of expression and s5 Public Order Act. Like *Norwood*, words and behaviour found to be threatening or abusive in accordance with s5, whether promoting political opinion or not, would not receive protection from the ECHR. Gross also praised the police for their management of the protest, stating, 'there is much to be said for the police efforts to keep the events of that day as low key as possible, concentrating on the more immediate matter of preventing outbreaks of violence.'[199]

Conclusion

The successive legislation and court judgments which have placed restrictions on freedom of expression demonstrate that English law has had a long tradition of prioritising the preservation of the peace over claims to free speech. The enactment of s54(13) Metropolitan Police Act 1839 highlighted the emergence of preventative powers which provided the police with the discretion to arrest those who used words or behaviour that was intended or likely to lead to a breach of the peace. The criminalisation of words in this way provided the police with

---

195 Ibid., at 55.
196 *Abdul and others v DPP* [2011] EWHC 247 (Admin)
197 C. Newman, 'Case Comment, Section 5 of the Public Order Act 1986: the Threshold of Extreme Protest', *Journal of Criminal Law 76*, no. 2 (2012), pp. 105–109.
198 *Abdul and others v DPP* at 31.
199 Ibid., at 52.

extensive and ambiguous powers. Although originally mandated to prevent violent confrontations and assaults between the lower classes, s54(13) was later used in the interwar era to prohibit political heckling at public meetings, demonstrating the scope of the provision.

Police responses to public meetings and their approach towards freedom of speech throughout this period have varied significantly. At different stages, police have controversially used their discretion to prevent potential breaches of the peace. These include the prohibition of meetings at Trafalgar Square in 1888, the treatment of the Manchester unemployed at Birmingham in 1908, the arrest of Katherine Duncan in 1934, the ban on the BUF speaker at Exeter in 1937, and the recent police actions which restricted the freedom of expression of Mark Norwood, Alison Redmond-Bate and Jane Laporte. The period studied has also demonstrated examples of police facilitation of potentially disorderly meetings or protests. These have included the reception of the Manchester unemployed at Coventry, the facilitation of both a fascist and anti-fascist demonstration at Hyde Park in 1934 as well as other volatile meetings of the fascists and communists before and after the Second World War, and the protests by Abdul and others at Luton which were facilitated and prosecuted only retrospectively. Since the HRA has fully incorporated the ECHR into UK law, some consistency in judgments can now be detected. In the realm of political activism or public protest, it is clear that extremist views will not be granted protection under Article 10. The cases of *Norwood* and *Abdul* have clarified this, while at the lower courts this has also been seen with the prosecutions of the MAC's Emdadur Choudhury and the EDL's Andrew Ryan.

The interwar years were a particularly explosive time as competing political extremes battled for dominance on the streets, leading to several complaints of police bias. Tactics applied were seen to have either focused on disorder coming from elements within the crowd or from the speakers themselves. It has been suggested that the application of this strategy predominantly focused on anti-fascist protesters at fascist meetings and speakers at communist or anti-fascist meetings. Yet a wider look at further events and the methods employed by both the far Right and the far Left in relation to existing law indicates that other pertinent reasons enlighten this debate. Examples of fascist speakers being compliant with requests to close or move meetings would have certainly helped their relationship with members of the police. In contrast, examples of left-wing activists who regularly resisted police authority and advocated unconstitutional methods in their propaganda naturally provoked conflict.

Whilst much of this activism can be morally vindicated for its anti-fascist stance, patronage for the hungry and unemployed, and support for the protection of civil liberties, the Home Office and police scepticism of revolutionary communist motivations must also be considered as an important factor that influenced the use of their discretion. In contrast, the BUF's respect for police authority and their cooperation with police during their demonstrations gave the police fewer opportunities or motivations to use force against them. The paradox is that the unethical policies of the BUF and other fascist movements had the power to provoke disorder whilst conducting their meetings in a largely lawful manner.[200] In *Norwood*, Auld LJ found that s5 was itself a statutory provision that protected the rights of others, yet in the context of political activism this alone still leaves the potential for partisanship and inconsistent police action. Indeed, Norwood would probably maintain that he was a victim of political oppression.

This chapter has demonstrated that there is no clear linear progression or regression of the status of free speech across this period, although free speech was regularly claimed as a 'right' by different activists. The Trafalgar Square Riot 1887 led to attempts to give the right of free speech and assembly positive legal status within constitutional law. Even the Public Order Act 1936 did not clarify to what extent free speech was attainable, as the provision under s5 provided an ambiguous definition of what words and behaviour were criminalised. Although ss4, 4A and 5 of the 1986 Act all have a similar vagueness in their approach of preventing harassment, alarm or distress, their more recent collaborative existence with the ECHR has demonstrated how these provisions can be applied more moderately.

In certain cases related to restrictive police tactics, where the activists may be seen as a nuisance rather than extremists, such as *R (o/a Laporte) v Chief Constable of Gloucestershire* and *Redmond-Bate v DPP*, the courts have taken a more libertarian approach to the protection of human rights, ruling against oppressive police measures. Nevertheless, in cases which involve more politically extreme offenders – such as *Norwood v DPP* and *Abdul and others v DPP* – the courts have taken the view that Convention Rights such as freedom of expression are necessarily limited to protect the rights of others and prevent disorder or crime. Even so, for the police officer on the street who has a duty to preserve the peace without political partiality, multiple dilemmas still remain. At what point should police act to prevent a breach of the peace? Who should be the target of their proactive response? And how is this achieved impartially, without making a political judgment on the activists or their opponents?

---

200 However, although BUF members did frequently engage in unlawful activities, such as attacks on Jews and Jewish property, they were committed more covertly and were usually committed independently of the movement's official activism.

7 Public meetings held on private premises

The roles of the steward and the police

You will find that interruptions at Fascist meetings do not last long.[1]

Introduction

Police responses to disorder at public meetings held on private premises have had a contentious and inconsistent history. This has a significant position in public order law as, contrary to the majority of public order policing which is concerned with preserving the peace in public places,[2] an ambiguous legal debate on the role of the police during disorder at public meetings held on private premises still endures. While disorder or the anticipation of disorder at a range of meetings has resulted in a proactive police response throughout 1829–2014, there are also incidents when the role of restoring order has been left to the appointed stewards. As the opening quotation by Sir Oswald Mosley reveals, some movements such as the BUF organised and trained their stewards to deal with interruptions efficiently. This chapter analyses the amount of force used to achieve this and the legal responses to coercive and even brutal stewarding. It also examines the different approaches of the police at different events and examines the inconsistency within provincial police practice, the allegations of political partiality and the ambiguity of the police's common law power to prevent a breach of the peace. All further references to public meetings in this chapter will denote those which are held on private premises, unless otherwise stated.

The development of police practice on the occasion of public meetings is examined from incidents in the nineteenth century, when the role of the police and the steward were legally highlighted in events involving the Chartists in 1848 and an assault case brought against a steward of a religious meeting by the ejected Major Edwards at the Dover magistrates in 1892. At the start of the twentieth century, the disruption of political meetings continued when prominent politicians, such

---

1 Sir Oswald Mosley, *Leicester Evening Mail*, 15 Apr 1935.
2 S9 Public Order Act 1936 defines 'public place' as 'any highway . . . and any other premises or place to which at the material time the public have or are permitted to have access, whether on payment or otherwise'.

as Sir Edward Grey in 1905 and Lloyd George in 1908, were victim to suffragette militancy and organised interruption, which influenced the Public Meeting Act 1908. Prominence is then given to the interwar years, especially the controversial and inconsistent use of police discretion when dealing with the BUF's rally at Olympia and the International Labour Defence Organisation's meeting in South Wales, which came to prominence in *Thomas v Sawkins*.[3] The inconsistent police tactics applied at these meetings have been used by Ewing and Gearty to advocate that police discretion was a clear demonstration of political partisanship which favoured fascist activism. They regard the Olympia meeting as 'one of the most dramatic occasions of the inter-war period' and argued that when policing right-wing groups, 'the police were invariably able to rediscover a nineteenth century style of dedication to political liberty and free speech' that was absent in respect to left-wing groups.[4] The debate in this chapter importantly differentiates between the dynamics of these two meetings, as well as other meetings during this era, and suggests that the difference in police responses were influenced by other elements than political motivation. An examination of the allegedly brutal ejections of the League of Empire Loyalists by Conservative stewards and Winter Garden staff at the 1958 conference at Blackpool and the resulting court cases demonstrates the continuation of violence at political meetings in the post War era. The use of police discretion in the context of public protest on private premises is then analysed in relation to *R v Chief Constable of Devon and Cornwall, ex parte Central Electricity Generating Board*[5] in 1982 and the amendments to police powers in s17 Police and Criminal Evidence Act 1984 (PACE). While there has been little disruption and disorder regarding political activism and protest in private spaces in recent years, the chapter concludes with an assessment of the potential for disorder and the preventive police tactics that have been used to prevent potential disorder at BNP meetings in the late twentieth century. While inconsistences within provincial police practice have been shown to exist throughout this period, this chapter demonstrates there is more uniformity within the legal responses to disorder held on private premises than may have originally been thought.

Legal definitions

The current legal definition of *public meeting*, found in s9 Public Order Act 1936, is examined in chapter six. A further meaning which is more applicable to meetings held on private premises, but has since been repealed by the Defamation Act 1952, is found in s4 Law of Libel Amendment Act 1888. Public meeting is defined within the 1888 Act as, 'any meeting bona fide and lawfully held for a lawful purpose, and for the furtherance or discussion of any matter of public concern, whether the admission thereto be general or restricted'. This provision

---

3 *Thomas v Sawkins* [1935] 2 KB 249.
4 Ewing and Gearty, *The Struggle*, p. 275.
5 *R v Chief Constable of the Devon and Cornwall Constabulary, ex parte Central Electricity Generating Board* [1982] QB 458.

was mandated to privilege newspapers with the authority to report the minutes of meetings, including those of a 'vestry, town council, school board, board of guardians, board or local authority form or constituted under the provisions of any Act of Parliament . . . [and print] at the request of any Government office or department, officer of state, commissioner of police, or Chief Constable of any notice or report issued by them for the information of the public', provided that the report of the meeting is not published with malicious intent, or with blasphemous or indecent matter. Although not legally bound by Statute, a similar definition was offered to the Report of the Departmental Committee on the Duties of the Police with respect to the Preservation of Order at Public Meetings in 1909 by the Chief Constable of Liverpool, Leonard Dunning:

> [A] public meeting may properly be defined to include any lawful meeting called for the furtherance or discussion of a matter of public concern, to which the public or any particular section of the public is invited or admitted, whether the admission thereto is general or restricted.

Dunning described this definition as 'an instruction to the police put in a language they are likely to understand'.[6]

The legal definition of *private premises* is more problematic. The Departmental Committee of 1909 clarified that 'If a public building is hired, or even lent, to an association or other section of the public for the purposes of a meeting, it becomes in law for the time being a non-public place.'[7] S9 Public Order Act 1936 defines private premises as 'premises to which the public have access (whether on payment or otherwise) only by permission of the owner, occupier, or lessee of the premises'. The implication of this distinction means that persons in attendance of a meeting on private premises are present only by the invitation of the organisers, meaning that if they refuse to leave when requested, they become trespassers. This entitles the organisers, or stewards acting on their behalf, to eject – without undue violence – any person who refuses to leave. Until the controversial judgment in *Thomas v Sawkins*,[8] it was widely understood that the police also required the invitation of the organisers to enter the premises if their assistance was required. Yet events have frequently developed that have compelled the police to take assertive action and enter private premises to either restore order or to prevent disorder.

As the law currently stands, the organisers of public meetings are entitled to refuse entry to the police, but this entitlement is subject to the police officer's power and duty to preserve the peace. A police officer can enter private premises to either prevent or deal with a breach of the peace, or to pursue a criminal. If

---

6 Cd. 4674, *Report of the Departmental Committee on the Duties of the Police With Respect to the Preservation of Order at Public Meetings* (1909), para 526.

7 Cd. 4673, *Report of the Departmental Committee on the Duties of the Police With Respect to the Preservation of Order at Public Meetings.* Volume 1: Report and Appendices (1909), p. 5.

8 *Thomas v Sawkins.*

no legal justification can be offered for the police officer's entry and the officer subsequently refuses to leave when requested by the organisers, then the police officer becomes a trespasser and ceases to be in the execution of their duty. The ambiguity of the law relating to public meetings and the importance of considering the individual facts of each case is highlighted by Peter Thornton QC, who states, 'The police might argue, for example, that a meeting convened to protest against the passage of a Race Relations Bill might permit their attendance if held in Bradford, but not if held in Devon.'[9] The availability of wide discretionary powers, although potentially justified on the reasonable apprehension of disorder, demonstrates the available scope of police practice and possible perceptions of partiality. This raises several questions: When a breach of the peace is only anticipated, what justification can validate the intrusive use of preventative police tactics? On the occasion of a suspected breach of the peace, at what point should the police enter the premises to restore order, and how can a breach of the peace in this case be defined?

Police responses to disorder in meetings in the nineteenth century

The Chartists and the Irish Confederates

The activism of the Chartist movement prompted a wide range of responses from the police and the Government which has been discussed in chapter four. In 1848, the activism of the Chartists and the Irish Confederates had briefly merged forging an alliance of the English and Irish working class, who shared a common interest in challenging the ruling establishment.[10] At a meeting held in the Chartist reading and assembly rooms in Soho, London, the unwanted presence of plain-clothed police officers led to the violent ejection of them by the doorkeeper, Michael McManus. The following case had the capacity to illuminate important legal issues, such as whether police presence at public meetings without the permission of the organisers could be legally justified, whether the meetings' designated stewards had the power to eject them, and the amount of physical force that the stewards could utilise. However, the resulting case failed to set any precedent for future directives to either police or steward.

In the event of the meeting of Irish Confederates, Police Constable Mitchell had attended in plain clothes and, giving evidence, declared that there were 200–300 people in attendance who listened to several extracts from newspapers. It was not recorded in the court reports if he disclosed whether he was there on duty or not. However, as Sergeant John Grey was also present and stated that

---

9 Thornton *et al., Public Order*, p. 122. This example reflects the greater ethnic diversity of Bradford as opposed to Devon, and the greater potential for hostility, provocation and disorder in the West Yorkshire city.

10 W. J. Lowe, 'The Chartists and the Irish Confederates: Lancashire, 1848', *Irish Historical Studies 24*, no. 94 (November 1984), pp. 172–196.

he had been 'sent there', it is likely their presence was to observe the meeting and record potentially seditious speeches. Mitchell stated that after being present for about 20 minutes there was a cry that the police were in the room. He was subsequently pointed out, shoved by several people and thrown to the ground. McManus then grabbed his collar and proceeded to drag him to the door, then throw him down the first flight of stairs shouting, 'If that don't do I'll kick you down the other flight of stairs.'[11] While this method of ejection from meetings was not uncommon, a successful charge of assault on a police officer would have relied on it being proved that the officer was in the course of his duty by being present at the meeting. The outcome of the case had the potential to either uphold or undermine this controversial police practice. However, the case never confronted this question.

At the Marlborough Police Court, McManus denied having laid violent hands on any person and he was fully committed by magistrate Hardwick. At the Central Criminal Court on 20 June 1848, McManus appeared with other members of the Chartist movement for other charges relating to riot and assault. Mr Bodkin, prosecuting for the Crown, stated that he did not wish to press the present charge against him. After explaining this decision, he stated,

> He hoped that this course would not be misunderstood, or that any doubt whatever would be entertained in any quarter of the fixed determination of the authorities to put down meetings of this dangerous character, and to prosecute with rigour all those who should be found promoting them or participating in the outrages which they but too frequently led to.[12]

The Common Serjeant reinforced this sentiment, declaring that a full example had been made by the other convictions and public justice had been answered.[13] As this charge was dropped, it prevented a legal judgment on whether the presence of the police at public meetings was lawful or not. Consequently, the police continued to attend meetings and this practice resulted in the convictions of other Chartists for sedition.[14] The uncertainty of whether the stewards had the authority to remove the police had not been answered. Furthermore, if the police did have the legal authority to attend public meetings without the permission of the organisers, an additional question of whether it was the duty of the police or the stewards to respond to disorder also remained unclear. This was deliberately addressed before the close of the nineteenth century in response to the increased use of organised disruption at political meetings and the contentious issue regarding the duty of the police and stewards.

---

11 *The Times*, 14 Jun 1848.
12 *The Times*, 21 Jun 1848.
13 Ibid.
14 A month later, Robert Crowe, Francis Looney and William Vernon were charged with sedition for speeches they had made at the Chartist assembly room in Soho.

Major Edwards' 'test' case 1892

On 5 October 1892, Major Edwards, a Labour candidate for Dover, was removed from the Dover Town Hall during a Church Congress meeting by Gunner Haseldine of the Royal Artillery. Consequently, Major Edwards brought a charge of assault against Haseldine, not for the purpose of securing a punishment against his violent behaviour, but in the hope of setting a legal precedent regarding the stewarding of public meetings. During the trial Edwards admitted that it was his intention to cause a disturbance in order to be ejected, but clarified that he did not 'wish to make more of the charge than necessary'.[15] He declared that the recent disorder at public meetings constituted a 'positive danger to liberty', explaining that the eviction of an interrupter who threatens that liberty should be ejected by the police, rather than other audience members or stewards. If his charge against the steward for assault was unsuccessful, and the assault was therefore justifiable, he requested that the magistrates condemn his conduct at the meeting in such severe terms that it made it quite clear to those who intentionally disrupt meetings 'that they need expect no mercy if their conduct brings them before your honourable bench'.[16]

During the proceedings it was recorded that there were three stewards on duty and they were all soldiers. The meeting's organiser gave them instructions only to show people to their seats as they did not expect any interruptions during the religious meeting. When the unwanted interlopers started singing, the Bishop of Manchester (who was visiting Dover) requested the Town Clerk to call the police in and have them removed.[17] It was admitted by Reverend Sarson that the Bishop did not expect that the removal of the interrupters would be performed by private persons. Conversely, Edwards highlighted that the police refused to interfere at his previous political meetings which were subjected to organised interruption. On hearing of the disruption these meetings, Reverend Sarson suggested to Edwards that if the same disruption should disturb the meeting with the Bishops from the House of Lords then it would highlight the issue of organised disruption in Dover and would 'stop that which seems to me at present, the greatest evil that is permitted to go on'.[18]

The magistrates' decision was unsatisfactory from Edwards' point of view. They dismissed the case with costs. When Edwards requested that they state their legal grounds for the decision, the Mayor responded that he could not answer that question. Edwards then requested that his conduct be condemned in order to 'make the ears tingle of those who take part in or instigate these disturbances of public meetings in Dover'. The Mayor replied, 'I don't think that that is part of our business.' As the judgment did not address whether the organised disruption of meetings

---

15 *The Dover Express*, 14 Oct 1892.
16 Ibid.
17 The request for the police potentially demonstrates the differences in provincial police practice. The differences highlighted demonstrate that it was common practice for the police in Manchester to enter and eject people from public meetings.
18 *The Dover Express*, 14 Oct 1892.

constituted a breach of the peace or a misdemeanour, it remained ambiguous whether the police had a duty to act when a disturbance broke out or not. Without clear legal instruction, the police could use their discretion in deciding when to act. The exact point of when a breach of the peace occurred was also a vague notion which left some degree of interpretation. If a steward used more force than necessary to eject an interrupter, he potentially committed a breach of the peace.

Pre-War disruption of political meetings

The suffragettes

The problems of keeping order at meetings came to the forefront during the militant practices of the suffragettes, whose high-profile campaign to disrupt political meetings was most prominent between 1905 and 1908. The suffragettes largely targeted Liberals after Prime Minister Sir Henry Campbell-Bannerman told one of the leading suffragettes, Christabel Pankhurst, that his cabinet was largely opposed to female enfranchisement. Historian Martin Pugh suggests that prominent Liberals of the time, such as Winston Churchill and Lloyd George, enjoyed the extra newspaper publicity and even used it to exercise their wit and humour. This was illustrated by the suffragette heckle, 'We have waited for forty years,' to which Lloyd George replied, 'I must say the lady rather looks it'.[19] Christabel Pankhurst argued that the publicity was beneficial to the suffrage movement, adding that it diverted press attention away from the ministers' speeches.[20] Suffragettes were often violently ejected by the stewards, who were acting under the orders of the organisers, which subsequently generated condemnation of the Liberal Party's attitude to civil liberty.

In 1905, Christabel Pankhurst and Annie Kenney were ejected from the Free Trade Hall, Manchester, during an address by Liberal MP Sir Edward Grey. Grey refused to answer their questions on female suffrage, which were ruled out of order. Following Pankhurst's cry, 'Treat us like men!' police forcibly removed the two agitators from the hall.[21] The charges of disorderly conduct, assault and obstruction, which were brought against Christabel Pankhurst, related to the events after the eviction when she spat in the face of a police officer and attempted to address a crowd on the street outside the hall. The extensive publicity that was gained as a result of the disruption of the high-profile political meeting in Manchester heralded the start of the suffragettes' defiance of the law as it became clear that militancy 'paid off'.[22] Political disruption became a common suffragette tactic.

19 M. Pugh, *The March of the Women: A Revisionist Analysis of the Campaign for Women's Suffrage, 1866–1914*, Oxford University Press: Oxford (2000), pp. 189–190.
20 Ibid., p.188; see also C. Pankhurst, 'Why We Protest at Cabinet Minister's Meetings', WSPU (1908).
21 *Daily Express*, 16 Oct 1905.
22 C. Rover, *Women's Suffrage and Party Politics in Britain 1866–1914*, Routledge and Kegan Paul Ltd: London (1967), p. 80.

At a Liberal Party meeting at the Albert Hall on 5 December 1908, the methods employed by the stewards in evicting female hecklers were subject to fierce criticism in the correspondence printed in *The Times*. Descriptions of the ejections included the powerful statements, 'Of the first half-dozen women ejected, four at least were fallen on with extreme violence by the stewards, sometimes thrown on the ground in the struggle, and . . . were pommelled and knocked about.'[23] Other descriptions from witnesses at the meeting recorded that the actions of the male stewards towards the female interrupters were 'regrettable and scandalous' asserting that the women were 'handled with a brutality which was a disgrace to our sex, and to any civilised country'.[24] The interruptions caused by the women were also subject to different interpretation. One letter described the female heckling as 'no more than ordinary interruptions made by men at political meetings for which they are never thrown out', adding that these women suffer missiles and assaults at their meetings but instead of ejecting people they 'control meetings by the ordinary political methods of good temper and firmness'.[25] The opposing view insisted that, 'Some of these ladies were so persistent in their attempt to interfere with the meeting that they had to be ejected' but continued to suggest that this should be done by 'muscular women . . . as it is very repulsive to see a woman struggling in the arms of men'.[26]

The interruptions organised by the suffragettes reveal the conflicting contemporary views regarding the disruption of meetings and the freedom to heckle political speakers. They also demonstrate the overt differences between Manchester and London regarding the duty of the police and the stewards. The legacy of the militant suffragettes' tactic of disrupting political meetings can be detected in a new offence that was introduced and passed through Parliament in the same month as the controversial Albert Hall meeting.

The Public Meeting Act 1908

The legal issue that was highlighted by the suffragettes' interjections was addressed in the memorandum which preceded the Public Meeting Bill 1908. It declared that no legal provision existed to remedy the problem of a person or body of persons breaking up a public meeting or preventing any of the speakers from being heard unless an actual assault took place. The object of the Bill was to create an offence of disorderly conduct at a meeting with the purpose of preventing the transaction of business.[27] The Bill was presented to Parliament by Conservative MP Lord Robert Cecil on Friday 18 December 1908 and was rushed through Parliament. There was a mixed response in the House of Commons to the

---

23 *The Times*, 8 Dec 1908.
24 *The Times*, 7 Dec 1908.
25 *The Times*, 8 Dec 1908.
26 Ibid.
27 House of Commons Parliamentary Papers. *Public Meeting. A Bill to Prevent Disturbance of Public Meetings* (1908).

Bill's effect on civil liberty. Liberal MP Josiah Wedgwood, who was critical of the Bill, declared it 'was the worst blow at the right of expressing individual political opinion that had been delivered for a long time'.[28] Other MPs, such as the Liberal William Byles, praised the clause as it offered to preserve the priceless liberties of free speech and free expression. He added that the object of the Bill was not to make an offence of disorderly conduct at political meetings, but disorderly conduct that was for the express purpose of preventing the transaction of business. In a response to those who opposed the Bill on the grounds of civil liberty, he stated, 'his hon. friends were championing the rights of those blackguards who came on purpose to prevent the object of the meeting being carried out.'[29]

An important theme of the Commons debate of the Public Meeting Bill was that experience of disruption and violence at political meetings was widespread. Labour MP William Crooks declared, 'My experience has been that it was the Liberals who broke up my meetings.'[30] Will Thorne, also a Labour MP, stated:

> No men in that House had been through the mill more than he had in regard to political meetings. On one occasion at Camborne he got an awful bashing, yet he was not prepared to vote for a Bill which would prevent anyone making inter[text missing – *interjections at*] such gatherings . . . It was for those who organized the meetings to make proper provision against those who would try to prevent the speakers being heard.[31]

The armament of a legal provision to protect public meetings from disruption was defended by Liberal MP Edward Hemmerde, who declared that most disruption could be attributed to women and socialists. He stated his praise of the Bill as the measure gave them a 'chance of clearing public meetings and public discussions of what was rapidly becoming an intolerable nuisance'.[32] A few speakers tolerated disorder in some circumstances. Crooks described interjections as 'the salt of public meetings'[33] while Wedgwood pleaded that the Bill 'would upset traditions which had obtained for 500 years,' and he therefore hoped that 'even at this eleventh hour it would be successfully opposed'.[34] Cecil successfully defended his Bill and it became law on 21 December 1908:

> If the small knot of people were not stopped it meant the denial of free speech, or if the other members of the meeting endeavoured to stop the interrupters it meant a free fight. Lynch law or the denial of free speech was the alternative with which they were confronted.[35]

---

28 *Hansard, HC Deb*, 19 Dec 1908, vol 198 cc2330.
29 Ibid., c2340.
30 Ibid., c2334.
31 Ibid., cc2331–2332.
32 Ibid., c2334.
33 Ibid., c2337.
34 Ibid., c2331.
35 Ibid., c2336.

However, despite the passing of the Public Meeting Act, the duty of the police at public meetings was still vague and inconsistent across the United Kingdom, which prompted further examination.

The Departmental Committee on the Duties of the Police with Respect to the Preservation of Order at Public Meetings 1908

The prevalence of political disruption in mainstream politics was highlighted in the 1908 by-elections at Chelmsford, which were contested by the Conservative Unionist Ernest Pretyman and the Liberal Mr A. Dence. Although the violence exercised at the meeting at Ingatestone was not necessarily unusual or any more severe than in other parts of the country – especially at election time – it was the practice of the police which gave the incident national attention. *The Times* described the Chelmsford division as 'old fashioned,' adding that the use of eggs as political weapons had 'not yet gone out of date in the elections here'. A description of one by-election meeting demonstrated the loudness and disorder that were prevalent: 'Mouth organs were played and fireworks were exploded in a crowded hall, and for half an hour the Liberal candidate tried in vain to obtain a hearing.'[36] The public meeting Dence was due to address at Ingatestone on 25 November 1908, which was abandoned at the last moment, revealed the variation of police practice. It was reported that the meeting was forcibly entered by fifty youths who threw aside the doorkeepers and violently ejected the Liberals inside. One was the temporary Liberal agent, Mr Martin, who was carried out to the street, dropped along the way, and rescued by friends who brought him into a side room of the hall where he fainted.

The report of Police Sergeant Willsmer to the Chief Constable of Essex Constabulary revealed that Mr Martin had requested a police presence inside the hall and informed the sergeant that 'a number of roughs were coming from Chelmsford and Brentwood to upset the meeting.'[37] However, Willsmer refused the request, stating that the police were not allowed to be present in the hall and it was up to the organisers to keep order at their own meeting. Following this disturbance, Liberal Unionist Austen Chamberlain asked the Home Secretary, Herbert Gladstone, whether he knew that different police forces in the country held different views of their duties regarding the preservation of order at public meetings and suggested that a committee should be appointed to inquire into the conduct of the police.

The Departmental Committee on the Duties of the Police with Respect to the Preservation of Order at Public Meetings was duly appointed, publishing its report on 14 April 1909. The Committee interviewed the Metropolitan Police Commissioner, as well as the Chief Constables of four counties and six large boroughs to establish the range of police practice. The Report determined that the varying practices of the Chief Constables could be classified by three distinct principles:

(1) That it is unwise for police to interfere with political meetings any further than they are bound to do in order to prevent actual breaches of the peace;

---

36 *The Times*, 26 Nov 1908.
37 Cd. 4673, para 22.

(2) That it is expedient to assist the promoters of public meetings to keep order inside, but that this is a special duty of the police which must be paid for by the persons desiring their assistance;

(3) That keeping order inside public meetings is part of the ordinary duties of the police, for which no payment ought to be asked.[38]

The Committee did not advocate any action to bring uniformity of police practice to public meetings as it was believed that the three different systems 'have in each case been adopted either in consequence of, or with the sanction of, the public opinion in each locality'.[39]

The Departmental Committee minutes of evidence revealed the consensus among the Chief Constables that the Public Meeting Act 1908 was a weak Statute that did not confer any additional powers or impose any additional duties on the police. With barely any exception, the Chief Constables would not direct the police to prosecute interrupters, but would require that the charge sheet be signed by the promoter or a steward of the meeting. The Committee considered the possibility of strengthening the Act by adding a power of arrest without warrant, but considered that the arrest of an interrupter would probably tend to further excite hostile opinion, and may even find disfavour among the supporters of the meeting. Chief Constable Dunning of Liverpool City Police expressed his dissatisfaction by stating that such a short Act of Parliament had too many pitfalls. In his questioning, it is established that if the police were to bring a prosecution under this Act, they would first have to prove that it was a lawful public meeting; second, that there was a disorderly act by someone that was preventing the transaction of the business for which the meeting was called; and third, that the intent of the person was to obstruct the meeting. Because of the wide discretion involved, Dunning explained that the Public Meeting Act should be instigated by the injured person only and not the police. Further to the inadequacy of the Act, he also clarified that there was no power of arrest under this Statute if the disorderly person refused to give his or her name to the police.[40]

The principal reason that the Departmental Committee refused to support any new legislation which would impose a duty on the police to undertake the role of stewards inside public meetings was that it would 'be resented by public sentiment as an apparent infringement of the liberty of public meeting'. It also added that the police force were the 'guardians of public order' and if such duty was imposed on them, they would be the first to 'resort to physical force, instead of merely "keeping the King's peace" as at present'.[41] The Report highlighted that the Chief Constables who followed a policy of noninterference at public meetings were unanimous against Chamberlain's proposals. Even those

38 Ibid., para 37.
39 Ibid.
40 Cd. 4674, paras 603–611.
41 Cd. 4673, para 14.

Constabularies who followed a policy of stationing police officers inside public meetings opposed the proposals, as their practice was to 'abstain from taking any action until they are called upon to assist the stewards in resisting violence or until a breach of the peace arises'. Under these two practices, the maintenance of police impartiality is declared to have been comparatively easy. Yet referring to the suggested proposals, the report concluded that 'an indiscretion or failure [on the police's] part would be more serious in its consequences than in the case of ordinary stewards.'[42]

Therefore, the maintenance of impartiality of police conduct was a decisive factor, and it was considered that this could be achieved with as little police interference as possible. However, by the 1920s the organised disruption of political meetings by the far Left was rendering them impossible to hold, with speakers unable to be heard. A letter from Conservative and Unionist Chairman J. Davidson to the Home Secretary William Joynson-Hicks stated that within two months it had been impossible for their speakers to attain a hearing at four of their meetings. A socialist pamphlet which instructed their members on how to disrupt meetings accompanied the letter. The pamphlet included the signals that the group marshal would use to initiate interruption by either the shouting of slogans or the singing of far-Left anthems.[43] The Home Office considered strengthening the Public Meeting Act, again highlighting that police practice at public meetings varied amongst different towns and boroughs. In the Metropolis, many other large towns and most counties, the practice was that police were not allowed to enter public meetings. In Manchester, Cardiff and a majority of boroughs, police officers were allowed in meetings on the application of the promoters; while in Birmingham and 'a few other places' it was considered that it was 'the ordinary course of their duty' for police to attend public meetings regardless of an application from the promoters or not.[44] Following a Home Office consultation with Chief Constables it emerged that no legislative action should be taken: the consensus was that the existing law was sufficient in its provisions to keep order at meetings, provided that the onus was on the promoters to prosecute interrupters under the Public Meeting Act 1908, which would effectively prevent future disturbances.[45]

The authorities' concern with maintaining public order at public meetings centred primarily on the disorder caused by interrupters. In the era of the suffragettes, the violent stewarding was mainly criticised on the basis of gender, arguing that it was more appropriate for females to be ejected by other females. The reassessment of the law regarding disorder at public meetings in the 1920s highlighted that the majority of Chief Constables were reluctant to have their powers increased, instead favouring the meeting promoters to make adequate arrangements and initiate their own legal proceedings against interrupters. However, in the 1930s when the BUF used their trained Defence Corps stewards to

42 Ibid., para 34.
43 HO 144/20069, Disturbances: Disturbances at public meetings (1925–1936).
44 Ibid.
45 Ibid.

keep order, the spotlight regarding the disorder at public meetings shifted its focus upon the stewards, rather than the interrupters. Additionally, with wide police discretion available regarding public meetings and varying police practice still present across England and Wales, the disparity between police responses was to come under intense focus.

Blackshirt brutality and the Olympia meeting 1934

The different application of police powers at the BUF meeting at Olympia, London on 7 June 1934 and the communist meeting in Caerau, Wales, just two months later on 17 August, have been frequently compared, yet vital differences that offer justification for police action that was not politically motivated have been neglected.[46] It is argued here that the police were hindered by wide discretion associated with ineffective legislation, ambiguous common law powers under the breach of the peace doctrine, and different past experiences with both political movements to consistently maintain public order.

During the interwar period the issue of police partisanship was addressed by Parliament and the NCCL.[47] The accusations had heightened in the aftermath of the BUF's public meeting at Olympia. For the BUF, the Olympia meeting represented a political triumph with an unprecedented 15,000 spectators.[48] Mosley had brought the spectacle of large-scale fascist rallies to British politics, emulating the methods of their Nazi counterparts. Eyewitness accounts have recorded the unnecessarily aggressive removal of hecklers and violent assaults conducted by the BUF stewards.[49] Despite the violent physical attacks exerted on members of the crowd, the Metropolitan Police did not intervene or attempt to prevent the BUF's gratuitously violent stewarding. The failure of the police to stop Blackshirt brutality and take effective control of the event attracted much criticism. The Home Secretary, Sir John Gilmour, defended the police, asserting that they had no legal authority to enter a public meeting unless they were invited to do so by the organiser, or had good reason to believe that a breach of the peace was being committed.[50] No legislation existed to confirm the legality of the police entering a meeting. In defending the police action at Olympia, Gilmour had to rely on

---

46 See Ewing and Gearty, *The Struggle*, pp. 282–295; also see D. S. Lewis, *Illusions of Grandeur: Mosley, Fascism and British Society 1931–1981*, Manchester University Press: Manchester (1987), p. 165.

47 For examples, see *Hansard, HC Deb*, 10 Jul 1936, vol 314 cc1566; *Hansard, HC Deb*, 25 Jun 1936, vol 313 cc1943; Kidd, *British Liberty*, pp. 123–158; and U DCL/75/2, NCCL Circular 'Police Discrimination'; U DCL/75/2 'Disturbances in East London', p. 8.

48 In *The Blackshirt*, 15 Jun 1934, p. 3, and other contemporary reports such as *The Times*, 8 Jun 1934, p. 16, it was claimed that 15,000 men and women were in the audience, yet the figure most accepted by historians is 12,000 audience members. See Pugh, *'Hurrah for the Blackshirts!'*, p. 156 and Thurlow, *Fascism*, p. 71.

49 For examples, see I. Montagu, *Blackshirt Brutality*, Workers Bookshop Limited (1934), and U DCL/40/1, NCCL enquiry into fascist meeting at Olympia (1934).

50 *Hansard, HC Deb*, 11 Jun 1934, vol 290 cc1343–1344.

the Report of the Departmental Committee from 1909. The uncertainty of police powers and their legal authority with regard to meetings held on private premises could potentially excuse the police of employing politically motivated methods at Olympia. However, this view does not vindicate the police decision not to enter the hall using common law powers when eyewitness accounts clearly demonstrated that severe disorder was occurring.

Anti-fascist views on Olympia

The NCCL, which had just formed in the February of 1934, collected numerous statements from spectators at Olympia in order to conduct an enquiry to investigate whether the allegations of Blackshirt brutality could be justified. The majority of the recordings were critical of the fascist stewards and it is clear that the police would have been aware that a breach of the peace was occurring in the hall, thereby giving them the right to enter:

> Wounded people began to leave the Hall. Hysterical women came out shrieking, "There's murder going on in there!" Then young men and women came out, all in a very distressed condition. Many women were holding their breasts and their faces displayed signs that they had been clawed by finger nails. The young men were in a deplorable condition. One man I saw, who was being assisted along by kind friends, looked as though an animal had attacked him, his face was mauled, his legs were dangling and his clothes were torn. Other men who were being assisted out had damaged faces and had the appearance that they were suffering from rupture. Practically all the men had smashed faces, not just bruised faces, but smashed faces.[51]

The NCCL's appeal for witnesses to the fascist brutality demonstrated that their position was sympathetic to the abused interrupters, namely the anti-fascists. Despite the horrific scenes described, it is difficult to form a critical view from these descriptions alone as they were collected with the objective of holding the BUF accountable for the violence that occurred. This bias was addressed by a critic of the enquiry, who wrote to the NCCL's founder and secretary, Ronald Kidd, stating that 'any body which has the temerity to call itself "The Council for Civil Liberties" should disdain even the appearance of impartiality' and underlined the actions of the interrupters, contending that the organised breaking up of a meeting with the use of weapons was also an infringement on civil liberties.[52] The NCCL did have an openly anti-fascist stance. For Sylvia Scaffardi, a co-founder of the Council, fascism represented 'the thunder of brute force [that threatened] to trample and overrun the sensitive humanitarian world'.[53] She acknowledged

---

51 U DCL/40/1, NCCL enquiry into fascist meeting at Olympia (1934), p. 9.
52 Ibid., letter from D. O'Conner, 16 Jun 1934.
53 S. Scaffardi, *Fire Under the Carpet: Working for Civil Liberties in the 1930s*, Lawrence and Wishart Ltd: London (1986) p. 49.

that in 1934 the image of fascism was still respectable to the wider public who were not involved in politics.[54] Reports from Germany on the treatment of the Jews and the *Brown Book of Hitler Terror*, published by Victor Gollancz in 1933, which contained statements and documents on Nazi violence, interrogation, torture and murder, also influenced the NCCL's contempt of fascism. Therefore, fascism represented an end to the ideals of individual freedom and liberty that the council were defending, which initiated their anti-fascist stance in Britain. The stated objective of the NCCL weakens the reliability of the extreme testimonies they collected. This does not absolve the Blackshirts from their violent actions but addresses the need to analyse the BUF account of the event.

The BUF's view on Olympia

The BUF's version of Olympia was recorded in their weekly newspaper *Blackshirt*.[55] Their propaganda predictably confirmed that the communists were responsible for the violence and were determined to 'Kill Mosley'.[56] BUF propaganda officer A. K. Chesterton's report detailed a 'frenzied Red minority' who were determined to prevent Mosley from being heard and that large groups of communists set upon stewards who tried to remove hecklers. He glorified the heroics of the Blackshirts who were 'fighting with their bare fists against the foulest weapons – daggers, razors, stockings filled with broken glass, everything that the criminal lunatic mentality could devise.'[57] In his autobiography, Sir Oswald Mosley quoted the Conservative MP Patrick Dormer's account from the *National Review*:

> [The Communists] marched from the East End, the police kindly escorting them, with the avowed purpose of wrecking the meeting . . . and with my own eyes I witnessed gangs of Communists . . . resisting ejection with the utmost violence.[58]

The article defended the 'vigour' of the Blackshirts on the account that they were faced by armed hooligans with only the use of their fists. This perception reversed the accusation of police partiality and also highlighted the nature of the resistance by those whom the stewards were ejecting. Mosley claimed that at their own dressing stations 'highly qualified medical personnel' treated sixty-three Blackshirts 'for injuries, mostly abdominal, and injuries caused by blunt instruments'. Mosley's descriptions of the injuries sustained to Blackshirts were just as brutal as the statements collected by the NCCL. These included a female

---

54 Ibid., p. 61.
55 *The Blackshirt*, 15 Jun 1934: see pages 1–2 for 'The Truth about the Olympia Disorder'; p. 3 for A. K. Chesterton's article, 'Reason's Triumph: Red Terror Smashed at Britain's Biggest Meeting'; and p. 8 for Oswald Mosley's account, 'Triumph of the Blackshirt Spirit'.
56 *The Blackshirt*, 15 Jun 1934, p. 1.
57 Ibid., p. 8.
58 Mosley, *My Life*, p. 247.

Blackshirt who suffered a cut to her eye and down her cheek and neck, finishing between her shoulder blades, as well as several Blackshirts who 'were laid up for three weeks' after being kicked in the head and stomach and attacked with blunt objects. Mosley also claimed that there were no serious injuries caused to the interrupters. Whatever the validity of the different accounts, there is no question that a breach of the peace had occurred.

Public attitudes towards Olympia and political violence

The Olympia meeting was a pivotal moment in the history of the BUF and has received much critical attention. Thurlow argued that although the initial effect of the meeting was to attract a large number of new recruits, with many new members being attracted to the BUF's dedication to the preservation of free speech and its stance against left-wing activism, they lost the long-term 'propaganda war concerning responsibility for the violence . . . and in retrospect it marked the turning-point in the fortunes of the movement'.[59] This is the general summary of textbook analysis, yet an evaluation of the responses to Olympia prompts further questioning of the contemporary political culture and reactions to political violence.

Lawrence introduces the pre-War political culture in which the 'old ways' of party politics and the disorder that occurred are referred to as a 'form of sport' and argued that it was commonly accepted by some politicians that the mobilisation of a private force was necessary to ensure successful political meetings.[60] He contends that this view changed after the First World War when 'the politics of misrule ceased to be tolerated by the vast majority of politicians.'[61] Pugh responded by stating that when old attitudes change they do so gradually and that 'many of the inter-war MPs had grown up in an era when political violence was routine and they retained the assumptions of an earlier generation.'[62] The historical debate between Lawrence and Pugh establishes that there was conflicting contemporary opinion on the acceptability of using violence in order to protect a political meeting. Despite the shock that the eyewitness accounts evoke from the modern reader, the conflicting contemporary attitudes concerning the entitlement of the organisers and their stewards to use 'reasonable necessary force' created a challenging situation for the use of police discretion in this era.

A greater understanding of the contemporary political culture and legal framework generate questions that demonstrate the complexity of the issues faced by the police and politicians. The situation at Olympia cannot be simplified by explaining police actions as either pro-fascist or anti-communist. While the nature of the fascist violence cannot be excused, it would be naïve, considering the advertised communist campaign to stop the meeting, to regard all of the ejected as innocent victims.

---

59 Thurlow, *Fascism*, pp. 64, 71.
60 Lawrence, 'Fascist violence', p. 241.
61 Ibid., p. 242.
62 M. Pugh, 'The National Government, the British Union of Fascists and the Olympia Debate' in *Historical Research 78*, no. 200 (May 2005), p. 255.

However, many of the reports recorded in the national press demonstrate that the Blackshirt brutality was indiscriminate and unjustifiable. *The Times* recorded some of the injuries sustained at the meeting, declaring that seventy patients were treated by doctors and several had to be detained in hospital. The injuries varied from a woman with external bleeding after blows to the abdomen, 'a man with five lacerated wounds in the scalp (said to be caused by a blow with a fire extinguisher)' and a man with a 'badly lacerated finger, obviously caused by some sharp cutting instrument'.[63] These examples demonstrate that women were also indiscriminately attacked (usually by female Blackshirts), but perhaps more importantly, that the Blackshirts were accused of using a variety of weapons to maintain order, including purposefully brought weapons of a discreet nature such as the 'sharp cutting instrument', or the use of nearby objects such as the fire extinguisher.

Correspondence from audience members published in *The Times* provided a balanced view of the event. In his short defence of Blackshirt action, Aylmer Haldane declared that the 'interrupters only received the treatment which they deserved' and that a 'forcible ejection of such intruders [was] the only remedy left' to preserve the meeting for the majority who wished to hear Mosley's speech.[64] Nonetheless, it would be incorrect to assume that Haldane's view on the necessity of force was common among other audience members. Haldane was an army officer who began his military career in 1881. In his account of how an insurgency was put down in *The Insurrection in Mesopotamia, 1920* he insisted that 'The Arabs of Iraq respect nothing but force, and to force only will they bend.'[65] Other members of the audience, attending the Olympia meeting out of curiosity of what fascism had to offer, were put off by the brutal exhibition of violence. This was the experience of T. S. Singleton-Fleming in his letter published the same day. He highlighted the 'disgusting display of force' and the 'un-English theatricalism and schoolboy hooliganism . . . [which] made it quite impossible for us to take fascism seriously.'[66]

Police accounts of the Olympia meeting

Police reports from the Olympia meeting demonstrate that not only were some police officers aware of the disruption inside, but that the graphic descriptions from the eyewitnesses were not necessarily exaggerated. One Special Branch Officer reported that:

> At 10.43 p.m. . . . A man was thrown through the entrance by three fascists into the street. One leg of his trousers had been torn off, and the other was

63 *The Times*, 9 Jun 1934.

64 Ibid.

65 A. Simpson, 'Haldane, Sir (James) Aylmer Lowthorpe (1862–1950)', *Oxford Dictionary of National Biography*, Oxford University Press, Oct 2008; online edn, May 2009 (www.oxforddnb. com/view/article/95438, accessed 12 Oct 2010).

66 Ibid.

round his ankle. His private parts were exposed, and he was bleeding freely from a head wound.[67]

Special Branch Sergeant Hunt, who was stationed inside the hall as an observer, witnessed 'about 50 persons ejected. They were handled in a most violent manner and in some cases were punched unconscious and their clothing torn.'[68] Another Special Branch Sergeant recorded that the strong opposition put up by interrupters, 'no doubt accounted for the great deal of the violence used upon them' but also witnessed hecklers that offered to walk out without fighting were still set upon by stewards and 'not allowed to do so without molestation'.[69]

In one instance, a Police Inspector assisted by ten Police Constables actually entered the building when a 'linkman' working for the Olympia venue informed him that a person inside needed assistance. Inspector O'Carroll's report stated that apart from the man 'in a state of semi-coma' he witnessed, 'six groups, each containing six to eight "Blackshirts" beating and kicking unmercifully a man in the centre of each group'.[70] He then rescued a youth being brutally beaten by four Blackshirts on the stairs. Interestingly, his account of the proceedings changed after he was interrogated by the Deputy Assistant Commissioner. The amended version of the events absolved O'Carroll from not making any arrests as he now stated that the youth '*appeared to have been* beaten in a brutal manner' rather than '*was being* beaten in a brutal manner' (italics mine) and that those responsible immediately ran making it impossible for him to restrain or identify them.[71] The seriousness of the assaults had also been lessened in the amended account, which highlighted that none of the individuals that he rescued accepted medical attention. The Deputy Assistant Commissioner defended O'Carroll's actions and stated, 'I am of the opinion that he acted with sound judgment in very difficult circumstances, and that his reasons for not making arrests are clear and sufficient.'[72] The difference of accounts does call into question the validity of police statements and their personal bias to protect or justify their own actions.

Lord Trenchard and Chief Constables on the duty of the police at public meetings

In the month following the Olympia meeting, the Metropolitan Police Commissioner, Lord Trenchard, wrote a Memorandum to the Home Secretary that emphasised that the fascists were the main cause of the recent disorder. Mosley frequently absolved his movement from any responsibility for violent

67 MEPO 2/4319, Police evidence sought about various happenings at Fascist meetings, in support of private prosecution (1934–1936).
68 Ibid., SB Sergeant Hunt, 8 June 1934.
69 Ibid., SB Sergeant Hilley, 8 June 1934.
70 Ibid., Inspector O'Carroll, 8 Jun 1934.
71 Ibid., DAC 1, 9 Jun 1934.
72 Ibid.

confrontations, arguing that the BUF Defence Corps was a necessary measure to ensure his movement's 'right' to freedom of speech. Trenchard highlighted that the main source of disruption at fascist meetings was caused by the 'abnormal provocation provided by the existence of a private uniformed "army" adopting continental methods and ideas'.[73] His memorandum does not demonstrate any sympathy for the fascist movement. He suggested that legislation should be introduced along the lines of a recent Swedish Act, which prohibited the formation of, or the taking part in, an organisation which was 'intended to serve as a defence corps for a political party or similar group'.[74] It was Trenchard's belief that this measure, along with prohibiting uniforms for political purposes, would prevent further disorder on a large scale.

Trenchard addressed the issue of freedom of speech with regard to the organised disruption of fascist speakers, arguing that political opponents were free to talk back and it should only become a concern of the authorities if the simultaneous communication leads to a breach of the peace. In the event of a public meeting the chairman had the right to ask an interrupter to leave, and stewards had the right to remove the person if they declined. On this issue, Trenchard stated that it was the responsibility of the police to interfere as little as possible and that the onus of keeping order in a meeting should stay with the stewards. The only detail that he would have liked to have changed was that it should be within the discretion of the Chief Officer of Police to deploy a sufficient number of men in the hall whether it was asked for by the organisers or not. This should be a power employed on rare occasions wherein the police should deal with unnecessary violence and fighting only if disturbances develop throughout the hall, and ultimately they should be empowered to order the chairman to close the meeting and withdraw his supporters.

Trenchard's suggestions demonstrated that although he did not want the police to become embroiled with the stewarding of public meetings, he was not politically motivated. Furthermore, as the police's responsibilities included the maintenance of public order, his post-Olympia suggestions represented a proportionate response that could have prevented further confrontations and brutality. Home Office papers demonstrate that many Chief Constables were in favour of new legislation to clarify police presence and powers at public meetings.[75] Fifteen Chief Constables participated in discussion with the Metropolitan Police Commissioner following the Olympia event for the purpose of drafting his memorandum and proposing new legislation. All of the Chief Constables agreed, to some extent, that

---

73   CAB 24/250, Preservation of Public Order: Memorandum by the Home Secretary and Commissioner of Police of the Metropolis (July 1934), p. 1.

74   Ibid., p. 2.

75   See HO 45/25386 (Disturbances: Wearing of uniform to denote membership of political organisations. Preservation of public order: disturbances arising out of public meetings and demonstrations, particularly those involving the British Union of Fascists [1933–1936]) for drafts of the 'Memorandum by the Commissioner of Police of the Metropolis' and minutes to the suggestions made by the fifteen other Chief Constables.

the police should assist stewards in removing interrupters when it became necessary. The object of this request was not just to support the stewards in keeping
order during their meetings but also, as the Chief Constable of Durham pointed
out, to empower the police to act when a breach of the peace occurred, whether
it was from organised interruption or excessively violent stewarding.[76] Although
there was an overwhelming consensus that the police should be present at public
meetings, there was some disagreement on the point at which the police should
intervene. This was either after a breach of the peace had occurred as already
suggested or, as the Chief Constable of Southport declared, when a breach of the
peace was likely, adding that any person who acted in a way which was likely
to cause a breach of the peace should also be prosecuted. He went even further
to check fascist aggression by stating that organisers should be required by law to
appoint stewards who should be subject to the direction of the police if they are
present.[77] Whether there to help preserve or to restore public order, the lawful
presence of the police at public meetings without requiring the invitation of the
organisers was the ultimate ideal.

Thomas v Sawkins

It was not the enactment of new legislation that enabled the police to legally
enter meetings when they apprehended a potential breach of the peace, but the
common law authority of *Thomas v Sawkins*. The background to this case needs
further clarification in order to elucidate the differences between the events at
Caerau and Olympia. Two months after the Olympia meeting, on 17 August 1934,
Police Inspector Parry, along with sergeants Lawrence and Sawkins of the Glamorgan County Police, entered the communist meeting at Caerau using common
law powers, anticipating that the meeting could become an unlawful assembly
or a riot, that a breach of the peace may occur, or that seditious speeches were
to be made. They refused to leave the premises after Alun Thomas, a speaker at
the meeting, lodged a complaint against the officers at the police station. When
Thomas proceeded to exercise his believed right to eject the police and placed his
hand on Parry's shoulder, Sawkins intervened by pushing Thomas' arm and hand
away, stating, 'I won't allow you to interfere with my superior officer.'[78] Thomas
brought a criminal prosecution against Sawkins under s42 of the Offences Against
the Person Act 1861. It was agreed that neither Thomas nor Sawkins used more
force than was reasonably necessary in the execution of their duty as steward or
police officer, but if the prosecution could prove that Sawkins had no right to be
in the hall at the time of the incident, his actions would have constituted assault.
The magistrates held that the police were entitled to be on the premises and the
charge of assault was dismissed. An appeal was taken to the Divisional Court

76　Ibid.
77　Ibid.
78　*Thomas v Sawkins* at 251.

where Lord Chief Justice Hewart asserted that 'a police officer has *ex virtute offi-cii* full right so to act when he has reasonable ground for believing that an offence is imminent or is likely to be committed' and dismissed the appeal.[79] This was a controversial outcome, and Thomas Kidd of the NCCL reflected on its potential effect, stating, 'Judge-made law, as binding as parliamentary law, could under-mine democracy.'[80]

For the respondent, Vaughan Williams KC argued that the police by oath swear to keep the peace and, by their duty of preventive justice, have a right to enter private premises to prevent a breach of the peace.[81] For the appellant, Sir Stafford Cripps KC argued that although the duty of the police was to preserve the King's Peace, they may enter private premises without a warrant, to either

> take a felon, where a felony has been committed and a particular person is reasonably suspected to be the offender, where a felony is likely, or about, to be committed, where he hears an affray on the premises, or to pursue and arrest those who have taken part in an affray.[82]

Other examples were used to demonstrate that existing provisions to empower a constable to enter private premises did not apply: 'There is no authority empow-ering a constable to enter private premises merely because he has a reasonable belief that an offence or a breach of the peace may be committed thereon.'[83]

In the original hearing held at Bridgend, W. H. Thompson, representing Thomas, quoted the Home Secretary's remarks from the Olympia debate in the Commons. This was a measure that could not be repeated in the appeal case. Despite the Home Secretary's ruling that the police could enter only when a sus-pected breach of the peace was actually being committed, the magistrates returned with the verdict that the police were entitled to be present and the summons on Sergeant Sawkins was dismissed. The magistrates also heard that the police in Caerau had been 'aggravated' by the 'considerable trouble' caused by recent meetings and marches and had every reason to have anticipated that a breach of the peace would occur.[84]

The reasonable anticipation of a breach of the peace was echoed by Lord Hew-art, who confirmed that it was part of the 'preventive power, and, therefore, part of the preventive duty, of the police . . . to enter and remain on the premises'.[85] Such a strong emphasis on the preventive power of the police has deep implications for civil liberties. This measure does in fact open the discretionary power of the police

79 Ibid., at 255.
80 Scaffardi, *Fire Under the Carpet*, p. 78.
81 *Thomas v Sawkins* at 253.
82 Ibid.
83 Ibid., at 252–253.
84 *The Times*, 14 Sep 1934.
85 *Thomas v Sawkins* at 254.

to act under the apprehension of an offence being committed and effectively pun-
ishes the person that the police are acting against without them even committing
an offence. Justice Avory reflected on the preventive power of the magistrates. He
quoted Justice Fitzgerald in *R v Queen's County Justices*[86] who declared that 'magistrates are invested with large judicial powers, for the maintenance of order and
the preservation of public peace.'[87] After referencing that that principle had been
approved in *Lansbury v Riley*[88] and *Wise v Dunning*,[89] he contended that the power
of a magistrate to bind someone over to be of good behaviour is no different to the
duty of the police constable to prevent a breach of the peace.

Although the preventive action described in *Thomas v Sawkins* was initiated by
the police, similarities can still be drawn with the decisions of the magistrates in
Wise v Dunning and *Lansbury v Riley*. The latter two cases dealt with the binding
over of speakers with a known history of using insulting words or words calculated to incite a breach of the peace. The appellants against the magistrates' decisions were a Protestant lecturer from Liverpool, George Wise, who was known to
cause breaches of the peace with anti-Catholic speeches and gestures, and George
Lansbury, a supporter of the Women's Social and Political Union, who was known
to incite militancy to advance pressure on the Government to extend the voting
franchise to women. Unfortunately, *Thomas v Sawkins* does not define the potential threat to a breach of the peace very clearly or document the history of the
appellant. Yet reasonable suspicion that seditious speeches would be made was
evidenced by the comments of Thomas at a previous meeting. In reference to the
police present, he said, 'If it were not for the presence of these people . . . I could
tell you a hell of a lot more.'[90] In the view of the respondent and the other officers,
their anticipation of an unlawful assembly, riot or a breach of the peace was based
on their knowledge and experience of previous meetings. Avory asserted the
authority of the police most clearly, confirming that 'no express statutory authority is necessary where the police have reasonable grounds to apprehend a breach
of the peace.'[91] This effectively set a new precedent by providing the police with
the power to enter public meetings when a breach of the peace was anticipated.

Regardless of the emphasis on preventive power, other factors were considered in the summing up. It was significant that the meeting was well advertised
and members of the public were invited to attend free of charge. Avory insisted
that 'There can be no doubt that the police officers who attended the meeting
were members of the public and were included in that sense in the invitation to
attend.'[92] Hewart added that it was remarkable to talk of trespass on the part of the

86 *R v Queen's County Justices* (1882) 10 LRI 294, 301.
87 *Thomas v Sawkins* at 256.
88 *Lansbury v Riley* [1914] 3 KB 229.
89 *Wise v Dunning* [1902] 1 KB 167.
90 *Thomas v Sawkins* at 250.
91 Ibid., at 257.
92 Ibid., at 255.

police after a public invitation had been issued, especially as part of the business of the meeting was the dismissal of the Chief Constable of the county.

Despite no statutory authority being mentioned to clarify the right of the police to be at the meeting, the justices accepted that common law had provided significant justification for their actions. *Humphries v Connor*[93] demonstrated the extent of the preventive powers available as it was held that a police officer was entitled to commit a technical assault on a person to preserve the public peace. Justice Lawrence referred to this in his summing up, stating that 'If a constable in the execution of his duty to preserve the peace is entitled to commit an assault, it appears to me that he is equally entitled to commit a trespass.'[94]

The BUF Olympia meeting and Thomas v Sawkins: compatibility for comparison?

The different approaches in exercising discretion evidenced by the Metropolitan Police and the Glamorgan County Police have been applied to demonstrate the existence of police partiality. The eyewitness accounts of the event at Olympia discussed in this chapter demonstrate the different attitudes of those present, who debated whether the Blackshirts used more than 'reasonable necessary force' when dealing with disrupters or not. This ambiguous phrase, which split the opinion of the audience, highlights the problem of police discretion. Although the Superintendent's decision not to enter the hall to prevent the violent ejection of interrupters was contentious, it was more likely to have been based on the perception of his legal power rather than pure partisanship. *Thomas v Sawkins* was a 'constitutional innovation' in which the Chair of Jurisprudence at Oxford, Arthur Goodhart, argued that no 'case was cited by counsel or in the judgments in which it had been specifically held that the police had this power, and no text-book contains a statement that it exists or has ever existed'.[95] As the scenes witnessed at Olympia happened a year before this decision, the Metropolitan Police were understandably more apprehensive about entering the meeting as their actions could have been interpreted as trespass by a court of law if sufficient reason could not be given to justify the use of this discretionary power.

The precedent set by *Thomas v Sawkins* directly conflicted with Gilmour's belief that the police had no legal right to enter meetings 'merely because they apprehend that disorder *may* occur'.[96] His Memorandum proposed that the law should be amended to empower the police to enter the premises of a public meeting if the Chief Officer of Police had reason to believe that disorder was likely to occur, whether invited to do so by the organisers or not.[97] This recommendation

---

93 *Humphries v Connor* (1864) 17 Ir CLR 1.

94 *Thomas v Sawkins* at 257.

95 A. L. Goodhart, '*Thomas v. Sawkins*: A Constitutional Innovation', The Cambridge Law Journal 6, no. 1 (1936), pp. 22–30.

96 CAB 24/250, 'Preservation of Public Order: Memorandum by the Home Secretary and Commissioner of Police of the Metropolis (July 1934), p. 1.

97 Ibid., p. 2.

would give the police statutory authority to enter meetings rather than relying on common law powers of anticipating a breach of the peace. In the Commons, Gilmour recognised that the police did have the right to enter if they had good reason to believe that a breach of the peace was being committed.[98] Therefore, it was perceived that the police did not have legal preventive powers to enter the Olympia hall on the apprehension of a breach of the peace, but they were empowered to do so on the occasion of a breach of the peace being committed. The Departmental Committee of 1909 addressed the disputable issue of what constituted a breach of the peace at a public meeting. The Chief Constable of Manchester suggested that 'it only occurs when the meeting is broken up by the opposition, and the conveners of the meeting resort to retaliatory methods.'[99] Although the Blackshirts' violent approach could accurately be described as retaliatory, the meeting was not broken up and instead was able to continue until its natural conclusion. Therefore, under this tenuous definition a breach of the peace did not occur.

Gilmour asserted the need to strengthen police powers, observing that the fascist policy of refusing police help had created a new problem that required the changing of the law.[100] The Public Meeting Act 1908 was effective only if the police were asked to assist when organised interruption disrupted a meeting, as it did not contain any provision for the police to enter private premises. The Act did not directly involve the police and by 1934 many Chief Constables considered it to be a 'dead letter'.[101] Another issue emphasised by the Departmental Committee of 1909 was that 'disorderly conduct' did not necessarily amount to a breach of the peace. The difference was highlighted that it was the duty of the police to keep the peace and not to secure a speaker's desire to be heard.[102] The Act was not amended until the Public Order Act 1936.

It is the experience of the Glamorgan County Police and the preventive action mentioned in *Wise v Dunning* and *Lansbury v Riley* that distinguish these events from the BUF meeting at Olympia. It has been suggested that the difference in police practice in *Thomas v Sawkins* and the Olympia meeting indicate the use of partial law enforcement.[103] The stimulus behind police action at Caerau was calculated to prevent seditious and inflammatory speeches being made and to prevent any potential disorder. In contrast, at Olympia, Mosley's fascist movement had not yet adopted an open anti-Semitic policy, and the authorities would have anticipated that any potential disturbances at Olympia would be caused by organised communist protest and not because of the potential of seditious speeches being made by Mosley. Therefore, it was still accepted that it was the stewards' responsibility, acting under the instructions of the chairman, to keep order at the meeting. The issue at Olympia was why the police did not enter the meeting

98   *Hansard, HC Deb*, 11 Jun 1934, vol 290 cc 1343–1344.
99   Williams, *Keeping the Peace*, p. 143.
100 CAB 24/250, pp. 1–2.
101 HO 45/25386.
102 Williams, *Keeping the Peace*, p. 139.
103 Pugh, '*Hurrah for the Blackshirts!*' p. 165.

despite it being evident that the stewards used more than reasonable necessary force. Yet if a breach of the peace were defined as disorder that prevented the business of the meeting were applied, then a breach was not present at Olympia offering justification for the police not entering the premises.

The Superintendent responsible for keeping order outside Olympia stated that he was satisfied that they had prevented a serious disturbance that would have led to injuries and serious damage to property.[104] His priorities demonstrate why more action was not taken by the police. If the police had entered the building, there was a risk that their presence would have inflamed the situation. Additionally, in the event of a riot, under s2(1) Riot (Damages) Act 1886, the Metropolitan Police would have been liable to pay compensation to any person who had sustained loss by injury, stealing or destruction. Another danger would have been that police action inside the hall could have been interpreted as pro-fascist. In the Commons, Conservative MP Geoffrey Lloyd upheld the view that had a breach of the peace occurred it was not the responsibility of the police to take charge of the meeting, but to help the stewards to restore order.[105] Therefore, if an interrupter, on refusing to leave the hall when requested, fought the Blackshirt stewards, the obligation of the police would have been to assist in that person's ejection. Although this may have helped regulate the force that was used by the stewards, it could still have been criticised as preferential policing in support of the fascists.

The danger of police intervention provoking serious disorder was reported in *The Times* following the action of the Glamorgan County Police at Caerau. Following the scuffle between Thomas and Sawkins, twenty police officers rushed into the back of the hall. Some had batons drawn, which created considerable disorder. *The Times* stated that 'It looked as though there was going to be serious trouble . . . but Inspector Parry then had the good sense to tell the police to withdraw.'[106] The Superintendent outside Olympia would have had similar concerns to the reaction to a significant number of police officers entering the hall. He stated that the police had 'successfully carried out and upheld the law'.[107] The police had fulfilled their duty impartially, albeit without some controversy.

The different uses of discretion applied at Olympia and Caerau raise the issue of diversity in police practice. Following the Olympia meeting, Labour MP Rhys Davies highlighted in the Commons that the Committee of 1909 did not come to any definite conclusions on the issue of policing public meetings. He stated that the report 'pointed out the three distinct ways of dealing with this issue, which they termed the Birmingham, the Liverpool and the Manchester police methods', adding that they were likely to differ again in London.[108] He defended the

---

104   MEPO 2/4319, Police evidence sought about various happenings at Fascist meetings, in support of private prosecution (1934–36), Superintendent Hammersmith Station, 8 June 1934.

105   *Hansard, HC Deb*, 14 Jun 1934, vol 290 c1937.

106   *The Times*, 14 Sep 1934.

107   MEPO 2/4319, Police evidence sought about various happenings at Fascist meetings, in support of private prosecution (1934–36), Superintendent Hammersmith Station to DAC 1, 8 June 1934.

108   *Hansard, HC Deb*, 14 Jun 1934, vol 290 cc1973–1974.

Metropolitan Police adding, 'The police carried out their duties in connection with the Olympia meeting very fairly,' declaring:

> Is it not possible to secure that the method employed in one of these three cities which is the most effective for the purpose of the proper conduct of public meetings shall be adopted throughout the whole of the country? I cannot conceive how the Manchester Watch Committee can issue instructions to its police force on how they should conduct themselves in connection with public meetings, while different instructions are issued by the Birmingham and the Liverpool Watch Committees respectively.[109]

Although responsible for the Metropolitan Police, the Home Office did not have the same level of authority over County and Borough police forces, which were organised on a local basis. Gilmour's interpretation of police powers at public meetings, and his belief that new legislation was required to allow police to enter public meetings, is reflected in the actions taken by the Metropolitan Police at Olympia.

Commonality between other public meetings in the interwar years

While the Olympia and South Wales meetings have been used to reinforce the charge of partisan policing in the 1930s,[110] it is important to select evidence from a range of events that demonstrate a more balanced view. The inconsistent approaches employed by different constabularies in the 1930s challenge the view of a dominant pro-fascist police culture. This is most significantly noted by the Manchester City Police and the Manchester Watch Committee, who showed very little tolerance of fascist activity or provocation.

A year before the Olympia meeting, Mosley spoke to a crowd of 3,000 in Manchester. The *Daily Mirror* reported that when 'pandemonium broke out [the police entered] and insisted that every "Black Shirt" should leave the hall.'[111] The fascist propaganda following the meeting predictably used the incident to criticise the police for protecting the communists who attempted to break up the meeting. The BUF newspaper *Blackshirt* reported:

> The red flag was under police protection for the night. Even a Communist who attempted to pull down the Union Jack was saved from Fascist retaliation by the police, and was escorted from the hall without arrest or punishment. Reds carrying bludgeons and razors were not touched by the police.

The Manchester Watch Committee was also involved in stifling fascist activity by refusing to grant permission for a uniformed BUF procession before the

---

109 Ibid., c1974.
110 See Ewing and Gearty, *The Struggle*, pp. 275–330, and Lewis, *Illusions of Grandeur*, p. 161.
111 *The Daily Mirror*, 13 Mar 1933.

prohibition of uniforms under s1 Public Order Act 1936. Four months after Olympia, Mosley addressed a BUF meeting at Plymouth Drill Hall on 5 October 1934 and the police entered to restore order. The meeting – which had an estimated audience of between 3,500 and 4,000 – was stewarded by just fifty Blackshirts.[112] There was some disorder at the meeting and the *Western Evening Herald* reported on the 'Blackshirt's Outrageous Conduct at Plymouth'. The most serious disturbance occurred near the end of the meeting when the platform was rushed by twenty anti-fascists, creating disorder and widespread fighting. The police subsequently entered the hall and restored order. Following the disorder, six fascists were summonsed with the charge of 'maliciously committing damage, injury and spoil to and upon a camera' belonging to the Western Morning News Company, contrary to s14(1) Criminal Justice Administration Act 1914. Four of the fascists were charged, and a second charge of assault (which related to a public meeting held outside Plymouth Pannier Market on the 11 October 1934) was also reflected in their sentence. Reports regarding the police practice at Plymouth varied. *The Times* stated that 'a large number of police who were present inside the hall took no part in the struggle'[113] while the *Western Morning News* reported that order was restored by the police, who were forced to enter the hall.[114]

In consequence of the criticism levelled at the Blackshirts' violent stewarding methods at the Olympia meeting, the BUF accepted the Metropolitan Police's request to station police officers within the premises of their next high-profile meeting, held at the Albert Hall on 28 October 1934. Significantly, this meeting fell a month after the Bridgend magistrates had ruled in Sawkins' favour, but a full seven months before the appeal at the Divisional Court. Mosley declared:

> We said we certainly had no objection to their coming in. We are always delighted to see the police. They are very influential members of the community . . . I have now held twenty-five meetings in this country and at only one of these were the police present – and at one only did disorder occur. Nevertheless we are delighted to see the police here tonight.[115]

The correspondence between the Metropolitan Police and the BUF prior to the Albert Hall meeting details arrangements such as the BUF instructions given to the Blackshirt stewards which included the directives, 'All interrupters are to be warned twice before action is taken . . . [and] If it is considered necessary to remove anyone from the Hall, it must be done as quickly and quietly as possible, force not being used unless absolutely necessary.'[116] The shortcomings of the Metropolitan Police, who did not enter the Olympia hall despite evident breaches

---

112 *Western Morning News*, 16 Nov 1934.
113 *The Times*, 6 Oct 1934.
114 Gray, *Blackshirts in Devon*, p. 67.
115 MEPO 2/3077, Fascist meetings, parade through West End and march past (1934–35), p. 4.
116 Ibid., 'British Union of Fascists: Instructions to Stewards'.

of the peace, were also addressed in the Albert Hall operation. The Commissioner's instructions included:

> In the event of a disturbance inside the Hall, one of the plain clothes men [from Special Branch] will go out to the nearest squad of uniform men and bring them in . . . [and] If the uniform men outside see a man ejected from the Hall looking as if he has been "knocked about" they should go in immediately.[117]

The Times reported that the event 'passed off without any disturbance'.[118]

Parallels can also be drawn with communist meetings in which stewards used violent methods of ejection. John Wynn initiated a private prosecution against a communist steward following a meeting at Ealing Town Hall held under the auspices of the Ealing Communist and Labour Parties to discuss affairs in Spain. Giving evidence at Ealing Police Court, Wynn accused the stewards of excessive violence towards the interrupters, declaring that one man was completely surrounded by stewards and was struck. Wynn, declaring his political impartiality, stated that he became involved only to assist a man who was being beaten following a melee of minor fights breaking out. Following his intervention, and the cry from the speaker to 'eject them all', he was repeatedly punched in the face and was thrown down a flight of stairs, which knocked him unconscious. This incident demonstrates the excessive force used by a communist steward that was akin to the exorbitance of the Blackshirts. In this case, the charge of grievous bodily harm was dismissed, as Wynn was deemed to have obstructed the stewards in their duty.[119] This judgment reveals that the magistrates in this case accepted a certain level of violence by stewards in order to protect their meeting from disruption even when the violent stewarding was conducted by a communist.

The Public Order Act 1936

S6 Public Order Act amended the Public Meeting Act 1908 and provided the police with the power to arrest anyone whom they reasonably suspected of acting in a disorderly manner in an attempt to break up a lawful public meeting, and who refused to give their name or address. More controversially, s2(6) was believed by many to give the fascists licence to continue their violent stewarding methods. In general s2 is mandated to proscribe quasi-military organisations, yet subsection 6 provides that

> Nothing in this section shall be construed as prohibiting the employment of a reasonable number of persons as stewards to assist in the preservation of order at any public meeting held upon private premises, or the making of arrangements for that purpose or the instruction of the persons to be so

117 Ibid., 'Notes made by the Commissioner at a meeting with ACA and ACC on 16.10.34.'
118 *The Times*, 29 Oct 1934.
119 *The Times*, 28 Sep 1936.

employed in their lawful duties as such stewards, or their being furnished with badges or other distinguishing signs.

During its progression through Parliament, Aneurin Bevan criticised the introduction of subsection 6, stating:

> We are now re-importing into the Bill the possibility of an organised, disciplined and semi-military force . . . The right hon. Gentleman suggests that he has safeguarded himself by putting in the word "lawful" before "duties." I have had no legal training whatever, but it, seems to me that the importation of the word "lawful" does nothing at all to strengthen the language, because no steward could in the discharge of his duties do an unlawful thing.[120]

The fear that this could safeguard unnecessarily violent fascist stewarding was eased by Dingle Foot, the Liberal MP who was also a member of the NCCL and critic of fascism. He stated:

> I think the insertion of the word "lawful" does something to avoid the precise evils which he has in mind, because if you have a group of stewards organised, not to use undue force, such as some of us think has been used in meetings in the last year or two; that would not come within the word "lawful."

The obligation of the organisers of meetings to appoint stewards was to ensure that police presence at meetings (especially political) was a last resort. Yet parameters had to be drawn in order that the violence at Olympia was not repeated. In defence of subsection 6, Foot suggested that 'unlawful' would cover stewards who were armed with knuckledusters and continued:

> [B]y using the word "lawful" here, we are drawing a distinction between the legitimate use of stewards for removing an interrupter who refuses to be silent and in fact holds up the meeting, and stewards who use very different methods and quite unnecessary force.[121]

Violent stewarding following the Public Order Act

According to Sylvia Scaffardi of the NCCL, the only reported incident of violence at a fascist meeting following the Public Order Act was on 25 January 1937 at Hornsey Town Hall.[122] At this meeting, the fascist stewards allegedly ejected

---

120 *Hansard, HC Deb*, 7 Dec 1936, vol 318 c1674.
121 Ibid., c1676.
122 The reduction in violence can be attributed to the growing prohibitions and conditions placed upon the BUF for the use of town and public halls across the country from 1935 onwards. See Benewick, *Political Violence*, p. 265. For an example of conditions being placed upon the BUF, see MEPO 2/3083, 'British Union of Fascists: attempts to ensure free policing of their meetings' (1936). Here, the Wandsworth Borough Council applies a charge on the BUF for the employment of police constables to preserve order inside the venue under clause 7 of the conditions of letting Streatham Bath Hall.

members of the audience in a violent manner.[123] The NCCL applied pressure on the Government to launch an official enquiry, but on the rejection of this, they proceeded to collect statements from eyewitnesses to record their own unofficial enquiry. One of the assaulted audience members was Norman Boulton, a stockbroker's clerk. He had witnessed an assault on a man in the row behind who had requested permission to ask Mosley a personal question. This was granted, and he asked Mosley, 'Can you deny that your wife was a Jew?' A number of stewards then assaulted him, striking him in the face and body. Following this assault, Boulton attempted to leave the hall and, on being questioned by a fascist steward, told him that he was going to fetch a policeman. The fascist steward subsequently him struck in the face, cutting his lip, and he was thrown out onto the pavement by four other fascists. He then reported that when he informed the Inspector in charge he refused to listen and 'told one of his subordinates to push me aside'.[124]

Another recorded assault at Hornsey Town Hall was upon E. McKercher. In response to some fascists sitting behind him who shouted 'castrate the bastards!', he asked them to moderate their language in the presence of ladies. After repeating his request a second time McKercher was punched in the face, causing him a cut to his eyebrow and cheek and breaking his glasses. The lady next to him agreed to be a witness to the assault. When McKercher reported this to the Inspector outside the hall, he was informed that he could do nothing without the name and address of the fascist, and he could not assist him on finding the suspect as he could only go inside the hall if he was requested to do so.

By 1938, many Labour-controlled Councils, including London County Council, had prevented the use of halls for BUF meetings. Copsey stated that this helped push the BUF further away from mainstream politics as they were left with little alternative than to conduct their activism on street corners and at open-air meetings.[125] By 1939, it was the fascists themselves who began to disrupt political meetings. In one instance, it was reported that 300 fascists had entered a Liberal meeting at York Hall, Bethnal Green on 16 February, allegedly by printing their own tickets, and proceeded to throw tomatoes and light bulbs at the speakers. A fight broke out and the police entered but only one arrest was made.[126] A letter from the Town Clerk to the Home Secretary submitted that the fascist retaliation came following the rejection of the fascists' application to use the hall. He suggested that the fascists may have been of the opinion that if they 'are not allowed the use of York Hall, no other political party shall have the quiet user thereof' and warned of the potential for further disruption in the future.[127] Home Office correspondence reveals that the police had already shared intelligence with the

---

123 Scaffardi, *Fire Under the Carpet*, p. 164

124 U DCL/40/6, NCCL enquiry into fascist meeting at Hornsey Town Hall, Letter from Witness to Town Clerk, 29 Jan 1937.

125 N. Copsey, *Anti-Fascism in Britain*, Macmillan Press Ltd: Hampshire (2000), p. 74.

126 *Western Morning News*, 17 Feb 1939.

127 HO 45/24996, Disturbances: Public Meeting Act (1908) Amendment Bill 1937: maintenance of order at public meetings, Letter from Bethnal Green Town Clerk to Samuel Hoare, 22 Feb 1939.

meeting's organiser that the fascists may try to enter with forged tickets to create disorder. During the meeting the police were repeatedly called upon. They criticised the inadequate provisions that were made to keep order, stating that, 'the stewards were too few in number and too weak to deal with the situation.'[128] Deputy Assistant Commissioner Ralph had instructed the Sub-Divisional Inspector to have 'a good number of police readily available to enter the hall if necessary'.[129] Sub-Divisional Inspector Robson's report reinforced the view that the police should not be present at meetings to act as stewards or to ensure the speaker receives a hearing. During the disorder at Bethnal Green, the police engaged only with fascists who resisted when they were asked to leave, which led to the arrest of the fascist Reginald Hewitt. In addition, Inspector Robson did not take any action against hecklers when a breach of the peace was not imminent.[130] This view was reinforced by the Superintendent's report, which stated that the only time the police could legally intervene was during the incident involving Hewitt.[131]

The BUF 'peace campaign' and Earl's Court 1939

In July 1939, the BUF hosted one last major rally at Earl's Court, London, where Mosley addressed a crowd of 15,000 to promote their peace campaign.[132] The timing of the Earl's Court meeting was particularly significant. In March that year, Hitler's military advance into Czechoslovakia had effectively torn up the Munich agreement, which Prime Minister Neville Chamberlain claimed would bring both 'peace with honour' and 'peace for our time'.[133] This signalled the increased threat of British involvement in a European war. Thurlow notes that this development had the effect of both changing the public's trust of Hitler and their perception of Nazism, whilst also showing Mosley as a potential leader, if only momentarily, who would keep Britain out of another war. The result was that although some BUF members left in protest, as the peace campaign was seen to put 'fascist loyalties above patriotic considerations', others 'flocked to the movement'.[134]

More importantly, from a public order perspective, the Earl's Court meeting did not attract any significant opposition. Copsey noted that militant opposition to Mosley had effectively dissipated as foreign events now took political prioritization.[135] In addition to this, the far Left also advocated peace. On 31 March 1939,

---

128 Ibid., Draft letter from Geoffrey Lloyd to Sir Percy Harris MP who reveals information from a Metropolitan Police Report.
129 Ibid., Letter from Carter of the Metropolitan Police to A Tudor of the Home Office, 23 Feb 1939.
130 HO 45/24996, Report by Sub Divisional Inspector Robson, 21 Feb 1939.
131 Ibid., Report by Superintendent Floyd Williams, 21 Feb 1939.
132 C. Cross, *The Fascists in Britain*, Barrie and Rockliff: London (1961), p. 189. However, Mosley claimed an audience of 20,000 and Special Branch estimated just 11,000. Thurlow, *Fascism in Britain*, p. 86.
133 Andrew, *The Defence of the Realm*, p. 203.
134 Thurlow, Fascism in Britain, pp. 86–87.
135 Copsey, *Anti-Fascism in Britain*, p. 75.

when the danger of a German invasion of Poland became apparent, Communist MP George Gallacher declared:

> The serious and important thing is that Members on this side of the House have continuously asserted that with collective security peace could be saved. The Prime Minister's policy has collapsed. Now he has led the country to the brink of war . . . I ask the Prime Minister to do a real service to the country and to give to those who believe in collective security an opportunity of forming a Government and saving the people of this country and the people of Europe from the menace of war.[136]

The British Government's reluctance to form a defensive pact with the Soviet Union over German aggression in East Europe was followed by the signing of the Nazi-Soviet pact in August 1939. Copsey argues that anti-fascist activism was now discarded by the Communist Party of Great Britain (CPGB), who now accommodated the 'dictates of Soviet foreign policy'.[137] Continued BUF activism in the months leading up to the War, such as the meeting at Earl's Court, as well as continued activism during the phoney war, therefore, did not provoke any organised opposition. There were exceptions, such as the attack on fascists in November 1939 who were travelling from a meeting in two double-decker buses, but Copsey pointed out that incidents like this 'proved exceptional'.[138]

Stewarding political meetings in the Post-War era

In the years after the War, the newly formed fascist movements never reached the same scale of the BUF's meetings at Albert Hall, Olympia or Earl's Court. Consequently, most fascist activism was performed on the streets and public disorder at indoor meetings became less of a political issue. However, there were exceptions. For example, Mosley's official launch of the UM was held at Wilfred Street School, Victoria on 8 February 1948 and it was reported that 'several hundred police . . . protected the meeting'.[139] Despite the incapacity of the far Right to hold large political rallies within hired premises, this did not prevent them from causing disturbances at other political meetings. Chesterton's League of Empire Loyalists (LEL), a Conservative pressure group which formed in 1953, advocated for the preservation of the British Empire. They disowned political violence and terrorism, regarded the Conservatives within the Macmillan administration as traitors and gained publicity by heckling at high-profile meetings.[140]

---

136 *Hansard, HC Deb*, 31 Mar 1939, vol 345 c2418. It should be noted that some Labour MPs rejected Gallacher's inclusion of the Labour benches during this speech.
137 Copsey, *Anti-Fascism in Britain*, p. 75.
138 Ibid.
139 S. Dorril, *Blackshirt: Sir Oswald Mosley and British Fascism*, Viking: London (2006), p. 569. Dorril's source is not referenced.
140 Thurlow, *Fascism in Britain*, p. 219.

The Conservative Party Conference at Blackpool 1958

The LEL's disruption of the Conservative Party Conference in Blackpool's Winter Gardens on 11 October 1958 is the most significant event regarding stewarding at a political meeting in the years following the Second World War. A graphic description of the level of violence used to evict the hecklers was recorded in *The Spectator* by Taper (a pseudonym used by Bernard Levin).[141] He declared that as Prime Minister Harold Macmillan rose to address the conference, a young man sounded a bugle three times from the balcony and cried, 'The League of Empire Loyalists sounds the retreat . . .' before he was cut off and the sound of a scuffle was heard.[142] Taper described how about seven people carried the man out, three of whom wore the uniform of the Winter Gardens venue and the others were either stewards or delegates of the conference. He continued to state that the youth was either flung or fell to the ground and was then kicked in the side by a group of those stood around him.

> He was then dragged to his feet and propelled along, being repeatedly punched in the head and body as he went; two very violent blows in particular (delivered by a Tory delegate) landing on the nape of his neck . . . At no time did the youth offer any resistance.[143]

Further hecklers were given similar treatment. Another youth who had his arms pinioned to his sides was attacked by a delegate who 'punched him repeatedly in the face'. The forth interrupter was marched out of the hall after being held and punched by members of the audience. Taper followed and witnessed the youth being taken into a room, which was guarded by two uniformed Winter Garden staff. He stated that the youth offered no resistance and was shouting 'I want the police, fetch the police' as he was escorted. Taper recalled the sound of violence that he heard from beyond the door. When the door was opened he described the boy's face as being marked and running with blood, and his clothes torn; he was at the point of collapse. Taper also saw a pool of blood on the floor.

As with the responses to Olympia, the violence used by stewards split opinion. The initial report in *The Times* did not describe the violence that was alleged to have been used; in referring to disorder, only reported that the hecklers were 'hustled from the gallery' or 'removed by attendants'.[144] However, the letters to the editor which were published in the days following the event reveal more illuminating contemporary attitudes on the use of violence at political meetings.

---

141 Taper was the pseudonym of journalist Bernard Levin who wrote a regular column for *The Spectator* as their political correspondent.
142 *The Spectator*, 17 Oct 1958, no. 6799. Accessed on 21 October 2013 from http://archive.spectator.co.uk/page/17th-october-1958/6
143 Ibid.
144 *The Times*, 13 Oct 1958.

Chesterton began the correspondence by criticising the violence used by the Conservative stewards. Unsurprisingly, his view on the stewarding of this meeting contradicted his description of the Blackshirts at Olympia. In his article 'Olympia and the Jews', Chesterton described the Blackshirt stewarding as the 'action of British manhood in defending their mighty rally from being wrecked by the mob'.[145] In his letter regarding the treatment of the LEL hecklers at the Winter Gardens, Chesterton highlighted that minimum force was not used, using as an example the experience of Donald Griffin, the LEL member who was allegedly beaten during his removal from the Winter Gardens venue. He also stated that the LEL activists had always left meetings quietly when they were asked.[146]

Lord Hailsham, chairman of the Conservative Party, declared that LEL members who entered the meeting 'were trespassers *ab initio*' as their tickets were obtained by 'one device or another.' He continued to state that the accusation of treason that a heckler aimed at the Prime Minister was calculated to cause a breach of the peace. On pointing out the potential criminality of the interrupters, Hailsham does note that members of the audience were not justified in physically intervening with them as this went against Conservative principles. However, he does not pass any judgment on the stewards or the Winter Garden staff, stating that his view of the audience was obstructed by the television lights.[147] The Labour response by MP Barbara Castle demonstrated a continuity of the desire to uphold the liberties of free speech, even though the hecklers in this case were from the far Right. Castle pointed out that when four LEL members heckled her meeting they were only asked to leave when the audience got tired of their 'childish interruptions . . . [she continued] What struck me at the time was how quietly these insult hurling gentlemen went as soon as they were told to leave'.[148] Former Mosleyite, Noel Symington,[149] showed remarkable consistency with the BUF line at Olympia in his attitude regarding hecklers even though the LEL hecklers were also of the far Right. He stated that as hecklers aim to get cheap publicity at the expense of the hosts, the 'use of deterrent force then comes into perspective'. He explicitly advocated that it 'is high time that the suspension of free speech through organized hecklers was brought to an end.' However, considering the opposition that Mosley's UM received at outdoor public meetings, this stance should be expected.[150]

The descriptions of the brutality used by the Winter Garden staff, stewards and delegates evoke comparisons to the fascist violence at Olympia. Yet, unlike Olympia, two of the victims at the Winter Gardens brought a charge of assault

---

145   A. K. Chesterton, *Oswald Mosley: Portrait of a Leader*, Action Press: London (1937).

146   It should be pointed out that Chesterton would not have seen a contradiction in his views between Olympia and Winter Gardens; he would have likely advocated the BUF line that the force was needed to eject the hecklers who fought the stewards with weapons.

147   *The Times*, 18 Oct 1958.

148   *The Times*, 21 Oct 1958.

149   Noel Symington stood as an Independent at Harborough during the 1950 General Election.

150   See chapter five.

against two of the alleged offenders. Donald Griffin and Stanley Hulka of the LEL brought summonses against William Lynch, a member of staff at the Winter Gardens, and George Finley, a Conservative Party agent for assault. R. Gordon Clover QC, defending Finley, argued that the interrupter was unwilling to leave and Finley only used as much force as necessary. The defence emphasised Griffin's deceitful character and the deliberate aggravation he caused:

> He gets into meetings using forged tickets, deliberately putting himself by dishonesty, trickery, and deception into situations where he can then proceed to behave with maximum amount of provocation and try to spoil meetings.[151]

Lynch also claimed that he did not hit the claimant or any other heckler. Levin gave evidence of the 'needless severity by stewards' and an Independent Television News reporter, Reginald Bosanquet, described the treatment of the hecklers as 'excessively violent'.[152] Despite this, the magistrates acquitted Lynch and Finley, and they ordered Griffin and Hulka to each pay £100 costs.

Harry Street has questioned the legality of the actions of the stewards and Winter Garden staff in consideration of the power of private citizens. Street argued that more facts needed to be ascertained in order to evaluate the legality of the ejections. He stated that if individuals had entered private property peaceably, then no force could be used to eject them unless they failed to comply to a request to leave. Furthermore, it would need to be ascertained whether the Conservative Party were the occupiers of the premises or had just paid a fee for their use. Street argued that if they were not the occupiers, then they had no power to eject anybody, and this could be done only by the owners of the Winter Gardens and their staff. Conversely, if the Conservative Party were the occupiers, then their stewards had the power to eject hecklers, but not the employees or owners of the venue.[153] Following Street's argument, as both employees and stewards were involved with the ejections, either the stewards or the venue staff had acted unlawfully.

Remarkably, a quarter century after Olympia, the violent tactics employed by stewards, audience members and venue staff was accepted in the courts. This demonstrated that there was still room for political violence within mainstream politics: it could still be justified and accepted within the compounds of the established conservative orthodoxy for the means of defending a political meeting. Many audience members, including women, were reported to have freely engaged in the violence against the protesters, which demonstrates that a continuation of old attitudes towards political violence had not completely vanished. Pugh's argument that there was a common acceptance of the Blackshirt violence at Olympia by Conservatives as the pre–First World War attitudes to political violence only

---

151 *The Times*, 2 Jun 1959.
152 P. Hitchens, *The Broken Compass: How British Politics Lost its Way*, Continuum: London (2009), p. 39.
153 Street, *Freedom, the Individual and the Law*, p. 52.

changed gradually can thus be extended. It can be shown that even in the post-Second World War era these attitudes had not yet been diminished.[154]

The imminence of disorder

The anti-nuclear protest Cornwall 1982

Towards the end of the twentieth century, political violence at indoor meetings became much less frequent. Organised disruption by political opponents tended to be conducted in the public realm. Even when meetings were conducted indoors, such as the National Front meetings in London at Conway Hall, Red Lion Square in 1974 and Southall Town Hall in 1979, the counter demonstrations on each occasion were held outside the venue. Both demonstrations led to considerable violence and were marked by the deaths of Kevin Gately and Blair Peach respectively. However, the duty of the police to intervene on private property to either prevent a breach of the peace or to disperse an unlawful assembly became a divisive legal issue involving the Chief Constable of Devon and Cornwall, John Alderson, and the Central Electricity Generating Board (CEGB) in 1982. In *R v Chief Constable of the Devon and Cornwall Constabulary, ex parte Central Electricity Generating Board*[155] the CEGB had sought an order of mandamus which would have required Alderson to order his police officers to either remove or assist in the removal of the protestors who were preventing the survey of a farm at Luxulyan, Cornwall, which was shortlisted as a possible site for a nuclear power station.

For the CEGB, it was argued that the police had a duty to take action because they believed that the actions of the protesters did constitute a breach of the peace and they reasonably anticipated that further and more serious breaches of the peace were likely. In addition, it was contended that the protest was an unlawful assembly as the obstruction that it caused constituted a criminal offence under s281(2) Town and Country Planning Act 1971. Although this offence does not include a power of arrest, it was contended that the power to arrest at common law was retained by s2(7) Criminal Law Act 1967, and that could be applied here as there was either a breach of the peace or a reasonable apprehension of it. *Thomas v Sawkins* was also cited to emphasise that the police were entitled to enter private land when there was reasonable grounds for believing that an offence is about to be committed.[156]

However, the presence of police on the private land was not an issue. Alderson did have officers stationed at the site to observe the protest, but no action was taken as – in the view of the officers present – a breach of the peace had not occurred nor was it reasonably anticipated. For Alderson, it was argued that there must either be violence or the apprehension of violence to constitute a breach of

---

154 Pugh, 'The National Government', p. 255.
155 *R v Chief Constable of the Devon and Cornwall Constabulary, ex parte Central Electricity Generating Board*.
156 Ibid., at 461–462.

the peace, not merely a breach of the law.[157] Furthermore, it was contested that the police had no greater powers than the CEGB in this situation. If the removal of an objector by the board would constitute an assault, then it would also be an assault if conducted by a police officer. Moreover, the anticipation of a breach of the peace and the decision of what actions were necessary lay within the discretion of the police officers present. This was highlighted by Alderson, who stated that, 'it was a case of vagueness of the law and an exercise of the resulting discretion in favour of no criminal procedure unless a breakdown of the peace was apprehended.'[158]

In his judgment, Lord Denning MR addressed the contentious issues of whether a breach of the peace had occurred or could be reasonably anticipated and whether the protest constituted an unlawful assembly. After quoting police reports which highlighted the 'passive manner' of the protestors, Denning disagreed with the police view that a breach of the peace could not be anticipated. In contrast, he stated that the actions of the protestors, such as laying down in front of a rig or putting their foot down to stop a hole being drilled, were criminal obstructions and did constitute a breach of the peace. He stated, 'There is a breach of the peace whenever a person who is lawfully carrying out his work is unlawfully and physically prevented by another from doing it.'[159] Alderson noted that this definition extended previous notions of a breach of the peace, as many contemporary police and lawyers believed that 'a degree of violence or its threat had been looked for'.[160] In addition, Denning also considered the protest constituted an unlawful assembly by using the definition, 'an assembly of three or more persons with the intent to commit a crime by open force'.[161] Furthermore, Lawton LJ stated that any police constables present when three or more obstructors show an intention to 'use violence to achieve their aims or otherwise act in a tumultuous manner' have a duty to disperse them as those present in the gathering would be committing the offence of unlawful assembly. Templeman LJ also highlighted that the protestors had engaged in six months of lawlessness 'characterised by physical interference with the rights of others'. Although all three judges highlighted the unlawful nature of the protest, the appeal was dismissed. Denning stated that his judgment provided a 'definitive legal mandate' and hoped that this would persuade Alderson to use his men to clear the protestors from the site, yet asserted

> I would not give any orders to the chief constable or his men. It is of the first importance that the police should decide on their own responsibility what action should be taken in any particular situation.[162]

157 Ibid., at 463.
158 Alderson, *Law and Disorder*, p. 185.
159 *Ibid.*
160 Alderson, *Law and Disorder*, p. 187.
161 *R v Chief Constable of the Devon and Cornwall Constabulary, ex parte Central Electricity Generating Board.*
162 Ibid., at 472.

This case demonstrates the wide discretion available to the police and the ambiguous nature of both the breach of the peace doctrine and the definition of unlawful assembly. Alderson was a pioneer of community policing in the United Kingdom and it was central to his decision making that police action was measured and proportionate. The case highlighted Alderson's reliance on the reports from Chief Inspector Bradley, who was at the protest and recorded that he did not believe that there was any intention for the protestors to use violence, and that their behaviour was perfectly peaceful. In addition, Bradley's reports also suggested that the positive relationship that the police had developed with the community would be put in jeopardy if they were to take more authoritative action.[163] With no arrest power for the breach of s281(2) Town and Country Planning Act 1971, the police officers present did not act; in their judgment, no breach of the peace had occurred or was likely to occur.

The situation mirrors some of the issues that were frequent during the policing of public meetings. While the police were able to remain on the property without any objection from the landowners, the issue of what point the police should intervene to prevent a breach of the peace was integral. Here, the discrepancies between the judgments in *R v Chief Constable of the Devon and Cornwall Constabulary* and the discretionary precaution shown by the police are evident. Moreover, the vagueness of the breach of the peace doctrine was highlighted by the different interpretations of Alderson and Denning. For Alderson, a breach of the peace was only considered likely when the protesters were to be removed but contested that it was 'the Board should take the first step.'[164] Sociologist Ian Welsh underlines the importance of the protest locally, which helped discover a new 'community' and breached the sense of isolation in the opposition of nuclear energy. The sense of Cornish identity was prominent and the CEGB was seen as 'an intruder from "up country"'. He states that it was widely commented in his fieldwork amongst the groups that it was 'the best thing to happen socially in Cornwall for ages'.[165] This sense of community was extended to the police for their approach in supervising the six-month protest. Following the ruling at the Court of Appeal, the protest ended peacefully, as Alderson met the protesters in person and asked them to leave. Alderson noted their response, 'You and your men have been very fair with us and we would not wish to cause you trouble. We do not want to embarrass you.' Furthermore, the protestors left with all their belongings and rubbish, and no arrests were made.[166] This was an early example of the facilitation of protest through negotiation and effective communication. It effectively allowed the protest and prevented any disorder.

163 Ibid., at p. 470.
164 Alderson, *Law and Disorder*, p. 187.
165 I. Welsh, *Mobilising Modernity: The Nuclear Movement*, Routledge: London (2000), p. 193
166 Alderson, *Law and Disorder*, p. 188.

Police and Criminal Evidence Act 1984

Additional powers relating to disorder on private premises have been provided by the Police and Criminal Evidence Act 1984 (PACE). Under s17(5) all previous common law powers relating to entry to private premises without a warrant were abolished, yet s17(6) provides that this excludes 'any power of entry to deal with or prevent a breach of the peace'. The changes under PACE therefore remain consistent with the judgment of *Thomas v Sawkins*. Yet this provision significantly extends the ambiguous judgment from 1935 which did not set any definite precedent regarding the police's power of entry regarding the type of private premises. The extension of the power to enter private premises in the anticipation of a breach of the peace in the domestic sphere was supported by Neill LJ in *McLeod v Commissioner of Police for the Metropolis*[167] in 1994, who stated:

> I am satisfied that Parliament in s 17(6) has now recognised that there is a power to enter premises to prevent a breach of the peace as a form of preventive justice. I can see no satisfactory basis for restricting that power to particular classes of premises such as those where public meetings are held.

The Representation of the People Act 1983 also provides extra protection of political meetings during parliamentary and local government elections under s97(1). In a similar power available by the Public Meeting Act 1908, the chairman of a meeting may request that a disorderly person provide a police constable with his name and address. If the person fails to comply, then a further offence is committed under s97(3) which also satisfies an arrest condition under s24 PACE. No significant changes were made in the Public Order Act 1986. In 1985, the White Paper Review of Public Order Law stated that it was neither necessary nor desirable to impose further controls on public meetings that were held on private premises. It was suggested that serious public disorder was less frequent at meetings held indoors and the substantive law was already adequate.

The British National Party

Political disorder and disruption have broadly abandoned the private sphere while the emphasis on public protest and activism has remained in public places. While far-Right parties such as the BNP have provoked significant disruption in the late twentieth and early twenty-first centuries, their political opponents have largely favoured counter-demonstrations in public places. Even when anti-fascist activists tried to enter BNP meetings, the police were able to use their preventative common law powers to avert an anticipated breach of the peace. Peter Waddington depicted an incident at a BNP general election meeting at Bethnal Green in 1992 where counter-demonstrators attempted to gain access to the public meeting and accused the police of protecting the fascists.[168] The problem that the police faced was that

---

167   *McLeod v Commissioner of Police for the Metropolis* (1994) 4 All ER 553, CA.
168   Waddington, *Liberty and Order*, p. 114.

the BNP had overestimated their support and seats remained unoccupied in the hall. Waddington describes how the officer in charge encountered some local councillors who showed hostility towards the BNP and their opponents but were able to solve the issue by entering the hall from a side entrance and removing the excess seating, and, as the hall rules proscribed standing during meetings, the officer was able to inform the demonstrators that there were no seats available.[169] While the actions of this officer may have prevented a breach of the peace inside the hall, he also contentiously restricted the liberty of those who wanted access to the public meeting. In this instance, the officer's use of discretion to restrict access to the meeting could only be justified if a breach of the peace was imminent. The *Evening Standard* reported that eight people were arrested during the 'mob violence' at Bethnal Green and described how the anti-racism protestors 'hurled sticks, bottles and beer glasses at the British National Party members'.[170] With high levels of disorder outside, the decision to deny entry to the protestors – albeit by questionable and liberty-inhibiting methods – likely prevented further disorder inside the hall.

The Human Rights Act 1998

Following the Human Rights Act 1998, it is unclear how much effect Articles 10 (freedom of expression) and 11 (freedom of assembly and association) may have on current police practice regarding public meetings. David Mead asserted that even in the era of the HRA it is difficult to assert what influence *Thomas v Sawkins* would have on the current domestic courts as there is no Strasbourg case that closely resembles it. However, Mead does conjecture that there is no reason to assume the outcome would have been any different, arguing that it is likely that the police would be capable of meeting several legitimate aims, such as public safety, crime prevention or protecting the rights of others.[171]

The application of the HRA to the duty of the police regarding public meetings demonstrates the conflict between prioritising either individual liberty or collective security. Despite the powers of the police regarding a breach of the peace on private premises being provided by Parliament courtesy of s17(6) PACE, the ambiguous nature of the breach of the peace doctrine will ultimately ensure that any future police intervention at public meetings will continue to be inconsistent and vulnerable to criticism from either the meetings' organisers or opposing protestors.

A recent claim by activist Jane Laporte in *Laporte and another v Commissioner of Police of the Metropolis*[172] has further clarified the legal legitimacy of the police to remove protestors from public meetings. On 24th February 2011, Laporte was involved in a protest at Haringey Civic Centre where the Council meeting was due to debate proposed cuts to the budget and services. Members of the public

---

169   Ibid., p. 126.
170   *Evening Standard (London)*, 7 Apr 1992.
171   Mead, *New Law of Peaceful Protest*, pp. 324–325.
172   *Laporte and another v Commissioner of Police of the Metropolis* [2014] EWHC 3574 (QB).

were allowed to attend in the public gallery. The police were aware of the protest outside the hall but they did not anticipate any disorder inside the building. Two police officers were stationed inside to facilitate the safe movement of the public to the gallery and prevent unauthorised access to the council chamber. When the doors opened, protestors rushed in and the policing tactics inside the Civic Centre were deemed inadequate. The supervising officer Inspector French requested the deployment of the Territorial Support Group.[173]

Some of the protesters entered the council chamber, others made calls for the resignation of the Council leader and others made inarticulate noise. They were warned that the meeting would be held behind closed doors if the disorder persisted. Laporte then called the protesters to the third floor, where she believed the councillors were attempting to hold the meeting away from public scrutiny. The police had locked a door to prohibit their incursion, but at this point a fire alarm was set off, releasing the doors. About fifteen protesters pushed past the two police officers to the canteen where the councillors had gathered. At this point, Inspector Wakeford shouted 'breach of the peace!' and ordered his officers to remove the protesters. This included the arrest, detention and prosecution of Laporte and fellow activist Nicolas Christian.

In Laporte and Christian's case against the Metropolitan Police Commissioner, they sought '(i) damages against the defendant for assault and battery, false imprisonment and malicious prosecution and (ii) a declaration that he has violated their rights under Articles 10 and 11 of the European Convention on Human Rights.' Although the decision of Inspector Wakeford to remove the protesters from the building was based his Breach of the Peace powers, Turner J ruled that this was not necessary as reasonable force could have been used to evict them on the basis of the law relating to exclusion and trespass.[174] The first claim was rejected on the basis that the police did not use any more force than was necessary to perform their duty in evicting the protesters. Turner J also rejected that both claimants were improperly prevented from exercising their rights to freedom of expression and highlighted that the machinery of local government should be protected from deliberately destructive conduct in a democratic society.[175] The description of the events demonstrates that the protest went beyond voicing their complaint to jeopardising the holding of the meeting. With this consideration the judgment should not be surprising. The decision reinforces the notion that if a protest is to occur on private property and prevent the lawful activities of others, then it is still unlikely to find support from the courts.

Conclusion

The role of the police at public meetings has had a turbulent and inconsistent history. Police presence at meetings on private premises has caused significant legal discussion and their duty to preserve order at them has been intensely debated.

---

173 Ibid., at 11.
174 Ibid., at 59.
175 Ibid., at 112 and 128.

Opportunities to establish some uniformity regarding the practice of the police in the nineteenth century failed. The abandonment of the case against McManus (the Chartist steward who ejected a police officer from a Soho meeting) in 1848 and the Major Edwards test case in 1892 both failed to provide any legal authority on the practice of the police at public meetings. In the twentieth century, the acceptance of the Departmental Committee in 1909 that police practice varied in different regions, and their refusal to advocate any changes as the differences were 'adopted either in consequence of, or with the sanction of, the public opinion in each locality' ensured that this inconsistency continued.

The events at Olympia and Caerau demonstrated the importance of uniformity and consistency in police practice to avoid allegations of political partisanship. However, despite the difference in established practices, other factors were also critical in addressing the use of police discretion at these two decisive meetings. The intelligence of the Glamorgan County Police of recent communist meetings gave them reasonable belief that their presence was required to prevent seditious speeches and prevent the disorder that may follow. Although disorder could have been reasonably anticipated by the Metropolitan Police at Olympia, as it was the threat of organised communist interruption that was the likely to be the cause, it was the duty of the steward, and not the police, to control the meeting. This does not mean that as the events of the evening unfolded and the brutality that occurred became apparent to the police that they were right not to enter the meeting. On the contrary, when it became apparent to the police that serious assaults were being committed inside, it became their duty to investigate and take control of the meeting and prevent further breaches of the peace, as was the case at the BUF meetings at Manchester and Plymouth. Despite knowledge of previous fascist violence, it is possible that the police did not expect such an outrageous display of brutality by the Blackshirts and were too apprehensive to deviate from their initial objective of keeping order outside the hall. The likelihood that the Police Superintendent in charge apprehended that police action could have inflamed the situation and caused a riot should not be discounted. Police presence could have provoked further disorder inside the meeting, and the 760 police on duty were also responsible for controlling an anti-fascist demonstration outside the Olympia hall. If a sufficient number of police had entered the meeting, it could have incensed the protest outside, leaving an inadequate number of police officers to control it. The involvement of police in the meeting would have also involved aiding the Blackshirts eject interrupters, which although that may have helped regulate the force used, it would have also provoked the anti-fascist crowd by witnessing police cooperation with the Blackshirts.

The differences in the policing of the meetings described in this chapter were largely the result of their different understandings of their legal powers which stemmed from the ambiguity of the breach of the peace doctrine. There is no clear definition of what constitutes a breach of the peace. At a meeting on private premises the issue is even more clouded by the power of the stewards to evict members of the audience. Therefore, at what point can it be said that a breach of the peace has occurred when physical force is necessary to remove a member of the audience? One measure of the consistency between the incidents discussed is that police intervention at the BUF meetings at Manchester and Plymouth and the Liberal meeting at Bethnal Green all occurred when the disorder became wide-spread and the stewards were unable to control it. However, when the stewards were able to contain order – albeit with the use of excessive force to remove the hecklers, such as at Olympia, the communist meeting at Ealing Town Hall, and the Conservative Party conference at Blackpool in 1958 – no police action was taken. In additional, in the case of the communist meeting and the Conservative Party Conference, the stewards charged with assault were acquitted by magistrates who recognised that the use of physical force was a necessary part of their power to fulfil their duty. These examples demonstrate a particular consistency in police practice across a varied spectrum of political activism.

The legal ground for the police to be present at a public meeting remains a contentious issue. The judgment of *Thomas v Sawkins* and the extent to which it can be enforced is still considered to be 'a murky area of the law, particularly when those present or those holding the meeting have decided that police officers should be excluded'.[176] Yet the discretion exercised in deciding which meetings require their attendance is necessarily a partial one, and open to the criticism of political prejudice. Even when the police are stationed inside the private premises of a public meeting (whether at the organiser's request or not) an explanation as to their duty is still required. It is commonly accepted that the maintenance of order is primarily the role of the appointed stewards, while the police ought to act only when requested to assist in the removal of a person who violently rejected their eviction. Yet this also puts the police in the difficult position of being accused of watching the violent ejection of hecklers by heavy-handed stewards. In the case of police practice voluntarily aiding the stewards, the appearance would also appear to have political motivation. The duty of the police at public meetings remains ambiguous and is still potentially inconsistent as it continually relies on their discretion and the breach of the peace doctrine. Yet unless the practice of organised interruption again begins to disrupt public meetings, then the duty of the police in this contentious area will not come under scrutiny again.

176 Thornton, *The Law of Public Order*, p. 122.

8 Dressed for disorder

The criminalisation of political uniforms

To-day any man may go about in any public place in any attire, so long as it is decent and is not female attire.[1]

Introduction

Throughout the last two centuries there have been numerous incidents where the choice of clothing apparel by either individuals or groups has warranted a legal response. This has been most prominent during the era of Sir Oswald Mosley's BUF when concern was raised by politicians and police officials that the Blackshirt uniform provoked public disorder. Countering this concern was the belief that the public should be at liberty to wear the attire of their choice without the interference of the government. The opening quote from Conservative MP Robin Turton highlighted the concerns of introducing legislation that would limit the liberty of people to dress as they pleased. Controversially, s1 Public Order Act 1936 created an offence which prohibited the wearing of a uniform in connection with a political object in a public place or public meeting. Yet even before this landmark provision – which is still in force today – there have been incidents which have prompted a response from the legal authorities based upon the wearing apparel of members of the public.

This chapter commences with an examination of criminal offences at both common law and Statute which proscribed, criminalised or suppressed certain garments in the early nineteenth century and considers the value of clothing in promoting political values or statements of protest. This includes an analysis of the enforcement tactics used during the Old Price Riots at Covent Garden Theatre in 1809. Even before the establishment of the modern police force, the Bow Street Runners were involved in policing disorder and arrested several audience members for wearing the initials 'OP' on their hats. Further into the nineteenth century in Swanlinbar, Ireland, police Sub-Inspector Connor removed an orange

---

1 *Hansard, HC Deb*, 16 Nov 1936, vol 317 cc1349–473 at 1426. This quote highlights the concern of Conservative MP Robin Turton, during the discussion of clause 1 Public Order Bill 1936 which was mandated to prohibit political uniforms. Incidentally, despite his belief that a man could not wear female attire, there was no law which proscribed this.

lily from a Protestant, Ann Humphries, who was walking past a Catholic church. These instances raise important questions regarding how garments or accessories can both promote and provoke disorder and probes an examination of the extent of preventative police powers related to the anticipation of a breach of the peace.

These issues were again revived in the interwar years as politically extreme movements such as the BUF sought recognition and publicity by wearing uniforms in public. In 1936, the Public Order Bill was introduced amidst significant debate in Parliament on the effect of clause 1, which prohibited the wearing of uniforms in connection with political objectives. Following the enactment of the Public Order Act 1936, several members of the BUF attempted to find loopholes in the new law and were subsequently arrested and tried at Magistrates Courts. As the Public Order Act did not include a definition of what constituted a uniform, the police have had to utilise their discretion when deciding when to take action against a suspect, and the subsequent cases become significant as it is the magistrates' role to interpret this ambiguous provision. The legacy of the infrequently utilised power under s1 is then examined with reference to the prosecution of Ku Klux Klan members who emulated the American model of the extreme right-wing movement in Rugby in 1965, and the IRA case a decade later, *O'Moran v DPP*.[2] In conclusion, the charges summonsed under s1 are compared and the interpretation of what constituted a political uniform reviewed.

Promoting and provoking disorder

The value of uniformity in dress to promote a particular opinion or grievance has been highlighted by historian Katrina Navickas:

> Political clothing was an articulation of both individual self and collective identity. Through the performance of wearing symbolic items, individuals used their bodies to claim a part in the wider body politic.[3]

The practice of wearing political adornments such as a coloured sash, ribbons or even jumpers to present a particular political identity has long been part of the mainstream political culture, especially at election time. However, when political dissidents pose a threat to national security or public order by either instigating or provoking violence the authorities have often been forced to consider the lawfulness of their attire.

Previous legislative responses that have proscribed certain objects of clothing have been mandated to secure the sovereignty of the state from internal threats. Most notably, the Dress Act 1746 proscribed the wearing of tartan and kilts in Scotland and was repealed in 1782. It was enacted following the Jacobite defeat at Culloden in the same year with an intention to abolish clan identity. For any man

2 *O'Moran and others v DPP* [1975] QB 864.
3 K. Navickas, "'That sash will hang you": Political Clothing and Adornment in England, 1780–1840', *The Journal of British Studies 49*, no. 3 (2010), pp. 540–565.

or boy who broke this proscription they were 'liable to be transported to any of His Majesty's plantations beyond the seas, there to remain for the space of seven years'. Even before this, Henry VII passed the Act of Livery and Maintenance in 1504 which prohibited private armies and uniforms; this Act survived until the Premiership of Lord Palmerston, when it was repealed in 1863. This ancient Act was mandated to prevent lords and estate owners from retaining followers and providing them with a livery in order to protect their interests. This included the formation of an army which, although may serve the monarch in the event of invasion, may also be used to threaten the Crown. In the nineteenth century significant events have highlighted how the wearing of particular adornments can either promote or provoke a public disorder.

The Old Price Riots 1809

When the Covent Garden Theatre reopened its doors on 18 September 1809, following months of restoration after a devastating fire the year before, sixty-seven days of protest and disorder ensued. While the symbol of the protest became the initials 'OP' – which focused on the demand for a return to the 'Old Prices' – this was only part of a more extensive struggle. The breadth of these grievances also included the removal of private boxes, authoritarian rule and foreign influence.[4] Jane Moody summarises the Old Price Riots as representing 'a rational response to what the protestors identified as Covent Garden's capitulation to decadent luxury and social exclusivity'.[5] Victor Emeljanow also highlights that parliamentary radicals were in part responsible for the organisation of the disorder, dispelling earlier assumptions that the Old Price Riots were an example of mob rule or class war.[6] As an expression of dissent which identified the protestors with the opposition to the changes at the Covent Garden Theatre, it became popular among protestors to brandish the initials OP on their hats. According to the authorities, this marked them as potential troublemakers and preventative legal action was taken against them.

On Saturday, 25 November 1809, the Bow Street magistrate was occupied from eight o'clock till half past one in the morning hearing various charges associated with the disorder at the theatre. The Bow Street officers used their discretion to bring Mr Wright before the magistrates charged with 'wearing the letters OP in his hat . . . and exciting riot and tumult in the pit.'[7] The magistrate, Mr Graham, ordered him to find bail. The significance of wearing the OP initials as an emblem of protest also had the consequence of being targeted by the authorities

4 J. Baker, 'The OP War, Libertarian Communication and Graphic Reportage in Georgian London', *European Comic Art 4*, no. 1 (2011), pp. 81–104.
5 J. Moody, *Illegitimate Theatre in London, 1770–1840*, Cambridge University Press: Cambridge (2000), p.62.
6 V. Emeljanow, 'The Events of June 1848: the 'Monte Cristo' Riots and the Politics of Protest', *New Theatre Quarterly 19*, no. 1 (2003), pp. 23–32. See also M. Baer, *Theatre and Disorder in Late Georgian London*, Clarendon: Oxford (1992).
7 *Morning Chronicle*, 27 Nov 1809.

for prosecution. James Brandon, the Box Keeper at the Covent Garden Theatre, also brought charges against William Allison, who wore the initials on his breast, also citing his demeanour as a contributing factor which, in the opinion of Brandon, expressed a 'wish to excite a continuance of the riot and tumult in the pit'.[8] He was also ordered to find bail.

The significance of whether wearing the initials themselves were a common law offence or not was addressed in *Clifford Esq. v Brandon*.[9] Henry Clifford Esq., a barrister, brought charges against Brandon for assault and false imprisonment following his arrest for wearing the initials at the theatre. The *Morning Chronicle* reported that those who had seized Clifford 'slunk away' after discovering the identity of their arrestee.[10] Brandon informed the magistrate that the charge was wearing the initials OP in his hat, and on further prompting from the magistrate added that he also made a noise. Clifford informed the magistrate that he wore the OP in order to ascertain whether any magistrate would consider that an offence. The magistrate informed him that there was no charge against him and he was discharged.[11] In his subsequent charge against Brandon for assault and false imprisonment, James Mansfield CJ advised the jury that,

> if any person encourages or promotes, or takes part in riots, whether by words, signs, or gestures, or by wearing the badge or ensign of the rioters, he is himself to be considered a rioter, and he is liable to be arrested for a breach of the peace . . . [adding] Why did he wear O. P. in his hat? Did he not know the meaning of these letters; and if he did, with what view did he exhibit them but to encourage the mob by his example, and to impress upon them the idea they were acting agreeably to law?[12]

The focus on the wearing of the initials was a significant aspect of this case: if the jury considered that Clifford was promoting the riot by wearing them, then his arrest could be justified and his charges against Brandon void. However, the jury found in Clifford's favour and he was awarded £5 damages. One reason cited by the jury for their verdict was that 'wearing the letters O. P. in a theatre was not any instigation to riot'.[13] In a social event known as 'the theatrical reconciliation dinner to celebrate the end of the Old Price Riots,' Clifford declared, 'May browbeating Judges ever be opposed by enlightened and impartial juries.'[14]

The disorder at the New Theatre Royal Covent Garden ceased by mid-December 1809, following negotiations between the theatre owner, John Kemble, and a party of protestors including Clifford. It was agreed that the prices for the pit

8 Ibid.
9 *Clifford Esq. v Brandon* (1810) 2 Campbell 358.
10 *Morning Chronicle,* 1 Nov 1809.
11 Ibid.
12 *Clifford Esq. v Brandon* at 370–371.
13 Ibid., at 372.
14 *Morning Chronicle*, 5 Jan 1810.

would be reduced to their former rate, the boxes were to be restored for the use of the public and all legal proceedings against anyone apprehended in the theatre were stopped.[15] Although this case preceded the formation of the modern police force, it demonstrated the breadth of discretion that law enforcers were willing to take, and the extent of support they would get from the magistrates, in order to prevent (or to hold people accountable for) breaches of the peace. While the initials OP were potentially perceived as a signal which promoted riot or disorder, other forms of dress also found attention from the police as they were perceived to provoke breaches of the peace from their opponents.

The orange lily: **Humphries v Connor (1864)**[16]

In Swanlinbar, Ireland, Anne Humphries wore an orange lily in her dress. This act, which provoked religious and political hostility from the Catholic inhabitants around her, threatened a breach of the peace. Using his preventive powers under the common law, Sub-Inspector Connor requested that she remove the emblem. After she failed to comply, he took it from her. Subsequently, Humphries brought an action against Connor for assault. The notable issue in this case is the tension between the individual liberty of the subject to wear the adornments of their choice without legal interference and the preventative power of the police to avert a breach of the peace. In Connor's defence it was highlighted that Humphries was threatened with violence by several persons who were following her. While O'Brien J and Hayes J acknowledged the right of Humphries to wear the lily, they judged that Connor was justified in his actions to remove it. Although Fitzgerald J also judged in favour of the defendant, he questioned whether Connor should have placed his attention on those threatening Humphries rather than the plaintiff. He warned that it may introduce mob rule and present a principle which would give 'police constables a power of interference with the personal liberty and rights of individuals'.[17] However, there was also doubt in the intention of the plaintiff when she wore the lily. For example, if she wore the 'emblem with intent to provoke a breach of the peace, then she became a wrongdoer' and Connor's actions were justified.[18]

The extension of police powers here greatly increased the discretion available to police officers and dangerously gave them more power to decide upon matters of religious or political significance. The wideness of discretion available in anticipating a breach of the peace, therefore, has the potential to facilitate partial and politicised policing. In the twentieth century, when extreme political bodies such as the BUF advanced their propaganda with members in full uniform, the issues of promotion and provocation of disorder were pertinent.

15 *Hampshire Chronicle*, 18 Dec 1809.
16 *Humphries v Connor* (1864) 17 Ir CLR 1.
17 *Cork Examiner*, 26 Feb 1864.
18 Ibid.

Political uniforms and interwar politics

Political uniforms played a major part in organisations of the British far Right in the 1920s and 1930s. The BUF, who were also known as the Blackshirts, paraded in uniform along the streets of Britain in public processions and held public meetings.[19] The Blackshirts were often seen as nuisances who provoked violent confrontation from opponents, and their political activities regularly threatened public order. Yet to what extent can the wearer of a political uniform be held responsible for the provocation of violence?

The Meaning of the Black Shirt

Many fascist groups were inspired by Benito Mussolini's black-shirted Fascist Party, who formed an Italian government in 1922. This included the British Fascisti and the Imperial Fascist League, who both adopted the Blackshirt uniform as well as many of Mussolini's fascist principles, but their numbers were relatively small. It was not until Mosley formed the BUF in 1932 that the Blackshirt uniform took a more prominent place in British society. The choice of wearing a uniform embodied the flavour of European politics, which seemed to contradict the patriotic message of the BUF. This foreign influence was commonly used to criticise the BUF as their uniform was referred to as 'alien elements making for conflict and disorder'.[20] Coupland argues that the black shirt added to the myths and dynamism of the BUF's political identity but added that they 'were all dressed up with nowhere to go; dressed for a struggle that never happened.'[21] More significantly, he argues that the Blackshirt uniform commonly conjured the image of the 'alien menace in anti-fascist discourse,' which negated the most vociferous claim of the BUF: 'Britain First'.[22]

The BUF was the largest and most organised fascist movement in Britain. Their adoption of the Blackshirt uniform and its frequent visible presence on the public streets gave them both exposure and notoriety. Officers were distinguished by wearing a black shirt with black trousers, while unit leaders and men wore a black shirt with grey trousers. Women wore a black blouse with a grey skirt and black beret, and they did not wear any lipstick or make-up.[23]

In official BUF literature, the value of the black shirt was attributed with numerous qualities. Mosley declared that the uniform and the spirit of those who wore it 'have been by far the biggest factors in the early success of Fascism'. He continued, 'Throughout modern Europe it has become the outward expression of

---

19 See chapters four and five for examples of BUF public processions and chapter six for examples of public meetings.
20 P. M. Coupland, 'The Black Shirt in Britain: The Meanings and Functions of Political Uniform' in J. Gottlieb and T. Linehan (eds), *The Culture of Fascism: Visions of the Far Right in Britain*, I. B. Taurus: London (2004), p. 106.
21 Ibid., p. 115.
22 Ibid.
23 Pugh, *'Hurrah for the Blackshirts!'*, pp. 134, 142.

manhood banded together in the iron resolve to save great nations from degeneration and decay.'[24] Despite the publicity that the uniform generated, its function was frequently aligned to fascist policy. For instance, Mosley stated that the uniform broke down class barriers: dressed in the same black shirt, all men look alike, 'whether they be on the "dole" or whether they be prosperous managers of big businesses'.[25] He stressed this point in a later publication: 'Already the Blackshirt has achieved within our own ranks that classless unity which we will ultimately secure within the nation as a whole.'[26] It was also asserted that the uniform had a practical quality which enables the fascist to 'distinguish friend from foe in the fights which Red violence forces upon us'.[27]

The official function or role of the political uniform may be comprehended only by someone who had read or heard the official literature. To the wider public, the uniform would have represented something else. Contemporary legal commentator Ivor Jennings asserted that uniforms create a feeling of security to those that wear them and feelings of insecurity in those who see them.[28] In consideration of this psychological impact, then that insecurity could have harnessed the hostile and violent responses which the Blackshirts were subjected to. The uniform could then be seen as a provocation in itself, in addition to the provocative far-Right policies which the fascists exhibited. Despite the emphasis on defence, the willingness to engage in political violence against their opponents must also be recognised. The uniform then can be seen not only as a provocation to disorder, but also as an element that promotes violent confrontation from its members by unifying them as a movement.

Political responses to the Blackshirt uniform

As early as June 1933, the correlation between public disorder and political uniforms was raised in the House of Commons. Following recent political disturbances in the West End of London, Labour MP Rhys Davies asked Sir Douglas Hacking, the Under Secretary for the Home Department, whether he would 'consider the desirability of suppressing all these organisations that are wearing uniforms and parading the streets'. Hacking replied, 'It may not always be desirable to prevent the wearing of uniforms. The wearing of uniform alone helps the police to find people guilty of any offence.'[29] But any benefit that political uniforms gave the police was soon to be reversed. Following discussions with the Metropolitan Police Commissioner, Home Secretary Sir John Gilmour claimed, 'recent developments have shown that any advantage in this direction is outweighed by the provocative effect of the wearing of such uniforms and the increasing number

24 O. Mosley, *Blackshirt Policy*, BUF Publications: London (1935), p. 16.
25 *Daily Mirror*, 25 Aug 1933.
26 Mosley, *Blackshirt Policy*, p. 16.
27 Ibid.
28 Jennings, 'Public Order', p. 177.
29 *Hansard, HC Deb*, 22 Jun 1933, vol 279 c920.

of street brawls which have occurred in consequence.'[30] The association of political uniforms with political violence remained and was frequently used in the mainstream political rhetoric.

In February 1934, Home Secretary John Gilmour was asked if he would consider introducing legislation to prohibit the wearing of uniforms by political parties. He reported that this question had been engaging his serious consideration. He continued to state that incidents of disorder which the police attributed to the wearing of political uniforms had escalated from eleven incidents in the first six months of 1933 in the Metropolitan Police District to no less than twenty-two disturbances in the last six months of the year.[31] This was the first in a series of questions aimed at the Home Secretary throughout 1934. Further questions came from Conservative MPs Vyvyan Adams,[32] Captain Sir Peter Macdonald[33] and Oswald Lewis,[34] Labour MPs John Tinker,[35] Jack Lawson[36] and William Thorne,[37] Liberal MP Robert Bernays,[38] and Scottish Unionist William Anstruther-Gray.[39] Gilmour's reply to these questions frequently suggested that the matter had seriously engaged his attention or that he had nothing further to add.

Despite the frequency of questions from all parties desiring the introduction of legislation to prohibit political uniforms, when a motion was made in May 1934 under the ten-minute rule to introduce a Bill by Conservative Mr Oliver Locker-Lampson, it found little support. Locker-Lampson argued:

> Violence breeds violence, and, if you want to turn England into a Communist camp, encourage Mosley to arm and dress and to break the law. Mosley breeds Bolshevism at every step, and he does it on purpose. Let his opportunities of appearing heroic be limited by a Bill like mine.[40]

Conservative Earl Winterton objected to the Bill, claiming that 'It would be quite impossible to define a political uniform for the purposes of this Bill.' His criticism continued: 'if this proposal were to be adopted, it would be the greatest

30 HO 45/25386, Disturbances: Wearing of uniform to denote membership of political organisations. Preservation of public order: disturbances arising out of public meetings and demonstrations, particularly those involving the British Union of Fascists (1933–36).
31 *Hansard, HC Deb*, 20 Feb 1934, vol 286 cc173–174.
32 *Hansard, HC Deb*, 1 Mar 1934, vol 286 c1249; *Hansard, HC Deb*, 19 Apr 1934, vol 288 cc1104–1105; *Hansard, HC Deb*, 2 May 1934, vol 289 cc311–312; *Hansard, HC Deb*, 30 May 1934, vol 290 cc167–168; *Hansard, HC Deb*, 30 Oct 1934, vol 293 c11.
33 *Hansard, HC Deb*, 30 Jul 1934, vol 292 c2289.
34 *Hansard, HC Deb*, 30 Oct 1934, vol 293 c11.
35 *Hansard, HC Deb*, 9 Apr 1934, vol 288 cc14–15.
36 *Hansard, HC Deb*, 16 May 1934, vol 289 cc1758–1760; *Hansard, HC Deb*, 16 May 1934, vol 289 cc1758–1760.
37 *Hansard, HC Deb*, 17 May 1934, vol 289 cc1922–1923.
38 *Hansard, HC Deb*, 16 May 1934, vol 289 cc1758–1760.
39 *Hansard, HC Deb*, 11 Jun 1934, vol 290 cc1341–1348 (question directed to Prime Minister) and *Hansard, HC Deb*, 30 Oct 1934, vol 293 c11.
40 *Hansard, HC Deb*, 16 May 1934, vol 289 c1767.

possible aid and advertisement for Sir Oswald Mosley's movement . . . what a cheap ready-made martyrdom it would provide.'[41]

In July 1934, Gilmour debated the existing law on public order with sixteen Chief Constables of England and Wales. Although Gilmour was still cautious about introducing any legislation prohibiting political uniforms at this time, the Chief Constables overwhelmingly supported the idea in some form or another. Of the sixteen questioned, only three Chief Constables did not support legislative action. The Chief Constable of Newcastle recognised that uniforms were the crux to the disorder but questioned the advisability of a ban.[42] In his following memorandum, Gilmour proposed

> That it should be an offence for any person, in pursuit of a political object, to form any body of persons into an organisation of a military character, by drill, or by the use of uniforms, or by the use of other military methods.[43]

The Lord Advocate suggested that targeting the use of political uniforms may be treated as an aggravation and that he preferred the banning of private armies in support of political organisations.[44] By mid-July, a cross-party conference was held which included Home Secretary John Gilmour, Attorney General Sir Thomas Inskip, Deputy Labour Leader Clement Attlee, and Labour MP Sir Stafford Cripps. Although this conference did not rule out the proscription of political uniforms, and there was a great deal of sympathy towards such legislative measures, no further action was taken. It was reported in the *News Chronicle* that the current view of the Government was that the Blackshirt movement had 'shot its bolt, and that no special legislation is now necessary'.[45]

Regional responses to the Blackshirt uniform

By 1936, questions were again directed to the Home Secretary, now Sir John Simon, on the matter of prohibiting political uniforms. The problem of how to define *uniform* was again used in response.[46] In July 1936, the BUF were denied an application to march in procession by the Manchester Watch Committee on account of the provocative nature of the fascists' uniforms. In response, the BUF publically reapplied, stating:

> In order to test whether the Watch Committee is animated by a genuine objection to political uniforms or by political prejudice against Fascism, I now

41 *Hansard, HC Deb*, 16 May 1934, vol 289 c1770.
42 HO 45/25386.
43 Ibid., 'Memorandum by the Home Secretary', 11 Jul 1934.
44 Ibid., 'Observations by the Lord Advocate', 9 Jul 1934.
45 U DCL/38, Filing case no. 38. Fascism (1934–1937); *News Chronicle*, 18 Jul 1934; *Daily Herald*, 24 Jul 1934.
46 *Hansard, HC Deb*, 07 May 1936, vol 311 cc1894–5W (Response by Under Secretary of State for the Home Department Geoffrey Lloyd).

make application for permission for a march of our members to the meeting in everyday clothes.[47]

Furthermore, when the BUF march was permitted, the route was stipulated by the Chief Constable. The Manchester Watch Committee was inevitably condemned by the fascist press, which claimed that the wearing of the uniform was an essential component of maintaining public order, as it distinguished the BUF from their opponents: 'the work of the police will be greatly increased, since our members are determined to abide by the law and the Red Hebrew front is determined to violate the law.'[48]

The effectiveness of this imposed condition, which essentially banned the wearing of the Blackshirt uniform for the procession on 19 July 1936, was subject to conflicting reports. The *Manchester Guardian* led with the headline, 'Disorder at Fascist Rally,' and described scenes in which numerous stones were thrown and sporadic fighting broke out. The police created the beginning of a stampede amongst the dense crowd as they attempted to reach the fighting, women with babies were removed to a safe distance, and there were eight arrests.[49] *The Times* reported that the demonstration, 'which had given the authorities some cause for anxiety beforehand, passed off fairly peaceably'. It made a brief reference to a stone being thrown and some trouble in front of the fascist platform, where some of the BUF's opponents 'shouted themselves hoarse and raised their clenched fists whenever the Fascists gave the Hitler salute'.[50] The Assistant Chief Constable claimed that the success of keeping order at the demonstration was because without their uniform, the fascists ceased to be provocative.[51] Following questions in the Commons, Home Secretary Sir John Simon could not assert whether the conditions imposed on the BUF march were made with any legal authority or not.[52] However, if any challenge was made to the decision, Ewing and Gearty suggest that, 'the police could have relied if they had chosen to do so on their breach of the peace jurisdiction.'[53] Even in the Police Courts, magistrates used their discretion to connect the wearing of the Blackshirt uniform with provocation. For example, in October 1936, Woolf Bensusan was accused of using insulting words and behaviour towards a fascist. In his judgment, the magistrate, Mr F. O. Langley stated, 'The existence of these Blackshirts is a provocation. I am not going to punish you because I think there was provocation.'[54] The Courts and Parliament recognised that political uniforms had the power to provoke disorder, and with the intensifying political violence associated with the BUF and their opponents, it was time for decisive legislative action.

---

47 *Manchester Guardian*, 17 Jul 1936.
48 *The Blackshirt*, 18 Jul 1936.
49 *The Manchester Guardian*, 20 Jul 1936.
50 *The Times*, 20 Jul 1936.
51 S. Cullen, 'Political Violence: The Case of the British Union of Fascists', *Journal of Contemporary History 28*, (1993), p. 256, quoting from HO 144/21061, 692, 242/172.
52 *Hansard, HC Deb*, 27 Jul 1936, vol 315 cc1095–1096.
53 Ewing and Gearty, *The Struggle*, p. 306, n150.
54 *The Manchester Guardian*, 10 Oct 1936.

S1 Public Order Act 1936

Reports following the disorder at Cable Street[55] frequently commented on the military-styled uniform worn by Mosley and other fascists. The *Western Morning News* recorded:

> Sir Oswald Mosley . . . yesterday wore the new uniform – a black military-cut jacket, grey riding breeches, and jack boots. He had a black peaked military hat and a red armband. Many of the Fascists on parade wore similar uniform.[56]

The scale of the violence at Cable Street was unprecedented in terms of BUF-related disorder. In combination with this, the escalating anti-Jewish attacks in East London and the new uniform – which was even more militarised and provocative – forced the Home Office to take action. There was renewed intensification over political uniforms and whether legislation should be introduced to prohibit them. Metropolitan Police Commissioner Sir Philip Game admitted that the police were not equipped to deal with the situation and asked the Cabinet to introduce legislation to prohibit political uniforms and political defence corps.[57]

When Home Secretary Sir John Simon introduced clause 1 Public Order Bill to Parliament, which prohibited the wearing of political uniform, he declared that:

> It is the unanimous view of the chief officers of police in the areas principally affected that the wearing of political uniforms is a source of special provocation, and testimony to the same effect has been offered to me at the Home Office by a number of deputations.[58]

The wording of clause 1, 'uniform signifying association with any political organisation or with the promotion of any political object', was carefully chosen. Simon stated that this clause would exclude the uniform of the Salvation Army, industrial organisations, benefit clubs, Boy Scouts and the Church Lads' Brigade.

Clause 1 was questioned by Mr Turton, who stated, 'To-day any man may go about in any public place in any attire, so long as it is decent and is not female attire' and questioned the advisability of adding any further restrictions on what people may wear, especially as no definition could be offered.[59] He moved that the clause should leave out the phrase, 'in any public place or' as he believed the Government were 'striking at a lot of people who are quite inoffensive and whom

---

55 See chapter four for analysis of the Battle of Cable Street 1936.
56 *Western Morning News*, 5 Oct 1936. Mosley later admitted that the adoption of a military uniform was a mistake. See Mosley, *My Life*, p. 253.
57 Pugh, '*Hurrah for the Blackshirts!*', p. 173; also see HO 144/20159, Disturbances: Public Order Bill (1936).
58 *Hansard, HC Deb*, 16 Nov 1936, vol 317 c1351.
59 Ibid. at c1426.

it is quite unnecessary to brand as criminals.' He mentioned the green shirts of the Social Credit Party, who were law abiding and should not fear the Attorney General when they walked out of their house.[60]

Simon made it clear that the clause would not carry a definition of the term *uniform*, as this would create potential loopholes that could be exploited. S1(1) Public Order Act 1936, which became law on 1 January 1937, states, 'any person who in any public place or at any public meeting wears uniform signifying his association with any political organisation or with the promotion of any political object shall be guilty of an offence'. Exceptions are permitted on occasion of ceremonial, anniversary or other special occasion, if the Chief Constable and the Secretary of State are satisfied that it will not be likely to involve any risk of public disorder. S1(2) confirms that the consent of the Attorney General is required for prosecutions to be instigated.

This section caused controversy on two fronts. First, it would affect other political organisations that were law abiding and did not threaten public order. Members of the Social Credit Party (SCP), recognisable by their green shirts, were the most noticeable victims of the new legislation. Other now-prohibited uniforms included the blue shirts of the Kensington Fascists, the grey shirts of the United Empire Fascist Party, the red shirts of the Independent Labour Party Guild of Youth, the brown or Khaki shirts of Communist Youth organisations, and the blue and white shirts used by Jewish anti-fascist organisations.[61] As s1 referred only to political uniforms, social and religious groups such as the Boy Scouts and the Salvation Army were omitted from the proscription. The only exception made in the Act was that uniforms could be worn on special occasions, which allowed the Ulster Orangemen to wear their uniforms for ceremonial processions. Second, as no definition of 'political uniform' was offered in the Act, it was controversially left for the Courts to interpret the meaning of this term. The question that this raises if a political uniform cannot be defined in legislation, how does a potential offender know whether his or her dress is considered to be prohibited or not?

Early prosecutions under s1

The BUF response to the new legislation demonstrated both their obedience to the law and their desire to circumvent it. A BUF cartoon which appeared in *Black-shirt*, reveals a fascist hanging up his uniform on 1 January 1937, demonstrating his respect of the law. The caption, 'Till the Day', emphasised the anticipated coming of a fascist state when the Blackshirt will again be worn. The BUF also submitted a request to the police to bring a test case against them so it could be ascertained whether a black shirt and tie worn with a regular suit would constitute an offence under the Act. They also issued a statement which declared: 'It is

---

60 *Hansard, HC Deb*, 23 Nov 1936, vol 318 cc49–50.
61 Anonymous, *Meetings, Uniforms and Public Order*, (a Guide to the Public Order Act 1936), Jordon and Sons: London (1937), p. 7.

incorrect to say that we either challenge or wish to defy the law. Our desire is, and always has been, to conform with the law.'[62] Yet in practice attempts were made to elude the proscription. In the first twelve days of 1937 there were at least thirty incidents where Blackshirts were stopped, had their names taken and were reported by the Metropolitan Police for an s1 offence. The Superintendent for N Division highlighted that the continued use of various items of the uniform associated with the BUF was to ascertain 'how far they will be able to go without police interference'.[63] It was also considered by the Attorney General that Mosley's adoption of wearing a plain black shirt under a grey lounge suit did not constitute a uniform under s1, although if a large number of fascists started to dress this way, such as at a procession, then that would require their attention.[64]

In January 1937, there were two prominent s1 prosecutions of BUF members. The different defences used demonstrate the way fascists sought loopholes in the new legislation. The first to be prosecuted was William Wood, a BUF paper seller, who was arrested on 2 January 1937 in Leeds. He was selling the newspapers *Action* and *Blackshirt* whilst wearing 'a peaked cap with a leather chin strap, and on the cap were two badges commonly associated with the BUF. He was also wearing a black shirt and a black tie'.[65] When Wood was approached by a police officer who asked him if he knew that wearing political uniforms was now an offence, he replied that he was told by his employers, the proprietors of the paper *Action*, 'that if he wore the uniform cap while he was selling the papers he was in the same position as the ordinary vendors of newspapers'.[66] In *R v Wood*[67] at Leeds Police Court, it was admitted by the police during cross-examination by Frederick Lawton[68] that other newspaper vendors also wore caps of a similar design. Defending, Lawton submitted that it was 'not a uniform, but a livery such as is worn by sellers of newspapers in all the big centres' and highlighted that the qualification to wear it was to sell papers to the value of 2s 2d per week for a period of one month.[69] It was argued by the prosecution that although the defendant was not attired in the full BUF uniform, the items that he was wearing were

62 *Nottingham Evening Post*, 2 Jan 1937.
63 DPP 2/433, 'Case papers, new series: Shepperd and Brien: Public Order Act'.
64 Ibid.
65 A Barrister, 'The Public Order Act 1936', *The Journal of Criminal Law 1*, no. 3 (1937), p. 451.
66 Ibid., p. 452.
67 *R v Wood* (1937) 81 Sol Jo 108.
68 Barrister Frederick Lawton, who was later to become Lord Chief Justice, was already an admirer of fascism before he became associated with the BUF, founding the Cambridge University Fascist Association as an undergraduate. He was called to the Bar by Inner Temple in 1935 and later that year watched Mosley, conducting his own case, sue John Marchbanks for slander at the King's Bench Division. After becoming acquainted with Mosley there, he joined the BUF and was later named as a prospective parliamentary candidate for the BUF in 1936. From then on, Mosley frequently employed Lawton to defend BUF members in court as well as to help set up a commercial radio station in Germany, an enterprise that Mosley hoped would aid the BUF's ailing financial situation. See A. De Courcy, *Diana Mosley*, Chatto and Windus: London (2003), p. 183.
69 *The Daily Mail (Hull)*, 27 Jan 1937.

complete enough to signify his association with the fascist party, submitting, 'It was not necessary that a uniform should be entirely complete to bring it within the mischief of section 1.'[70] The prosecutor described the Act as 'vaguely nebulous' claiming that 'the police and other people were anxious to know what the exact position was.'[71]

The Stipendiary Magistrate stressed that he did not want to lay down any general principles in regard to the law, declaring that all cases must be treated on their own merits. Regarding the dress worn by Wood, he was of the opinion that it could properly be described as a uniform within the meaning of the Act, stating, 'I think that the average person who had seen him would have said not "Oh, there's a man representing the Action Press," but "Oh, there's a Fascist."'[72] Although the maximum punishment for a s1 offence was three months imprisonment and a fine of £50, Wood was fined 40 shillings because the Stipendiary Magistrate stated that as it was a test case he would only impose a nominal penalty. Following the failed 'livery' defence in *R v Wood*, Lawton was called upon to defend four Blackshirts who had been arrested for the s1 offence in Hull.

In *R v Charnley*,[73] Sidney Charnley, Eric Webster, John Charnley and Peter Smith were summonsed before the Hull Stipendiary Magistrate on 29 January 1937 for wearing a uniform signifying their association with the BUF on 7 January at a public meeting. Sidney Charnley, the meeting's chairman, was described as wearing a 'dark navy blue woollen pull-over, black trousers, black belt with the Fascist badge on the buckle, and also a red brassard on the left arm'.[74] His brother John was similarly dressed, and Smith wore a black jacket and a red armband. For the defence it was argued that the garments worn constituted ordinary clothing and there was no intention of them being associated with a political object. The only items purchased from the same source were the armlets and belts. As for these items, Lawton argued that a distinctive mark such as an armlet may be considered part of a uniform but it was not a uniform in itself. He quoted the Attorney General, who stated during the House of Commons debates on clause 1 that the wearing of a distinctive tie would not constitute an offence under the Act, arguing that the object of the Act was to prevent the wearing of a complete outfit, stating, 'If they wanted to stop the wearing of badges they could have said so.'[75]

In giving judgment, the magistrate dismissed this argument, stating that if uniform meant a complete outfit, then Parliament would have stated so. Therefore, uniform must mean something less than that, yet, like the Leeds magistrate before him, he declared that he would not be drawn into defining the limits upon which a uniform could be described. The defendants were said to have been honest in their replies in trying to remain lawful, and the magistrate believed that they were

70 Anonymous, 'Cases in Magisterial and Other Courts: Public Order Act, 1936 – Political Uniforms', *Justice of the Peace and Local Government Review CI*, no. 6 (6 Feb 1937), p. 90.
71 *Nottingham Evening Post*, 27 Jan 1937.
72 *The Daily Mail (Hull)*, 27 Jan 1937.
73 *R v Charnley* (1937) 81 Sol Jo 108.
74 *The Journal of Criminal Law 1*, no. 3 (1937), p. 453.
75 *The Times*, 30 Jan 1937.

not deliberately attempting to break the law. They were 'bound over on their own recognizances each in £5 to be of good behaviour for six months and order to pay 10s each towards the costs of prosecution, with the exception of Smith, who was ordered to pay 5s'.[76] Whether the magistrate's view that the Blackshirts' intentions were honest was correct or not, the fascists were testing the boundaries of the new law and trying to exploit its vagueness. The lack of a definition only proved to strengthen the position of the magistrates to implement a wide interpretation of the meaning of 'political uniform'.

The attire described in *R v Wood* was very similar to the militaristic uniform worn by the BUF before the Public Order Act, but the clothes described in *R v Charnley*, which were claimed to be normal everyday clothes, were still considered to be political uniforms because of the various armlets and badges worn. Mosley continued to wear a black shirt after the Act and even challenged the Government to prosecute him at a speech delivered at Hornsey Town Hall, London, on 25 January 1937. In his speech, Mosley accused the police of bullying and blackmail, alleging that they frequently took the names and addresses of BUF members who wore a plain black shirt and threatened them with prosecution. He used this platform to forbid his followers to wear a black shirt in order to stop this intimidation. His black shirt was worn under a light coloured suit and there were no visible badges or armlets on display to signify association with any political party. Therefore, no prosecution was ever likely. Mosley used this sign of defiance to intensify his rhetoric against the Public Order Act, which he described as 'grossly partisan' and 'designed by our opponents to damage and to impede our organisation'.[77]

In contrast to the successful prosecutions of the uniformed fascists, the magistrates' judgments in two cases involving the green-shirted members of the SCP had quite a different outcome. The first was in Luton, where three members were charged with the s1 offence with the approval of the Attorney General. *The Times* recorded that 'The criterion appeared to be whether or not a collection of persons dressed in similar articles of distinctive apparel gave a reasonable onlooker the appearance of persons dressed in uniform.'[78] Although the defendants wore their distinctive green shirt and tie, one wore them with an ordinary suit, and others with either a mackintosh or overcoat. However, they all wore armlets with the emblem of their party on them. The solicitor for the defence read the definition of the word *uniform* from the *New English Dictionary* and argued that, 'it was perfectly obvious that they were not wearing a "distinctive dress of the same pattern, colour and appearance."'[79] The Bench dismissed the case.

On 16 June 1937, another member of the SCP was summonsed under s1 Public Order Act 1936. He wore 'a light green shirt, green collar, green tie (the tie

76 Ibid.
77 *Action*, 30 Jan 1937.
78 *The Times*, 3 Jun 1937.
79 Ibid.

bearing an inscription or initials), a black belt, grey flannel trousers, and a green armlet, the last marked with a "double K" in white'.[80] For the defence, it was argued that his green shirt was only revealed because he removed his coat because of the warm weather, and his shirt was light green, rather than the dark green that was associated with the party. Further, the defendant was not wearing a beret which was part of the usual uniform of the SCP, and the shirt and tie were quite 'ordinary' and ones 'that anyone might buy'.[81] Although the magistrate, Paul Bennett, held that the shirt, tie and armlet constituted a uniform, *The Times* reported that he 'did not take a serious view of that case' and he dismissed the summons under the Probation of Offenders Act on payment by the defendant of £5 5s costs.

The discretion utilised by the magistrates in these cases demonstrates that the members of the SCP were treated more leniently than the Blackshirts who violated s1, despite the similarities in the garments which constituted their uniform. This was also reflected in the Parliamentary debates, which implicitly stated that the main function of the uniform ban was to counter the provocation caused by the BUF and to prevent other extremist bodies creating uniformed divisions themselves. A certain amount of sympathy had been imparted for members of the SCP, who were not considered to be a provocation or a source of political violence by Parliament, but would have their liberty to dress in uniform curtailed. The Blackshirts did experience a higher conviction rate, but the sentencing consistently reflected a temperate view of the offence by the magistrates. A further Blackshirt conviction in August 1937 validates this view, when Reginald Dawson was fined £5 and ordered to pay £2 2s costs at Hampstead. The full punishment available to the magistrates on summary conviction under s7(2) was imprisonment for a term not exceeding three months, a fine not exceeding £50, or both. Dawson was dressed in a 'black stockinette jersey' with a polo collar two inches deep and a fascist badge on the lefthand side, grey trousers and a wide black leather belt with a chromium-plated buckle consisting of 'slots which appeared to have been used for holding a badge'.[82] During Dawson's public address at Carlingford Road, Hampstead, he responded to a heckler from the crowd who commented on his uniform by stating, 'All right. If you don't know what a uniform is, don't show your ignorance.' The clothes worn by Dawson were the same as those worn by certain members of the BUF before the Act came into force, although the badge had been removed from the belt, and no armlet was worn (which had been a recent development of the fascist uniform).

The relatively few reported cases of s1 Public Order Act violations would indicate that the provision was successful in preventing political activists from

---

80 *The Times*, 17 Jun 1937.
81 Ibid. Also, the 'Double K' was likely to stand for 'Kibbo Kift' which was a youth organisation founded in 1921 by John Hargrave who was a former Commissioner of Baden-Powell's boy scout movement. Hargrave was later influenced by Major C.H. Douglas' theories of social credit and adopted these ideas into the official policy of his movement which became the Greenshirt Movement for Social Credit in 1931, and then Social Credit Party of Great Britain in 1935.
82 *The Times*, 26 Aug 1937.

causing provocation by wearing political uniforms. In giving evidence, Reginald Dawson declared that he had worn the same outfit in Kilburn and Camden Town.

At Camden Town, an Inspector took a different view of his powers under s1 and asked Dawson if any others were going to join him wearing the black polo jumper, stating that if they did then it would constitute a political uniform. This demonstrates that it was not just the courts that had difficulty defining what constituted a political uniform – at street level, the vague Statute also allowed for inconsistency among police action. If it proved difficult for the authorities to interpret this ambiguous criminal offence, the choice of dress for the political activist had to be carefully selected. The real value of s1 was that the Blackshirt uniform was not worn again in public processions or by their stewards at public meetings, and it ended the provocation of the uniformed Fascist Defence Force, subduing their appearance as a private army and removing a certain level of the provocation that the BUF generated. However, s1 did not end the violence and public disorder that was associated with the BUF and their anti-fascist opposition.[83] Anderson argues that since the provisions of the Public Order Act 'are inhibitive rather than repressive, [its effects] are impossible to assess'.[84] Coupland also adds that, without their uniforms, the BUF attracted a mass of new members that were previously put off by their military appearance.[85] In fact, despite the uniform ban, the BUF had a sudden growth in membership before the Second World War, due to their peace campaign.

Post-War prosecutions under s1

Ku Klux Klan activism in Rugby 1965

S1 Public Order Act 1936 continues to remain in force; it was not repealed or amended when the 1936 Act was reformed by the Public Order Act 1986. The most prominent s1 convictions since the Second World War were of members of the British Ku Klux Klan (KKK) in October 1965, and the Provisional Sinn Fein for offences committed in June and August 1974. For the KKK case, s1 was a convenient provision to prevent the dangerous growth in Britain of a racist far-Right movement that emulated the American model.

On 19 June 1965, twelve members of the KKK held a cross-burning ceremony in Rugby, Warwickshire. Despite being on private land, it was argued by the prosecution in *R v Robert Edward Relf and others*[86] that the ceremony constituted a public meeting as members of the press were invited, and the burning cross could

---

83 See 'The application of s3 from 1937–1939' in chapter five and 'The police, anti-Semitism and the Public Order Act' in chapter 6 for examples of BUF violence after the Blackshirt uniform was proscribed under the Public Order Act 1936.

84 Anderson, *Fascists*, p. 191.

85 Coupland, 'The Black Shirt in Britain', p. 115.

86 *R v Robert Edward Relf and others*, unreported (1965), Rugby Magistrates Court.

be seen for miles around; therefore, fulfilling one of the requirements under s1.[87] The eight members who faced charges were all convicted, three of whom received three month prison sentences, two were fined, and three were bound over.

Seven members wore uniforms. With the exception of Relf, who was convicted of aiding and abetting Thomas Allen and William Duncan to commit the offence, the dress of the uniformed members consisted of 'white gowns with a black cross over the heart and cloth headdresses with slits for the eyes and mouth which were not unlike dunce's caps'.[88] At the meeting it was recorded that the aims of the KKK were 'to rid Britain of Jews, Roman Catholics and Coloureds . . . by every possible means including violence'.[89] It was also stated that the punishment for betraying the KKK was death.[90] In an interview with the invited members of the press, Relf stated that 'if candidates could be found they would put them up at the general election'.[91] The prosecution also successfully argued that these statements, indicated a 'political organization, and . . . the promotion of political objectives' which further guaranteed a successful prosecution under s1.[92]

Sinn Fein activism in 1975

The two separate Sinn Fein cases were brought together on appeal to the Queen's Bench Division in December 1975. The first, *O'Moran and others v DPP*[93] consisted of eight appellants who were convicted at Old Street Magistrates for offences contrary to s1(1) Public Order Act 1936. They had dressed in black or dark blue berets, dark glasses, dark pullovers and other dark clothing during the funeral procession of their colleague and hunger striker Michael Gaughan, who died in Pankhurst Prison on the Isle of Wight. In the second case, *Whelan and Others v DPP*,[94] the twelve appellants had been convicted following an attempted political procession from Speaker's Corner to Downing Street. The members were arrested at the start of the procession under s1(1) after several warnings from Chief Inspector Cooksley, who informed them that wearing a political uniform was against the law and that if they did not remove their berets they would be arrested.

The significance of the appeal was that it was the first time that matters relating to s1 had been brought before a superior court. In giving judgment on the first case, Lord Widgery CJ ruled that although the appellants were 'dressed in a

---

87 *The Times*, 8 Oct 1965.

88 Ibid.

89 DPP 2/4009, RELF, Robert; WEBB, Michael; WEBB, Patrick and others: wearing political uniform at public meeting; S1(1) Public Order Act, 1936. Ku Klux Klan ceremony held on 19 June 1965, at Long Lawford, Warwickshire. First prosecution involving Ku Klux Klansmen (1965–1966).

90 Ibid. 'Summary of facts'. In his statement the speaker William Duncan declared that this was only a line for publicity and not serious.

91 *The Times*, 8 Oct 1965.

92 Ibid.

93 *O'Moran and others v DPP* [1975] QB 864.

94 *Whelan and others v DPP* [1975] QB 864.

similar but not identical fashion', the fact that they all wore berets, and were seen together rather than in isolation, ruled that that article constituted a uniform as its adoption was for 'the purposes of showing association between the men in question'.[95] He continued to point out that the uniform in *O'Moran* went beyond the berets in any case and ruled that the pullover, dark glasses and dark clothes, on that occasion, constituted a uniform within the meaning of the Act.

Further to this, Widgery had to judge whether it was necessary under s1(1) for the prosecution to prove which political organisation was concerned. At the Old Street Magistrates court, Police Sergeant Garnham stated that the berets had been previously associated with members of the Irish Republican Army, who wore them with combat jackets, and were also becoming a common feature amongst other Irish republican organisations at demonstrations in London. He claimed that people wearing berets were frequently seen in the close proximity of Sinn Fein banners or were carrying them.[96] Widgery stressed that it was not necessary to prove the previous use of the article as uniform, but that their style of dress showed a mutual association with one another. He continued that this could be judged from the events when the alleged uniform was worn. The particular events in this case were that the men wore what Widgery had already judged to have been uniforms at a funeral service associated with a member of the Irish republican movement, and they delivered an address of a political character. Bearing this in mind, he stated that it was 'abundantly clear that they were activities of an organisation of a political character. Thus the chain of responsibility under the section would be complete'[97] and consequently dismissed the appeals headed by O'Moran.

The appeals headed by Whelan were also dismissed. Widgery's judgment here was even more explicit: 'I see no reason why a beret in itself, if worn in order to indicate association with a political body, should not be a uniform for present purposes.'[98] In his reasoning, he concurred with the magistrate's view that 'An independent bystander, seeing the approach of a group of marchers wearing identical headgear under the banner of the Provisional Sinn Fein, would conclude that it was their uniform.'[99] This ruling indicated that a single item of clothing, such as a beret, could be legally described as a political uniform within the meaning of the Act.

Britain First activism in 2014

Paul Golding, the leader of the new far-Right party Britain First (BF), was charged with a s1 offence at Chelmsford Magistrates' Court on 5 January 2015. At the same time that he wore the prohibited uniform, he allegedly harassed Munazza Munawar outside her home. Golding had mistaken Munawar's address for the home of her brother-in-law Sajeel Shahid, who was a leader of the proscribed

95 *O'Moran and others v DPP* at 872–873.
96 *The Times*, 30 Jul 1974.
97 *O'Moran and others v DPP* at 874.
98 *Whelan and others v DPP* at 876–877.
99 Ibid. at 876.

Islamist group Al-Muhajiroun. District Judge David Woollard said, 'It was a polit-ical stunt which was designed to further the cause of the party and to generate the kind of material which is later placed on the Britain First website.'[100] Golding was found guilty on both counts; he was fined £325 for harassment and £100 for wearing a political uniform. This is the first significant prosecution under s1 for forty years, but demonstrates how this little-used provision continues to prevent the use of uniforms which potentially provoke violence and insecurity in others.

Members of this political movement are often seen in public together either wearing green bomber jackets, green polo shirts or green fleeces with the BF emblem on and flat caps. The uniformity of this dress corresponds with the requirements necessary for a s1 prosecution in *O'Moran*. In addition, BF have political ambitions which have included standing in local elections and mounting a campaign for the 2015 general election. In Golding's video published on the BF website and Facebook page, he has insisted that the prosecution needs to prove that it is compulsory for BF members to wear these items for him to be found guilty of this offence. As there is no mention of compulsion in the wording of this provision, it is expected that that this defence will fail.

The wearing of articles which denote support of a proscribed organisation

Under Terrorism Act 2000 s13(1) it is an offence if a person in a public place (a) wears an item of clothing, or (b) wears, carries or displays an article, in such a way or in such circumstances as to arouse reasonable suspicion that he or she is a member or supporter of a proscribed organisation. Under this provision, items such as badges, flags, emblems and armbands (which would not otherwise fall under the meaning of uniform in s1 Public Order Act 1936) are included. The judgment in *Rankin v Murray*[101] demonstrates the extent of this far-reaching provision.

James Rankin was convicted for a s13(1) offence following his arrest at the Seacat Terminal in Troon, Scotland, when officers were suspicious about his jew-ellery, which included a ring with the initials UVF (possibly indicating his mem-bership or support of the Ulster Volunteer Force). For Rankin, it was argued that the ring was a gift from his wife, that he regularly visited Northern Ireland, that he participated in lawful Loyalist activities, and that he was not a member or sup-porter of the Ulster Volunteer Force. The appeal was refused by the High Court. It was the opinion of the Court that

> on the assumption that these facts are to be taken as having been established, they go no way, in our view, to negative the actual suspicion entertained by the officers nor the objectively reasonable basis for that suspicion.[102]

---

100 *Essex Chronicle*, 6 Jan 2015.
101 *Rankin v Murray* (2004) S.L.T. 1164.
102 Ibid., para 8.

The emphasis on the term *suspicion* demonstrates the remarkable extent of this law which by s13(3) is punishable on summary conviction to (a) imprisonment for a term not exceeding six months, (b) a fine not exceeding level 5 on the standard scale or (c) both.

Conclusion

Different types of clothing or adornments have intermittently prompted legal responses from the police and the Government. While the Court rulings in *Clifford, Esq. v Brandon* and *Humphries v Connor* are seemingly inconsistent, there are important factors that account for the largely different verdicts. The jury at the Court of Common Pleas found Brandon guilty of assault and false imprisonment after Clifford's arrest for wearing the letters OP in his hat and declared that wearing the initials was not instigation to riot. The police officer in *Humphries v Connor* was cleared of assault for removing the orange lily despite the judges' acknowledgment that Humphries was at liberty to wear the emblem. The main difference is that the lily had the power to provoke a violent reaction from those who were opposed to her making the political and religious statement, and in the view of the officer, a breach of the peace was imminent. In *Clifford* there was no suggestion that the initials OP would provoke a reaction from opponents, but would promote disorder and instigate riotous behaviour from Clifford's allies. Also, there was no imminent threat to a breach of the peace when he was arrested, demonstrating that police responses which utilise the breach of the peace doctrine under the common law need to consider the immediacy of the disorder before taking action. In the twentieth century, the controversial method used by the Manchester Watch Committee to restrict the wearing of the Blackshirt uniform in public procession was not legally challenged but succeeded in prohibiting the attire.

Since the enactment of the Public Order Act 1936, there have been several instances when a defendants' attire has been judged to have been a political uniform within the meaning of s1. A key feature of all these decisions, however, has been the unwillingness of the presiding judges to lay down any general principles. Instead, their judgments have highlighted an importance to the specific events recorded and conduct of the defendants. Therefore, no conclusive definition of what constitutes a political uniform can be offered, but the common features found in such judgments can elucidate a better understanding of the phrase. Yet the elasticity of the wording has allowed for the conviction of members of politically extreme groups.

In the interwar period, respective magistrates have convicted Blackshirts who provided varied and innovative defences. For the Blackshirt newspaper vender, Wood, it was argued in his defence that his uniform was a livery from the company Action Press, and that other newspaper venders wore similarly styled dress. In this case it was judged that a complete uniform need not be worn and that a general member of the public would have recognised him as a fascist rather than an employee of Action Press. The second defence for Charnley and others was that their clothes were purchased within the everyday course of their lives, and that only their badges signified an association with a political organisation. It was also judged by the magistrate that the uniform does not need to be complete to fall within the meaning of the Act, and the brassard or armband 'with the emblem of the political party was certainly an identification and a uniform'.[103] The Blackshirt prosecution of Dawson relied on the previous association of the black polo-styled jersey with the BUF before the Act was passed. These three judgments reflect the subsequently wide scope that s1(1) holds without a definition of what constitutes a political uniform.

However, the leniency given to the green shirts worn by members of the SCP questions the consistency of the application of the Act. The descriptions provided to the courts of the defendants' attire had overwhelming similarities with those worn by the Blackshirts. Yet these cases were dismissed. In the case against Douglas Wright it was reported that he was dismissed under the Probation of Offenders Act 1907 on payment of £5 5s costs. Although this was a similar figure to the fines issued to the Blackshirts, the defendant was spared a criminal conviction. This inconsistency was highlighted by *The Blackshirt*, which alleged discrimination against the fascists, stating that it was proof that the Public Order Act was supposed to work only against them. The BUF challenged Parliament to include a definition of 'political uniform' within the law, to allow the magistrates to 'keep their just reputation of impartiality'.[104] The full sentence of three months' imprisonment and the maximum fine of £50 to members of the KKK certainly reflects that the more extreme the political organisation, the more severe the punishment may be. Yet this chapter has also demonstrated that police discretion is prominent when dealing with possible offenders who may provoke disorder by their dress or who may violate s1 Public Order Act. When faced with an imminent breach of the peace, does the police officer direct his or her action at the provoker or the provoked? Recent case law, which applies the ECHR, takes into account the action of the provoker.[105]

The judgments regarding s1 prosecutions demonstrate the flexibility that is provided by not including a definition. It is clear from the Parliamentary debates that the uniform ban was primarily aimed at preventing the provocation caused by the Blackshirts, and it was regretted that small political groups without a reputation for public disorder like the SCP would be affected by the Act. Yet any statutory provision should be applied equally to each defendant regardless of their political persuasion. This vague provision has offered tribunals an opportunity to apply a broad interpretation to their judgment. In practice this has demonstrated that a more lenient view has been afforded to those whose uniforms and political methods have not had a history or reputation of provocation or serious disorder. Political movements that represent a threat to public order or national security such as the BUF, KKK and Sinn Fein have consequently found that the courts have taken a more serious view when they have breached s1.

---

103 *The Daily Mail (Hull)*, 29 Jan 1937.
104 *The Blackshirt*, 5 Jun 1937.
105 For example, see *Redmond-Bate v DPP* for a judgment which ruled that the police officer should direct their action towards the threat of violence. This was discussed in chapter six.

Conclusion

This socio-legal examination of the police and their role as guardians of public order has established a history of inconsistent attitudes and practice towards the liberties of free expression and assembly on the one hand to the protection of the general public and property on the other. The changing tension between these two forces constitutes an ebb and flow within the history of public protest and political activism that, despite significant milestones such as the Human Rights Act 1998, has not necessarily guaranteed that such rights have a higher status today than they have had during certain moments in recent history. In this respect, there has been no 'Whig' history of public order which has observed the increasing importance of human rights and civil liberties within police practice. Nor has there been a steadily increasing efficiency in police tactics. These variations not only changed through time but there were also regional variants which demonstrate how multifaceted this history is.

Since the formation of the modern police service in 1829, there has effectively been a tug of war between these competing rights (free expression and assembly versus the protection of the general public and property) which have struggled for supremacy. The use of unarmed police in public order scenarios itself represented a move away from the use of both amateur and professional military agencies. However, in the century that followed the introduction of the police, the army still played a significant role. A series of legislative developments and common law judgments have contributed to this ongoing narrative of police responses. The rights of freedom of assembly and expression have continued to have a contentious existence even after the HRA. In the 200 years which preceded the HRA, the responses to potential public disorder by the police and successive Governments have also added to this chequered history. One major aspect of policing public order has been to directly place the role of the police into an arena which involves making decisions with political consequences. The demands for constitutional and social change which have been led by the political Left (highlighted by Henry Hunt at St Peter's Field in 1819, the Chartists in the mid nineteenth century, the Social Democratic Party in the late and nineteenth and early twentieth century, the CPGB and the NUWM in the interwar period and numerous anti-capitalist, anti-war and anti-austerity demonstrations since) have protested against the reactionary tendencies of the Government, who resisted calls for pro-gressive social policies, and the reactionary tendencies of the Government and the conservative function of the police. John Alderson importantly noted how the activists on the Left targeted the police and the establishment. This is not surpris-ing when it has been the establishment that has frequently disregarded demands for social change. Key issues which we now take for granted, such as universal suffrage, have been the result of long and often violent battles with the authorities. The police's duty to keep the peace has often placed them in direct opposition to these campaigners. The memories of past conflicts and battles live long through the generations. Even after seventy-five years, the Battle of Cable Street is still fondly remembered and celebrated by the East End community and anti-fascists. Although it is remembered as the day that checked the march of fascism through the East End of London, this was achieved only by confronting and fighting the police. Generational suspicion and contempt for the police has long lived among some aspects of the far Left; evidence of police suspicion of the far Left has also been witnessed.

The police's relationship with the far Right has had a contrasting history. How-ever, this difference is more subjected to the inherently different methods of activ-ism that the far Right have employed rather than any dominant notions of police partiality. In their official activism the BUF pioneered methods of political activ-ism that marginally stayed within the realms of the law, which problematised the police response. The evidence presented here demonstrates how successive Metropolitan Police Commissioners and many Chief Constables of the interwar period were frustrated by fascist activism and advocated changes in the law as they felt their current powers were insufficient to suppress fascist-related disorder.[1]

Throughout this book it has been demonstrated that the breadth of decision making that the police were afforded under the breach of the peace doctrine has led to inconsistent policing. Police decision making in public order scenarios is vital as it has the power to both prevent and provoke disorder. Robust police responses to small disorder within larger crowds often aggravated further disor-der by altering group identities within the crowd, therefore changing the crowd dynamics. Advances within public order policing, such as the employment of PLTs, demonstrate an important development which recognises the provocative nature of an overzealous police response to public protest. Therefore, the use of positive strategies which include public engagement, negotiation and facilitation have become more appropriate measures to prevent disorder.

Seen in the context of its development, the law relating to freedom of assembly was vague and ambiguous in the latter half of the nineteenth century, which was highlighted by the Home Secretary William Harcourt's confusing advice to local authorities regarding the Salvation Army. The judgment in *Beatty v Gillbanks* pro-vided a clear maxim that people could not be prevented from engaging in lawful

---

1 See the discussion on the Public Order Bill 1934 in chapter four.

activity because of the predicted unlawful response of others. This placed a clear emphasis on the police, as keepers of the peace, to protect lawful public assemblies and processions. Yet this concept became more ambiguous following the judgment in *Wise v Dunning*. This uncertainty was particularly notable in the interwar years by the inconsistency in practice of the provincial police in response to various hunger and unemployed marches. The processions of the BUF and the confrontations they provoked became catalysts for precise legal powers. The Public Order Act 1936 provided the police with the ability to regulate processions as well as apply for a banning order. The provision to proscribe processions under both the 1936 and 1986 Act have been predominantly used against the far Right (including the BUF, UM, NF and EDL), which demonstrates the provocative nature of right-wing objectives and activism. More recently, the use of 'kettling' and its support from the Courts as a common law method to prevent disorder has provided the police with further restrictive and coercive powers to stifle and suppress public protest. Again, this Breach of the Peace power has some ambiguity in the question of how imminent the breach of the peace was for it to be supported by the judiciary. The discomfort caused to activists and members of the public when this tactic is utilised also has the 'perhaps' unintentional consequence of deterring participation in public protest.

Inconsistency in the law relating to freedom of expression was particularly notable in the era of the BUF and the CPGB. While there were instances where the police obstructed and prevented meetings of the far Left, this time period also revealed how the police also used their Breach of the Peace powers to close fascist meetings. These are not cited so regularly in the historiography as the Blackshirts obeyed such instruction without confrontation and disorder, exciting very little interest. Yet they do show how policing in this era was not always as partial as has perhaps been argued. The inconsistency in police practice within this era is demonstrated by the differing levels of activism that different provincial police forces tolerated. Although there was no linear progression towards the recognition of freedom of speech as a right, the consistency that has been identified in the era since the HRA is that the more politically extreme the speech or the activist, the less likely they are to have their claim to the right of freedom of expression supported by the courts.

The inconsistent responses of the police to political activism are most noticeably highlighted by their different methods used when policing activism on private premises. The ambiguity of their legal powers led to the adoption of several different policing methods across the country. This need for uniformity was highlighted by the use of police inside the hall at a far-Left meeting in South Wales and the reluctance of the Metropolitan Police to enter the BUF meeting at Olympia, despite the evident brutality of the stewards. Although *Thomas v Sawkins* provided the police with a common law power to enter a meeting when disorder was anticipated there was still a question over when they should intervene. As the steward has the primary role in keeping order and ejecting interrupters at meetings on private premises, there is naturally going to be some physical confrontation. Even when the stewarding had been of a particularly brutal nature (such as at the communist meeting at Ealing Town Hall in 1936 and the Conservative Party conference at Blackpool in 1958), the magistrates in each case were prepared to accept that the stewards were acting within their duty when they ejected those who obstructed them in doing their duty.

The State's responses to extremism have been noticeably demonstrated by the enactment of the infrequently used s1 Public Order Act 1936. Its success in gaining a successful prosecution and therefore denying political movements of the extra publicity and provocation relied on the ambiguity of the definition of *uniform*, which has tended to favour the prosecution. This has been emphasised again by the successful prosecution of BF leader Paul Golding on 5 January 2015. While the prosecution looks likely to succeed given the vague definition of uniform accepted in *O'Moran and others v DPP*, the interest will be in the sentencing which has varied significantly in the cases examined.

Although the Public Order Act 1936 and 1986 were both significant milestones in public order law, as they recognised and addressed the need for national consistency in police practice, the quest for uniformity has been hindered by the wide discretion still available to the police. This drive for uniformity has continued, yet provincial police forces still have significant independence and manoeuvrability within the law to employ different tactics at public protests and political actions.

The future direction of police strategies at public order events is currently positioned at a crossroads, with the dual developments in tactical operations demonstrating the practical antithesis of each other. On one hand, the increasing practice of 'kettling' which has found support from the domestic courts and the ECtHR in particular circumstances, the increasing use of paramilitary style uniforms and equipment, the continued use of coercive methods of dispersion and the likelihood that the water cannon will soon be commissioned in London, represent the robust style of policing which responds to the threat of disorder with force, intimidation and pressure. On the other, the development of PLTs and the use of plain-clothed officers to gain trust, negotiate and facilitate public protest, represent the competing end of the spectrum which seemingly places a greater emphasis on the rights of expression and assembly. However, it may be misleading to summarise the motivations behind these two strands of policing in such crude terms as their position on civil liberties and human rights. As recent studies on crowd psychology have revealed, the facilitation of public demonstrations and political activism that does not rely on coercive and confrontational policing methods is less likely to provoke frustration, opposition and ultimately retaliative violence from members of a crowd.

Crowds throughout history that have been frustrated by the lack of facilitation of protests or the suppression of protests by authorities have frequently responded with violence and disorder. Incidents of disorder, such as those described at Featherstone in 1893, the Manchester marchers in Birmingham in 1908, the NUWM in Hyde Park in 1932, the Poll Tax Riot in 1990, and the English Riots 2011 have all escalated largely as a response to indiscriminate and overzealous policing which had either presented an oppositional front to the demonstration or had presented a forceful and constricting presence which changed crowd dynamics, generated hostility and exacerbated the seriousness of the disorder. While serious public disorder and riot may compel a robust police response to restore order, the preventative measures employed by the police in the first instance must demonstrate neutrality, facilitation and cooperation. The warnings from history demonstrate that the use of indiscriminate coercive tactics which have been utilised in the past should not be seen as viable strategies for the future. Such discerning tactics, or the threat of them through their visibility, must be recognised as a provocation which marks the battle lines between crowd and the police.

Bibliography

Primary sources

The National Archives

CAB 24/250, Preservation of public order: Memorandum by the Home Secretary and Commissioner of Police of the Metropolis (July 1934).

CAB 24/264, March of the unemployed on London: Memorandum by the Home Secretary (1936).

CAB 24/271, Prohibition of political processions in London: Memorandum by the Home Secretary (1937).

DPP 2/433, Case papers, new series: Shepperd and Brien: Public Order Act.

DPP 2/4009, RELF, Robert; WEBB, Michael; WEBB, Patrick and others: Wearing political uniform at public meeting; S1(1) Public Order Act, 1936. Ku Klux Klan ceremony held on 19 June 1965, at Long Lawford, Warwickshire. First prosecution involving Ku Klux Klansmen (1965–1966).

HO 45/25383, Disturbances: Anti-fascist activities; anti-fascist demonstrations and activities directed against meeting of the British Union of Fascists in Hyde Park on 9 Sept 1934 (1929–1934).

HO 45/25386, Disturbances: Wearing of uniform to denote membership of political organisations. Preservation of public order: Disturbances arising out of public meetings and demonstrations, particularly those involving the British Union of Fascists (1933–1936).

HO 45/24996, Disturbances: Public Meeting Act (1908) Amendment Bill 1937: Maintenance of order at public meetings.

HO 144/18294, Police: Powers and duties of the police at meetings, processions and demonstrations.

HO144/20069, Disturbances: Disturbances at public meetings (1925–1936).

HO 144/20159, Disturbances: Public Order Bill (1936).

HO 144/21064. Disturbances: British Union of Fascists: Activities

HO 144/8014, Disturbances: Trade Disputes and Trade Unions Bill, 1927.

MEPO 2/3077, Fascist meetings, parade through West End and march past (1934–1935).

MEPO 2/3083, British Union of Fascists: attempts to ensure free policing of their meetings (1936).

MEPO 2/3115, Fascist: Provoking a breach of peace with insulting words (1937).

MEPO 2/3116, Disturbances at Fascist meetings: Complaint by Sir Oswald Mosley (1937).

MEPO 2/4319, Police evidence sought about various happenings at Fascist meetings, in support of private prosecution (1934–1936).

MEPO 2/10651, Case of riotous assembly at Worthing, Sussex against Sir Oswald Mosley, William Joyce, Bernard Mullen and Captain Charles Bentinck Budd: Reports, and correspondence.
MEPO 3/551, Fascist march and communist rally 4 Oct 1936.
MEPO 3/2940, Fascist: Disorder at public meetings (1934–1938).
MEPO 3/3093, Disturbances at Union Movement meetings: Result of proceedings against offenders (1948).

The Hull History Centre

U DCL/8/6, Police and demonstrations, Arms for Spain; fascist and anti-fascist (1934–1940).
U DDC/5/364, Pamphlet: 'Eye Witnesses at Olympia' (1934).
U DCL/75/2, Duplicated circulars issued by NCCL (1937–1938).
U DCL/38, Filing case no. 38. Fascism (1934–1937).
U DCL/40/1, NCCL enquiry into fascist meeting at Olympia (1934).
U DCL/40/6, NCCL enquiry into fascist meeting at Hornsey Town Hall (1937)

Newspapers and journals (electronic and print)

Aberdeen Journal
Action
BBC News
Birmingham Evening Mail
Birmingham Journal
Bradford Telegraph
Cork Examiner
Daily Mail
Daily Post (Liverpool)
Daily Star Sunday
Daily Telegraph
Daily Worker
Derby Daily Telegraph
Dundee Courier
Evening Standard (London)
Evening Telegraph
Gloucester Citizen
Gloucestershire Echo
Hampshire Chronicle
Hull Daily Mail
Justice of the Peace and Local Government Review
Leicester Evening Mail
Leicester Mercury
Lichfield Mercury
London Standard
Luton On Sunday
Luton Today
Manchester Courier and Lancashire General Advertiser
Manchester Guardian
Morning Chronicle

News Chronicle
Nottingham Evening Post
Police Oracle
Reading Mercury
Staffordshire Gazette and County Standard
The Blackshirt
The Bristol Mercury and Daily Post
The Daily Express
The Daily Mirror
The Dover Express
The Huddersfield Daily Chronicle
The Independent on Sunday
The Journal of Criminal Law
The Leeds Times
The Morning Post
The Mail on Sunday
The Newcastle Guardian
The Pall Mall Gazette
The Spectator
The Star
The South Western Labour Journal
The Times
Western Daily Press
Western Evening Herald
Western Gazette
Western Morning News
Western Times

Official publications

Cd. 4673, *Report of the Departmental Committee on the Duties of the Police With Respect to the Preservation of Order at Public Meetings.* Volume 1: Report and Appendices (1909).

Cd. 4674, *Report of the Departmental Committee on the Duties of the Police With Respect to the Preservation of Order at Public Meetings* (1909).

Cmd. 5457, *Report of the Commissioner of Police of the Metropolis for the Year 1936.*

Cmd. 5761, *Report of the Commissioner of Police of the Metropolis for the year 1937.*

Cmnd. 7891, *Review of the Public Order Act 1936 and Related Legislation* (1980).

Cmnd. 9510, *Review of Public Order Law* (1985).

Featherstone Inquiry. *Minutes of evidence taken before the Committee appointed to inquire into the circumstances connected with the disturbances at Featherstone on 7th September 1893* [C.7234i].

Featherstone Inquiry. *Report of the Committee appointed to inquire into the circumstances connected with the disturbances at Featherstone on 7th September 1893* [C.7234].

Her Majesty's Chief Inspector of Constabulary (HMIC), 'Adapting to Protest' (2009).

Her Majesty's Chief Inspector of Constabulary (HMIC), 'Policing Public Order: An overview and review of progress against the recommendations of *Adapting to Protest* and *Nurturing the British Model of Policing*' (2011).

House of Commons Parliamentary Papers. *Public Meeting. A Bill to Prevent Disturbance of Public Meetings* (1908).

House of Commons Written Answers, 24 Jan 2011, col 55W.

Law Com No. 123, *Report on Criminal Law; Offences Relating to Public Order* (1983)

Report from the Select Committee on Metropolis Police Offices; with the minutes of evidence, appendix and index (1837).

Other publications

Anonymous, *Meetings, Uniforms and Public Order* (a Guide to the Public Order Act 1936). Jordon and Sons: London (1937).

Chesterton, A. K., *Oswald Mosley: Portrait of a Leader*, Action Press: London (1937).

Crossman, G., *Draft Terrorism Bill: Liberties Briefing*, Sept 2005.

JUST West Yorkshire, *When Hate Came to Town* (2010), accessed from www.jrf.org.uk/work/work-area/bradford-programme/when-hate-came-to-town

Mosley, O., *Blackshirt Policy*, BUF Publications: London (1935).

Mosley, O., *Fascism: 100 Questions Asked and Answered*, BUF Publications: London (1936).

Pankhurst, C., 'Why we Protest at Cabinet Minister's Meetings', WSPU (1908).

Shelley, P., *The Mask of Anarchy* (1819).

Swain, V., *Report on the Policing of the English Defence League and Counter Protests in Leicester on October 9th 2010,* Network for Police Monitoring (2011).

The Guardian and the London School of Economics, *Reading the Riots: Investigating England's Summer of Disorder*, London (2011), available at www.theguardian.com/uk/interactive/2011/dec/14/reading-the-riots-investigating-england-s-summer-of-disorder-full-report.

Miscellaneous primary sources

Cameron, C., PM's speech on the fightback after the riots, 15 Aug 2011, accessed from www.gov.uk/government/speeches/pms-speech-on-the-fightback-after-the-riots

Carroll, K., speech at Dewsbury 30 June 2012 at www.youtube.com/watch?v=Pa2TO7 zYYZQ accessed on 19 Nov 2014.

Freedom of Information request by the author to the Home Office. Reference: 31049.

Johnson, B., *Letter to May, T.,* 6 Jan 2014, accessed from www.london.gov.uk/priorities/policing-crime/consultations/water-cannon

May, T., *Letter to Boris Johnson*, 23 Jan 2014, accessed from www.london.gov.uk/priorities/policing-crime/consultations/water-cannon

Mayor of London Office for Policing and Crime, *Water Cannon: Responses to Consultation* (2014), accessed from www.london.gov.uk/sites/default/files/140318%20-%20Water%20Cannon%20-%20Responses%20to%20Consultation%20_0.pdf

Politics.co.uk, 'Ed Miliband riot statement in full', accessed from www.politics.co.uk/comment-analysis/2011/08/11/ed-miliband-riot-statement-in-full

Secondary sources

Books and chapters in edited collections

Alderson, J., *Law and Disorder*, Hamish Hamilton Ltd: London (1984).

Anderson, G. D., *Fascists, Communists and the National Government: Civil Liberties in Great Britain, 1931–1937*, University of Missouri Press: Columbia and London (1983).

Andrew, C., *The Defence of the Realm: The Authorised History of MI5*, Penguin: London (2009).

Baer, M., *Theatre and Disorder in Late Georgian London*, Clarendon: Oxford (1992).

Bailey, V., *Order and Disorder in Modern Britain: Essays on Riot, Crime, Policing and Punishment*, Breviary Stuff Publications: London (2014).

Beggs QC, J., Thomas G. and Rickard, S., *Public Order: Law and Practice*, Oxford University Press: Oxford (2012).

Benewick, R., *Political Violence and Public Order*, Allen Lane The Penguin Press: London (1969).

Bentley, M., *Politics Without Democracy 1815–1914*, second edition, Blackwell: Oxford (1996).

Bloom, C., *Riot City: Protest and Rebellion in the Capital*, Palgrave Macmillan: London (2012).

Branson, N., *The History of the Communist Party of Great Britain 1927–1941*, Lawrence and Wishart: London (1985).

Brown D., and Ellis, T., *Policing Low-Level Disorder: Police Use of Section 5 of the Public Order Act 1986*, Home Office Research Study 135 (1994).

Burke, E., *Reflections on the Revolution in France* (1790).

Card, R. *Public Order Law*, Jordans Ltd: Bristol (2000).

Channing, I., *Blackshirts and White Wigs: Reflections on Public Order Law and the Political Activism of the British Union of Fascists*, unpublished PhD thesis (2014), Plymouth University.

Channing, I., *Poverty and the Poor Law in Plymouth, 1900–1930: Guardians of the Poor or Guardians of the Ratepayers?*, unpublished MRes thesis (2009), Plymouth University.

Chase, M., *Chartism: A New History*, Manchester University Press: Manchester (2007).

Clark, J., *Striving to Preserve the Peace: The National Council for Civil Liberties, the Metropolitan Police and the Dynamics of Disorder in Inter-war Britain*, PhD thesis, Open University (2008).

Copsey, N., *Anti-Fascism in Britain*, Macmillan Press Ltd: Hampshire (2000).

Coupland, P. M., 'The Black Shirt in Britain: The Meanings and Functions of Political Uniform' in J. Gottlieb and T. Linehan (eds), *The Culture of Fascism: Visions of the Far Right in Britain*, I. B. Taurus: London (2004).

Cross, C., *The Fascists in Britain*, Barrie and Rockliff: London (1961).

Dicey, A. V., *An Introduction to the Study of the Law of the Constitution*, tenth edition, Macmillan Press Ltd: London (1959).

Dorril, S., *Blackshirt: Sir Oswald Mosley and British Fascism*, Viking: London (2006).

Emsley, C., *The English Police: A Political and Social History*, Pearson Education Ltd: Harlow (1996).

Emsley, C., *The Great British Bobby: A History of British Policing From the 18th Century to the Present*, Querus: London (2010).

Emsley, C., *Policing and Its Context 1750–1870*, Macmillan Press Ltd: London (1983).

Emsley, C., 'The birth and development of the police' in T. Newburn (ed), *Handbook of Policing*, second edition, Routledge: London (2011).

Ewing, K. D., and Gearty, C. A., *The Struggle for Civil Liberties: Political Freedom and the Rule of Law in Britain, 1914–1945*, Oxford University Press: Oxford (2004).

Ewing, K. D., *Bonfire of the Liberties: New Labour, Human Rights, and the Rule of Law*, Oxford University Press: Oxford (2010).

Gray, T., *Blackshirts in Devon*, The Mint Press: Exeter (2006).

Hannington, W., *Unemployed Struggles 1919–1936*, Lawrence and Wishart Ltd: London (1979).

Hitchens, P., *The Broken Compass: How British Politics Lost Its Way*, Continuum: London (2009).

Jackson, P., Pitchford, M., Feldman, M., and Preston, T., *The EDL: Britain's 'New Far Right' Social Movement*, The University of Northampton's Radicalism and New Media Research Group: Northhampton (2011).

James, P. S., *Introduction to English Law*, eighth edition, Butterworths: London (1972).

Jefferson, T., *The Case Against Paramilitary Policing*, Open University Press: Milton Keynes (1990).

Jones, D., *The Last Rising, The Newport Insurrection of 1839*, Clarendon Press: Oxford (1985).

Keller, L., *Triumph of Order: Democracy and Public Space in New York and London*, Columbia University Press: New York (2010).

Kidd, R., *British Liberty in Danger*, Lawrence and Wishart Ltd: London (1940).

Kingsford, P., *The Hunger Marches in Britain 1920–1939*, Lawrence and Wishart Ltd: London (1982).

Le Bon, G., *The Crowd: A Study of the Popular Mind*, T. Fisher Unwin: London (1895).

Lewis, D. S., *Illusions of Grandeur: Mosley, Fascism and British Society 1931–1981*, Manchester University Press: Manchester (1987).

Lustgarten, L., *The Governance of Police*, Sweet and Maxwell: London (1986).

Marlowe, J., *The Peterloo Massacre*, Rapp & Whiting: London (1969).

Marston, J. and Tain, P., *Public Order: The Criminal Law*, Callow Publishing: London (2001).

Mather, F. C., *Public Order in the Age of the Chartists*, Manchester University Press: Manchester (1959).

Mather, F. C., 'The Government and the Chartists' in A. Briggs (ed), *Chartist Studies*, Macmillan (1967).

Mead, D., *The New Law of Peaceful Protest: Rights and Regulation in the Human Rights Act Era*, Hart Publishing Ltd: Oxford (2010).

Moody, J., *Illegitimate Theatre in London, 1770–1840*, Cambridge University Press: Cambridge (2000).

Montagu, I., *Blackshirt Brutality*, Workers Bookshop Ltd (1934).

Morgan, J., *Conflict and Order: The Police and Labour Disputes in England and Wales, 1900–1939*, Clarendon Press: Oxford (1987).

Mosley, O., *My Life*, Friends of Oswald Mosley: London (2006), downloaded from www.oswaldmosley.com/downloads/My%20Life.pdf on 15 April 2010.

Muir Jr., W. K., *Police: Streetcorner Politicians*, University of Chicago Press: Chicago and London (1977).

Mullally, F., *Fascism Inside England*, Claud Morris Books Ltd: London (1946).

Palmer, S., *Police and Protest in England and Ireland 1780–1850*, Cambridge University Press: Cambridge (1988).

Paine, T., *Rights of Man*, J. S. Jordan: London (1791).

Pugh, M., '*Hurrah for the Blackshirts! Fascists and Fascism in Britain Between the Wars*', Pimlico: London (2006).

Pugh, M., *The March of the Women: A Revisionist Analysis of the Campaign for Women's Suffrage, 1866–1914*, Oxford University Press: Oxford (2000).

Reiman, J., 'Is Police Discretion Justified in a Free Society?' in J. Kleinig (ed), *Handled with Discretion: Ethical Issues in Police Decision Making*, Rowman & Littlefield Publishers: Maryland, USA (1996).

Reiner, R., *The Politics of the Police*, second edition, Harvester Wheatsheaf: Hertfordshire (1992).

Renton, D., *Fascism, Anti-Fascism and Britain in the 1940s*, Macmillan Press Ltd: Hampshire and London (2000).

Rover, C., *Women's Suffrage and Party Politics in Britain 1866–1914*, Routledge and Kegan Paul Ltd: London (1967).

Scaffardi, S., *Fire Under the Carpet: Working for Civil Liberties in the 1930s*, Lawrence and Wishart Ltd: London (1986).

Simon, J., *Retrospect: The Memoir of the Rt. Hon. Viscount Simon*, Hutchinson and Co Ltd: London (1952).

Smith, J. C. and Hogan, B., *Criminal Law*, third edition, Butterworths: London (1973).

Stelfox, P., *Criminal Investigation: An Introduction to Principles and Practice*, Routledge Willan Publishing: Cullompton (2009).

Stott C., and Gorringe, H., 'From Peel to PLTs: Adapting to Liaison Based Public Order Policing in England and Wales', in J. Brown (ed), *The Future of Policing: Papers Prepared for the Stevens Independent Commission into the Future of Policing in England and Wales*, Routledge: London and New York (2013).

Street, H., *Freedom, the Individual and the Law*, Penguin Books: Middlesex (1963).

Supperstone, M., *Brownlie's Law of Public Order and National Security*, second edition, Butterworth and Co: London (1981).

Thompson, D., (ed) *The Early Chartists*, Macmillan: New York (1971).

Thompson, E. P., *The Making of the English Working Class*, Penguin Books: London (1991).

Thornton, HHJ P. QC, Brander, R., Thomas, R., Rhodes, D., Schwarz, M., and Rees, E., *the Law of Public Order and Protest*, Oxford University Press: Oxford (2010).

Tosh, J., *The Pursuit of History*, Pearson Education Ltd: Harlow (2006).

Townshend, C., *Making the Peace: Public Order and Public Security in Modern Britain*, Oxford University Press: Oxford (1993).

Thurlow, R., *Fascism in Britain, From Oswald Mosley's Blackshirts to the National Front*, I. B. Tauris: London (2009).

Thurlow, R., *The Secret State: British Internal Security in the Twentieth Century*, Blackwell Publishers: Oxford (1994).

Thurlow, R., 'The Straw that Broke the Camel's Back: Public Order, Civil Liberties and the Battle of Cable Street' in T. Kushner and N. Valman (eds), *Remembering Cable Street: Fascism and Anti-Fascism in British Society*, Vallentine Mitchell: Middlesex (2000).

Vogler, R., *Reading the Riot Act: The Magistracy, the Police and the Army in Civil Disorder*, Open University Press: Milton Keynes (1991).

Waddington, D., *Policing Public Order: Theory and Practice*, Willan Publishing: Cullompton (2007).

Waddington, P.A.J., *Liberty and Order: Public Order Policing in a Capital City*, UCL Press Ltd: London (1994).

Waddington, P.A.J., 'Controlling protest in contemporary historical and comparative perspective', in D. della Porta and H. Reiter (eds), *Policing Protest: the Control of Mass Demonstrations in Western Democracies*, University of Minnesota Press (1998).

Welsh, I., *Mobilising Modernity: The Nuclear Movement*, Routledge: London and New York (2000).

Winter, J., *London's Teeming Streets: 1830–1914*, Routledge: London and New York (1993).

Williams, C., 'Rotten Boroughs: The Crisis of Urban Policing and the Decline of Municipal Independence 1914–64', in J. Moore and J. Smith (eds), *Corruption in Urban Politics and Society, Britain 1780–1950*, Ashgate: Surrey (2007).

Williams, D., *Keeping the Peace: The Police and Public Order*, Hutchinson & Co Ltd: London (1967).

Williams, D., *John Frost. A Study in Chartism*, University of Wales Press: Cardiff (1939).

Wisler D., and Tackenberg, M., 'The Role of the Police: Image or Reality?' in R. Bessel and C. Emsley (eds), *Patterns of Provocation: Police and Public Disorder*, Berghahn Books: Oxford and New York (2000).

Worley, M., *Labour Inside the Gate: A History of the British Labour Party Between the Wars*, I. B. Tauris: London (2005).

Journal articles

Allen of Abbeydale, 'Newsam, Sir Frank Aubrey (1893–1964)', *Oxford Dictionary of National Biography*, Oxford University Press: Oxford (2004); online edition, Jan 2008, www.oxforddnb.com/view/article/35219?docPos=1, accessed 14 February 2015.

Baker, J., 'The OP War, Libertarian Communication and Graphic Reportage in Georgian London', *European Comic Art 4*, no. 1 (2011), pp. 81–104.

Bartlett, P., '"On Historical Contextualisation": A Lawyer Responds', *Crimes and Misdemeanours 1*, no. 2 (2007), pp. 102–106.

Catterall, P., (ed), 'The Battle of Cable Street: Witness Seminar', *Contemporary Record 8*, no. 1 (Summer 1994), pp. 105–132.

Charlesworth, L., 'On Historical Contextualisation: Some Critical Socio-Legal Reflections', *Crimes and Misdemeanours 1*, no. 1 (2007), pp. 1–40.

Cullen, S., 'Political Violence: The Case of the British Union of Fascists', *Journal of Contemporary History 28* (1993), pp. 245–267.

Emeljanow, V., 'The Events of June 1848: The 'Monte Cristo' Riots and the Politics of Protest', *New Theatre Quarterly 19*, no. 1 (2003), pp. 23–32.

Fenwick, H., 'Marginalising Human Rights: Breach of the Peace, "Kettling", the Human Rights Act and Public Protest', *Public Law*, no. 4, (2009), pp. 737–765.

Glover, R., 'The Uncertain Blue Line – Police Cordons and the Common Law', *Criminal Law Review* (2012), pp. 245–260.

Goodhart, A. L., '*Thomas v. Sawkins*: A Constitutional Innovation', *The Cambridge Law Journal 6*, no. 1 (1936), pp. 22–30.

Gorringe, H. and Rosie, M., '"We *Will* Facilitate Your Protest': Experiments With Liaison Policing', *Policing 7*, no. 2 (2013), pp. 204–211.

Hoggett J., and Stott, C., 'Crowd Psychology, Public Order Police Training and the Policing of Football Crowds', *Policing: An International Journal of Police Strategies and Management 33*, no. 2 (2010), pp. 218–235.

Hunt, A., 'Criminal Prohibitions on Direct and Indirect Encouragement of Terrorism', *Criminal Law Review* (June 2007), pp. 441–458.

Jennings, W. I., 'Public Order', *The Political Quarterly in the Thirties 42*, no. 5(1971), pp. 175–186.

Lawrence, J., 'Fascist Violence and the Politics of Public Order in Inter-War Britain: The Olympia debate revisited', *Historical Research 76*, no. 192 (May 2003), pp. 238–267.

Lowe, W. J., 'The Chartists and the Irish Confederates: Lancashire, 1848', *Irish Historical Studies 24*, no. 94 (Nov 1984), pp. 172–196.

Mead, D., 'Case Comment: Kettling Comes to the Boil Before the Strasbourg Court: Is It a Deprivation of Liberty to Contain Protesters En Masse?', *Cambridge Law Journal 71*, no. 3 (2012), pp. 472–475.

Navickas, K., '"That sash will hang you": Political Clothing and Adornment in England, 1780–1840', *The Journal of British Studies 49*, no. 3 (2010), pp. 540–565.

Newman, C., 'Case Comment, Section 5 of the Public Order Act 1986: The Threshold of Extreme Protest', *Journal of Criminal Law 76*, no. 2 (2012), pp. 105–109.

Parpworth, N., 'Processions or Public Disorder?' *Criminal Law and Justice Weekly 178* (2014), pp. 178–180.

Poole, R., 'The March to Peterloo: Politics and Festivity in Late Georgian England', *Past and Present*, no. 192 (Aug 2006), pp. 109–153.

Pugh, M., 'The National Government, the British Union of Fascists and the Olympia Debate' *Historical Research 78*, no. 200 (May 2005), pp. 253–262.

Reiman, J., 'Against Police Discretion: Reply to John Kleinig', *Journal of Social Philosophy 29*, no. 1 (1998), pp. 132–142.

Reicher, S., Stott, C., Cronin, P., and Adang, O., 'An Integrated Approach to Crowd Psychology and Public Order Policing', *Policing: An International Journal of Police Strategies & Management 27*, iss. 4 (2004), pp. 558–572.

Simpson, A., 'Haldane, Sir (James) Aylmer Lowthorpe (1862–1950)', *Oxford Dictionary of National Biography*, Oxford University Press: Oxford (Oct 2008); online edition, May 2009, www.oxforddnb.com/view/article/95438, accessed 12 Oct 2010.

Smith, E., 'Once as History, Twice as Farce? The Spectre of the Summer of '81 in Discourses on the August 2011 Riots', *Journal for Cultural Research 17*, no. 2 (2013), pp. 124–143.

Stanko, B., and Dawson, P., 'Reflections on the Offending Histories of Those Arrested During the Disorder', *Policing 7*, no. 2 (2012), pp. 3–11.

Stone, R., 'Breach of the Peace: The Case for Abolition' (2001), 2 *Web JCLI* accessed at http://webjcli.ncl.ac.uk/2001/issue2/stone2.html

Stott, C., and Drury, J., 'Crowds, Context and Identity: Dynamic Categorization Processes in the "Poll Tax Riot"', *Human Relations 53*, no. 2 (2000), pp. 247–273.

Stott, C., Scothern, M., and Gorringe, H., 'Advances in Liaison Based Public Order Policing in England: Human Rights and Negotiating the Management of Protest?', *Policing 7*, no. 2 (2013), pp. 212–226.

Swift, R., 'Policing Chartism, 1839–1848: The Role of the "Specials" Reconsidered' English *Historical Review CXXII*, no. 497 (2007), pp. 669–699.

Taylor, M., 'Rethinking the Chartists: Searching for Synthesis in the Historiography of Chartism' in *The Historical Journal 39*, no. 2 (1996), pp. 479–495.

Thurlow, R., review of *The Struggle for Civil Liberties: Political Freedom and the Rule of Law in Britain, 1914–1945* by K. D. Ewing and C. A. Gearty in *Albion: A Quarterly Journal Concerned with British Studies 33*, no. 2 (Summer 2001), pp. 350–351.

Trilling, D., 'The Lost Weekend', *The New Statesman 141*, no. 5107, (28 May 2012), pp. 30–35.

Waddington, D., 'The Madness of the Mob? Explaining the 'Irrationality' and Destructiveness of Crowd Violence', *Sociology Compass 2*, no. 2 (2008), pp. 675–687.

Waddington, P. A. J., 'The Case Against Paramilitary Policing Considered', *British Journal of Criminology 33*, no. 3 (1993), pp. 353–373.

Williams, C., 'Britain's Police Forces: Forever Removed from Democratic Control?' *History and Policy* (5 Nov 2003), accessed from www.historyandpolicy.org/policy-papers/papers/britains-police-forces-forever-removed-from-democratic-control.

Index